You, Too, Can Find Anybody

Other books by Joseph J. Culligan:

When In Doubt, Check Him Out (also on video)

Requirements To Become a P.I. In The 50 States And Elsewhere

Adoption Searches Made Easier

You, Too, Can Find Anybody
A Reference Manual
Copyright © 1997 by Joseph J. Culligan

Hallmark Press, Incorporated
Miami, Florida 33169

Please note that all government agencies, including driving and motor vehicle records departments, are constantly changing policies insorfar as what access to records and files will be accorded the public.

Library of Congress Catalog Card Number: 91-91166
ISBN: 0-9630621-0-7
Printed in the United States of America
10 9 8 7 6 5 4 3 2

Culligan, Joseph J.
    You, too, can find anybody : a reference manual by Joseph J. Culligan.
    p. cm.
    Includes directories.

    1. Missing persons—Investigations.   I. Title.

HV6762.A3C8 1992   362.233'6
                             QBI92-10608

Neither the author nor publisher assumes any responsibility for the use or misuse of information and sources contained in this book.

*This book is dedicated
to my grandson, Mitchell*

Preface

This reference manual is being published because of the overwhelming response received due to television shows featuring cases of mine in which regular, everyday people were able, with a minimal amount of guidance from me, to find loved ones by simply searching public records.

The reader of this manual will be able to access a myriad of public records with the aplomb and dexterity of an experienced investigator. Of course, a subject missing for forty years will be found using different sources than those applied when attempting to find an individual missing for four months. The reader will instinctively know which sources are to be utilized. Most importantly, the reader will be able to achieve success using legal sources. There is no reason why any missing person case needs to employ surreptitious methods or means. For example, you can call 202-307-3126 and the federal government will tell you if someone is now or has ever been an inmate in any federal prison. Because you may not have a clue where to start on your search, on page 3-11, I give the address of a company that investigators and governments have used for years to run social security numbers, death files and telephone numbers. For the first time, this company has consented to accept orders from the public.

I have been asked to write about many of the high-profile cases that my firm has worked on, including the case of the exiled General from Central America, the case of the game show inventor who was sued for palimony, the case involving a member of a well-known political family in Palm Beach charged with assault, the case of the children's show host who was arrested on the west coast of Florida, the case of the nations's largest failed savings and loan institution, the case of the Wall Street arbitrageur whose actions changed the way the stock market conducts business. These and many other assignments have required comprehensive and exacting investigations, including locating witnesses and extensive background checks. I feel that readers will benefit if they understand some of the inner workings of investigations which *You, Too, Can Find Anybody*, will provide. By knowing the sources used and the mechanics applied in investigations, the readers will be able to follow the cases in my footsteps when I write the book on my cases. The whos, whats, whys, wheres and whens will not seem so mysterious.

I have met many fine professionals, such as Dan Meenan, news editor of the "A *Current Affair*," and you will, no doubt, become acquainted with numerous individuals after you initiate your search. Take the time to thank everyone along the way for their valued assistance. Since you will, most likely, be successful in your search, you might as well sow a path that will be pleasant and memorable.

My investigative firm only accepts assignments from clientele that includes attorneys, private investigators and government for investigative services. Most of our cases are termed "impossible" by our clients but we have had a 100% success rate in locating missing persons and have used the same sources that are contained herein. Since many readers may gain enough confidence from reading this book and wish to further pursue an investigative career, I have also produced another book titled *Requirements to Become a P.I. in the 50 States and Elsewhere*. This book is over 570 pages and you will be able to see what background and experience is needed to become a private investigator. There are currently 12 states that do not require statewide licensing.

If you find the person you are looking for using this book and you think that your case would translate into good television, then write to me immediately. I do not want to delay your reunion and I can't promise you that your story will fit into a talk show's schedule at that moment but, as I am sure you are aware, I do many shows each month on national television where I reunite families who did the "finding" themselves. I have appeared on *The Maury Povich Show*, *Donahue*, *Ricki Lake*, *Montel Williams*, *Hard Copy* and *Leeza* among others.

I may be contacted by writing to: 4995 Northwest 79th Avenue, Suite 115, Miami, Florida 33166.

CONTENTS

1

Driving Records, Registrations & Titles

Many readers of this book will be able to locate their subject by simply contacting motor vehicle departments.

The best hit rate will be for males since they do not change their name as often as females do. Motor vehicles departments maintain license records for females with their previous surname(s) for years, so you will want to write, even though you believe that your female subject has had a name change. Many of my "impossible" cases have been solved because I simply requested the subject's driving record.

You will, no doubt, want to start with the last known state of the subject. Even if the subject has moved to another state, each motor vehicle department maintains a record going back from two years to thirty years (each state varies) indicating what state the subject's license was surrendered to.

When writing to request a copy of the subject's driving record, include the date of birth. If you do not have an exact date of birth for the subject, write and ask for an alpha search.

Here is a sample letter requesting a driving record when you do not have a date of birth:

Date

John Anyone
123 Anywhere Drive
Anytown, New York 12345
Telephone: 212-555-1234

Dear Commissioner of Motor Vehicles:
   Kindly send me the driving record of Robert Hamilton. I am sorry I do not have a date of birth but please do an alpha search for the year of 1943. Find attached a check for the appropriate fee. I am also submitting an additional check for $15.00. This will cover any additional costs should there be more than one Robert Hamilton.
   If your search reveals that there are numerous Robert Hamiltons, please advise me and I will decide on what course of action I wish to pursue.

Sincerely,
John Anyone

The above letter does wonders. If the driving record division writes to you and says there are many individuals who have your subject's name with that year of birth, you will want to write back and give the area of the state that you feel the subject may now reside or had resided in. If you receive several driving records and do not know which is your subject, don't despair. Driving records may contain some or all of the following which will assist you in determining which of the licensees is your subject:

Addresses	Social Security Number
Height	Date of Birth
Weight	Dates and Locations of Accidents
Hair Color	Dates and Locations of Traffic Tickets
Eye Color	Restrictions, i.e. Eyeglasses

DRIVERS LICENSES

ALABAMA
Driver Licenses
State of Alabama
Post Office Box 1471–H
Montgomery, Alabama 36192

ALASKA
Driver Licenses
State of Alaska
Post Office Box 20020–E
Juneau, Alaska 99802

ARIZONA
Driver Licenses
State of Arizona
Post Office Box 2100–L
Phoenix, Arizona 85001

ARKANSAS
Driver Licenses
State of Arkansas
Post Office Box 1272–L
Little Rock, Arkansas 72203

CALIFORNIA
Driver Licenses
State of California
Post Office Box 944231–O
Sacramento, California 94244

COLORADO
Driver Licenses
State of Colorado
140 West 6th Avenue
Denver, Colorado 80204

CONNECTICUT
Driver Licenses
State of Connecticut
60 State Street
Wethersfield, Connecticut 06109

DELAWARE
Driver Licenses
State of Delaware
Post Office Box 698–M
Dover, Delaware 19903

DISTRICT OF COLUMBIA
Drivers Licenses
District of Columbia
301 C Street, N.W.
Washington, D.C. 20001

FLORIDA
Driver Licenses
State of Florida
Neil Kirkman Building
Tallahassee, Florida 32399

GEORGIA
Driver Licenses
State of Georgia
Post Office Box 1456–I
Atlanta, Georgia 30371

HAWAII
Driver Licenses
State of Hawaii
530 South King Street
Honolulu, Hawaii 96813

IDAHO
Driver Licenses
State of Idaho
Post Office Box 7129–T
Boise, Idaho 83707

ILLINOIS
Driver Licenses
State of Illinois
2701 South Dirksen Parkway
Springfield, Illinois 62723

INDIANA

Driver Licenses
State of Indiana
State Office Building
Indianapolis, Indiana 46204

IOWA

Driver Licenses
State of Iowa
100 Euclid Avenue
Des Moines, Iowa 50306

KANSAS

Driver Licenses
State of Kansas
Docking Office Building
Topeka, Kansas 66626

KENTUCKY

Driver Licenses
State of Kentucky
State Office Building
Frankfort, Kentucky 40622

LOUISIANA

Driver Licenses
State of Louisiana
Post Office Box 64886–C
Baton Rouge, Louisiana 70896

MAINE

Driver Licenses
State of Maine
State House, Room 29
Augusta, Maine 04333

MARYLAND

Driver Licenses
State of Maryland
6601 Ritchie Highway, N.E. Room 211
Glen Burnie, Maryland 21062

MASSACHUSETTS

Driver Licenses
Commonwealth of Massachusetts
100 Nashua Street
Boston, Massachusetts 02114

MICHIGAN

Driver Licenses
State of Michigan
7064 Crowner Drive
Lansing, Michigan 48918

MINNESOTA

Driver Licenses
State of Minnesota
Transportation Building, Room 108
Saint Paul, Minnesota 55155

MISSISSIPPI

Driver Licenses
State of Mississippi
Post Office Box 958–H
Jackson, Mississippi 39205

MISSOURI

Driver Licenses
State of Missouri
Post Office Box 200–E
Jefferson City, Missouri 65105

MONTANA

Driver Licenses
State of Montana
303 North Roberts
Helena, Montana 59620

NEBRASKA

Driver Licenses
State of Nebraska
301 Centennial Mall South
Lincoln, Nebraska 68509

NEVADA

Driver Licenses
State of Nevada
555 Wright Way
Carson City, Nevada 89711

NEW HAMPSHIRE

Driver Licenses
State of New Hampshire
10 Hazen Drive
Concord, New Hampshire 03305

NEW JERSEY

Driver Licenses
State of New Jersey
25 South Montgomery Street
Trenton, New Jersey 08666

NEW MEXICO

Drivers Licenses
State of New Mexico
Post Office Box 1028–L
Santa Fe, New Mexico 87504

NEW YORK

Driver Licenses
State of New York
Empire State Plaza
Albany, New York 12228

NORTH CAROLINA

Driver Licenses
State of North Carolina
1100 New Bern Avenue
Raleigh, North Carolina 27697

NORTH DAKOTA

Driver Licenses
State of North Dakota
Capitol Grounds
Bismarck, North Dakota 58505

OHIO

Driver Licenses
State of Ohio
Post Office Box 7167–L
Columbus, Ohio 43266

OKLAHOMA

Driver Licenses
State of Oklahoma
Post Office Box 11415–F
Oklahoma City, Oklahoma 73136

OREGON

Driver Licenses
State of Oregon
1905 Lana Avenue, N.E.
Salem, Oregon 97314

PENNSYLVANIA

Driver Licenses
State of Pennsylvania
Post Office Box 8695–L
Harrisburg, Pennsylvania 17105

PUERTO RICO

Driver Licenses
Commonwealth of Puerto Rico
Post Office Box 41243–O
Santurce, Puerto Rico 00940

RHODE ISLAND

Driver Licenses
State of Rhode Island
345 Harris Avenue
Providence, Rhode Island 02909

SOUTH CAROLINA

Driver Licenses
State of South Carolina
Post Office Box 1498–R
Columbia, South Carolina 29216

SOUTH DAKOTA

Driver Licenses
State of South Dakota
118 West Capitol Avenue
Pierre, South Dakota 57501

TENNESSEE

Driver Licenses
State of Tennessee
Post Office Box 945–E
Nashville, Tennessee 37202

TEXAS

Driver Licenses
State of Texas
Post Office Box 4087–S
Austin, Texas 78773

UTAH

Driver Licenses
State of Utah
1095 Motor Avenue
Salt Lake City, Utah 84116

VERMONT

Driver Licenses
State of Vermont
120 State Street
Montpelier, Vermont 05603

VIRGINIA

Driver Licenses
State of Virginia
2300 West Broad Street
Richmond, Virginia 23269

WASHINGTON

Driver Licenses
State of Washington
211 12th Avenue, S.E.
Olympia, Washington 98504

WEST VIRGINIA

Driver Licenses
State of West Virginia
1800 Washington Street, East
Charleston, West Virginia 25317

WISCONSIN

Driver Licenses
State of Wisconsin
Post Office Box 7918
Madison, Wisconsin 53707

WYOMING

Driver Licenses
State of Wyoming
122 West 25th Street
Cheyenne, Wyoming 82002

NOTE:

If your subject appears to be a person that will not give proper information on any licenses or other documents, then the traffic ticket will possibly be able to lead you to the subject's location. If your subject's driving record indicates traffic violations, take note of the jurisdiction or location that issued the ticket. Write to that authority and request a photocopy of the ticket.

On the ticket will be the make, model and license number of the vehicle the subject was driving when stopped for the citation.

Write to the motor vehicle registration department, supplying the license plate number of the vehicle. Many times the registration that you receive to the vehicle will indicate ownership of a person other than your subject. You will now have a new address to check and a new person that may be questioned as to the whereabouts of your subject.

ACCIDENT REPORTS

If your subject's driving record indicates an accident then you will want to order a copy of the accident report. This report will, of course, contain much information such as address, vehicles involved in the accident, location of accident, etc. but what I use this report for is primarily to find out about the other party in the accident. You will have the name, address, drivers license number, vehicle information and other important details listed in the report.

If the accident report indicates that your subject was at fault and there was damage to the vehicles and injuries then your subject may have been sued or will be facing a court date in the near future. You will need the other parties information because you will want to search the public records for a suit filed by this party. The address of this other party is important because they may file suit where they reside which may not be necessarily in the same court jurisdiction where the accident occurred or where your subject lives.

Pay particular attention to the subpoena the subject was served and the address they were served at. If any damages were awarded that exceeded the subject's insurance coverage then there will be numerous records indicating the liens and attachments that have been filed. You may be able to glean numerous addresses for the subject by reviewing these public records.

If your subject was not at fault then they may have filed suit. You will want to review the files of any litigation. You can be assured that any address listed for your subject will be accurate because the subject had filed this suit with the intent of collecting damages and, of course, a correct address would have been supplied by the subject so they would be able to collect any damages.

You may order the accident report from the jurisdiction that is noted on the driving record. The following list of state police agencies is included in this chapter because the state will usually have a copy of every accident involving damage and injuries. If the jurisdiction on the accident report is unclear then the state police will be able to either provide you a copy of the accident report or will evaluate the accident location from the information on the driving record and advise you exactly where to make your inquiry.

STATE POLICE AGENCIES

ALABAMA

Alabama Department of Public Safety
State of Alabama
Post Office Box 1511
Montgomery, Alabama 36192

ALASKA

Department of Public Safety
State of Alaska
Post Office Box N
Juneau, Alaska 99811

ARIZONA

Department of Public Safety
State of Arizona
2102 West Encanto Boulevard
Phoenix, Arizona 85005

ARKANSAS

Department of Public Safety
State of Arkansas
Three Natural Resources Drive
Little Rock, Arkansas 72215

CALIFORNIA

State Department of Justice
State of California
Post Office Box 944255
Sacramento, California 94244

COLORADO

Colorado Bureau of Investigation
State of Colorado
690 Kipling Street
Lakewood, Colorado 80215

CONNECTICUT

State Police Department
State of Connecticut
294 Colony Street
Meriden, Connecticut 06450

DELAWARE

Delaware State Police Department
State of Delaware
Post Office Box 430
Dover, Delaware 19903

DISTRICT OF COLUMBIA

Department of Public Safety
District of Columbia
Post Office Box 1606
Washington, D.C. 20013

FLORIDA

Department of Law Enforcement
State of Florida
Post Office Box 1489
Tallahassee, Florida 32302

GEORGIA

Department of State Police
State of Georgia
Post Office Box 370748
Decatur, Georgia 30037

HAWAII

Department of Public Safety
State of Hawaii
465 South King Street
Honolulu, Hawaii 96813

IDAHO

Department of State Police
State of Idaho
6083 Clinton Street
Boise, Idaho 83704

ILLINOIS

Department of State Police
State of Illinois
260 North Chicago Street
Joliet, Illinois 60431

INDIANA

Indiana State Police
State of Indiana
100 North Senate Avenue
Indianapolis, Indiana 46204

IOWA

Department of Public Safety
State of Iowa
Wallace State Office Building
Des Moines, Iowa 50319

KANSAS

Kansas Bureau of Public Safety
State of Kansas
1620 Southwest Tyler
Topeka, Kansas 66612

KENTUCKY

Kentucky State Police
State of Kentucky
1250 Louisville Road
Frankfort, Kentucky 40601

LOUISIANA

Department of Public Safety
State of Louisiana
Post Office Box 66614
Baton Rouge, Louisiana 70896

MAINE

Maine State Police
State of Maine
36 Hospital Street
Augusta, Maine 04330

MARYLAND

Maryland State Police
State of Maryland
1201 Reisterstown Road
Pikesville, Maryland 21208

MASSACHUSETTS

Department of Public Safety
Commonwealth of Massachusetts
One Ashburton Place
Boston, Massachusetts 02108

MICHIGAN

Department of State Police
State of Michigan
714 South Harrison Road
East Lansing, Michigan 48823

MINNESOTA

Department of Public Safety
State of Minnesota
1246 University Avenue
Saint Paul, Minnesota 55104

MISSISSIPPI

Department of Public Safety
State of Mississippi
Post Office Box 958
Jackson, Mississippi 39205

MISSOURI

Department of Public Safety
State of Missouri
1510 East Elm Street
Jefferson City, Missouri 65102

MONTANA

Department of State Police
State of Montana
303 North Roberts
Helena, Montana 59620

NEBRASKA

Nebraska State Police
State of Nebraska
Post Office Box 94907
Lincoln, Nebraska 68509

NEVADA

Department of Public Safety
State of Nevada
555 Wright Way
Carson City, Nevada 89711

NEW HAMPSHIRE

New Hampshire State Police
State of New Hampshire
10 Hazen Drive
Concord, New Hampshire 03305

NEW JERSEY

New Jersey State Police
State of New Jersey
Post Office Box 7068
West Trenton, New Jersey 08628

NEW MEXICO

Department of Public Safety
State of New Mexico
Post Office Box 1628
Santa Fe, New Mexico 87504

NEW YORK

New York State Police
State of New York
Executive Park Tower
Albany, New York 12203

NORTH CAROLINA

Department of Public Safety
State of North Carolina
407 Blount Street
Raleigh, North Carolina 27602

NORTH DAKOTA

North Dakota Bureau of Investigation
State of North Dakota
Post Office Box 1054
Bismarck, North Dakota 58502

OHIO

Department of Investigations
State of Ohio
Post Office Box 365
London, Ohio 43140

OKLAHOMA

Department of Public Safety
State of Oklahoma
Post Office Box 11497
Oklahoma City, Oklahoma 73136

OREGON

Oregon State Police
State of Oregon
3772 Portland Road
Salem, Oregon 97310

PENNSYLVANIA

Pennsylvania State Police
Commonwealth of Pennsylvania
1800 Elmerton Avenue
Harrisburg, Pennsylvania 17110

RHODE ISLAND

Department of Public Safety
State of Rhode Island
72 Pine Street
Providence, Rhode Island 02903

SOUTH CAROLINA

Department of Law Enforcement
State of South Carolina
Post Office Box 21398
Columbia, South Carolina 29221

SOUTH DAKOTA

Division of Criminal Investigation
State of South Dakota
500 East Capitol Avenue
Pierre, South Dakota 57501

TENNESSEE

Department of Public Safety
State of Tennessee
1150 Foster Avenue
Nashville, Tennessee 37224

TEXAS

Texas State Police
State of Texas
Post Office Box 4143
Austin, Texas 78765

UTAH

Department of Public Safety
State of Utah
4501 South 2700 West Avenue
Salt Lake City, Utah 84119

VERMONT

Vermont State Police
State of Vermont
103 South Main Street
Waterbury, Vermont 05676

VIRGINIA

State Police of Virginia
State of Virginia
Post Office Box 27272
Richmond, Virginia 23261

WASHINGTON

Washington State Police
State of Washington
Post Office Box 2527
Olympia, Washington 98504

WEST VIRGINIA

West Virginia State Police
State of West Virginia
725 Jefferson Road
South Charleston, West Virginia 25309

WISCONSIN

Wisconsin Law Enforcement Bureau
State of Wisconsin
Post Office Box 2718
Madison, Wisconsin 53701

WYOMING

Criminal Investigation Bureau
State of Wyoming
316 West 22nd Street
Cheyenne, Wyoming 85002

After you have the subject's driving record and address, you may discover that the address is not the current one. Of course, there are many ways to receive a person's new address but you may want to write to the appropriate motor vehicle department and, armed with the subject's date of birth from the driving record, request a list of all motor vehicles listed in the subject's name. Many times the search will reveal that the subject is co-owner of a vehicle with a spouse, friend or business associate.

Motor vehicle registrations are important to request in the event that the address on the subject's driving record is not current. A drivers license may be **renewed as infrequently as every eight years**. Since motor vehicle registrations are **renewed every year**, you will obtain a more current address.

Here is a sample of a letter:

Date
John Anyone
123 Anywhere Drive
Anytown, New York 12345
Telephone Number: 212-555-1234

Dear Commissioner of Motor Vehicles:
Kindly send me the motor vehicle information for vehicles owned by : Robert Hamilton, Date of Birth: 03/04/43. Please find attached a check to cover the costs of the requested registration information for up to five vehicles. If there are more than five vehicles, please contact me and I will be glad to remit the amount requested.

Sincerely,
John Anyone

Fees were not included in this chapter because most of the states will adjust prices within the next twenty-four months. Write to the states for their current price structure. Please note that all government agencies, including driving and motor vehicle records departments, are constantly changing policies insofar as what access to records and files will be accorded the public.

For instance, a marriage record is public record in Dade County Florida whereas a marriage record is NOT public in any of the five boroughs of New York City. Also, for example, California restricts access to driving records. However, Florida will not only send you the driving record you requested but will give the individual's social security number as part of the record.

Now that you have the registration information, you may want to do additional research. Every state keeps a record of all transactions regarding the sale of a motor vehicle because of the need to ensure continuity of odometer readings and to prove that the records followed a specific sequence in case the validity of a vehicle identification number is questioned in the event of tampering.

You may want to request a "body file" or "vehicle history" of a particular motor vehicle of the subject. You will receive a packet that may occasionally include up to thirty pages.

The photocopies will include paperwork with the subject's signature. This may help you to compare what you have on record as positive proof that you are on the right track pursuing leads for the location of the correct subject.

You will also see that the history of the motor vehicle will indicate what previous addresses were contained on the yearly registrations. You may need these addresses so that you can contact the current occupants and inquire as to where your subject may have moved to.

The information will indicate the name and address of the previous owner. This individual may have known the subject and may be able to provide you with more information. Even if the previous owner did not know the subject ask the individual if, through casual conversation, when the sale of the vehicle was being consummated, there was any mention of employment or other personal information. If you recall the last time you bought or sold a vehicle, look how much information you and the other person exchanged just chatting.

If you write and request the file on a vehicle that the subject does not own anymore this may provide new information relating to the location of the subject. The packet of information you will receive about the sold vehicle will indicate the new owner's address. Your subject may have sold the vehicle to this person because the subject needed money, was leaving the state and wanted to sell an extra vehicle, wanted the money from the sale so that they could buy a new vehicle, etc. The point is the subject, like all of us, had to explain to the buyer why the vehicle was being sold. There will be many possibilities for new information regarding the location of your subject from this simple method of inquiry.

Here is a sample letter to order a "body file" or "vehicle history":

Date

John Anyone
123 Anywhere Drive
Anytown, New York 12345
Telephone Number: 212-558-1234

Dear Tag Department:
   Kindly send the complete vehicle history of the following vehicle:

>   *Title number: 74651201*
>   *Vehicle Identification Number: 2398UTG670KR453H6*

   *I have attached a check for $8.00. If this is not sufficient, please contact
me and I will remit the requested amount.*

Sincerely,
John Anymore

REGISTRATION AND TITLES

ALABAMA

Department of Motor Vehicles
State of Alabama
Post Office Box 104-G
Montgomery, Alabama 36101

ALASKA

Department of Motor Vehicles
State of Alaska
5700 Todor Road
Anchorage, Alaska 99507

ARIZONA

Department of Motor Vehicles
State of Arizona
1801 West Jefferson Street
Phoenix, Arizona 85001

ARKANSAS

Department of Motor Vehicles
State of Arkansas
Post Office 1272-R
Little Rock, Arkansas 72203

CALIFORNIA

Department of Motor Vehicles
State of California
Post Office Box 932328-A
Sacramento, California 94232

COLORADO

Department of Motor Vehicles
State of Colorado
140 West 6th Street
Denver, Colorado 80204

CONNECTICUT

Department of Motor Vehicles
State of Connecticut
60 State Street
Wethersfield, Connecticut 06109

DELAWARE

Department of Motor Vehicles
State of Delaware
State Office Building
Dover, Delaware 19903

DISTRICT OF COLUMBIA

Department of Motor Vehicles
District of Columbia
301 C Street
Washington, D.C. 20001

FLORIDA

Department of Motor Vehicles
State of Florida
2900 Apalachee Parkway
Tallahassee, Florida 32399

GEORGIA

Department of Motor Vehicles
State of Georgia
104 Trinty Washington Building
Atlanta, Georgia 30334

HAWAII

Department of Motor Vehicles
State of Hawaii
896 Punchbowl Street
Honolulu, Hawaii 96813

IDAHO

Department of Motor Vehicles
State of Idaho
Post Office Box 34-N
Boise, Idaho 83731

ILLINOIS

Department of Motor Vehicles
State of Illinois
Centennial Government Building
Springfield, Illinois 62756

INDIANA

Department of Motor Vehicles
State of Indiana
State Office Building, Room 416
Indianapolis, Indiana 46204

IOWA

Department of Motor Vehicles
State of Iowa
Park Fair Mall, Box 9204
Des Moines, Iowa 50306

KANSAS

Department of Motor Vehicles
State of Kansas
Post Office Box 12021-D
Topeka, Kansas 66616

KENTUCKY

Department of Motor Vehicles
State of Kentucky
State Building, Room 204
Frankfort, Kentucky 40622

LOUISIANA

Department of Motor Vehicles
State of Louisiana
Post Office Box 64886-P
Baton Rouge, Louisiana 70896

MAINE

Department of Motor Vehicle
State of Maine
State Building
Augusta, Maine 04333

MARYLAND

Department of Motor Vehicles
State of Maryland
6601 Ritchie Highway, N.E.
Glen Burnie, Maryland 21062

MASSACHUSETTS

Department of Motor Vehicles
Commonwealth of Massachusetts
100 Nashua Street, Room 100
Boston, Massachusetts 02114

MICHIGAN

Department of Motor Vehicles
State of Michigan
Mutual Government Building
Lansing, Michigan 48918

MINNESOTA

Department of Motor Vehicles
State of Minnesota
Transportation Building, Room 159
Saint Paul, Minnesota 55155

MISSISSIPPI

Department of Motor Vehicles
State of Mississippi
Post Office Box 1140-A
Jackson, Mississippi 39205

MISSOURI

Department of Motor Vehicles
State of Missouri
Post Office Box 100-J
Jefferson City, Missouri 65105

MONTANA

Department of Motor Vehicles
State of Montana
925 Main Street
Deer Lodge, Montana 59722

NEBRASKA

Department of Motor Vehicles
State of Nebraska
Post Office Box 94789-O
Lincoln, Nebraska 68509

NEVADA

Department of Motor Vehicles
State of Nevada
State Building
Carson City, Nevada 89111

NEW HAMPSHIRE

Department of Motor Vehicles
State of New Hampshire
James H. Hayes Building
Concord, New Hampshire 03305

NEW JERSEY

Department of Motor Vehicles
State of New Jersey
135 East State Street
Trenton, New Jersey 08666

NEW MEXICO

Department of Motor Vehicles
State of New Mexico
Post Office Box 1028-E
Santa Fe, New Mexico 87504

NEW YORK

Department of Motor Vehicles
State of New York
State Office Building North
Albany, New York 12228

NORTH CAROLINA

Department of Motor Vehicles
State of North Carolina
1100 New Bern Avenue, Room 124
Raleigh, North Carolina 27697

NORTH DAKOTA

Department of Motor Vehicles
State of North Dakota
806 East Boulevard
Bismarck, North Dakota 58505

OHIO

Department of Motor Vehicles
State of Ohio
Post Office Box 16520
Columbus, Ohio 43266

OKLAHOMA

Department of Motor Vehicles
State of Oklahoma
409 Northeast 28 Street
Oklahoma City, Oklahoma 73105

OREGON

Department of Motor Vehicles
State of Oregon
1905 Lana Avenue, N.E.
Salem, Oregon 97314

PENNSYLVANIA

Department of Motor Vehicles
Commonwealth of Pennsylvania
Post Office Box 8691
Harrisburg, Pennsylvania 17105

PUERTO RICO

Department of Motor Vehicles
Commonwealth of Puerto Rico
Post Office Box 41269
Santurce, Puerto Rico 00940

RHODE ISLAND

Department of Motor Vehicles
State of Rhode Island
State Office Building
Providence, Rhode Island 02903

SOUTH CAROLINA

Department of Motor Vehicles
State of South Carolina
Post Office Box 1498-L
Columbia, South Carolina 29216

SOUTH DAKOTA

Department of Motor Vehicles
State of South Dakota
118 West Capitol Avenue
Pierre, South Dakota 57501

TENNESSEE

Department of Motor Vehicles
State of Tennessee
500 Deaderick Street
Nashville, Tennessee 37242

TEXAS

Department of Motor Vehicles
State of Texas
5805 North Lamar Boulevard
Austin, Texas 78773

UTAH

Department of Motor Vehicles
State of Utah
1095 Motor Avenue
Salt Lake City, Utah 84116

VERMONT

Department of Motor Vehicles
State of Vermont
120 State Street
Montpelier, Vermont 05603

VIRGINIA

Department of Motor Vehicles
State of Virginia
Post Office Box 27412-O
Richmond, Virginia 23269

WASHINGTON

Department of Motor Vehicles
State of Washington
Post Office Box 9909-V
Olympia, Washington 98504

WEST VIRGINIA

Department of Motor Vehicles
State of West Virginia
State Office Building
Charleston, West Virginia 25305

WISCONSIN

Department of Motor Vehicles
State of Wisconsin
4802 Sheboygan Avenue
Madison, Wisconsin 53707

WYOMING

Department of Motor Vehicles
State of Wyoming
122 West 25th Street
Cheyenne, Wyoming 82002

ALBERTA

Department of Motor Vehicles
10365 97th Street
Edmonton, Alberta T5J 3W7

BRITISH COLUMBIA

Department of Motor Vehicles
2631 Douglas Street
Victoria, British Columbia V8T 5A3

MANITOBA

Department of Motor Vehicles
1075 Portage Avenue
Winnipeg, Manitoba R3G 0S1

NEW BRUNSWICK

Department of Motor Vehicles
Post Office Box 6000-E
Fredericton, New Brunswick E3B 5H1

NEWFOUNDLAND

Department of Motor Vehicles
Post Office Box 8710-S
Saint John's, Newfoundland A1B 4J5

NORTHWEST TERRITORIES

Department of Motor Vehicles
Post Office Box 1320-Y
Yellowknife, N.W.T. X1A 2L9

NOVA SCOTIA

Department of Motor Vehicles
Post Office Box 54-O
Halifax, Nova Scotia B3J 2L4

ONTARIO

Department of Motor Vehicles
2680 Keele Street
Downsview, Ontario M3M 3E6

PRINCE EDWARD ISLAND

Department of Motor Vehicles
Post Office Box 2000
Charlottetown,
Prince Edward Island C1A 7N8

QUEBÉC

Department of Motor Vehicles
1037 de la Chevrotiere Street
Quebéc, Quebéc G1R 4Y7

SASKATCHEWAN

Department of Motor Vehicles
2260 11th Avenue
Regina, Saskatchewan S4P 2N7

YUKON

Department of Motor Vehicles
Post Office Box 2703-U
Whitehorse, Yukon Y1A 2C6

The following two articles will show how regular people have retrieved motor vehicle records with great success. In the first article, Harry Pugh was able to access his daughter's driving record and found her after 28 years. In the second article, Annie Boyd Hill located her son after 48 years and he was found because of a simple inquiry to the driver's license bureau.

St. Petersburg Times

Friday, November 13th, 1992

Happy Tears for Dad and Daughter

After more than 28 years, a father and daughter are reunited while The Flower of Scotland is heard on the bagpipes.

By Matthew Sauer
Times Staff Writer

The pipers may have never sounded so sweet.

Harry Pugh of Indian Rocks Beach was reunited Thursday with his daughter, Mary Kay Craig, after a separation of more than 28 years. The last time Pugh, 62, saw Mary Kay, now 30, she was 1 1/2 years old.

The two met at Tampa International Airport to the sounds of Highland Games pipe major Henry Boyd playing The Flower of Scotland. Pugh takes part in the Highland Games in Treasure Island every year, and Boyd volunteered to play the bagpipes in full regalia when Mary Kay arrived.

The day before his daughter's ar-

rival, Pugh was wondering whether he would cry when she arrived. He did, saying the sound of the bagpipe took him over the edge.

"All they have to do is play The Flower of Scotland and it gets me every time," Pugh said as he talked with his new-found daughter.

Pugh's two other daughters, Lorraine and Allison, came to the airport to meet their sister. Lorraine had been introduced to Mary Kay years earlier as a friend, but they had never met as sisters. Allison is Pugh's daughter from his second marriage.

Mary Kay, who is eight months pregnant, said it would take her time to adjust to having a father who, for years, she thought was dead.

"I'm just a little overwhelmed with this right now," she said.

Mary Kay's child will be Pugh's second grandchild. Allison's son, Aaron, will be a year old Sunday.

As Boyd played his bagpipe, a curious crowd of about 50 people gathered to see what the emotional reunion was all about. Several people in the crowd seemed to be as caught up in the reunion as Pugh and his daughter.

Pugh lost touch with his daughter after he was divorced in 1965. He was granted custody of Lorraine, who was then 9, and Mary Kay who was then 1 1/2. Pugh said that soon afterward he allowed Mary Kay to lover with her mother because he didn't have the time to take care of her and to work.

Pugh returned to his native England to be with his mother and sister. He said he wanted his daughter to have female figures to relate to.

"At a time like that, you need to be around people that know you well", Pugh said. "Friends can say what they think are the right things to say, but you really need your family."

Pugh lost touch with his ex-wife. Mary Kay's stepfather and mother moved around, and Pugh said it was difficult to keep track of those changes.

Later, Pugh was transferred back to the United States and he made trips to Canada with Lorraine to attempt to find Mary Kay, who he thought was living in Ontario.

"It seemed impossible to contact them," Pugh said.

Pugh retired five years ago with a disability after an accident. More free time in front of the TV eventually led to Thursday's reunion.

Pugh saw an interview on the Maury Povich Show with a private detective who was explaining how easy it was to track people using their driver's license. Pugh decided to use daughter's Canadian license to find her.

After a telephone call to Canada and a little paperwork, Pugh had his daughter's phone number.

Two weeks later, Pugh called her.

"She was really shocked," Pugh said, describing their conversation. "I said 'Mary Kay . . . This is your father.' She said, "My real father?' I said 'Yes.' She told me that she had to sit down. . . .She had been told that I was dead."

Pugh said he's glad he took the advice of the television detective.

"He said it was so easy, but to the layman, it seemed tough," Pugh said. "In the end, it took me three weeks and $5. I've got to thank Maury Povich for that."

(Reprinted by permission, the St. Petersburg Times)

Mom finds missing son who was taken in '45

By Ron Avery
Daily News Staff Writer

Annie Boyd Hill was a live-in nanny of a wealthy Germantown family in the early 1940s.

She made $6 a week and paid $2 to a woman in West Philadelphia who cared for her baby boy, whom she visited on her days off.

One day in 1945, the West Philadelphia woman disappeared with 2-year-old Albert "Billy" Boyd.

About a week ago, Annie, now 69, was finally reunited with her baby - now approaching his 50th birthday.

They sit in the living room of Albert Boyd's home in Logan trying to tell their story, but every paragraph is punctuated by tears.

The emotions are so overwhelming, the story so complicated, but they have no doubt that they are truly mother and son.

They say the woman who took the baby and raised him as her own son was Carrie May Jones, who died in 1972.

Albert's earliest years are vague. The woman he called "Mom" kept moving from place to place, job to job. Like his real mother, she worked mostly in the houses of the wealthy as a servant or nanny.

She finally settled in East Orange, N.J., when Albert was about 10. He used the family name "Jones" throughout his school years.

But at 18, he needed his birth certificate to get a Social Security card and to register for the draft.

At this point, "Mom" decided to reveal part of the truth. "She told me she wasn't my biological mother," says Boyd. "She had a copy of my real birth certificate, showing my name as Albert William Boyd.

"She said my mother was a teenager who got pregnant, but couldn't keep me," says Boyd. "She said the grandparents sent her back down South. I did learn my mother's name was Annie Boyd.

"But she told me, 'I'm the only mother you've ever known,' " recalls Boyd. " 'I'm the person who has loved and raised you.' She had been a good mother in most ways. I just accepted the story. I had no other recourse."

Although he decided not to search for the woman who seemed to have abandoned him, he did change his name from Jones to Boyd.

Annie married but she never had another child. And she never gave up her dream of finding her lost baby.

"I was young. I didn't know what to do," she explains. "I went to a lawyer. He hired a detective. The detective traced her to Broomall and Bryn Mawr and New Jersey. He said he lost her tracks in Atlanta.

"By that time, we had spent $5,000. It was a lot of money back then. I couldn't afford to search anymore," she says softly.

But she never stopped hoping. She always told friends the story of her missing baby. From time to time, she or friends attempted to find Albert. Once she wrote the armed services requesting help. But Albert never served in the military.

Albert moved to Philadelphia in 1970 and lived for many years in Germantown. His mother lived in West Philadelphia. Their paths never crossed.

Two years ago, Annie moved back to her native North Carolina, where she has a huge number of relatives.

Late last year, she was at the hairdresser in Zebulon, N.C. The shop's television was tuned to the Maury Povich Show. The guest was the author of a book on how to trace missing people.

"He was talking about cases just like mine, and I started crying," Annie recalls.

She wound up telling her story to everyone in the beauty parlor. Shop owner Edith Harris decided to buy the book on tracing missing persons and renew Annie's search.

The beautician's efforts paid off quickly. Following the advice of the **author, she wrote to the Pennsylvania driver's licensing bureau. She asked for addresses of any Boyds or Jones with the birth date of June 15, 1943.**

Harris got Boyd's name and address from the state and wrote about a month ago. Mother and son spoke every day on the telephone until Annie arrived in Philadelphia for an extended visit. "I thought I would have an anxiety attack the day Mom arrived," says Boyd. "All my wife's family was here and this whole place was crying.

"When my mom and I talk, it's like reading a book," says Boyd. She tells me about her life...I've met some of my family here in Philadelphia. There's one cousin that looks so much like me, it's like looking in a mirror."

Annie says "I prayed every night for 50 years...Mother's Days were the hardest for me, to see other women in my family surrounded by grandchildren.

"I always asked God just to see Albert again," she adds. "It took all this time. I'll be 70 in May. My biggest worry was that he might be dead."

"That was my fear, too," adds the son. "I was afraid that if I spent time searching for my mother and discovered she was dead, it would be too devastating. I didn't want to go through that."

This Mother's Day will be Annie's happiest, with a newfound son, daughter-in-law and four grandchildren.

Every July there's a massive family reunion in North Carolina, where Boyd will meet about 500 kinfolk he never knew existed.

(Reprinted by permission, the Philadelphia Daily News)

Births, Deaths, Marriages & Divorces

BIRTH RECORDS

Birth Records will usually contain the following information:

Complete name
Subject's exact date of birth
Place of birth
Name of the father and mother
Age of the father and mother
Occupation of the father and mother
Mother's maiden name
Address of the father and mother
Place of birth of the father and mother

Complete name: You will need an exact name when checking the motor vehicle records. A middle name is of importance because many individuals use a middle name prominently later on. For example: G. Gordon Liddy, J. Edgar Hoover, F. Scott Fitzgerald, H. Norman Schwartzkopf.

Subject's exact date of birth: If you did not have the exact date of birth of your subject, you would have ordered a search for a particular year or a span of several years. Now that you have the birth record, you now have the exact date of birth.

Place of birth: There is much research that can be done when you are aware of the place of birth of your subject. You may want to search for other relatives at the city of birth. You will see elsewhere in this book a firm mentioned that does specialized computer work called the Research Investigative Services. They will run on a city, state or nationwide basis any name for a listing for a telephone number so if the birth certificate of your subject lists the name Robert Rowland of Hialeah, Florida as the father, you may run the name Robert Rowland nationwide or have Research Investigative Services run all the Robert Rowland names in the southern part of Florida. You may also run just the last name Rowland with no first name for Southern Florida or Hialeah. You will probably be able to contact a sibling, cousin, uncle, aunt or a grandparent who may be able to give you the location of your subject. Of course, the leads that can be provided by relatives of the subject speaks for itself and you can be assured that the information is accurate because of the source.

Name of father and mother: From the birth record, you now have the complete name of the father and mother. If you feel that the subject's parents may be alive then you can conduct a search of the motor vehicle records for their location. They may be able to provide information.

Age of the father and mother: Birth records will usually contain the age but not the exact date of birth of the parents. The age of the parents at the time of birth of the subject will give you an approximate year of birth.

Occupation of the father and mother: The occupations, professions or trades of both parents are listed on the birth certificate. If you have a problem with finding the parents of the subject, you may want to check trade associations and unions if the parents had occupations that required participation or membership in an organization. The occupation listing may list physician, attorney, barber, taxi driver, certified public accountant, or any of a myriad of professions that necessitate licensing which generate records that are public information. You will want to inquire if the parent is still licensed or order a record from the archives if many years have passed. Again, contacting a parent of the subject is another avenue you will want to evaluate.

Mother's maiden name: The mother's name is of importance because this will be one of the only records you will be able to retrieve to access the mother's maiden name from. You may want to conduct a search for the family of the mother and question them on the whereabouts of your subject who, of course, is their relative.

Address of father and mother: The address of the parents at the time of birth may be different from the place of birth of your subject. You may want to check property records. The family may still own the residence or, as has happened before, the subject may own property through an inheritance. If you discover that the property the address matches was a rental by the parents you may want to inquire through the real estate records who owned the property then and who owns the property now. An inquiry to the owner may provide information as to the whereabouts of the parents.

Place of birth of the father and mother: Because of the need to contact the parents in certain cases, the place of birth of the parents is of value. Remember that the parents may be divorced and together with the fact that many years may have passed, a place of birth of either parent will yield a starting point for a search for each parent.

In difficult cases where the subject can just not be located, I have found that contact with the family will provide information that could not have been developed independently. To locate a missing person requires a coalition of resources. If every avenue fails in the search for your subject, the contact with the family is a key that many do not utilize because their location at the present time seems hopeless to ascertain. But as you see from the birth record you have enough information regarding the parents to conduct a search.

DEATH RECORDS

Death records provide the following:

> **A person's complete name**
> **Date of death**
> **Date of birth**
> **Social Security Number of the deceased**
> **Place of birth of the deceased**
> **Occupation of the deceased**
> **Place of death**
> **Cause of death**
> **Name of the father and mother of the deceased**
> **Mother's maiden name**
> **Name and address of cemetery or crematory**
> **Name of physician that certified cause of death**

Death records are of value because you may want to order a search to be conducted on the parent or a relative of the subject you are trying to find. From the death record you will be able to have enough information to possibly contact persons who know your subject.

Step one was to order a sweep done on several years if you do not know when a parent or sibling died. Now that you have the death record you will see there are several avenues to explore. You may want to contact the funeral home listed on the death record. The funeral home maintains records in hard copy form. On record will be the person responsible for making and paying for the arrangement of internment. Many times, as you can imagine, this person may be your subject or at the very least a relative that may know where your subject is.

Cause of death is important because one of the most successful methods of locating a subject is through autopsy records. Check to see if a parent, sibling or relative has died. If the cause of death is homicide, automobile accident, industrial accident, etc., an autopsy is performed. In many locales, the autopsy is public record. The routine entries in the files will provide very specific information. The medical examiner makes notes regarding who was contacted to make arrangements for disposition of the body. The full names, telephone numbers and addresses of relatives are entered on the record.

If you do not have an autopsy to review, you may want to contact the probate court. If the parent of the subject died without a will (intestate), there will be a wealth of information in the probate court files. Information in the file will contain the names, addresses and amounts of monies of each of the persons who are recognized by the court as heirs. If your subject's whereabouts is unknown at the time the estate is distributed, there will be a note in the file under distribution of assets that reads: "Registry of the County Probate Court will hold for John Doe (subject's name), son of decedent, all monies in escrow until whereabouts of this heir has been determined." When you see this written, search through the entire file because professional heir finders have most likely located the subject and the release forms and other information are in the file.

MARRIAGE RECORDS

Marriage records will provide the following information about the bride and groom:

> **Name**
> **Address**
> **Date of birth**
> **Place of birth**
> **Previous marriage status (married or never married)**
> **Last marriage ended by: (death, divorce or annulment)**
> **Number of previous marriages**
> **If divorced, where**
> **Name of person performing the ceremony**
> **Signatures of bride and groom**
> **Names of the witnesses**

There are a myriad of uses for the information gleaned from the marriage record. If you do not know if your male or female subject is married, order a search conducted for a span of several years. If you do locate a marriage record then review the certificate for the above noted information. If there is a divorce indicated, you may want to order a copy of the divorce file. The witnesses and person who performed the ceremony may be contacted. They may know obscure details about the bride and groom, and may even know the whereabouts of your subject.

Marriage records are one of the best ways to find the changes in a female name. Start with an age at which you believe the first marriage occurred. You will have the first marriage searched by the maiden name. After you have that record, you may want to now search the marriage records with the new name. Then, of course, this can be done until you are satisfied that you have the current name.

DIVORCE RECORDS

A review of a complete divorce file will yield information that is unattainable anywhere else. The file will contain the names and ages of the children of the subject. If time has passed and the children are of age, they may be of assistance in locating the subject. You may, of course, use all the regular means of locating one or all of the children.

The divorce file will contain a list of vehicles owned by the couple and will include the vehicle identification number (VIN) in many instances. See which vehicle your subject took possession of. Even if this case is years old, the VIN will never change on a vehicle, so you may want to order a body history on the vehicle. If your subject does not own the vehicle anymore, you will be able to see all the documentation that will include the name of the person who purchased it. You will then contact that individual and they may be able to provide information about your subject.

Many times the divorce file will specify what boats or vessels the couple owned. You will want to follow the course outlined in the above paragraph.

The divorce file will contain a listing of property owned. You will learn what real estate your subject retained. If your subject keeps even a small undeveloped piece of land, this will be of help. The mailing address for the tax bill will be public record and may lead you to your subject.

Place of event	Cost of copy	Address	Remarks
Alabama			
Birth or Death	$5.00	Center for Health Statistics State Department of Public Health 434 Monroe Street Montgomery, AL 36130-1701	State office has had records since January 1908. Additional copies at same time are $2.00 each. Fee for special searches is $5.00 per hour. Money order or certified check should be made payable to **Center for Health Statistics**. Personal checks are not accepted. To verify current fees, the telephone number is **(205) 242-5033**.
Marriage	$5.00	Same as Birth or Death	State office has had records since August 1936.
	Varies	See remarks	Probate Judge in county where license was issued.
Divorce	$5.00	Same as Birth or Death	State office has had records since January 1950.
	Varies	See remarks	Clerk or Register of Court of Equity in county where divorce was granted.
Alaska			
Birth or Death	$7.00	Department of Health and Social Services Bureau of Vital Statistics P.O. Box H-02G Juneau, AK 99811-0675	State office has had records since January 1913. Money order should be payable to **Bureau of Vital Statistics**. Personal checks are not accepted. To verify current fees, the telephone number is **(907) 465-3391**. This will be a **recorded** message.
Marriage	$7.00	Same as Birth or Death	State office has had records since 1913.
Divorce	$7.00	Same as Birth or Death	State office has had records since 1950.
	Varies	See remarks	Clerk of Superior Court in judicial district where divorce was granted. Juneau and Ketchikan (First District), Nome (Second District), Anchorage (Third District), Fairbanks (Fourth District).

Place of event	Cost of copy	Address	Remarks
American Samoa			
Birth or Death	$2.00	Registrar of Vital Statistics Vital Statistics Section Government of American Samoa Pago Pago, AS 96799	Registrar has had records since 1900. Money order should be made payable to **ASG Treasurer**. Personal checks are not accepted. To verify current fees, the telephone number is **(684) 633-1222, extension 214**. Personal identification required before record will be sent.
Marriage	$2.00	Same as Birth or Death	
Divorce	$1.00	High Court of American Samoa Tutuila, AS 96799	
Arizona			
Birth (long form)	$8.00	Vital Records Section	State office has records since July
Birth (short form)	$5.00	Arizona Department of Health Services P.O. Box 3887	1909 and abstracts of records filed in counties before then.
Death	$5.00	Phoenix, AZ 85030	Check or money order should be made payable to **Office of Vital Records**. Personal checks are accepted. To verify current fees, the telephone number is **(602) 542-1080**. This will be a **recorded** message. Applicants must submit a copy of picture identification or have their request notarized.
Marriage	Varies	See remarks	Clerk of Superior Court in county where license was issued.
Divorce	Varies	See remarks	Clerk of Superior Court in county where divorce was granted.
Arkansas			
Birth	$5.00	Division of Vital	State office has had records since
Death	$4.00	Records Arkansas Department of Health 4815 West Markham St. Little Rock, AR 72201	February 1914 and some original Little Rock and Fort Smith records from 1881. Additional copies of death record, when requested at the same time, are $1.00 each.

Place of event	Cost of copy	Address	Remarks
Arkansas (cont)			
			Check or money order should be made payable to **Arkansas Department of Health**. Personal checks are accepted. To verify current fees, call **(501) 661-2336**. This will be a **recorded** message.
Marriage	$5.00	Same as Birth or Death	Coupons since 1917.
	Varies	See remarks	Full certified copy may be obtained from County Clerk in county where license was issued.
Divorce	$5.00	Same as Birth or Death	Coupons since 1923.
	Varies	See remarks	Full certified copy may be obtained from Circuit or Chancery Clerk in county where divorce was granted.
California			
Birth	$11.00	Vital Statistics Section	State office has had records since
Death	$7.00	Department of Health Services 410 N Street Sacramento, CA 95814	July 1905. For earlier records, write to County Recorder in county where event occurred.
			Check or money order should be made payable to **State Registrar, Department of Health Services** or **Vital Statistics**. Personal checks are accepted. To verify current fees, the telephone number is **(916) 445-2684**.
Heirloom Birth	$30.00	Same as Birth or Death	Decorative birth certificate (11" x 14") suitable for framing.
Marriage	$11.00	Same as Birth or Death	State office has had records since July 1905. For earlier records, write to County Recorder in county where event occurred.
Divorce	$11.00	Same as Birth or Death	Fee is for search and identification of county where certified copy can be obtained. Certified copies are not available from State Health Department.
	Varies	See remarks	Clerk of Superior Court in county where divorce was granted.

Place of event	Cost of copy	Address	Remarks
Canal Zone			
Birth or Death	$2.00	Panama Canal Commission Vital Statistics Clerk APO Miami, FL 34011	Records available from May 1904 to September 1979.
Marriage	$1.00	Same as Birth or Death	Records available from May 1904 to September 1979.
Divorce	$0.50	Same as Birth or Death	Records available from May 1904 to September 1979.
Colorado			
Birth or Death	$6.00 Regular service $10.00 Priority service	Vital Records Section Colorado Department of Health 4210 East 11th Avenue Denver, CO 80220	State office has had death records since 1900 and birth records since 1910. State office also has birth records for some counties for years before 1910. Regular service means the record is mailed within 3 weeks. Priority service means the record is mailed within 5 days. Check or money order should be made payable to **Colorado Department of Health**. Personal checks are accepted. To verify current fees, the telephone number is **(303) 320-8474**. This will be a **recorded** message.
Marriage	See remarks	Same as Birth or Death	Certified copies are not available from State Health Department. Statewide index of records for 1900-39 and 1975 to present. Fee for verification is $6.00.
	Varies	See remarks	Copies available from County Clerk in county where license was issued.
Divorce	See remarks	Same as Birth or Death	Certified copies are not available from State Health Department. Statewide index of records for 1900-39 and 1968 to present. Fee for verification is $6.00
	Varies	See remarks	Copies available from Clerk of District Court in county where divorce was granted.

Place of event	Cost of copy	Address	Remarks
Connecticut			
Birth or Death	$5.00	Vital Records Department of Health Services 150 Washington Street Hartford, CT 06106	State office has had records since July 1897. For earlier records, write to Registrar of Vital Statistics in town or city where event occurred.
			Check or money order should be made payable to **Department of Health Services**. Personal checks are accepted. FAX requests are not accepted. Must have original signature on request. To verify current fees, the telephone number is **(203) 566-2334**. This will be a **recorded** message.
Marriage	$5.00	Same as Birth or Death	Records since July 1897.
		See remarks	Registrar of Vital Statistics in town where license was issued.
Divorce		See remarks	Index of records since 1947. Applicant must contact Clerk of Superior Court where divorce was granted. State office does not have divorce decrees and cannot issue certified copies.
Delaware			
Birth or Death	$5.00	Office of Vital Statistics Division of Public Health P.O. Box 637 Dover, DE 19903	State office has death records since 1930 and birth records since 1920. Additional copies of the same record requested at the same time are $3.00 each.
			Check or money order should be made payable to **Office of Vital Statistics**. Personal checks are accepted. To verify current fees, the telephone number is **(302) 736-4721**.
Marriage	$5.00	Same as Birth or Death	Records since 1930. Additional copies of the same record requested at the same time are $3.00 each.
Divorce	See remarks	Same as Birth or Death	Records since 1935. Inquiries will be forwarded to appropriate office. Fee for search and verification of

Place of event	Cost of copy	Address	Remarks
Delaware (cont)			essential facts of divorce is $5.00 for each 5-year period searched. Certified copies are not available from State office.
	$2.00	See remarks	Prothonotary in county where divorce was granted up to 1975. For divorces granted after 1975 the parties concerned should contact Family Court in county where divorce was granted.
District of Columbia			
Birth or Death	$8.00	Vital Records Branch Room 3009 425 I Street, NW Washington, DC 20001	Office has had death records since 1855 and birth records since 1874 but no death records were filed during the Civil War.
			Cashiers check or money order should be made payable to **DC Treasurer**. To verify current fees, call **(202) 727-9821**.
Marriage	$5.00	Marriage Bureau 515 5th Street, NW Washington, DC 20001	
Divorce	$2.00	Clerk, Superior Court for the District of Columbia, Family Division 500 Indiana Avenue, NW Washington, DC 20001	Records since September 16, 1956.
	Varies	Clerk, U.S. District Court for the District of Colombia Washington, DC 20001	Records since September 16, 1956.
Florida			
Birth *Death*	$8.00 $4.00	Department of Health and Rehabilitative Services Office of Vital Statistics 1217 Pearl Street Jacksonville, FL 32202	State office has some birth records dating back to April 1865 and some death records dating back to August 1877. The majority of records date from January 1917. (If the exact date is unknown, the fee is $8.00 (births) or $4.00 (deaths) for the first year searched and $2.00 for each additional year up to a maxi-

Place of event	Cost of copy	Address	Remarks
Florida (cont)			mum of $50.00. Fee includes one certification of record if found or certified statement stating record not on file.) Additional copies are $3.00 each when requested at the same time.
			Check or money order should be made payable to **Office of Vital Statistics**. Personal checks are accepted. To verify current fees, the telephone number is **(904) 359-6900**. This will be a **recorded** message.
Marriage	$4.00	Same as Birth or Death	Records since June 6, 1927. (If the exact date is unknown, the fee is $4.00 for the first year searched and $2.00 for each additional year up to a maximum of $50.00. Fee includes one copy of record if found or certified statement stating record not on file.) Additional copies are $3.00 each when requested at the same time.
Divorce	$4.00	Same as Birth or Death	Records since June 6, 1927. (If the exact date is unknown, the fee is $4.00 for the first year searched and $2.00 for each additional year up to a maximum of $50.00. Fee includes one copy of record if found or certified statement stating record not on file.) Additional copies are $3.00 each when requested at the same time.
Georgia			
Birth or Death	$3.00	Georgia Department of Human Resources Vital Records Unit Room 217-H 47 Trinity Avenue, SW Atlanta, GA 30334	State office had records since January 1919. For earlier records in Atlanta or Savannah, write to County Health Department in county where event occurred. Additional copies of same record ordered at same time are $1.00 each except birth cards, which are $4.00 each.
			Money order should be made payable to **Vital Records, GA. DHR**.

Place of event	Cost of copy	Address	Remarks
Georgia (cont)			Personal checks are not accepted. To verify current fees, the telephone number is **(404) 656-4900**. This is a **recorded** message.
Marriage	$3.00	Same as Birth or Death	Centralized State records since June 9, 1952. Certified copies are issued at State office. Inquiries about marriages occurring before June 9, 1952, will be forwarded to appropriate Probate Judge in county where license was issued.
	$3.00	See remarks	Probate Judge in county where license issued.
Divorce	Varies	See remarks	Centralized State records since June 9, 1952. Certified copies are not issued at State office. Inquiries will be forwarded to appropriate Clerk of Superior Court in county where divorce was granted.
	$3.00	See remarks	Clerk of Superior Court in county where divorce was granted.
Guam			
Birth or Death	$5.00	Office of Vital Statistics Department of Public Health and Social Services Government of Guam P.O. Box 2816 Agana, GU, M.I. 96910	Office has had records since October 16, 1901.

Money order should be made payable to **Treasurer of Guam**. Personal checks are not accepted. To verify current fees, the telephone number is **(671) 734-7292**. |
Marriage	$5.00	Same as Birth or Death	
Divorce	Varies	Clerk, Superior Court of Guam Agana, GU, M.I. 96910	
Hawaii			
Birth or Death	$2.00	Office of Health Status Monitoring State Department of Health P.O. Box 3378 Honolulu, HI 96801	State office has had records since 1853.

Check or money order should be made payable to **State Department of Health**. Personal checks are |

Place of event	Cost of copy	Address	Remarks
Hawaii (cont)			accepted for the correct amount only. To verify current fees, the telephone number is **(808) 548-5819**. This is a **recorded** message.
Marriage	$2.00	Same as Birth or Death	
Divorce	$2.00	Same as Birth or Death	Records since July 1951.
	Varies	See remarks	Circuit Court in county where divorce was granted.
Idaho			
Birth or Death	$8.00	Vital Statistics Unit Idaho Department of Health and Welfare 450 West State Street Statehouse Mail Boise, ID 83720-9990	State office has had records since 1911. For records from 1907 to 1911, write to County Recorder in county where event occurred.

Check or money order should be made payable to **Idaho Vital Statistics**. Personal checks are accepted. To verify current fees, the telephone number is **(208) 334-5988**. This is a **recorded** message. |
Marriage	$8.00	Same as Birth or Death	Records since 1947. Earlier records are with County Recorder in county where license was issued.
	Varies	See remarks	County Recorder in county where license was issued.
Divorce	$8.00	Same as Birth or Death	Records since 1947. Earlier records are with County Recorder where divorce was granted.
	Varies	See remarks	County records in county where divorce was granted.
Illinois			
Birth or Death	$15.00 certified copy $10.00 certification	Division of Vital Records Illinois Department of Public Health 650 West Jefferson Street Springfield, IL 62702-5079	State office has had records since January 1916. For earlier records and for copies of State records since January 1916, write to County Clerk in county where event occurred (county fees vary). The fee for a search of the State files is $10.00. If the record is found, one certified copy is issued at no additional

Place of event	Cost of copy	Address	Remarks
Illinois (cont)			charge. Additional certified copies of the same record ordered at the same time are $2.00 each. The fee for a full certified copy is $15.00. Additional certified copies of the same record ordered at the same time are $2.00 each.
			Money orders, certified checks, or personal checks should be made payable to **Illinois Department of Public Health**. To verify current fees, the telephone number is **(217) 782-6553**. This will be a **recorded** message.
Marriage	$5.00	Same as Birth or Death	Records since January 1962. All items may be verified (fee $5.00). For certified copies, inquires will be forwarded to appropriate office. Certified copies are NOT available from State office.
Divorce	$5.00	Same as Birth or Death	Records since January 1962. Selected items may be verified (fee $5.00). Certified copies are NOT available from State office.
			For certified copies, write to the Clerk of Circuit Court in county where divorce was granted.
Indiana			
Birth *Death*	$6.00 $4.00	Vital Records Section State Board of Health 1330 West Michigan Street P.O. Box 1964 Indianapolis, IN 46206-1964	State office has had birth records since October 1907 and death records since 1900. Additional copies of the same record ordered at the same time are $1.00 each. For earlier records, write to Health Officer in city or county where event occurred.
			Check or money order should be made payable to **Indiana State Board of Health**. Personal checks are accepted. To verify current fees, the telephone number is **(317) 633-0274**.

Place of event	Cost of copy	Address	Remarks
Indiana (cont)			
Marriage	See remarks	Same as Birth or Death	Marriage index since 1958. Certified copies are not available from State Health Department.
	Varies	See remarks	Clerk of Circuit Court or Clerk of Superior Court in county where license was issued.
Divorce	Varies	See remarks	County Clerk in county where divorce was granted.
Iowa			
Birth or Death	$6.00	Iowa Department of Public Health Vital Records Section Lucas Office Building 321 East 12th Street Des Moines, IA 50319	State office has had records since July 1880. Check or money order should be made payable to **Iowa Department of Public Health**. To verify current fees, the telephone number is **(515) 281-5871**. This will be a **recorded** message.
Marriage	$6.00	Same as Birth or Death	State office has had records since July 1880.
Divorce	See remarks	Same as Birth or Death	Brief statistical record only since 1906. Inquiries will be forwarded to appropriate office. Certified copies are not available from State Health Department.
	$6.00	See remarks	Clerk of District Court in county where divorce was granted.
Kansas			
Birth or Death	$6.00	Office of Vital Statistics Kansas State Department of Health and Environment 900 Jackson Street Topeka, KS 66612-1290	State office has had records since July 1911. For earlier records, write to County Clerk in county where event occurred. Additional copies of same record ordered at same time are $3.00 each. Check or money order should be made payable to **State Registrar of Vital Statistics**. Personal checks are accepted. To verify current fees, the telephone number is **(913) 296-1400**. This will be a **recorded** message.

Place of event	Cost of copy	Address	Remarks
Kansas (cont)			
Marriage	$6.00	Same as Birth or Death	State office has had records since May 1913.
	Varies	See remarks	District Judge in county where license was issued.
Divorce	$6.00	Same as Birth or Death	State office has had records since July 1951.
	Varies	See remarks	Clerk of District Court in county where divorce was granted.
Kentucky			
Birth *Death*	$5.00 $4.00	Office of Vital Statistics Department for Health Services 275 East Main Street Frankfort, KY 40621	State office has had records since January 1911 and some records for the cities of Louisville, Lexington, Covington, and Newport before then.
			Check or money order should be made payable to **Kentucky State Treasurer**. Personal checks are accepted. To verify current fees, the telephone number is **(502) 564-4212**.
Marriage	$4.00	Same as Birth or Death	Records since June 1958.
	Varies	See remarks	Clerk of County Court in county where license was issued.
Divorce	$4.00	Same as Birth or Death	Records since June 1958.
	Varies	See remarks	Clerk of Circuit Court in county where decree was issued.
Louisiana			
Birth (long form) *Birth (short form)* *Death*	$8.00 $5.00 $5.00	Vital Records Registry Office of Public Health 325 Loyola Avenue New Orleans, LA 70112	State office has had records since July 1914. Birth records for City of New Orleans are available from 1790, and death records from 1803.
			Check or money order should be made payable to **Vital Records**. Personal checks are accepted. To verify current fees, the telephone number is **(504) 568-2561**.

Place of event	Cost of copy	Address	Remarks
Louisiana (cont)			
Marriage			
Orleans Parish	$5.00	Same as Birth or Death	
Other Parishes	Varies	See remarks	Certified copies are issued by Clerk of Court in parish where license was issued.
Divorce	Varies	See remarks	Clerk of Court in parish where divorce was granted.
Maine			
Birth or Death	$5.00	Office of Vital Records Human Services Building Station 11 State House Augusta, ME 04333	State office has had records since 1892. For earlier records, write to the municipality where the event occurred. Additional copies of same record ordered at same time are $2.00 each.
			Check or money order should be made payable to **Treasurer, State of Maine**. Personal checks are accepted. To verify current fees, the telephone number is **(207) 289-3184.**
Marriage	$5.00	Same as Birth or Death	Additional copies of same record ordered at same time are $2.00 each.
Divorce	$5.00	Same as Birth or Death	Records since January 1892.
	Varies	See remarks	Clerk of District Court in judicial division where divorce was granted.
Maryland			
Birth or Death	$4.00	Division of Vital Records Department of Health and Mental Hygiene Metro Executive Building 4201 Patterson Avenue P.O. Box 68760 Baltimore, MD 21215-0020	State office has had records since August 1898. Records for City of Baltimore are available from January 1875.
			Will not do research for genealogical studies. Must apply to State of Maryland Archives, 350 Rowe Blvd., Annapolis, MD 21401, (301) 974-3914.
			Check or money order should be made payable to **Division of Vital**

Place of event	Cost of copy	Address	Remarks
Maryland (cont)			**Records**. Personal checks are accepted. To verify current fees, the telephone number is **(301) 225-5988**. This will be a **recorded** message.
Marriage	$4.00	Same as Birth or Death	Records since June 1951.
	Varies	See remarks	Clerk of Circuit Court in county where license was issued or Clerk of Court of Common Pleas of Baltimore City (for licenses issued in City of Baltimore).
Divorce *Verification only*	$4.00	Same as Birth or Death	Records since January 1961. Certified copies are not available from State office. Some items may be verified.
	Varies	See remarks	Clerk of Circuit Court in county where divorce was granted.
Massachusetts			
Birth or Death	$6.00	Registry of Vital Records and Statistics 150 Tremont Street, Room B-3 Boston, MA 02111	State office has records since 1896. For earlier records, write to The Massachusetts Archives at Columbia Point, 220 Morrissey Boulevard, Boston, MA 02125 (617) 727-2816.
			Check or money order should be made payable to **Commonwealth of Massachusetts**. Personal checks are accepted. To verify current fees, the telephone number is **(617) 727-7388**. This will be a **recorded** message.
Marriage	$6.00	Same as Birth or Death	Records since 1896.
Divorce	See remarks	Same as Birth or Death	Index only since 1952. Inquirer will be directed where to send request. Certified copies are not available from State office.
	$3.00	See remarks	Registrar of Probate Court in county where divorce was granted.

Place of event	Cost of copy	Address	Remarks
Michigan			
Birth or Death	$10.00	Office of the State Registrar and Center for Health Statistics Michigan Department of Public Health 3423 North Logan Street Lansing, MI 48909	State office has had records since 1867. Copies of records since 1867 may also be obtained from County Clerk in county where event occurred. Fees vary from county to county. Detroit records may be obtained from the City of Detroit Health Department for births occurring since 1893 and for deaths since 1897.
			Checks or money orders should be made payable to **State of Michigan**. Personal checks are accepted. To verify current fees, the telephone number is **(517) 335-8655**. This will be a **recorded** message.
Marriage	$10.00	Same as Birth or Death	Records since April 1867
	Varies	See remarks	County Clerk in county where license was issued.
Divorce	$10.00	Same as Birth or Death	Records since 1897.
	Varies	See remarks	County Clerk in county where divorce was granted.
Minnesota			
Birth	$11.00	Minnesota Department of Health Section of Vital Statistics 717 Delaware Street, SE P.O. Box 9441 Minneapolis, MN 55440	State office has had records since January 1908. Copies of earlier records may be obtained from Court Administrator in county where event occurred or from the St. Paul City Health Department, if the event occurred in St. Paul. Additional copies of the birth record when ordered at the same time are $5.00 each. Additional copies of the death record when ordered at the same time are $2.00 each.
Death	$8.00		
			Check or money order should be made payable to **Treasurer, State of Minnesota**. Personal checks are accepted. To verify current fees, the telephone number is **(612) 623-5121**.

Place of event	Cost of copy	Address	Remarks
Minnesota (cont)			
Marriage	See remarks	Same as Birth or Death	Statewide index since January 1958. Inquiries will be forwarded to the appropriate office. Certified copies are not available from State Department of Health.
	$8.00	See remarks	Court Administrator in county where license was issued. Additional copies of the marriage record when ordered at the same time are $2.00 each.
Divorce	See remarks	Same as Birth or Death	Index since January 1970. Certified copies are not available from State Office.
	$8.00	See remarks	Court Administrator in county where divorce was granted.
Mississippi			
Birth	$11.00	Vital Records	State office has had records since 1912. Full copies of birth certificates obtained within 1 year after the event are $5.00. Additional copies of same record ordered at same time are $2.00 each for birth; $1.00 each for death.
Birth (short form)	$6.00	State Department of	
Death	$5.00	Health	
		2423 North State Street	
		Jackson, MS 39216	
			For out-of-State request only bank or postal money orders are accepted and should be made payable to **Mississippi State Department of Health**. Personal checks are accepted only for in-State requests. To verify current fees, the telephone number is **(601) 960-7981**. A **recorded** message may be reached on (601) 960-7450.
Marriage	$5.00	Same as Birth or Death	Statistical records only from January 1926 to July 1, 1938, and since January 1942.
	$3.00	See remarks	Circuit Clerk in county where license was issued.

Place of event	Cost of copy	Address	Remarks
Mississippi (cont)			
Divorce	See remarks $0.50 per page plus $1.00 for certification	Same as Birth or Death	Records since January 1926. Certified copies are not available from State office. Inquiries will be forwarded to appropriate office.
	Varies	See remarks	Chancery Clerk in county where divorce was granted.
Missouri			
Birth or Death	$4.00	Department of Health Bureau of Vital Records 1730 East Elm P.O. Box 570 Jefferson City, MO 65102	State office has had records since January 1910. If event occurred in St. Louis (City), St. Louis County, or Kansas City before 1910, write to the City or County Health Department. Copies of these records are $3.00 each in St. Louis City and $5.00 each in St. Louis County. In Kansas City, $6.00 for first copy and $3.00 for each additional copy ordered at the same time.
			Check or money order should be made payable to **Missouri Department of Health**. Personal checks are accepted. To verify current fees on birth records, the telephone number is **(314) 751-6387**; for death records, **(314) 751-6376**.
Marriage	No fee	Same as Birth or Death	Indexes since July 1948. Correspondent will be referred to appropriate Recorder of Deeds in county where license was issued.
	Varies	See remarks	Recorder of Deeds where license was issued.
Divorce	No fee	Same as Birth or Death	Indexes since July 1948. Certified copies are not available from State Health Department. Inquiries will be forwarded to appropriate office.
	Varies	See remarks	Clerk of Circuit Court in county where divorce was granted.

Place of event	Cost of copy	Address	Remarks
Montana			
Birth or Death	$5.00	Bureau of Records and Statistics State Department of Health and Environmental Sciences Helena, MT 59620	State office has had records since late 1907. Check or money order should be made payable to **Montana Department of Health and Environmental Sciences**. Personal checks are accepted. To verify current fees, the telephone number is **(406) 444-2614**.
Marriage	See remarks	Same as Birth or Death	Records since July 1943. Some items may be verified. Inquiries will be forwarded to appropriate office. Apply to county where license was issued if known. Certified copies are not available from State Office.
	Varies	See remarks	Clerk of District Court in county where license was issued.
Divorce	See remarks	Same as Birth or Death	Records since July 1943. Some items may be verified. Inquiries will be forwarded to appropriate office. Apply to court where divorce was granted if known. Certified copies are not available from State Office.
	Varies	See remarks	Clerk of District Court in county where divorce was granted.
Nebraska			
Birth *Death*	$6.00 $5.00	Bureau of Vital Statistics State Department of Health 301 Centennial Mall South P.O. Box 95007 Lincoln, NE 68509-5007	State office has had records since late 1904. If birth occurred before then, write the State office for information. Check or money order should be made payable to **Bureau of Vital Statistics**. Personal checks are accepted. To verify current fees, the telephone number is **(402) 471-2871**.
Marriage	$5.00	Same as Birth or Death	Records since January 1909.
	Varies	See remarks	County Court in county where license was issued.

Place of event	Cost of copy	Address	Remarks
Nebraska (cont)			
Divorce	$5.00	Same as Birth or Death	Records since January 1909.
	Varies	See remarks	Clerk of District Court in county where divorce was granted.
Nevada			
Birth or Death	$7.00	Division of Health-Vital Statistics Capitol Complex 505 East King Street #102 Carson City, NV 89710	State office has records since July 1911. For earlier records, write to County Recorder in county where event occurred.
			Check or money order should be made payable to **Section of Vital Statistics**. Personal checks are accepted. To verify current fees, the telephone number is **(702) 885-4480**.
Marriage	See remarks	Same as Birth or Death	Indexes since January 1968. Certified copies are not available from State Health Department. Inquiries will be forwarded to the appropriate office.
	Varies	See remarks	County Recorder in county where license was issued.
Divorce	See remarks	Same as Birth or Death	Indexes since January 1968. Certified copies are not available from State Health Department. Inquiries will be forwarded to the appropriate office.
	Varies	See remarks	County Clerk in county where divorce was granted.
New Hampshire			
Birth or Death	$3.00	Bureau of Vital Records Health and Human Services Building 6 Hazen Drive Concord, NH 03301	State office has had records since 1640. Copies of records may be obtained from State office or from City or Town Clerk in place where event occurred.
			Check or money order should be made payable to **Treasurer, State of New Hampshire**. Personal checks are accepted. To verify cur-

Place of event	Cost of copy	Address	Remarks
New Hampshire (cont)			rent fees, the telephone number is **(603) 271-4654**. This will be a **recorded** message.
Marriage	$3.00	Same as Birth or Death	Records since 1640.
	Varies	See remarks	Town Clerk in town where license was issued.
Divorce	$3.00	Same as Birth or Death	Records since 1808.
	Varies	See remarks	Clerk of Superior Court where divorce was granted.
New Jersey			
Birth or Death	$4.00	State Department of Health Bureau of Vital Statistics South Warren and Market Streets CN 370 Trenton, NJ 08625	State office has had records since June 1878. Additional copies of same record ordered at same time are $2.00 each. If the exact date is unknown, the fee is an additional $1.00.
		Archives and History Bureau State Library Division State Department of Education Trenton, NJ 08625	For records from May 1848 to May 1878. Check or money order should be made payable to **New Jersey State Department of Health**. Personal checks are accepted. To verify current fees, the telephone number is **(609) 292-4087**. This will be a **recorded** message.
Marriage	$4.00	Same as Birth or Death	If the exact date is unknown, the fee is an additional $1.00 per year searched.
	$2.00	Archives and History Bureau State Library Division State Department of Education Trenton, NJ 08625	For records from May 1848 to May 1878.

Place of event	Cost of copy	Address	Remarks
New Jersey (cont)			
Divorce	$2.00	Superior Court Chancery Division State House Annex Room 320 CN 971 Trenton, NJ 08625	The fee is for the first four pages. Additional pages cost $0.50 each.
New Mexico			
Birth	$10.00	Vital Statistics	State office has had records since
Death	$5.00	New Mexico Health Services Division 1190 St. Francis Drive Santa Fe, NM 87503	1920 and delayed records since 1880. Check or money order should be made payable to **Vital Statistics**. Personal checks are accepted. To verify current fees, the telephone number is **(505) 827-2338**. This will be a **recorded** message.
Marriage	Varies	See remarks	County Clerk in county where license was issued.
Divorce	Varies	See remarks	Clerk of Superior Court where divorce was granted.
New York			
(except New York City)			
Birth or Death	$15.00	Vital Records Section State Department of Health Empire State Plaza Tower Building Albany, NY 12237-0023	State office has had records since 1880. For records before 1914 in Albany, Buffalo, and Yonkers, or before 1880 in any other city, write to Registrar of Vital Statistics in city where event occurred. For the rest of the State, except New York City, write to State office. Check or money order should be made payable to **New York State Department of Health**. Personal checks are accepted. To verify current fees, the telephone number is **(518) 474-3075**. This will be a **recorded** message.
Marriage	$5.00	Same as Birth or Death	Records from 1880 to present.

Place of event	Cost of copy	Address	Remarks

New York (cont)

Place of event	Cost of copy	Address	Remarks
Marriage (cont)	$5.00	See remarks	For records from 1880-1907 and licenses issued in the cities of Albany, Buffalo, or Yonkers, apply to — Albany: City Clerk, City Hall Albany, NY 12207; Buffalo: City Clerk, City Hall, Buffalo, NY 14202; Yonkers: Registrar of Vital Statistics, Health Center Building, Yonkers, NY 10701.
Divorce	$15.00	Same as Birth or Death	Records since January 1963.
	Varies	See remarks	County Clerk in county where divorce was granted.

New York City

Place of event	Cost of copy	Address	Remarks
Birth or Death	$5.00	Bureau of Vital Records Department of Health of New York City 125 Worth Street New York, NY 10013	Office has birth records since 1898 and death records since 1930. For Old City of New York (Manhattan and part of the Bronx) birth records for 1865-97 and death records for 1865-1929 write to Archives Division, Department of Records and Information Services, 31 Chambers Street, New York, NY 10007.
			Money order should be made payable to **New York City Department of Health**. To verify current fees, the telephone number is **(212) 619-4530**. This will be a **recorded** message.
Marriage **Bronx Borough**	$10.00	City Clerk's Office 1780 Grand Concourse Bronx, NY 10457	Records from 1847 to 1865, Archives Division, Department of Records and Information Services, 31 Chambers Street, New York, NY 10007, except Brooklyn records for this period which are filed with County Clerk's Office, Kings County, Supreme Court Building, Brooklyn, NY 11201. Additional copies of same record ordered at same time are $5.00 each. Records from 1866 to 1907. City Clerk's Office in borough where marriage
Brooklyn Borough	$10.00	City Clerk's Office Municipal Building Brooklyn, NY 11201	
Manhattan Borough	$10.00	City Clerk's Office Municipal Building New York, NY 10007	

Place of event	Cost of copy	Address	Remarks
New York City (cont)			was performed. Records from 1908 to May 12, 1943. New York City residents write to City Clerk's Office in the borough of bride's residence; nonresidents write to City Clerk's Office in Borough where license was obtained. Records since May 13, 1943. City Clerk's Office in borough where license was issued.
Queens Borough	$10.00	City Clerk's Office 120-55 Queens Boulevard Kew Gardens, NY 11424	
Staten Island Borough (no longer called Richmond)	$10.00	City Clerk's Office Staten Island Borough Hall Staten Island, NY 10301	
Divorce			See New York State.
North Carolina			
Birth or Death	$5.00	Department of Environment, Health, and Natural Resources Division of Epidemiology Vital Records Section 225 North McDowell Street P.O. Box 27687 Raleigh, NC 27611-7687	State office has had birth records since October 1913 and death since January 1, 1930. Death records from 1913 through 1929 are available from Archives and Records Section, State Records Center, 215 North Blount Street, Raleigh, NC 27602. Check or money order should be made payable to **Vital Records Section**. Personal check are accepted. To verify current fees, the telephone number is **(919) 733-3526**.
Marriage	$5.00	Same as Birth or Death	Records since January 1962.
	$3.00	See remarks	Registrar of Deeds in county where marriage was performed.
Divorce	$5.00	Same as Birth or Death	Records since January 1958.
	Varies	See remarks	Clerk of Superior Court where divorce was granted.
North Dakota			
Birth	$7.00	Division of Vital Records State Capital 600 East Blvd. Avenue Bismark, ND 58505	State office had some records since July 1893. Years from 1894 to 1920 are incomplete. Additional copies of birth records are $4.00 each; death records are $2.00 each.
Death	$5.00		

Place of event	Cost of copy	Address	Remarks
North Dakota (cont)			
			Money order should be made payable to **Division of Vital Records**. To verify current fees, the telephone number is **(701) 224-2360**.
Marriage	$5.00	Same as Birth or Death	Records since July 1925. Requests for earlier records will be forwarded to the appropriate office. Additional copies are $2.00 each.
	Varies	See remarks	County Judge in county where license was issued.
Divorce	See remarks	Same as Birth or Death	Index of records since July 1949. Some items may be verified. Certified copies are not available from State Health Department. Inquiries will be forwarded to appropriate office.
	Varies	See remarks	Clerk of District Court in county where divorce was granted.
Northern Mariana Islands			
Birth or Death	$3.00	Office of Vital Statistics Superior Court Commonwealth of Northern Mariana Islands Saipan, MP 96950	No information available on years for which records are available. If any questions, contact the address below.
Marriage	$3.00	Same as Birth or Death	Money order or Bank Cashiers Check should be made payable to **Treasurer, CNMI**. Personal checks are not accepted. To verify current fees, the telephone number is **(607) 234-6401**.
Divorce	$2.50 plus $0.50 per page for Divorce Decree	Same as Birth or Death	

Place of event	Cost of copy	Address	Remarks
Ohio			
Birth or Death	$7.00	Division of Vital Statistics Ohio Department of Health G-20 Ohio Department Building 65 South Front Street Columbus, OH 43266-0333	State office has had birth records since December 20, 1908. For earlier birth and death records, write to the Probate Court in the county where the event occurred. The State Office has death records which occurred less than 50 years ago. Death records which occurred 50 or more years ago-through December 20, 1908—can be obtained from the Ohio Historical Society, Archives Library Division, 1985 Velma Avenue, Columbus, OH 43211-2497.
			Check or money order should be made payable to **State Treasury**. Personal checks are accepted. To verify current fees, the telephone number is **(614) 466-2531**. This will be a **recorded** message.
Marriage	See remarks	Same as Birth or Death	Records since September 1949. All items may be verified. Certified copies are not available from State Health Department. Inquiries will be referred to appropriate office.
	Varies	See remarks	Probate Judge in county where license was issued.
Divorce	See remarks	Same as Birth or Death	Records since September 1949. All items may be verified. Certified copies are not available from State Health Department. Inquiries will be forwarded to appropriate office.
	Varies	See remarks	Clerk of Court of Common Pleas in county where divorce was granted.
Oklahoma			
Birth or Death	$5.00	Vital Records Section State Department of Health 1000 Northeast 10th St. P.O. Box 53551 Oklahoma City, OK 73152	State office has had records since October 1908. Check or money order should be made payable to **Oklahoma State Department of Health**. Personal checks are accepted. To verify cur-

Place of event	Cost of copy	Address	Remarks
Oklahoma (cont)			rent fees, the telephone number is **(405) 271-4040.**
Marriage	Varies	See remarks	Clerk of Court in county where license was issued.
Divorce	Varies	See remarks	Clerk of Court in county where divorce was granted.
Oregon			
Birth or Death	$8.00	Oregon Health Division Vital Statistics Section P.O. Box 116 Portland, OR 97207	State office has had records since January 1903. Some earlier records for the City of Portland since approximately 1880 are available from the Oregon State Archives, 1005 Broadway, NE, Salem, OR 97310.
Heirloom Birth	$25.00	Same as Birth or Death	Presentation style calligraphy certificate suitable for framing.
			Check or money order should be payable to **Oregon Health Division.** To verify current fees, the telephone number is **(503) 229-5710.** This will be a **recorded** message.
Marriage	$8.00	Same as Birth or Death	Records since January 1906.
	Varies	See remarks	County Clerk in county where license was issued. County Clerks also have some records before 1906.
Divorce	$8.00	Same as Birth or Death	Records since 1925.
	Varies	See remarks	County Clerk in county where divorce was granted. County Clerks also have some records before 1925.
Pennsylvania			
Birth	$4.00	Division of Vital Records	State office has had records since January 1906.
Wallet card	$5.00		
Death	$3.00	State Department of Health Central Building 101 South Mercer St. P.O. Box 1528 New Castle, PA 16103	For earlier records, write to Register of Wills, Orphans Court, in county seat of county where event occurred. Persons born in Pittsburgh from 1870 to 1905 or in Allegheny

Place of event	Cost of copy	Address	Remarks
Pennsylvania (cont)			City, now part of Pittsburgh, from 1882 to 1905 should write to Office of Biostatistics, Pittsburgh Health Department, City-County Building, Pittsburgh, PA 15219. For events occurring in City of Philadelphia from 1860 to 1915, write to Vital Statistics, Philadelphia Department of Public Health, City Hall Annex, Philadelphia, PA 19107. Check or money order should be made payable to **Division of Vital Records**. Personal checks are accepted. To verify current fees, the telephone number is **(412) 656-3147**. This will be a **recorded** message.
Marriage	See remarks	Same as Birth or Death	Records since January 1906. Certified copies are not available from State Health Department. Inquiries will be forwarded to appropriate office.
	Varies	See remarks	Marriage License Clerks, County Court House, in county where license was issued.
Divorce	Varies	Same as Birth or Death	Records since January 1946. Certified copies are not available from State Health Department. Inquiries will be forwarded to appropriate office.
	Varies	See remarks	Prothonotary, Court House, in county seat of county where divorce was granted.
Puerto Rico			
Birth or Death	$2.00	Department of Health Demographic Registry P.O. Box 11854 Fernández Juncos Station San Juan, PR 00910	Central office has had records since July 22, 1931. Copies of earlier records may be obtained by writing to local Registrar (Registrador Demografico) in municipality where event occurred or by writing to central office for information.

Place of event	Cost of copy	Address	Remarks

Puerto Rico (cont)

			Money order should be made payable to **Secretary of the Treasury**. Personal checks are not accepted. To verify current fees, the telephone number is **(809) 728-7980**.
Marriage	$2.00	Same as Birth or Death	
Divorce	$2.00	Same as Birth or Death See remarks	Superior Court where divorce was granted.

Rhode Island

Birth or Death	$5.00	Division of Vital Records Rhode Island Department of Health Room 101, Cannon Building 3 Capitol Hill Providence, RI 02908-5097	State office has had records since 1853. For earlier records, write to Town Clerk in town where event occurred. Additional copies of the same record ordered at the same time are $3.00 each. Money order should be payable to **General Treasurer, State of Rhode Island**. To verify current fees, the telephone number is **(401) 277-2811**. This will be a **recorded** message.
Marriage	$5.00	Same as Birth or Death	Records since January 1853. Additional copies of the same record ordered at the same time are $3.00 each.
Divorce	$1.00	Clerk of Family Court 1 Dorrance Plaza Providence, RI 02903	

South Carolina

| *Birth or Death* | $6.00 | Office of Vital Records and Public Health Statistics South Carolina Department of Health and Environmental Control 2600 Bull Street Colombia, SC 29201 | State office has had records since January 1915. City of Charleston births from 1877 and deaths from 1821 are on file at Charleston County Health Department. Ledger entries of Florence City births and deaths from 1895 to 1914 are on file at Florence County Health Department. Ledger entries of Newberry City births and deaths from the late 1800's are on file at |

Place of event	Cost of copy	Address	Remarks
South Carolina (cont)			Newberry County Health Department. These are the only early records obtainable.
			Check or money order should be made payable to **Office of Vital Records**. Personal checks are accepted. To verify current fees, the telephone number is **(803) 734-4830**.
Marriage	$6.00	Same as Birth or Death	Records since July 1950.
	Varies	See remarks	Records since July 1911. Probate Judge in county where license was issued.
Divorce	$6.00	Same as Birth or Death	Records since July 1962.
	Varies	See remarks	Records since April 1949. Clerk of county where petition was filed.
South Dakota			
Birth or Death	$5.00	State Department of Health Center for Health Policy and Statistics Vital Records 523 E. Capitol Pierre, SD 57501	State office has had records since July 1905 and access to other records for some events that occurred before them.
			Money order should be made payable to **South Dakota Department of Health.** Personal checks are accepted. To verify current fees, the telephone number is **(605) 773-3355**. This will be a **recorded** message.
Marriage	$5.00	Same as Birth or Death	Records since July 1905.
		See remarks	County Treasury in county where license was issued.
Divorce	$5.00	Same as Birth or Death	Records since July 1905.
	Varies	See remarks	Clerk of Court in county where divorce was granted.

Place of event	Cost of copy	Address	Remarks
Tennessee			
Birth (long form)	$10.00	Tennessee Vital Records	State office has had birth records
Birth (short form)	$5.00	Department of Health and Environment Cordell Hull Building Nashville, TN 37219-5402	for entire State since January 1914, for Nashville since June 1881, for Knoxville since July 1881, and for
Death	$5.00		Chattanooga since January 1882. State office has had death records for entire State since January 1914, for Nashville since July 1874, for Knoxville since July 1887, and for Chattanooga since March 6, 1872. Birth and death enumeration records by school district are available for July 1908 through June 1912. For Memphis birth records from April 1874 through December 1887 and November 1898 to January 1, 1914, and for Memphis death records from May 1848 to January 1, 1914, write to Memphis-Shelby County Health Department, Division of Vital Records, Memphis, TN 38105. Additional copies of the same birth, marriage or divorce record, requested at the same time, are $2.00 each.
			Check or money order should be made payable to **Tennessee Vital Records**. Personal checks are accepted. To verify current fees, the telephone number is **(615) 741-1763**. In Tennessee call **1-800-423-1901**.
Marriage	$10.00	Same as Birth or Death	Records since July 1945.
	Varies	See remarks	County Clerk in county where license was issued.
Divorce	$10.00	Same as Birth or Death	Records since July 1945.
	Varies	See remarks	Clerk of Court in county where divorce was granted.

Place of event	Cost of copy	Address	Remarks
Texas			
Birth or Death	$8.00	Bureau of Vital Statistics Texas Department of Health 1100 West 49th Street Austin, TX 78756-3191	State office has had records since 1903. State office has had records since 1903. Additional copies of same record ordered at same time are $2.00 each. Check or money order should be made payable to **Texas Department of Health**. Personal checks are accepted. To verify current fees, the telephone number is **(512) 458-7451**. This is a **recorded** message.
Marriage	See remarks	Same as Birth or Death	Records since January 1966. Certified copies are not available from State office. Fee for search and verification of essential facts of marriage is $8.00.
	Varies	See remarks	County Clerk in county where license was issued.
Divorce	See remarks	Same as Birth or Death	Records since January 1968. Certified copies are not available from State office. Fee for search and verification of essential facts of divorce is $8.00.
	Varies	See remarks	Clerk of District Court in county where divorce was granted.
Utah			
Birth **Death**	$11.00 $8.00	Bureau of Vital Records Utah Department of Health 288 North 1460 West P.O. Box 16700 Salt Lake City, UT 84116-0700	State office has had records since 1905. If event occurred from 1890 to 1904 in Salt Lake City or Ogden, write to City Board of Health. For records elsewhere in the State from 1898 to 1904, write to County Clerk in county where event occurred. Additional copies, when requested at the same time, are $4.00 each. Check or money order should be made payable to **Utah Department**

Place of event	Cost of copy	Address	Remarks
Utah (cont)			of **Health**. Personal checks are accepted. To verify current fees, the telephone number is **(801) 538-6105**. This is a **recorded** message.
Marriage	$8.00	Same as Birth or Death	State office has had records since 1978. Only short form certified copies are available.
Divorce	Varies	See remarks	County Clerk in county where license was issued.
	$8.00	Same as Birth or Death	State office has had records since 1978. Only short form certified copies are available.
	Varies	See remarks	County Clerk in county where divorce was granted.
Vermont			
Birth or Death	$5.00	Vermont Department of Health Vital Records Section Box 70 60 Main Street Burlington, VT 05402	State has had records since 1955. Check or money order should be made payable to **Vermont Department of Health**. Personal checks are accepted. To verify current fees, the telephone number is **(802) 863-7275**.
Birth, Death, or Marriage	$5.00	Division of Public Records 6 Baldwin Street Montpelier, VT 05602	Records prior to 1955.
	$5.00	See remarks	Town or City Clerk of town where birth or death occurred.
Marriage	$5.00	Same as Birth or Death	State has had records since 1955.
	$5.00	See remarks	Town Clerk in town where license was issued.
Divorce	$5.00	Same as Birth or Death	State has had records since 1968.
	$5.00	See remarks	Town Clerk in town where divorce was granted.

Place of event	Cost of copy	Address	Remarks
Virginia			
Birth or Death	$5.00	Division of Vital Records State Health Department P.O. Box 1000 Richmond, VA 23208-1000	State office has had records from January 1853 to December 1896 and since June 14, 1912. For records between those dates, write to the Health Department in the city where the event occurred.
			Check or money order should be made payable to **State Health Department**. Personal checks are accepted. To verify current fees, the telephone number is **(804) 786-6228**.
Marriage	$5.00	Same as Birth or Death	Records since January 1853.
	Varies	See remarks	Clerk of Court in county or city where license was issued.
Divorce	$5.00	Same as Birth or Death	Records since January 1918.
	Varies	See remarks	Clerk of Court in county or city where divorce was granted.
Virgin Islands			
Birth or Death St.Croix	$10.00	Registrar of Vital Statistics Charles Harwood Memorial Hospital St. Croix, VI 00820	Registrar has had birth and death records on file since 1840.
St. Thomas and St. John	$10.00	Registrar of Vital Statistics Knud Hansen Complex Hospital Ground Charlotte Amalie St. Thomas, VI 00802	Registrar has had birth records on file since July 1906 and death records since January 1906.
			Money order for birth and death records should be made payable to **Bureau of Vital Statistics**. Personal checks are not accepted. To verify current fees, call **(809) 774-9000 ext. 218 or 298**.
Marriage	See remarks	Bureau of Vital Records and Statistical Services Virgin Islands Department of Health Charlotte Amalie St. Thomas, VI 00801	Certified copies are not available. Inquiries will be forwarded to the appropriate office.

Place of event	Cost of copy	Address	Remarks

Virgin Islands (cont)

Place of event	Cost of copy	Address	Remarks
St. Croix	$2.00	Chief Deputy Clerk Family Division Territorial Court of the Virgin Islands P.O. Box 929 Christiansted St. Croix, VI 00820	

St. Thomas and St. John	$2.00	Clerk of the Territorial
		  Court of the Virgin
		  Islands
		Family Division
		P.O. Box 70
		Charlotte Amalie
		St. Croix, VI 00801	

Divorce	See remarks	Same as Marriage	Certified copies are not available. Inquiries will be forwarded to the appropriate office.
St. Croix	$5.00	Same as Marriage	Money order for marriage and divorce records should be made payable to **Territorial Court of the Virgin Islands**. Personal checks are not accepted.
St. Thomas and St. John	$5.00	Same as Marriage	

Washington

Place of event	Cost of copy	Address	Remarks
Birth or Death	$11.00	Vital Records 1112 South Quince P.O. Box 9709, ET-11 Olympia, WA 98504- 9709	State office has had records since July 1907. For King, Pierce, and Spokane counties copies may also be obtained from county health departments. County Auditor of county of birth has registered births prior to July 1907. Money order should be made payable to **Vital Records**. To verify current fees, the telephone number is **(206) 753-5936**. Recorded messages for out of State, call **1-800-551-0562**; in State, call **1-800-331-0680**.

Place of event	Cost of copy	Address	Remarks
Washington (cont)			
Marriage	$11.00	Same as Birth or Death	State office has had records since January 1968.
	$2.00	See remarks	County Auditor in county where license was issued.
Divorce	$11.00	Same as Birth or Death	State office has had records since January 1968.
	Varies	See remarks	County Clerk in county where divorce was granted.
West Virginia			
Birth or Death	$5.00	Vital Registration Office Division of Health State Capitol Complex Bldg. 3 Charleston, WV 25305	State office has had records since January 1917. For earlier records, write to Clerk of County Court in county where event occurred.
			Check or money order should be made payable to **Vital Registration**. Personal checks are accepted. To verify current fees, the telephone number is **(304) 348-2931**.
Marriage	$5.00	Same as Birth or Death	Records since 1921. Certified copies available from 1964.
	Varies	See remarks	County Clerk in county where license was issued.
Divorce	See remarks	Same as Birth or Death	Index since 1968. Some items may be verified (fee $5.00). Certified copies are not available from State office.
	Varies	See remarks	Clerk of Circuit Court, Chancery Side, in county where divorce was granted.
Wisconsin			
Birth *Death*	$8.00 $5.00	Vital Records 1 West Wilson Street P.O. Box 309 Madison, WI 53701	State Office has scattered records earlier than 1857. Records before October 1, 1907, are very incomplete. Additional copies of the same record ordered at the same time are $2.00 each.

Place of event	Cost of copy	Address	Remarks
Wisconsin (cont)			
			Check or money order should be made payable to **Center for Health Statistics**. Personal checks are accepted. To verify current fees, the telephone number is **(608) 266-1371**. This will be a **recorded** message.
Marriage	$5.00	Same as Birth or Death	Records since April 1836. Records before October 1, 1907, are incomplete. Additional copies of the same record ordered at the same time are $2.00 each.
Divorce	$5.00	Same as Birth or Death	Records since October 1907. Additional copies of the same record ordered at the same time are $2.00 each.
Wyoming			
Birth	$5.00	Vital Records Services	State office has had records since
Death	$3.00	Hathaway Building Cheyenne, WY 82002	July 1909.
			Money order should be made payable to **Vital Records Services**. To verify current fees, the telephone number is **(307) 777-7591**.
Marriage	$5.00	Same as Birth or Death	Records since May 1941.
	Varies	See remarks	County Clerk in county where license was issued.
Divorce	$5.00	Same as Birth or Death	Records since May 1941.
	Varies	See remarks	Clerk of District Court where divorce took place.

NOTES

NOTES

3

Social Security Administration

The Social Security Administration permits the public to check if a death has occurred for anyone that has died since 1962. Later in this chapter, I will discuss what value knowing the location of death of an individual will have to your search.

Most of you are aware that a social security number is of great use in finding someone. You can find out the social security number of someone through voter's registration records, driving records from certain states, mortgage paperwork that is on file at the county records department, etc. This chapter will contain a source you will be able to use to run social security numbers to obtain an address of an individual. The next two pages will show you that you can find the social security number of your subject by looking through public records such as a summons and a child support order.

☐ IN THE CIRCUIT COURT OF THE ELEVENTH JUDICIAL CIRCUIT IN AND FOR DADE COUNTY, FLORIDA.
☐ IN THE COUNTY COURT IN AND FOR DADE COUNTY, FLORIDA.

CIVIL DIVISION	CIVIL ACTION SUMMONS Personal Service on a Natural Person (En Espanol al Dorso)　(Francais Au Verso)	CASE NUMBER 92-635

PLAINTIFF(S) LINDA ELLIS	VS. DEFENDANT(S) MARVIN BARN　327-98-8852	CLOCK IN

To Defendant(s): MARVIN BARN	Address: 176 NW 36 Ave FT. LAUDERDALE, FL. 33311

A lawsuit has been filed against you. You have 20 calendar days after this summons is served on you to file a written response to the attached Complaint with the clerk of this court. A phone call will not protect you; your written response, including the case number given above and the names of the parties, must be filed if you want the Court to hear your side of the case. If you do not file your response on time, you may lose the case, and your wages, money and property may thereafter be taken without further warning from the Court. There are other legal requirements. You may want to call an attorney right away. If you do not know an attorney you may call an attorney referral service or a legal aid office (listed in the phone book).

IV-D ORIGINAL PROCESS

If you choose to file a written response yourself, at the same time you file your written response to the Court, located at:

Dade County Courthouse
Clerk of Courts
Room 13
3 West Flagler Street
Miami, Florida 33130

Additional Court locations are printed on the back of this form.

You must also mail or take a copy of your written responses to the "Plaintiff/Plaintiff's Attorney" named below.

Plaintiff/Plaintiff Attorney SANDRA GREE	Address 10　SOUTH BISCAYNE BOULEVARD MIAMI FLORIDA 33131

TO EACH SHERIFF OF THE STATE OF FLORIDA: You are commanded to serve this Summons and a copy of the Complaint of this lawsuit on the above named defendant.

CLERK OF COURTS	BY: _____ DEPUTY CLERK	DATE 1-16-92

State of Florida, Department
of Health and Rehabilitative
Services, Child Support
Enforcement, on behalf of:
PATRICIA COHE
LAURA COHE
by and through LIGIA E COHE
As Custodian and next friend,
     Petitioner,

vs.

ALBERTO D COHE
     Respondent,
   SSN:
      271-98-8095

PETITION TO ESTABLISH CHILD SUPPORT AND FOR OTHER RELIEF

COMES NOW the Plaintiff, Department of Health and Rehabilitative Services, et. al., by and through the undersigned attorney, and files this Petition for Child Support and other Relief, and as grounds states as follows:

1. This is an action to establish child support and for other relief for the dependent child(ren):

    PATRICIA COHE   BORN ON MARCH 25th 1984 in VENEZUELA
    LAURA COHE   BORN ON AUGUST 17th 1982 in VENEZUELA.

2. This Court has personal jurisdiction of the Defendant in that the Defendant is currently or was preceding commencement of this action a resident of the State of Florida.

3. LIGIA E COHE and the child(ren) reside in DADE COUNTY, Florida.

4. Defendant is legally responsible parent of the child(ren).

5. The child(ren) needs and has needed since birth, support from the Defendant who has had the ability to provide support.

6. The Defendant is over 18 years of age and is not a member of the Armed Forces of the United States or its allies.

7. The Department has incurred administrative costs, fees for legal services and court costs in this action which Defendant is able to pay.

8. The child(ren) is or has been a beneficiary of Public Assistance or is otherwise eligible for services of the Department pursuant to Chapter 409, F.S.

9. The participation of the Department and the representation of the undersigned attorney are limited in scope as set forth in s. 409.2564 (5), F.S.

WHEREFORE, the Plaintiff prays that the court will:

1. Determine the Defendant to be a legally responsible parent of the child(ren).

2. Order the Defendant to pay child support pursuant to s. 61.30, F.S., or an amount deemed reasonable by this Court payable through the child support depository plus depository fees.

3. Order the Defendant to pay child support retroactive to date of birth of the child(ren).

4. Determine there is a past period child support in the amount of $1,188.00 as of 12/10/1991, plus any amount paid through the date of the final hearing and require the Defendant to repay the total past period child support.

5. Allow the Department to certify for intercept by the United States Internal Revenue Service any arrears or past period child support owed by Defendant.

AREA NUMBERS

The following chart may be of assistance to you if you know what your subject's Social Security Number is. The first three digits are "area numbers." These numbers will indicate what state or territory the subject resided in when they applied for their Social Security card. This information may give a lead on what area the subject may be in or have returned to.

001-003	New Hampshire	429-432	Arkansas
004-007	Maine	433-439	Louisiana
008-009	Vermont	440-448	Oklahoma
010-034	Massachusetts	449-467	Texas
035-039	Rhode Island	468-477	Minnesota
040-049	Connecticut	478-485	Iowa
050-134	New York	486-500	Missouri
135-158	New Jersey	501-502	North Dakota
159-211	Pennsylvania	503-504	South Dakota
212-220	Maryland	505-508	Nebraska
221-222	Delaware	509-515	Kansas
223-231	Virginia	516-517	Montana
232-236	West Virginia	518-519	Idaho
237-246	North Carolina	520	Wyoming
247-251	South Carolina	521-524	Colorado
252-260	Georgia	525,585	New Mexico
261-267	Florida	526-527	Arizona
268-302	Ohio	528-529	Utah
303-317	Indiana	530	Nevada
318-361	Illinois	531-539	Washington
362-386	Michigan	540-544	Oregon
387-399	Wisconsin	545-573	California
400-407	Kentucky	574	Alaska
408-415	Tennessee	575-576	Hawaii
416-424	Alabama	577-579	District of Columbia
425-428	Mississippi	580	Virgin Islands

581-585	Puerto Rico, Guam,	589-595	Florida
	American Samoa,	596-599	Puerto Rico
	Philippine Islands	600-601	Arizona
586	Guam, American	602-626	California
	Samoa, Mariana Island,	627-645	Texas
	Philippines	646-647	Utah
588	Mississippi	648-649	New Mexico

Social Security Death Master File

I will explain how the Master Death File is accessed because it may prove to be one of the most time-saving and cost-effective techniques you will use.

The Social Security Administration releases an updated list every three months that contains the names of all persons who have died. The information that is available to the public is:

1. Social Security Number
2. First and last name
3. Date of birth
4. Date of death
5. Zip Code of exact place of death
6. Zip Code where the lump sum Death Payment was made

The total number of persons listed in the Master Death File is currently at 58 million and includes deaths since 1937. Several companies have bought the magnetic tapes that the Social Security Administration makes available for sale that contain the Master Death File. They have spent $32,000.00 to convert the tapes over to computer disks and the quarterly updates cost $1,700.00.

Here are the various ways the Master Death File can be accessed:

1. **By name only**
2. **By name and date of birth**
3. **By Social Security Number**
4. **By name and date of death**
5. **By first name only with date of birth**

If the subject I am trying to find has been missing for more than several years, I will order a check of the Master Death File. If the subject does appear, then I will order a copy of the death record to give to the client as proof that the subject is deceased. Case closed. But the most important use of the Death Master File is to quickly and with a minimum of information find a death record of a parent. If I believe that a parent of the subject has died I will request a Death Master File record be run on their name. Even though you will usually not have the date of birth, Social Security Number, or even the place of death of the parent, a search can be conducted. Of course, a name like John Smith will not yield good results because of the long list that will be produced. But if you have the year of birth, then the field can be narrowed down considerably.

When I review the Death Master File record of a parent, I look for the zip code that states the place of death. I will order a death certificate and then contact the funeral home that is listed. The funeral home's records will indicate the next of kin, which may be your subject. Even if your subject is not listed, the home address and telephone number of the spouse or other family member will be contained in the funeral home's records. These close relatives may be queried about the location of your subject.

A great way to find your subject is to look for the obituary of a parent. Find out the names of the newspapers that were published at the time of death of the parent. Then check with that newspaper or the public library to order a microfilm copy of the obituary which was printed a few days after the death. The obituary will list the names of the spouse of the deceased and children's name (the female offspring will usually have the married name listed) and town where they live.

Your subject may be listed along with location of residence. If not, then you may have a surviving parent or siblings who may know where your subject is.

Since you now have the place of death of the parent, you may want to contact the probate court of jurisdiction. If the parent had died intestate (no will), there will be a file that contains much information, including the names and addresses of all persons that were paid monies by the probate court for the estate. Since your subject was an offspring, they will be entitled to part of the estate and the subject's address may be listed along with the amount of money they received.

On many occasions, I have ordered from the Probate Court a copy of the check that was cashed by a subject. Many times the subject will have their drivers license number listed on the back of the check because they were required to show identification when cashing the check. At the very least, you will know what city the subject's bank is in.

The information that is contained on the Death Master File is as follows:

```
St Soc Sec Num Last Name    First Name Birth Date Death Date Resi  Zip1  Zip2
-- ----------- ------------------- ---------- ---------- ---- ----- -----
```

St – This indicates what state the subject lived in when they applied for a Social Security Number.

Soc Sec Num – Social Security Number

Last Name – The name that the death benefits list as account holder.

First Name – Walt would be Walter, Larry would be Lawrence, and Bob would be Robert if this is the formal name used by the decedent when they applied for their Social Security Number but a name of Harry could very well be Harry instead of Harold if this is what was written on the original application.

Birth Date – The full birth date is usually printed on the Death Master File.

Death Date – The exact day is sometimes missing from the Master Death File but the month and year is usually displayed.

Resi – This stands for residence and indicates in which state the death occurred.

Zip 1 – Indicates the Zip Code area in which the death occurred.

Zip 2 – Indicates the Zip Code that the lump sum payment was mailed to.

The following sample records of well-known persons will be used to illustrate different information that may or may not appear on the Death Master Record.

```
St Soc Sec Num Last Name   First Name Birth Date Death Date Resi  Zip1  Zip2
-- ----------- ----------------------- ---------- ---------- ---- ----- -----
   CA 563-66-4692 ASTAIRE       ANN      12/22/1878 07/00/1975 (CA) 91202
  *CA 568-05-4206 ASTAIRE       FRED     05/10/1899*06/00/1987 (CA) 90213
   ME 004-12-2305 ASTAIRE       THEODORE 08/12/1913 09/00/1979 (CT) 06503 06511

06503 CT New Haven .....  06511 CT New Haven .....  90213 CA Beverly Hills..
91202 CA Glendale  .....
```

The record for the last name Astaire will show that certain names will not produce a lengthy list which will make your search that much easier. Since 1962, only three people with the name Astaire have died.

```
St Soc Sec Num Last Name   First Name Birth Date Death Date Resi  Zip1  Zip2
-- ----------- ----------------------- ---------- ---------- ---- ----- -----
   MD 215-09-2405 DISNEY       WALTER   03/21/1878 08/00/1967 (MD) 21228
   IL 342-10-3698 DISNEY       WALTER   10/17/1890 05/00/1973 (IL) 61734
   DC 577-07-8270 DISNEY       WALTER   05/31/1894 01/00/1979 (MD) 61734
   NY 110-12-1395 DISNEY       WALTER   08/14/1897 10/00/1980 (FL) 33062
   KY 402-07-4149 DISNEY       WALTER   09/09/1899 06/00/1983 (KY) 40906
  *CA 562-10-0296 DISNEY       WALTER   12/05/1901*12/00/1966 ( ) 00000
   TN 413-09-3359 DISNEY       WALTER   03/20/1908 10/00/1972 (TN) 37311
   VA 228-10-8454 DISNEY       WALTER   09/24/1912 03/00/1978 (KY) 40391 24277
   KY 401-24-1418 DISNEY       WALTER   09/11/1921 03/00/1972 (KY) 40272
   TN 408-76-5315 DISNEY       WALTER   04/20/1947 09/00/1985 (TN) 37714

20782 MD Hyattsville....  21228 MD Baltimore .....   24277 VA Pennington Gap.
38062 FL Pompano Beach..  37311 TN Cleveland .....   37714 TN Caryville .....
40272 KY Louisville.....  40391 KY Winchester.....   40906 KY Barbourville...
61734 IL Delavan   .....
```

The above list contains all the Walter Disneys that have died since 1962. When you have a record that does not indicate a place of death then look at the beginning of the record. The Social Security Number of the highlighted Walter Disney shows that this individual applied for his number in California. This would be where you would start a search for a will that will show the distribution of assets. If this was the father of your subject, in this hypothetical sample, his will would be a good record to review for the address of your subject.

```
St  Soc Sec Num  Last Name       First Name  Birth Date  Death Date  Resi  Zip1   Zip2
--  -----------  --------------  ----------  ----------  ----------  ----  -----  -----
PA  164-09-9984  EISENHOWER      DAVID       10/05/1898  02/00/1983  (PA)  19124  33526
PA  185-30-5818  EISENHOWER      DAVID       12/25/1914  12/00/1978  (PA)  18102
PA  204-40-5790  EISENHOWER      DESSIE      07/29/1881  05/00/1970  (PA)  17044
PA  205-20-0582  EISENHOWER      DOLORES     11/01/1906  08/00/1972  (PA)  17834
PA  182-36-0274  EISENHOWER      DOROTHY     10/05/1885  12/00/1975  (PA)  19026
PA  203-20-9135  EISENHOWER      DOROTHY     09/27/1899  06/00/1979  (PA)  17751  17745
PA  208-18-5794  EISENHOWER      DOROTHY     10/08/1904  12/00/1981  (PA)  19607
PA  209-20-7686  EISENHOWER      DOROTHY     06/17/1927  11/00/1987  (PA)  18201
OK  440-12-7856  EISENHOWER      DOWELL      10/16/1903  09/00/1966  (TX)  78401
```
*CA 572-64-0315 EISENHOWER   DWIGHT   10/14/1890*03/00/1969 (PA) 17325

```
10504 NY Armonk     .....   17044 PA Lewistown .....    17325 PA Gettysburg.....
17745 PA Lock Haven.....    17751 PA Mill Hall  .....   17834 PA Kulpmont  .....
18102 PA Allentown  .....   18201 PA Hazletown  .....   19026 PA Drexel Hill....
19124 PA Philadelphia...    19607 PA Shillington....    33526 FL Dade City  .....
78401 TX Corpus Christi.
```

Every Eisenhower with the first name initial D was requested. If you are not sure of the exact first name of the person you are searching for in the Death Master File list, you may want to use this technique of not giving a first name, but just the first initial of the first name. After you receive the list, then you will be able to review other information and determine the correct decedent. The year of death, state of death, and the issuing state of Social Security Number would have helped find the subject of the search in this hypothetical case.

```
St  Soc Sec Num  Last Name       First Name  Birth Date  Death Date  Resi  Zip1   Zip2
--  -----------  --------------  ----------  ----------  ----------  ----  -----  -----
KY  402-03-2297  TRUMAN          HARRY       10/16/1884  10/00/1966  (KY)  41015
```
*MO 488-40-6969 TRUMAN   HARRY   05/08/1884*12/00/1972 (MO) 64050
```
PA  170-03-8745  TRUMAN          HARRY       05/15/1866  03/00/1973  (PA)  15223
MI  386-01-1149  TRUMAN          HARRY       08/08/1887  07/00/1963  (MI)  00000
KY  402-20-8745  TRUMAN          HARRY       01/27/1890  03/00/1978  (KY)  40205
WA  535-20-8745  TRUMAN          HARRY       10/30/1896  05/00/1980  (WA)  98611  98532
PA  178-05-8291  TRUMAN          HARRY       07/04/1897  10/00/1965  (PA)  00000
MI  367-26-8037  TRUMAN          HARRY       03/12/1901  11/00/1978  (OH)  43023
AZ  527-01-2253  TRUMAN          HARRY       02/17/1905  02/00/1968  (CA)  95258
NY  119-26-6047  TRUMAN          HARRY       08/19/1905  02/00/1985  (IN)  47130
```

```
15223 PA Pittsburgh.....    40205 KY Louisville.....    41015 KY Covington  .....
43023 OH Granville  .....   47130 IN Jeffersonville.    49415 MI Fruitport  .....
64050 MO Independence...    92646 CA Huntington Beac    95258 CA Woodbridge.....
98532 WA Chehalis   .....   98611 WA Castle Rock....
```

St	Soc Sec Num	Last Name	First Name	Birth Date	Death Date	Resi	Zip1	Zip2
*MO	495-50-5300	TRUMAN	BESS	02/13/1885	*10/00/1982	(MO)	64050	
WV	234-80-3101	TRUMAN	BESSIE	04/18/1889	12/30/1989	(WV)	25276	
IN	305-70-2063	TRUMAN	BESSIE	08/07/1889	09/00/1983	(IN)	46806	
OR	542-22-6633	TRUMAN	BESSIE	01/15/1893	07/00/1976	(OR)	97034	
OK	445-32-1574	TRUMAN	BESSIE	10/05/1936	11/00/1969	(OK)	73502	

```
25276 WV Spencer    .....   46806 IN Fort Wayne.....   64050 MO Independence...
73502 OK Lawtow     .....   97034 OR Lake Oswego....
```

The two Truman Master Death Records were ordered by name only. There are numerous decedents with the name Harry Truman but if you knew that the person you were searching for was from Missouri, then you would have isolated the focus of your search easily.

You will notice that there is only one Bess Truman that has died since 1962. In this case, you did not need to know what area the person was from.

St	Soc Sec Num	Last Name	First Name	Birth Date	Death Date	Resi	Zip1	Zip2
TN	408-50-1182	PRESLE	EARL	07/09/1930	03/00/1985	(TN)	38555	
GA	256-48-7374	PRESLEY	EARL	05/08/1936	02/00/1987	(GA)	31904	
MS	428-58-7758	PRESLEY	EDDIE	05/25/1934	05/00/1983	(MS)	39501	
WV	232-58-9834	PRESLEY	EDWARD	01/11/1930	03/00/1983	( )		24830
AL	424-52-7031	PRESLEY	EDWARD	07/22/1937	03/00/1980	(AL)	36256	
TN	409-64-5512	PRESLEY	ELMER	08/06/1940	09/22/1990	( )	38134	
*TN	409-52-2002	PRESLEY	ELVIS	01/08/1935	*08/16/1977	( )		38116
MS	425-11-0453	PRESLEY	ELVIS	10/24/1957	04/00/1987	(MS)	38858	
TX	455-46-8412	PRESLEY	ERNEST	12/24/1930	03/00/1979	( )		76179

```
24830 WV ELBERT    .....   31904 GA Columbus   .....   36256 AL Daviston  .....
38116 TN Memphis   .....   38134 TN Memphis    .....   38555 TN Crossville.....
38858 MS Nettleton .....   39501 MS Gulfport   .....   76179 TX Saginaw   .....
```

The above record is a result of a request for all persons with the last name Presley and the first name containing the letter E as the first letter. You will notice that in this case, the highlighted Presley does not show a place of death under Zip Code 1, but Zip Code 2 indicates where the lump sum Social Security was sent. For each space on a death master file record there may be no information entered. You can see that there are several death date, Resi, Zip1 and Zip 2 spaces that have no information.

The Master Death Record is responsible for the successful resolution of more missing persons cases than any other source. There is no quicker or precise method for ascertaining someone's death. It has been a great tool to use for the past several years. The Social Security Administration will not accept any requests for Death Master File searches. I use a company in Miami that is in the same business area I am located in that charges $45.00 for each name search. This fee covers a list of up to one hundred duplicate names returned for each name submitted that you request. The fee for over one hundred duplicate names is $30.00 per hundred.

Research Investigative Services
7907 Northwest 53rd Street, Suite 420
Miami, Florida 33166

Research Investigative Services does not advertise as its clients are investigative firms, such as mine, and governments and they keep their telephone number unlisted. However, orders are accepted from the public for the items mentioned here. In fact, you may remember Pam Casey of Northern California who was reunited with her sister after 42 years on The Maury Povich Show, on December 3rd, 1992. She along with three other families on that particular program had used the Research Investigative Services.

NATIONWIDE TELEPHONE SEARCH

Research Investigative Services has an excellent system for **nationwide** checks of listed telephone numbers. They charge $40 for the first hundred names and $25 for every increment of one hundred names thereafter. Research Investigative Services will run a name such as Robert Hamilton and the system will respond with every Robert Hamilton who has a **listed** telephone number, plus the address. In some cases, the name will appear with an address and just the area code, indicating an unlisted number, but you now have a location for this person.

This system is of tremendous assistance in cases where people have been missing for a period of time. Many times a subject will move to a different part of the country. After the subject feels comfortable that the search for them is over, they will resume listing their telephone number as they make a move to the mainstream of life. Another use for the nationwide check of a telephone number to a particular name is to find relatives. I recently ran the name Joseph Culligan and came up with many people with my name. Several were directly related to me from two generations ago.

SOCIAL SECURITY NUMBER ADDRESS UPDATE REPORT

Another service that the Research Investigative Services provides is the Social Security Number Address Update Report. If you have gleaned your subject's Social Security Number from research, you may submit a request for a search to be conducted on this number.

Any addresses that the subject had used for any dealings with certain businesses, governments, credit card companies and other entities may be given. This system is perfectly legal because no credit information is given. Research Investigative Services charges a fee of $35.00 dollars and is the only company I know of that will not charge a fee if the computer search fails to return at least one address.

I do not believe in hourly charges for searches because I have heard of many horror stories (and I am sure you have) in which people have been charged for many hours of time plus expenses and received nothing for their money except the response from the searcher or investigator saying he/she needs more and more money to complete the search. Research Investigative Services has had many requests for searches from the public and you may write to have a representative contact you. A search will be done on a NO TRACE/NO CHARGE basis for the fee of $900 (Nine hundred dollars). The guarantee of finding the person you are seeking or be charged nothing may make it worth the expense.

Another system that this company offers are files comprising data pertaining to World War II Prisoners of War from both the Pacific and European theaters. If you know that your subject was a POW, then you may want to access this file or you may want to consider accessing you subject's father's file. The search is run by name. Locating your subject's father is, of course, another technique used in your quest for the location of your subject and the search will be aided by the information supplied by the POW file. There are over 175,000 names listed.

WORLD WAR II POW — EUROPEAN THEATER
MOREY, FRANCIS R.

Serial Number: (36652216)
Grade Code:(4) Staff Sergeant
Service Branch: (1) US Army
Service Code #1:(AC) Army Air Corps
Service Code #2: (20) Air Corps
Residence State:( ) Unknown
Race:( ) Unknown

Organization:(s53)
Unit Number & Type: (0456-06)
Area of Casualty: (78) Austria
Latest Reported Date:06/06/1945
Source of Report: (official)
Detained By: (Germany)
Camp Imprisoned: ( ) Unknown Location

Francis R. Morey, Staff Sergeant, US Army, was reported taken prisoner in Austria on 12/11/1944. He was imprisoned at a camp in unknown location and was liberated on 06/06/1945.

WORLD WAR II POW — EUROPEAN THEATER
MOREY, HOWARD R.

Serial Number: (0&749652)
Grade Code:(G) Second Lieutenant
Service Branch: (1) US Army
Service Code #1:(AC) US Army
Service Code #2: (20) Air Corps
Residence State:(13) Massachusetts
Race:(1) White

Organization:(215)
Unit Number & Type: (0449-06)
Area of Casualty: (72) Germany
Latest Reported Date:05/07/1945
Source of Report: (official)
Detained By: (Germany)
Camp Imprisoned:(032) Barth-Vogelsang, Prussia

Howard R. Morey, Second Lieutenant, US Army, was reported taken prisoner in Germany on 02/22/1944. He was imprisoned at a camp in Barth-Vogelsang, Prussia, and was liberated on 05/07/45.

WORLD WAR II POW — EUROPEAN THEATER
MOREY, RALPH A.

Serial Number:(16173674)
Grade Code: (7) Private First Class
Service Branch:(1) US Army
Service Code #1: (INF) Infantry
Service Code #2: (10) Infantry
Residence State: ( ) Unknown
Race:(1) White

Organization:(740)
Unit Number & Type:(0275-06)
Area of Casualty:(76) France
Latest Reported Date:12/30/1945
Source of Report: (official)
Detained By: (Germany)
Camp Imprisoned:(007)Ludwigsburg, Wurttemberg

Ralph A. Morey, Private First Class, US Army, was reported taken prisoner in France on 01/01/1945. He was imprisoned at a camp in Ludwigsburg, Wurttemberg, and was liberated on 12/30/1945.

WORLD WAR II POW — PACIFIC THEATER
WAINWRIGHT, J. M.

Serial Number: (0&002131)
Grade Code: (A) LT GENERAL
Service Branch: (1) US Army
Service Code #1: (USA) Unknown
Service Code #2: (00) Unknown
Date Reported: 05/07/1942
Residence State: (23) New York
Race: (1) White

Organization: (J32)
Unit Number & Type: (7260-41)
Area of Casualty: (45) Philippine Islands
Latest Reported Date: / /194
Source of Report: (official)
Status Reported: (8) Was Liberated
Detained By: (Japan)
Camp Imprisoned: (709) Manchuria

J.M. Wainwright, Lt General, US Army, was reported taken prisoner on the Philippine Islands on 05/07/1942. He was imprisoned at a camp in Manchuria and was liberated later.

If you are aware of the fact that the subject's father had died in Korea or Vietnam then a good source is to order a printout of your subject's father's casualty file. This file contains information for every conflict casualty that occurred in the Korean or Vietnam War. There are over 100,000 listings for these two wars.

KOREAN CONFLICT — CASUALTY FILE
LINTON, ROBERT S.

Military Service: (A) U.S. Army
Country of Casualty: (KR) Korea
Type of Casualty: (A1) was Killed in
                  Hostile Action
Ref No — Proc Date: (14474L-11/79)
Soc Sec or SVC No: (55079227)
Military-Pay Grade: (PVT-E2)
Date of Death: (09/26/51)

Home City: (Cheyenne)
Home State: (28) Nebraska
Date of Birth (/ /25)
Cause of Death (*) Unknown
Air, Ground, or Sea: (*) Unknown
Race: (C) Caucasian
Sex: (M) Male

Robert S. Linton, PVT, U.S. Army was born 1925. His home city was listed as Cheyenne, Nebraska. He was killed in hostile action in Korea on 09/26/51.

VIETNAM CONFLICT — CASUALTY FILE
BURGESS, STANLEY WAYNE

Military Service: (M) U.S. Marine Corps

Country of Casualty: (VS) South Vietnam

Type of Casualty: (A1) was Killed in Hostile Action

Air, Ground or Sea: (7) Ground Casualty

Ref No - Proc Date: (11256-05/69)

Soc Sec or SVC No: (2412647)

Military-Pay Grade: (LCPL-E3)

Date of Death: (05/10/69)

Home City: (Las Vegas)

Service Occupation: (0311)

Date of Birth: (01/24/51)

Cause of Death: (D) Gunshot or Small Arms Fire

Race: (C) Caucasian

Religious Affiliate: (00) No Religious Preference

Age/Sex/Svc/Marital: (18/Male/01/Single)

Date Tour Begin: (04/25/69)

Body Recovered (*) Recovered

Province: (03) Quang Nam

Stanley Wayne Burgess, LCPL, U.S. Marine Corps was born on 01/24/51 and began his tour in Vietnam on 04/25/69. He was killed in hostile action in Quang Nam, South Vietnam on 05/10/69.

There is much that can be gleaned about the father because you will, in many cases, be able to obtain the father's home city, Social Security Number, marital status, etc. from the printout ordered. Even though the information may be as much as forty years old, you will be able to contact relatives who may live in the hometown. They may know your subject. This technique is not used, of course, if you know the subject's family.

The World War II POW list of the Pacific and European theaters and the Korean and Vietnam Conflict Casualty file will all be searched for the one fee for the name you supply. You do not need to furnish a date of birth or Social Security Number. This search is conducted strictly by name. The cost is $40.00 for a list of up to 100 persons with the same name you submit.

Since you are using this book for public research, you may want to consider doing what others have done. As you can see from the following article, there is a profit to be made from public records. Apparently, some people are making a big business from wills. Most wills are public record. You may want to order them from the county probate courts and do something similar to what Betty Johnson did. Her investment was just $45 for Elvis Presley's will and, as you can see, her profit at the time of this article was over $28,000. Research Investigative Services has provided the following wills to their clients: **John F. Kennedy** (18 pages), **Marilyn Monroe** (3 pages), **Elvis Presley** (13 pages), **John Lennon** (3 pages), **Jerry Garcia** (16 pages) and **Clark Gable** (2 pages). They will provide all five wills to you for $46. You may get them from this company or, of course, the probate office.

The Miami Herald

WEDNESDAY, AUGUST 14, 1991

Wherether e' sawill there' sabigpr ofit

By JONATHAN S. COHN
© The Miami Herald

No, Betty Johnson does not think Elvis Presley is still alive.

In fact, she's sort of glad he's dead, since she's making a killing off the King's Demise.

About three weeks ago, Johnson, who runs a Pompano Beach courtroom records business, figured there might be a market for selling copies of Elvis's will.

Since taking out a classified ad in USA Today, Johnson had received more than 1300 orders for the 13-page will, from as far away as England and Australia. She obliges — $22 a pop. This makes up for her initial investment — a $45 court fee.

RECORD KEEPER: Betty Johnson is tapping an open market by selling copies of Elvis' will.

Full of legal jargon, the document, complete with Presley's signature, comes with all the appropriate Memphis markings. Still, though, there are skeptics — from Hawaii.

"Because he's supposed to be living there, you know," Johnson says.

The folks at Graceland aren't overjoyed, either. "Just kind of sad that people would want to buy somebody's will," says spokesman Steve Marshall. Johnson, of course, thought of it first. And it is **public record** and all perfectly legal.

So are the final testament of John F. Kennedy and Marilyn Monroe. Look for 'em soon.

(Reprinted by permission, The Miami Herald)

4

County Records

T here are a myriad of public records that can be accessed on the county level. The following is a list of the types of records you will find that may contain your subject's name and address:

Assumption Agreement

Abstract

Affidavit

Agreement

Agreement for Deed

Agreement Not To Encumber

Amended Judgment

Assignment

Assignment of Judgment

Assignment of Lien

Assignment of Mortgage

Assignment of Proprietary Lease

Breach of Agreement

Breach of Contract

Breach of Lease

Certificate

Certificate of Additional Intangible Tax

Certificate of Approval

Certificate of Merger

Certificate of Organization	Notice of Federal Tax Lien
Certificate of Title	Notice of Lis Pendens
Change of Name	Notice of Tax Lien (State)
Condominium Rider	Partial Release of Lien
Corporation	Personal Representative's Deed
Cost Judgment	Power of Attorney
Declaration of Trust	Public Defender's Claim
Deed	Quit Claim Deed
Discharge	Restrictions (Covenants)
Disclaimer	Receipt of Advance
Dismissal	Release of Estate Tax
Divorce	Release of Federal Tax Lien
Easement	Release of Lien (Mechanic's Lien)
Easement Deed	Resolution
Eminent Domain	Restoration of Incompetency
Estate Tax Closing Letter	Restored Corporation
Estate Tax Lien	Revocation of Power of Attorney
Fictitious Name	Satisfaction of Final Decree
Foreclosure of Chattel Mortgage	Satisfaction of Judgment
Guardianship	Satisfaction or Release of Lien
Incompetency	Satisfaction or Release of Mortgage
Incorporation	Satisfaction of Tax Executions
Involuntary Bankruptcy	Separation
Judgment	Support Agreement
Lease	Tax Warrant
Levy	Title Opinion
Lien	Trust Agreement
Modification Agreement	Trustee Resignation
Mortgage Modification Agreement	Voluntary Bankruptcy
Name Restoration	Warranty Deed
Nontaxable Certificate or Receipt	Writ of Garnishment

You may search for any of these records with just the name of your subject. You will note that the list contains public documents that range from Federal and State tax liens to writs of garnishment.

COUNTY MAILING ADDRESSES

ALABAMA

Autauga County
4th & Court Streets
Prattville, Alabama 36067

Baldwin County
Post Office Box 639
Bay Minette, Alabama 36507

Barbour County
Post Office Box 398
Clayton, Alabama 36016

Bibb County
Court Square
Centreville, Alabama 35042

Blount County
220 2nd Avenue East
Oneonta, Alabama 35121

Bullock County
Post Office Box 230
Union Springs, Alabama 36089

Butler County
Post Office Box 756
Greenville, Alabama 36037

Calhoun County
1702 Noble Street
Anniston, Alabama 36201

Chambers County
County Courthouse
Lafayette, Alabama 36862

Cherokee County
Courthouse Annex
Centre, Alabama 35960

Chilton County
Post Office Box 557
Clanton, Alabama 35045

Choctaw County
117 South Mulberry Avenue
Butler, Alabama 36904

Clarke County
117 Court Street
Grove Hill, Alabama 36451

Cleburne County
406 Vickery Street
Heflin, Alabama 36264

Coffee County
Post Office Box 402
Elba, Alabama 36323

Colbert County
201 North Main Street
Tuscumbia, Alabama 35674

Conecuh County
Post Office Box 347
Evergreen, Alabama 36401

Coosa County
Post Office Box 218
Rockford, Alabama 35136

Covington County
County Courthouse
Andalusia, Alabama 36420

Crenshaw County
Post Office Box 227
Luverne, Alabama 36049

Cullman County
500 2nd Avenue Southwest
Cullman, Alabama 35055

Dale County
Post Office Box 246
Ozark, Alabama 36361

Dallas County
Post Office Box 997
Selma, Alabama 36702

Dekalb County
300 Grand Avenue Southwest
Fort Payne, Alabama 35967

Elmore County
Post Office Box 338
Wetumpka, Alabama 36092

Escambia County
Post Office Box 848
Brewton, Alabama 36427

Etowah County
800 Forrest Avenue
Gadsen, Alabama 35901

Fayette County
Post Office Box 819
Fayette, Alabama 35555

Franklin County
410 North Jackson Street
Russellville, Alabama 35653

Geneva County
Post Office Box 430
Geneva, Alabama 36340

Greene County
Post Office Box 656
Eutaw, Alabama 35462

Hale County
1001 Main Street
Greensboro, Alabama 36744

Henry County
101 West Court Square Street
Abbeville, Alabama 36310

Houston County
Post Office Box 6406
Dothan, Alabama 36302

Jackson County
Post Office Box 397
Scottsborro, Alabama 35768

Jefferson County
716 North 21st Street
Birmingham, Alabama 35263

Lamar County
Pond Street
Vernon, Alabama 35592

Lauderdale County
Post Office Box 1059
Florence, Alabama 35631

Lawrence County
750 Main Street
Moulton, Alabama 35650

Lee County
215 South 9th Street
Opelika, Alabama 36801

Limestone County
310 West Washington Street
Athens, Alabama 35611

Lowndes County
Post Office Box 65
Haynesville, Alabama 36040

Macon County
210 North Elm Street
Tuskegee, Alabama 36083

Madison County
100 Courthouse Square Southeast
Huntsville, Alabama 35801

Marengo County
101 East Coats Avenue
Linden, Alabama 36748

Marion County
Post Office Box 1595
Hamilton, Alabama 35570

Marshall County
540 Ringo Street
Guntersville, Alabama 35976

Mobile County
109 Government Street
Mobile, Alabama 36602

Monroe County
South Mount Plaza Avenue
Monroeville, Alabama 36461

Montgomery County
Post Office Box 1667
Montgomery, Alabama 36192

Morgan County
302 Lee Street Northeast
Decatur, Alabama 35601

Perry County
Post Office Box 505
Marion, Alabama 36756

Pickens County
Post Office Box 418
Carrollton, Alabama 35447

Pike County
120 West Church Street
Troy, Alabama 36081

Randolph County
Post Office Box 328
Wedowee, Alabama 36278

Russell County
Post Office Box 518
Phenix City, Alabama 36867

Saint Clair County
Post Office Box 397
Ashville, Alabama 35953

Shelby County
Main Street
Columbiana, Alabama 35051

Sumter County
Franklin Street
Livingston, Alabama 35470

Talladega County
Post Office Box 755
Talladega, Alabama 35160

Tallapoosa County
101 North Broadnax Street
Dadeville, Alabama 36853

Tuscaloosa County
714 Greensboro Avenue
Tuscaloosa, Alabama 35401

Walker County
Post Office Box 749
Jasper, Alabama 35502

Washington County
Post Office Box 146
Chatom, Alabama 36518

Wilcox County
Post Office Box 656
Camden, Alabama 36726

Winston County
Post Office Box 309
Double Springs, Alabama 35553

ALASKA

Bristol Bay Borough
Post Office Box 189
Naknek, Alaska 99633

Haines Borough
Post Office Box 1209
Haines, Alaska 99827

Juneau Borough
155 South Seward Street
Juneau, Alaska 99801

Kenai Peninusula Borough
144 North Binkley Street
Soldolna, Alaska 99669

Ketchikan Borough
344 Front Street
Ketchikan, Alaska 99901

Kodiak Borough
710 Mill Bay Road
Kodiak, Alaska 99615

Matanuska-Susltna Borough
Post Office Box 1608
Palmer, Alaska 99645

Municipality of Anchorage
Post Office Box 196650
Anchorage, Alaska 99519

North Slope Borough
Post Office Box 69
Barrow, Alaska 99723

North Star Borough
809 Pioneer Road
Fairbanks, Alaska 99701

Northwest Arctic Borough
Post Office Box 1110
Kotzebue, Alaska 99752

Silka Borough
304 Lake Street
Sitka, Alaska 99835

ARIZONA

Apache County
Post Office Box 428
Saint Johns, Arizona 85936

Cochise County
Post Office Box CK
Bisbee, Arizona 85603

Coconino County
100 East Birch Avenue
Flagstaff, Arizona 86001

Glla County
1400 Ash Street
Globe, Arizona 85501

Graham County
800 West Main Street
Safford, Arizona 85546

Groonlee County
Post Office Box 1027
Clifton, Arizona 85533

La Paz County
1713 South Kola Avenue
Parker, Arizona 85344

Maricopa County
111 South 3rd Avenue
Phoenix, Arizona 85003

Mohave County
401 East Spring Street
Kingman, Arizona 86401

Navajo County
Post Office Box 668
Holbrook, Arizona 86025

Pima County
150 West Congress Street
Tuscon, Arizona 85701

Pinal County
100 North Florence
Florence, Arizona 85232

Santa Cruz County
Post Office Box 1265
Nogales, Arizona 85628

Yavapal County
255 East Gurley Street
Prescott, Arizona 86301

Yuma County
168 South 2nd Avenue
Yuma, Arizona 85364

ARKANSAS

Arkansas County
Post Office Box 719
Stuttgart, Arkansas 72160

Ashley County
215 East Jefferson Avenue
Hamburg, Arkansas 71646

Baxter County
County Courthouse
Mountain Home, Arkansas 72653

Benton County
Post Office Box 699
Bentonville, Arkansas 72712

Boone County
Post Office Box 846
Harrison, Arkansas 72602

Bradley County
County Courthouse
Warren, Arkansas 71671

Calhoun County
Main Street
Hampton, Arkansas 71744

Carroll County
210 West Church Avenue
Berryville, Arkansas 72616

Chicot County
County Courthouse
Lake Village, Arkansas 71653

Clark County
County Courthouse Square
Arkadelphia, Arkansas 71923

Clay County
2nd Street
Piggott, Arkansas 72454

Cleburne County
301 West Main Street
Heber Springs, Arkansas 72543

Cleveland County
Main & Magnolia Streets
Rison, Arkansas 71665

Columbia County
1 Court Square
Magnolia, Arkansas 71753

Conway County
Moose & Church Streets
Morrilton, Arkansas 72110

Craighead County
511 South Main Street
Jonesboro, Arkansas 72401

Crawford County
3rd & Main Streets
Van Buren, Arkansas 72956

Crittenden County
County Courthouse
Marion, Arkansas 72364

Cross County
705 East Union Avenue
Wynne, Arkansas 72396

Dallas County
3rd & Oak Streets
Fordyce, Arkansas 71742

Desha County
Post Office Box 188
Arkansas City, Arkansas 71630

Drew County
210 South Main Street
Monticello, Arkansas 71655

Faulkner County
801 Locust Street
Conway, Arkansas 72032

Franklin County
Commercial Street
Ozark, Arkansas 72949

Fulton County
Post Office Box 278
Salem, Arkansas 72576

Garland County
501 Ouachita
Hot Springs, Arkansas 71901

Grant County
Main & Center Streets
Sheridan, Arkansas 72150

Greene County
Post Office Box 364
Paragould, Arkansas 72451

Hempstead County
Post Office Box 1420
Hope, Arkansas 71801

Hot Springs County
3rd & Locust Street
Malvern, Arkansas 72104

Howard County
421 North Main Street
Nashville, Arkansas 71852

Independence County
192 East Main Street
Batesville, Arkansas 72501

Izard County
Post Office Box 95
Melbourne, Arkansas 72556

Jackson County
Main Street
Newport, Arkansas 72112

Jefferson County
Post Office Box 6317
Pine Bluff, Arkansas 71611

Johnson County
Post Office Box 278
Clarksville, Arkansas 72830

Lafayette County
Post Office Box 754
Lewisville, Arkansas 71845

Lawrence County
Post Office Box 553
Walnut Ridge, Arkansas 72476

Lee County
15 East Chestnut Street
Marianna, Arkansas 72360

Lincoln County
Drew & Wiley Streets
Star City, Arkansas 71667

Little River County
351 North 2nd Street
Ashdown, Arkansas 71822

Logan County
Broadway Street
Booneville, Arkansas 72927

Lonoke County
Post Office Box 431
Lonoke, Arkansas 72086

Madison County
Post Office Box 37
Huntsville, Arkansas 72740

Marlon County
Courthouse Square
Yellville, Arkansas 72687

Miller County
4 Laurel Street
Texarkana, Arkansas 75502

Mississippi County
Walnut & 2nd Streets
Blytheville, Arkansas 72315

Monroe County
123 Madison Street
Clarendon, Arkansas 72029

Montgomery County
Post Office Box 717
Mount Ida, Arkansas 71957

Nevada County
County Courthouse
Prescott, Arkansas 71857

Newton County
Post Office Box 435
Jasper, Arkansas 72641

Ouachita County
145 Jefferson Street
Camden, Arkansas 71701

Perry County
Post Office Box 358
Perryville, Arkansas 72126

Phillips County
626 Cherry Street
Helena, Arkansas 72342

Pike County
Washington Street
Murfreesboro, Arkansas 71958

Poinsett County
Courthouse Square
Harrisburg, Arkansas 72432

Polk County
507 Church Avenue
Mena, Arkansas 71953

Pope County
100 West Main Street
Russellville, Arkansas 72801

Prairie County
Post Office Box 278
Des Arc, Arkansas 72040

Pulaski County
401 West Markham Street
Little Rock, Arkansas 72201

Randolph County
201 Marr Street
Pocahontas, Arkansas 72455

Saint Francis County
313 South Izard Street
Forrest City, Arkansas 72335

Saline County
200 North Main Street
Benton, Arkansas 72015

Scott County
Post Office Box 1578
Waldron, Arkansas 72958

Searcy County
Post Office Box 297
Marshall, Arkansas 72650

Sebastian County
6th & Rogers
Fort Smith, Arkansas 72901

Sevier County
115 North 3rd Street
De Queen, Arkansas 71832

Sharp County
County Courthouse
Ash Flat, Arkansas 72513

Stone County
Post Office Box 427
Mountain View, Arkansas 72560

Union County
Main & Washington Streets
El Dorado, Arkansas 71730

Van Buren County
Post Office Box 80
Clinton, Arkansas 72031

Washington County
2 South College Avenue
Fayetteville, Arkansas 72701

White County
300 North Spruce Street
Searcy, Arkansas 72143

Woodruff County
Post Office Box 356
Augusta, Arkansas 72006

Yell County
Post Office Box 219
Danville, Arkansas 72833

CALIFORNIA

Alameda County
1225 Fallon Street
Oakland, California 94612

Alpine County
Post Office Box 158
Markleeville, California 96120

Amador County
108 Court Street
Jackson, California 95642

Butte County
25 County Center Drive
Oroville, California 95965

Calaveras County
891 Mountain Ranch Road
San Andreas, California 95249

Colusa County
546 Jay Street
Colusa, California 95932

Contra Costa County
725 Court Street
Martinez, California 94553

Del Norte County
625 6th Street
Crescent City, California 95531

El Dorado County
495 Main Street
Placerville, California 95667

Fresno County
2281 Tulare Street
Fresno, California 92721

Glenn County
526 West Sycamore Street
Willows, California 95988

Humboldt County
825 5th Street
Eureka, California 95501

Imperial County
852 Broadway Street
El Centro, California 92243

Inyo County
168 North Edwards Street
Independence, California 93526

Kern County
1415 Truxton Avenue
Bakersfield, California 93301

Kings County
1400 West Lacey Boulevard
Hanford, California 93230

Lake County
255 North Forbes Street
Lakeport, California 95453

Lassen County
220 South Lassen Street
Susanville, California 96130

Los Angeles County
111 North Hill Street
Los Angeles, California 90012

Madera County
209 West Yosemite Avenue
Madora, California 93637

Marin County
1501 Civic Center Drive
San Rafael, California 94903

Mariposa County
Post Office Box 247
Mariposa, California 95338

Modoc County
Post Office Box 131
Alturas, California 96101

Mondocino County
State & Perkins
Ukiah, California 95482

Mono County
Post Office Box 537
Bridgeport, California 93517

Monterey County
Post Office Box 1819
Salinas, California 93902

Morcod County
2222 M Street
Mercod, California 95340

Napa County
Post Office Box 880
Napa, California 94559

Nevada County
201 Church Street
Nevada City, California 95959

Orange County
700 Civic Center Drive, West
Santa Ana, California 92701

Placer County
11960 Heritage Oak Place
Auburn, California 95604

Plumas County
Post Office Box 10207
Quincy, California 95971

Riverside County
4050 North Main Street
Riverside, California 92501

Sacramento County
720 9th Street
Sacramento, California 95814

San Benito County
440 5th Street
Hollister, California 95023

San Bernardino County
777 East Rialto Avenue
San Bernardino, California 92415

San Diego County
1600 Pacific Highway
San Diego, California 92101

San Francisco
400 Van Ness Avenue
San Francisco, California 94102

San Joaquin County
222 East Weber
Stockton, California 95202

San Luis Obispo County
1035 Palm Street
San Luis Obispo, California 93408

San Mateo County
401 Marshall Street
Redwood City, California 94063

Santa Barbara County
1100 Anacapa Street
Santa Barbara, California 93101

Santa Clara County
70 West Hedding Street
San Jose, California 95110

Santa Cruz County
701 Ocean Street
Santa Cruz, California 95060

Shasta County
1500 Court Street
Redding, California 96001

Sierra County
Post Office Box D
Downieville, California 95936

Siskiyou County
311 4th Street
Yreka, California 96097

Solzno County
580 West Texas Street
Fairfield, California 94533

Sonoma County
Post Office Box 11187
Santa Rosa, California 95406

Stanislaus County
Post Office Box 1098
Modesto, California 95353

Sutter County
433 2nd Street
Yuba City, California 95991

Tehama County
Post Office Box 250
Red Bluff, California 96080

Trinity County
Post Office Box 1258
Weaverville, California 96093

Tulare County
2900 West Burrel Avenue
Visalia, California 93291

Tuolumne County
2 South Green Street
Sonora, California 95370

Ventura County
800 South Victoria Avenue
Ventura, California 93009

Yolo County
725 Court Street
Woodland, California 95695

Yuba County
215 5th Street
Marysville, California 95901

COLORADO

Adams County
450 South 4th Avenue
Brighton, Colorado 80601

Archuleta County
Post Office Box 1507
Pagosa Springs, Colorado 81147

Atamosa County
402 Edison Avenue
Alamosa, Colorado 81101

Baca County
741 Main Street
Springfield, Colorado 81073

Bent County
Post Office Box 350
Las Animas, Colorado 81054

Boulder County
Post Office Box 471
Boulder, Colorado 80306

Chaffee County
132 Crestone Avenue
Salida, Colorado 81201

Cheyenne County
Post Office Box 67
Cheyenne Wells, Colorado 80810

Clear Creek County
Post Office Box 2000
Georgetown, Colorado 80444

Conejos County
Post Office Box 157
Conejos, Colorado 81129

Costilla County
Post Office Box 100
San Luis, Colorado 81152

Crowley County
6th & Main Streets
Ordway, Colorado 81063

Custer County
205 South 6th Street
Westcliffe, Colorado 81252

Delta County
501 Palmer Street
Delta, Colorado 81416

Denver County
City county Building
Denver, Colorado 80202

Dolores County
4th & Main Streets
Dove Creek, Colorado 81324

Douglas County
301 Wilcox Street
Castle Rock, Colorado 80104

Eagle County
Post Office Box 850
Eagle, Colorado 81631

El Paso County
20 East Vermijo Avenue
Colorado Springs, Colorado 80903

Elbert County
Post Office Box 37
Kiowa, Colorado 80117

Fremont County
615 Macon Avenue
Cannon City, Colorado 81212

Garfield County
109 8th Street
Glenwood Springs, Colorado 81601

Giipin County
Post Office Box 366
Central City, Colorado 80427

Grand County
308 Byers Avenue
Hot Sulphur Springs, Colorado 80451

Gunnison County
200 East Virginia Avenue
Gunnison, Colorado 81230

Hinsdale County
Post Office Box 277
Lake City, Colorado 81235

Huerfano County
400 Main Street
Walsenburg, Colorado 81089

Jackson County
Post Office Box 337
Walden, Colorado 80480

Jefferson County
1700 Arapahoe Street
Golden, Colorado 80419

Kiowa County
1305 Golf Street
Eads, Colorado 81036

Kit Carson County
Post Office Box 249
Burlington, Colorado 80807

La Plata County
1060 East 2nd Avenue
Durango, Colorado 81301

Lake County
Post Office Box 917
Leadville, Colorado 80461

Larimer County
Post Office Box 1190
Fort Collins, Colorado 80522

Las Animas County
1st & Maple Streets
Trinidad, Colorado 81082

Lincoln County
718 3rd Avenue
Hugo, Colorado 80821

Logan County
315 Main Street
Sterling, Colorado 80751

Mesa County
Post Office Box 20000
Grand Junction, Colorado 81502

Mineral County
Creede Avenue
Creede, Colorado 81130

Moffat County
221 West Victory Way
Craig, Colorado 81625

Montezuma County
109 West Main Street
Cortez, Colorado 81321

Montrose County
Post Office Box 1289
Montrose, Colorado 81402

Morgan County
231 Ensign Street
Fort Morgan, Colorado 80704

Otero County
Post Office Box 511
La Junta, Colorado 81050

Ouray County
541 4th Street
Ouray, Colorado 81427

Park County
501 Main Street
Fairplay, Colorado 80440

Phillips County
221 South Interocean Avenue
Holyoke, Colorado 80734

Pitkin County
506 East Main Street
Aspen, Colorado 81611

Prowers County
301 South Main Street
Lamar, Colorado 81052

Pueblo County
215 West 10th Street
Pueblo, Colorado 81003

Rio Blanco County
Post Office Box 1067
Meeker, Colorado 81641

Rio Grande County
Post Office Box 160
Del Norte, Colorado 81132

Routt County
Post Office Box 773598
Steamboat Springs, Colorado 80477

Saguache County
Post Office Box 655
Saguache, Colorado 81149

San Juan County
Post Office Box 466
Silverton, Colorado 81433

Sedgwick County
Post Office Box 3
Julesburg, Colorado 80737

Summitt County
Post Office Box 68
Breckenridge, Colorado 80424

Teller County
Post Office Box 959
Cripple Creek, Colorado 80813

Washington County
150 Ash Avenue
Akron, Colorado 80720

Weld County
915 10th Street
Greeley, Colorado 80631

Yuma County
Post Office Box 426
Wray, Colorado 80758

CONNECTICUT

Fairfield Judicial District
1061 Main Street
Bridgeport, Connecticut 06601

Hartford Judicial District
95 Washington Street
Hartford, Connecticut 06106

Litchfield Judical District
20 West Street
Litchfield, Connecticut 06759

Middlesex Judical District
265 Dekoven Drive
Middletown, Connecticut 06457

New Haven County
200 Orange Street
New Haven, Connecticut 06510

Tolland Judicial District
69 Brooklyn Street
Rockville, Connecticut 06066

Windham Judical District
155 Church Street
Putnam, Connecticut 06280

DELAWARE

Kent County
414 Federal Street
Dover, Delaware 19901

New Castle County
800 North French Street
Wilminton, Delaware 19801

Sussex County
Post Office Box 609
Georgetown, Delaware 19947

FLORIDA

Alachua County
21 East University Avenue
Gainesville, Florida 32601

Baker County
55 North 3rd Street
MacClenny, Florida 32063

Bay County
300 East 4th Street
Panama City, Florida 32401

Bradford County
Post Office Box 8
Starke, Florida 32091

Brevard County
700 South Park Avenue
Titusville, Florida 32780

Broward County
Post Office Box 14668
Fort Lauderdale, Florida 33302

Calhoun County
425 East Central Avenue
Blountstown, Florida 32424

Charlotte County
115 West Olympia Avenue
Punta Gorda, Florida 33950

Citrus County
110 North Apopka Avenue
Inverness, Florida 32650

Clay County
Post Office Box 698
Green Cove Springs, Florida 32043

Collier County
3301 Tamiami Trail East
Naples, Florida 33962

Dade County
111 Northwest 1st Avenue
Miami, Florida 33128

De Soto County
201 East Oak Street
Arcadia, Florida 33821

Dixie County
Post Office Box 1206
Cross City, Florida 32628

Duval County
330 East Bay Street
Jacksonville, Florida 32202

Escambia County
223 South Palafox Place
Pensacola, Florida 32501

Flagler County
200 East Moody Boulevard
Bunnell, Florida 32110

Franklin County
Market Street
Apalachicola, Florida 32320

Gadsden County
10 East Jefferson Street
Quincy, Florida 32351

Gilchrist County
112 South Main Street
Trenton, Florida 32693

Glades County
Post Office Box 10
Moore Haven, Florida 33471

Gulf County
1000 5th Street
Port Saint Joe, Florida 32456

Hamilton County
207 Northeast 1st Street
Jasper, Florida 32052

Hardee County
412 West Orange Street
Wauchula, Florida 33873

Hendry County
Highways 80 & 29
La Belle, Florida 33935

Hernando County
20 North Main Street
Brooksville, Florida 34601

Highlands County
430 South Commerce Avenue
Sebring, Florida 33870

Hillsborough County
419 North Pierce Street
Tampa, Florida 33602

Holmes County
201 North Oklahoma Street
Bonifay, Florida 32425

Indian River County
1840 25th Street
Vero Beach, Florida 32960

Jackson County
Post Office Box 510
Marlanna, Florida 32446

Jefferson County
US Highways 90 & 19
Monticello, Florida 32344

Lafayette County
Main Street
Mayo, Florida 32066

Lake County
315 West Main Street
Tavares, Florida 32778

Lee County
2115 2nd Street
Fort Myers, Florida 33901

Leon County
301 South Monroe Street
Tallahassee, Florida 32301

Levy County
Post Office Box 610
Bronson, Florida 32621

Liberty County
Highway 20
Bristol, Florida 32321

Madison County
Post Office Box 237
Madison, Florida 32340

Manalee County
Post Office Box 1000
Bradenton, Florida 34206

Marlon County
601 Southeast 25th Avenue
Ocala, Florida 32671

Martin County
2401 Southeast Monterey Road
Stuart, Florida 34996

Monroe County
500 Whitehead Street
Key West, Florida 33040

Nassau County
416 Centro
Fernandina Beach, Florida 32034

Okaloosa County
Highway 90
Crestview, Florida 32536

Okeechobee County
304 Northwest 2nd Street
Okeechobee, Florida 34972

Orange County
201 South Rosalind Avenue
Orlando, Florida 32801

Osceola County
12 South Vernon Avenue
Kissimmee, Florida 34741

Palm Beach County
301 North Olive Avenue
West Palm Beach, Florida 33401

Pasco County
7530 Little Road
New Port Richey, Florida 34654

Pinellas County
315 Court Street
Clearwater, Florida 34616

Polk County
255 North Broadway Avenue
Barlow, Florida 33830

Pulnam County
410 Street Johns Avenue
Palatka, Florida 32177

Saint Johns County
99 Cordova Street
Saint Augustine, Florida 32084

Saint Lucie County
221 Indian River Drive
Fort Pierce, Florida 34950

Santa Rosa County
801 Caroline Street Southeast
Milton, Florida 32570

Sarasota County
2000 Main Street
Sarasota, Florida 34237

Seminole County
301 North Park Avenue
Sanford, Florida 32771

Sumter County
209 North Florida Street
Bushnell, Florida 33513

Suwannee County
200 Ohio Avenue South
Live Oak, Florida 32060

Taylor County
Post Office Box 620
Perry, Florida 32347

Union County
55 West Main Street
Lake Butler, Florida 32054

Volusia County
123 West Indiana Avenue
De Land, Florida 32720

Wakulla County
Post Office Box 337
Crawfordville, Florida 32327

Walton County
Post Office Box 1260
De Funiak Springs, Florida 32433

Washington County
201 West Cypress Avenue
Chipley, Florida 32428

GEORGIA

Appling County
100 North Oak Street
Baxley, Georgia 31513

Bacon County
502 West 12th Street
Alma, Georgia 31510

Baker County
Courthouse Way
Newton, Georgia 31770

Baldwin County
201 West Hancock Street
Milledgeville, Georgia 31061

Banks County
Post Office Box 130
Homer, Georgia 30547

Barrow County
310 South Broad Street
Windor, Georgia 30680

Bartow County
PO Box 543
Cartersville, Georgia 30120

Ben Hill County
401 East Central Avenue
Fitzgerald, Georgia 31750

Berrien County
105 East Washington Avenue
Nashville, Georgia 31639

Bibb County
601 Mulberry Street
Macon, Georgia 31201

Bleckley County
306 2nd Street Southeast
Cochran, Georgia 31014

Brantley County
Highways 76 & 33
Quitman, Georgia 31643

Bryan County
401 South College Street
Pembroke, Georgia 31321

Bullock County
North Main Street
Statesboro, Georgia 30458

Burke County
6th & Liberty Street
Waynesboro, Georgia 30830

Butts County
Post Office Box 320
Jackson, Georgia 30233

Calhoun County
Courthouse Square
Morgan, Georgia 31766

Camden County
4th Street
Woodbine, Georgia 31569

Candier County
Courthouse Square
Metter, Georgia 30439

Carroll County
311 Newnan Street
Carrollton, Georgia 30117

Catoosa County
206 East Nashville Street
Ringgold, Georgia 30736

Charlton County
100 3rd Street
Folkston, Georgia 31537

Chatham County
133 Montgomery Street
Savannah, Georgia 31401

Chattahoochee County
Post Office Box 299
Cussola, Georgia 31805

Chattooga County
Post Office Box 211
Summmerville, Georgia 30747

Cherokee County
100 North Street
Canton, Georgia 30114

Clarke County
325 East Washington Street
Athens, Georgia 30601

Clay County
Post Office Box 550
Fort Gaines, Georgia 31751

Clayton County
121 South McDonough Street
Jonesboro, Georgia 30236

Clinch County
100 Court Square
Homerville, Georgia 31634

Cobb County
10 East Park Square
Marietta, Georgia 30090

Coffee County
210 South Coffee Avenue
Douglas, Georgia 31533

Colquitt County
Main Street
Moultrie, Georgia 31776

Columbia County
Post Office Box 100
Appling, Georgia 30802

Cook County
212 North Hutchinson Avenue
Adel, Georgia 31620

Coweta County
Post Office Box 945
Newnan, Georgia 30264

Crawford County
Post Office Box 389
Knoxville, Georgia 31050

Crisp County
210 7th Street South
Cordele, Georgia 31015

Dade County
Post Office Box 417
Trenton, Georgia 30752

Dawson County
Post Office Box 192
Dawsonville, Georgia 30534

Dekalb County
556 North McDonough Street
Decatur, Georgia 30030

Decatur County
122 West Water Street
Bainbridge, Georgia 31717

Dodge County
Post Office Box 818
Eastman, Georgia 31023

Dooly County
Post Office Box 322
Vienna, Georgia 31092

Dougherty County
6754 Broad Street
Douglasville, Georgia 30134

Early County
105 Courthouse Square
Dlakely, Georgia 31723

Echois County
Post Office Box 190
Statenville, Georgia 31648

Effingham County
901 North Pine Street
Springfield, Georgia 31329

Elbert County
14 North Oliver Street
Elberton, Georgia 30635

Emanuel County
101 North Main Street
Swainsboro, Georgia 30401

Evans County
3 Freeman Street
Claxton, Georgia 30417

Fannin County
Post Office Box 487
Blue Ridge, Georgia 30513

Fayette County
200 Courthouse Square
Fayetteville, Georgia 30214

Floyd County
Post Office Box 946
Rome, Georgia 30162

Forsyth County
Post Office Box 128
Cumming, Georgia 30130

Franklin County
Courthouse Square
Carnesville, Georgia 30521

Fulton County
160 Pryor Street Southwest
Atlanta, Georgia 30303

Gilmer County
1 Westside Square
Ellijay, Georgia 30540

Glascock County
Post Office Box 231
Gibson, Georgia 30810

Glynn County
701 G Street
Brunswick, Georgia 31520

Gordon County
100 South Wall Street Annex 1
Calhoun, Georgia 30701

Grady County
250 North Broad Street
Cairo, Georgia 31728

Greene County
201 North Main Street
Greensboro, Georgia 30642

Gwinnett County
75 Langley Drive
Lawrenceville, Georgia 30245

Habersham County
Post Office Box 227
Clarkseville, Georgia 30523

Hall County
116 Spring Street East
Gainesville, Georgia 30501

Hancock County
Courthouse Square
Sparta, Georgia 31087

Haralson County
Post Office Box 488
Buchanan, Georgia 30113

Harris County
Post Office Box 528
Hamilton, Georgia 31811

Hart County
Post Office Box 279
Hartwell, Georgia 30643

Heard County
Post Office Box 40
Franklin, Georgia 30217

Henry County
345 Phillips Drive
McDonough, Georgia 30253

Houston County
200 Carl Vinson Parkway
Warner Robbins, Georgia 31088

Irwin County
710 North Irwin Avenue
Ocilla, Georgia 31774

Jackson County
Post Office Box 68
Jefferson, Georgia 30549

Jasper County
County Courthouse
Monticello, Georgia 31064

Jeff Davis County
Jeff Davis Street
Hazlehurst, Georgia 31539

Jenkins County
Post Office Box 797
Millen, Georgia 30442

Johnson County
Post Office Box 269
Wrightsville, Georgia 31096

Jones County
Post Office Box 1359
Gray, Georgia 31032

Lamar County
327 Thomaston Street
Barnesville, Georgia 30204

Lanier County
100 West Main Street
Lakeland, Georgia 31635

Laurens County
101 North Jefferson Street
Dublin, Georgia 31021

Liberty County
Courthouse Square
Hinesville, Georgia 31313

Lincoln County
Humphrey Street
Lincolnton, Georgia 30817

Loe County
Post Office Box 56
Leesburg, Georgia 31763

Long County
McDonald Street
Ludowici, Georgia 31316

Lowndes County
Post Office Box 1349
Valdosta, Georgia 31603

Lumpkin County
280 Courthouse Circle Northeast
Dahlonega, Georgia 30533

Macon County
Sumter Street
Oglethorpe, Georgia 30168

Madison County
Post Office Box 147
Danielsville, Georgia 30633

Marion County
Courthouse Square
Buena Vista, Georgia 31803

McDuffie County
Post Office Box 28
Thomson, Georgia 30824

McIntosh County
Post Office Box 428
Greenville, Georgia 30222

Miller County
155 South 1st Street
Colquitt, Georgia 31737

Mitchell County
12 Broad Street
Camilla, Georgia 31730

Monroe County
Post Office Box 189
Forsyth, Georgia 31029

Montgomery County
Railroad Avenue
Mount Vernon, Georgia 30445

Morgan County
Post Office Box 168
Madison, Georgia 30650

Murray County
3rd Avenue
Chatsworth, Georgia 30705

Muscogee County
100 10th Street
Columbus, Georgia 31901

Newton County
1113 Usher Street
Covington, Georgia 30209

Oconee County
15 Water Street
Watkinsville, Georgia 30677

Oglethorpe County
Post Office Box 261
Lexington, Georgia 30648

Paulding County
1 Courthouse Square
Dallas, Georgia 30132

Peach County
205 West Church Street
Fort Valley, Georgia 31030

Pickens County
211-1 North Main Street
Jasper, Georgia 30143

Pierce County
Post Office Box 679
Blackshear, Georgia 31516

Pike County
Post Office Box 377
Zubulon, Georgia 30295

Polk County
Post Office Box 268
Cedartown, Georgia 30125

Pulaski County
Post Office Box 29
Hawkensville, Georgia 31036

Putnam County
108 South Madison Avenue
Eatonton, Georgia 31024

Quitman County
Post Office Box 114
Georgetown, Georgia 31754

Rabun County
Post Office Box 925
Clayton, Georgia 30525

Randolph County
Court Street
Cuthbert, Georgia 31740

Richmond County
530 Green Street
Augusta, Georgia 30911

Rockdale County
922 Court Street Northeast
Conyers, Georgia 30207

Schley County
Post Office Box 352
Ellaville, Georgia 31806

Screven County
Post Office Box 159
Sylvania, Georgia 30467

Seminole County
County Courthouse
Donalsonville, Georgia 31745

Spalding County
132 East Solomon Street
Griffin, Georgia 30223

Stephens County
Post Office Box 386
Toccoa, Georgia 30577

Stewart County
Post Office Box 157
Lumpkin, Georgia 31815

Sumter County
Post Office Box 295
Americus, Georgia 31709

Talbot County
Courthouse Square
Talbotton, Georgia 31827

Tallaferro County
Courthouse Square
Crawfordville, Georgia 30631

Tattnall County
Main & Brazell Streets
Reidsville, Georgia 30453

Taylor County
Post Office Box 278
Butler, Georgia 31006

Telfair County
Courthouse Square
McRae, Georgia 31055

Terrell County
955 Forrester Drive Southeast
Dawson, Georgia 31742

Thomas County
Post Office Box 920
Thomasville, Georgia 31799

Tift County
225 North Tift Avenue
Tifton, Georgia 31704

Toombs County
Courthouse Square & Highway 280
Lyons, Georgia 30436

Towns County
Post Office Box 178
Hiawassee, Georgia 30546

Troup County
Post Office Box 1149
La Grange, Georgia 30241

Troutlen County
2nd Street
Soperton, Georgia 30457

Turner County
200 East College Avenue
Ashburn, Georgia 31714

Twiggs County
101 Magnolia Street
Jeffersonville, Georgia 31044

Union County
Rural Route 8 Box 8005
Blairsville, Georgia 30512

Upson County
Post Office Box 889
Thomaston, Georgia 30286

Walker County
Court Street Annex 1
Monroe, Georgia 30655

Ware County
800 Church Street
Waycross, Georgia 31501

Warren County
100 Main Street
Warrenton, Georgia 30828

Washington County
Post Office Box 271
Sandersville, Georgia 31082

Wayne County
174 North Brunswick Street
Jesup, Georgia 31545

Webster County
Washington Street & Highway 280
Preston, Georgia 31824

Wheeler County
Pearl Street
Alamo, Georgia 30411

White County
1657 South Main Street
Cleveland, Georgia 30528

Whitfield County
300 West Crawford Street
Dalton, Georgia 30720

Wilcox County
Courthouse Square
Abbeville, Georgia 31001

Wilkes County
23 East Court Street
Washington, Georgia 30673

Wilkinson County
Post Office Box 161
Irwinton, Georgia 31042

HAWAII

Hawaii County
25 Aupuni Street
Hilo, Hawaii 96720

Honolulu County
530 South King Street
Honolulu, Hawaii 96813

Kauai County
4396 Rice Street
Lihue, Hawaii 96766

Maui County
200 South High Street
Wailuku, Hawaii 96793

IDAHO

Ada County
650 Main Street
Boise, Idaho 83702

Adams County
Post Office Box 48
Council, Idaho 83612

Banneck County
624 East Center Street
Paris, Idaho 83261

Bear Lake County
7 East Center Street
Paris, Idaho 83261

Benewah County
7th & College Avenue
Saint Maries, Idaho 83861

Bingham County
501 North Maple Street
Blackfoot, Idaho 83221

Blaine County
Post Office Box 400
Hailey, Idaho 83333

Boise County
Post Office Box 157
Idaho City, Idaho 83631

Bonner County
215 South 1st Avenue
Sandpoint, Idaho 83864

Bonneville County
605 North Capital Avenue
Idaho Falls, Idaho 83402

Boundary County
315 Kootnal Street
Bonners Ferry, Idaho 83805

Butte County
Post Office Box 737
Arco, Idaho 83213

Camas County
Post Office Box 30
Fairfielda, Idaho 83327

Canyon County
1115 Albany Street
Caldwell, Idaho 83605

Caribou County
Post Office Box 775
Soda Springs, Idaho 83276

Cassia County
County Courthouse
Durley, Idaho 83318

Clark County
Post Office Box 205
Dubois, Idaho 83423

Clearwater County
Post Office Box 586
Orofino, Idaho 83544

Custer County
Post Office Box 597
Challis, Idaho 83226

Elmore County
150 South 4th East Street
Mountain Home, Idaho 83647

Franklin County
39 West Oneida Street
Preston, Idaho 83263

Fremont County
151 West 1st North
Saint Anthony, Idaho 83445

Gem County
415 East Main Street
Emmett, Idaho 83617

Gooding County
Post Office Box 417
Gooding, Idaho 83330

Idaho County
320 West Main Street
Grangeville, Idaho 83530

Jefferson County
134 North Clark Street
Rigby, Idaho 83442

Jerome County
300 North Lincoln Avenue
Jerome, Idaho 83338

Kootenal County
501 North Government Way
Coeur D'Alene, Idaho 83814

Lalah County
522 South Adams Street
Moscow, Idaho 83843

Lemhi County
206 Courthouse Drive
Salmon, Idaho 83467

Lewis County
510 Oak Street
Neperce, Idaho 83543

Lincoln County
111 West B Street
Shoshone, Idaho 83352

Madison County
Post Office Box 389
Rexburg, Idaho 83440

Minidoka County
715 G Street
Rupert, Idaho 83350

Noz Parisherce County
Post Office Box 896
Lewiston, Idaho 83501

Oneida County
10 Court Street
Malad City, Idaho 83252

Owyhee County
Post Office Box 128
Murphy, Idaho 83650

Payette County
Post Office Box D
Payette, Idaho 83661

Power County
543 Bannock Avenue
American Falls, Idaho 83211

Shoshone County
Post Office Box 1049
Wallace, Idaho 83873

Teton County
Post Office Box 756
Driggs, Idaho 83422

Twin Falls County
Post Office Box 126
Twin Falls, Idaho 83303

Valley County
Post Office Box 737
Cascade, Idaho 83611

Washington County
Post Office Box 670
Weisor, Idaho 83672

ILLINOIS

Adams County
521 Vermont Street
Quincy, Illinois 62301

Alexander County
2000 Washington Avenue
Cairo, Illinois 62914

Bond County
Post Office Box 407
Greenville, Illinois 62246

Boone County
601 North Main Street
Belvidere, Illinois 61008

Brown County
21 West Court Street
Mount Sterling, Illinois 62353

Bureau County
County Courthouse
Princeton, Illinois 61356

Calhoun County
County Road
Hardin, Illinois 62047

Carroll County
Route 78 & Rapp Road
Mount Carroll, Illinois 61053

Cass County
County Courthouse
Virginia, Illinois 62691

Champaign County
204 East Elm Street
Urbana, Illinois 61801

Christian County
600 North Main Street
Taylorville, Illinois 62568

Clark County
501 Archer Avenue
Marshall, Illinois 62441

Clay County
County Courthouse
Louisville, Illinois 62858

Clinton County
850 Fairfax
Carlyle, Illinois 62231

Coles County
Post Office Box 207
Charleston, Illinois 61920

Cook County
118 North Clark Street
Chicago, Illinois 60602

Crawford County
Douglas Street
Robinson, Illinois 62454

Cumberland County
Courthouse Square
Toledo, Illinois 62468

De Witt County
201 West Washington Street
Clinton, Illinois 61727

Dekalb County
110 East Sycamore Street
Sycamore, Illinois 60178

Douglas County
401 South Center Street
Tuscola, Illinois 61953

Du Parishage County
421 North County Farm Road
Wheaton, Illinois 60187

Edgar County
County Courthouse
Paris, Illinois 61944

Edwards County
50 East Main Street
Albion, Illinois 62806

Effingham County
Post Office Box 628
Effingham, Illinois 62401

Fayette County
221 South 7th Street
Vandalia, Illinois 62471

Ford County
200 West State Street, Room 101
Paxton, Illinois 60957

Franklin County
100 Public Square
Benton, Illinois 62812

Fulton County
100 North Main Street
Lewistown, Illinois 61542

Gallatin County
Post Office Box K
Shawneetown, Illinois 62984

Greene County
519 North Main Street
Carrollton, Illinois 62016

Grundy County
111 East Washington Street
Morris, Illinois 60450

Hamilton County
Public Square
McLeansboro, Illinois 62859

Hancock County
Court House
Carthage, Illinois 62321

Hardin County
Main Street
Elizabethtown, Illinois 62931

Henderson County
Post Office Box 308
Oquawka, Illinois 61469

Henry County
100 South Main Street
Cambridge, Illinois 61238

Iroquois County
550 South 10th Street
Watseka, Illinois 60970

Jackson County
1001 Walnut Street
Murphysboro, Illinois 62966

Jasper County
100 West Jourdan Street
Newton, Illinois 62448

Jefferson County
County Courthouse
Mount Vernon, Illinois 62864

Jersey County
201 West Pearl Street
Jerseyville, Illinois 62052

Jo Daviess County
330 North Bench Street
Galena, Illinois 61036

Johnson County
Post Office Box 96
Vienna, Illinois 62995

Kane County
100 South 3rd Street
Geneva, Illinois 60134

Kankakee County
450 East Court Street
Kankakee, Illinois 60901

Kendall County
110 West Ridge Street
Yorkville, Illinois 60560

Knox County
200 South Cherry Street
Galesburg, Illinois 61401

Lake County
18 North County Street
Waukegan, Illinois 60085

Lasalle County
707 East Etna Road
Ottawa, Illinois 61350

Lawrence County
County Courthouse
Lawrenceville, Illinois 62439

Lee County
Galena & 3rd Streets
Dixon, Illinois 61021

Livingston County
112 West Madison Street
Pontiac, Illinois 61764

Logan County
601 Broadway Street
Lincoln, Illinois 62656

Macon County
253 East Wood Street
Decatur, Illinois 62523

Macoupin County
County Courthouse
Carlinville, Illinois 62626

Madison County
155 North Main Street
Edwardsville, Illinois 62025

Marion County
Broadway & Main Street
Salem, Illinois 62881

Marshall County
122 North Prairie Street
Lacon, Illinois 61540

Mason County
County Courthouse
Havana, Illinois 62644

Massac County
Post Office Box 429
Metropolis, Illinois 62960

McDonough County
County Courthouse
Macomb, Illinois 61455

McHenry County
2200 North Seminary Avenue
Woodstock, Illinois 60098

McLean County
104 West Front Street
Bloomington, Illinois 61701

Menard County
Post Office Box 456
Petersburg, Illinois 62675

Mercer County
College Avenue & Southwest 3rd Street
Aledo, Illinois 61231

Monroe County
100 South Main Street
Waterloo, Illinois 62298

Montgomery County
1 Courthouse Square
Hillsboro, Illinois 62049

Morgan County
300 West State Street
Jacksonville, Illinois 62650

Moultrie County
Courthouse
Sullivan, Illinois 61951

Ogle County
Post Office Box 357
Oregon, Illinois 61061

Peoria County
324 Main Street
Peoria, Illinois 61602

Perry County
Town Square
Pinckneyville, Illinois 62274

Piatt County
101 West Washington Street
Monticello, Illinois 61856

Pike County
Route 36
Pittsfield, Illinois 62363

Pope County
Post Office Box 216
Golconda, Illinois 62938

Pulaski County
Post Office Box 218
Mound City, Illinois 62963

Putnam County
4th Street
Hennepin, Illinois 61327

Randolph County
1 Taylor Street
Chester, Illinois 62233

Richland County
Main Street
Olney, Illinois 62450

Rock Island County
1504 3rd Avenue
Rock Island, Illinois 61201

Saint Clair County
10 Public Square
Belleville, Illinois 62220

Saline County
10 East Poplar Street
Harrisburg, Illinois 62946

Sangamon County
800 East Monroe Street
Springfield, Illinois 62701

Schuyler County
Post Office Box 190
Rushville, Illinois 62681

Scott County
101 East Market Street
Winchester, Illinois 62694

Shelby County
324 East Main Street
Shelbyville, Illinois 62565

Stark County
130 West Main Street
Toulon, Illinois 61483

Stephenson County
15 North Galona Avenue
Freeport, Illinois 61032

Tazewell County
4th & Court Streets
Pekin, Illinois 61554

Union County
311 West Market Street
Jonesboro, Illinois 62952

Vermilion County
7 North Vermilion Street
Danville, Illinois 61832

Wabash County
4th & Market Street
Mount Carmel, Illinois 62863

Warren County
Public Square
Monmouth, Illinois 61462

Washington County
Saint Louis Street
Nashville, Illinois 62263

Wayne County
300 East Main Street
Fairfield, Illinois 62837

White County
Main Street
Carmi, Illinois 62821

Whiteside County
200 East Knox Street
Morrison, Illinois 61270

Will County
302 North Chicago Street
Joliet, Illinois 60431

Williamson County
200 West Jefferson Street
Marion, Illinois 62959

Winnebago County
400 West State Street
Rockford, Illinois 61101

Woodford County
Post Office Box 38
Eureka, Illinois 61530

INDIANA

Adams County
112 South 2nd Street
Decatur, Indiana 46733

Allen County
1 East Main Street
Fort Wayne, Indiana 46802

Bartholomew County
Post Office Box 924
Columbus, Indiana 47202

Benton County
700 East 5th Street
Fowler, Indiana 47944

Blackford County
110 West Washington Street
Hartford City, Indiana 47348

Boone County
1 Courthouse Square
Lebanon, Indiana 46052

Brown County
Van Buren & Main Streets
Nashville, Indiana 47448

Carroll County
County Courthouse
Delphi, Indiana 46923

Cass County
200 Court Parkway
Logansport, Indiana 46947

Clark County
City Court Building 501 East Court Ave.
Jeffersonville, Indiana 47130

Clay County
1206 East National Avenue
Brazil, Indiana 47834

Clinton County
50 North Jackson Street
Frankfort, Indiana 46041

Crawford County
Post Office Box 375
English, Indiana 47118

Davless County
County Courthouse
Washington, Indiana 47501

Dearborn County
215-B West High Street
Lawrenceburg, Indiana 47025

Decatur County
150 Courthouse Square
Greensburg, Indiana 47240

Dekalb County
100 Main Street
Auburn, Indiana 46706

Delaware County
Post Office Box 1089
Muncie, Indiana 47308

Dubois County
Main Street
Jasper, Indiana 47546

Elkhart County
117 North 2nd Street
Goshen, Indiana 46526

Fayette County
401 North Central Avenue
Connersville, Indiana 47331

Floyd County
211 West 1st Street
New Albany, Indiana 47150

Fountain County
County Courthouse
Covington, Indiana 47932

Franklin County
459 Main Street
Brookville, Indiana 47012

Fulton County
815 Main Street
Rochester, Indiana 46975

Gibson County
Courthouse Square
Princeton, Indiana 47670

Grant County
County Courthouse
Marion, Indiana 46952

Greene County
Main & Washington Streets
Bloomfield, Indiana 47424

Hamilton County
Public Square
Noblesville, Indiana 46060

Hancock County
9 East Main Street
Greenfield, Indiana 46140

Harrison County
300 North Capitol Avenue
Corydon, Indiana 47112

Hendricks County
County Courthouse
Danville, Indiana 46122

Henry County
Broad Street
New Castle, Indiana 47362

Howard County
Main & Sycamore
Kokomo, Indiana 46901

Huntington County
North Jefferson Street
Huntington, Indiana 46750

Jackson County
Post Office Box 122
Brownstown, Indiana 47220

Jasper County
Courthouse Square
Rensselaer, Indiana 47978

Jay County
120 North Court Street
Portland, Indiana 47371

Jefferson County
300 East Main Street
Madison, Indiana 47250

Jennings County
County Courthouse
Vernon, Indiana 47282

Johnson County
5 East Jefferson Street
Franklin, Indiana 46131

Knox County
7th & Broadway
Vincennes, Indiana 47591

Kosciusko County
100 West Center Street
Warsaw, Indiana 46580

La Grange County
114 West Michigan Street
La Grange, Indiana 46761

La Parishorte County
Courthouse Square
La Porte, Indiana 46350

Lake County
2293 North Main Street
Crown Point, Indiana 46307

Lawrence County
Bedford Square
Bedford, Indiana 47421

Madison County
16 East 9th Street
Anderson, Indiana 46016

Marion County
200 East Washington Street
Indianapolis, Indiana 46204

Marshall County
211 West Madison Street
Plymouth, Indiana 46563

Martin County
Post Office Box 170
Shoals, Indiana 47581

Miami County
21 Court Street
Peru, Indiana 46970

Monroe County
Post Office Box 547
Bloomington, Indiana 47402

Montgomery County
100 East Main Street
Crawfordsville, Indiana 47933

Morgan County
Post Office Box 1556
Martinsville, Indiana 46151

Newton County
Courthouse Square
Kentland, Indiana 47951

Noble County
101 North Orange Street
Albion, Indiana 46701

Ohio County
Main Street
Rising Sun, Indiana 47040

Orange County
Court Street
Paoli, Indiana 47454

Owen County
County Courthouse
Spencer, Indiana 47460

Parke County
County Courthouse
Rockville, Indiana 47872

Perry County
8th Street
Cannelton, Indiana 47520

Pike County
Main Street
Petersburg, Indiana 47567

Porter County
16 East Lincolnway
Valparaiso, Indiana 46383

Posey County
County Courthouse
Mount Vernon, Indiana 47620

Pulaski County
112 East Main Street
Winamac, Indiana 46996

Putnam County
Post Office Box 546
Greencastle, Indiana 46135

Randolph County
County Courthouse
Winchester, Indiana 47394

Ripley County
Post Office Box 177
Versailles, Indiana 47042

Rush County
Post Office Box 429
Rushville, Indiana 46173

Saint Joseph County
227 West Jefferson Boulevard
South Bend, Indiana 46601

Scott County
1 East McClain Avenue
Scottsburg, Indiana 47170

Shelby County
315 South Harrison Street
Shelbyville, Indiana 46176

Spencer County
541 Main Street
Rockport, Indiana 47635

Starke County
Washington Street
Knox, Indiana 46534

Steuben County
Southeast Public Square
Angola, Indiana 46703

Sullivan County
County Courthouse
Sullivan, Indiana 47882

Switzerland County
County Courthouse
Vevay, Indiana 47043

Tippecanoe County
20 North 3rd Street
Lafayette, Indiana 47901

Tipton County
County Courthouse
Tipton, Indiana 46072

Union County
26 West Union Street
Liberty, Indiana 47353

Vanderburgh County
Post Office Box 3356
Evansville, Indiana 47732

Vermillion County
Post Office Box 8
Newport, Indiana 47966

Vigo County
3rd & Wabash
Terre Haute, Indiana 47807

Wabash County
1 West Hill Street
Wabash, Indiana 46992

Warren County
North Monroe Street
Williamsport, Indiana 47993

Warrick County
County Courthouse
Boonville, Indiana 47601

Washington County
County Courthouse
Salem, Indiana 47167

Wayne County
401 East Main Street
Richmond, Indiana 47374

Wells County
102 West Market Street
Bluffton, Indiana 46714

White County
Post Office Box 350
Monticello, Indiana 47960

Whitley County
302 South Chauncey Street
Columbia City, Indiana 46725

IOWA

Adair County
Post Office Box L
Greenfield, Iowa 50849

Adams County
Davis & 9th
Corning, Iowa 50841

Allamakee County
Post Office Box 248
Waukon, Iowa 52172

Appanoose County
County Courthouse
Centerville, Iowa 52544

Audubon County
County Courthouse
Audubon, Iowa 50025

Benton County
100 East 4th Street
Vinton, Iowa 52349

Black Hawk County
316 East 5th Street
Waterloo, Iowa 50703

Boone County
County Courthouse
Boone, Iowa 50036

Bremer County
415 East Bremer Avenue
Waverly, Iowa 50677

Buchanan County
210 5th Avenue Northeast
Independence, Iowa 50644

Buena Vista County
Post Office Box 1186
Storm Lake, Iowa 50588

Butler County
Post Office Box 325
Allison, Iowa 50602

Calhoun County
Post Office Box 273
Rockwell City, Iowa 50579

Carroll County
Post Office Box 867
Carroll, Iowa 51401

Cass County
7th Street Courthouse
Atlantic, Iowa 50022

Cedar County
400 Cedar Street
Tipton, Iowa 52772

Cerro Gordon County
220 North Washington Avenue
Mason City, Iowa 50401

Cherokee County
Post Office Box F
Cherokee, Iowa 51012

Chickasaw County
Prospect Street
New Hampton, Iowa 50659

Clarke County
117 South Main Street
Osceola, Iowa 50213

Clay County
215 West 4th Street
Spencer, Iowa 51301

Clayton County
111 High Street
Elkader, Iowa 52043

Clinton County
Post Office Box 157
Clinton, Iowa 52732

Crawford County
Post Office Box 546
Denison, Iowa 51442

Dallas County
801 Court Street
Adel, Iowa 50003

Davis County
Courthouse Square
Bloomfield, Iowa 52537

Decatur County
207 North Main Street
Leon, Iowa 50144

Delaware County
Post Office Box 527
Manchester, Iowa 52057

Des Moines County
Post Office Box 158
Burlington, Iowa 52601

Dickinson County
18th & Hill County Courthouse
Spirit Lake, Iowa 51360

Dubuque County
720 Central Avenue
Dubuque, Iowa 52001

Emmel County
609 1st Avenue North
Estherville, Iowa 51334

Fayette County
Vine Street
West Union, Iowa 52175

Floyd County
101 South Main Street
Charles City, Iowa 50616

Franklin County
121st Avenue Northwest
Hampton, Iowa 50441

Fremont County
Courthouse Square
Sidney, Iowa 51652

Greene County
County Courthouse
Jefferson, Iowa 50129

Grundy County
700 G Avenue
Grundy Center, Iowa 50638

Guthrie County
200 North 5th Street
Guthrie Center, Iowa 50115

Hamilton County
County Courthouse
Webster City, Iowa 50595

Hancock County
855 State Street
Garner, Iowa 50438

Hardin County
Edgington Avenue
Eldora, Iowa 50627

Harrison County
113 North 2nd Avenue
Logan, Iowa 51546

Henry County
100 East Washington Street
Mount Pleasant, Iowa 52641

Howard County
218 North Elm Street
Cresco, Iowa 52136

Humboldt County
County Courthouse
Dakota City, Iowa 50529

Ida County
401 Moorehead Street
Ida Grove, Iowa 51445

Iowa County
Court Avenue
Marengo, Iowa 52301

Jackson County
201 West Platt Street
Maquoketa, Iowa 52060

Jasper County
100 1st Street
Newton, Iowa 50208

Jefferson County
Post Office Box 984
Fairfield, Iowa 52556

Johnson County
417 South Clinton Street
Iowa City, Iowa 52240

Jones County
High Street
Anamosa, Iowa 52205

Keokuk County
Courthouse Square
Sigourney, Iowa 52591

Kossuth County
114 West State Street
Algona, Iowa 50511

Lee County
Post Office Box 1443
Fort Madison, Iowa 52627

Linn County
50 3rd Avenue Bridge
Cedar Rapids, Iowa 52401

Louisa County
117 South Main Street
Wapello, Iowa 52653

Lucas County
County Courthouse
Chariton, Iowa 50049

Lyon County
206 South 2nd Avenue
Rock Rapids, Iowa 51246

Madison County
Post Office Box 152
Winterset, Iowa 50273

Mahaska County
Post Office Box 30
Oskaloosa, Iowa 52577

Marion County
Post Office Box 497
Knoxville, Iowa 50138

Marshall County
17 East Main Street
Marshalltown, Iowa 50158

Mills County
418 Sharp Street
Glenwood, Iowa 51534

Mitchell County
County Courthouse
Osage, Iowa 50461

Monona County
610 Iowa Avenue
Onawa, Iowa 51040

Monroe County
County Courthouse
Albia, Iowa 52531

Montgomery County
105 Coolbaugh Street
Red Oak, Iowa 51566

Muscatine County
Post Office Box 327
Muscatine, Iowa 52761

O'Brien County
155 South Hayes
Primghar, Iowa 51245

Osceola County
614 5th Avenue
Sibley, Iowa 51249

Page County
112 East Main Street
Clarinda, Iowa 51632

Palo Alto County
11th & Broadway
Emmetsburg, Iowa 50536

Plymouth County
3rd Avenue & 2nd Street Southeast
Le Mars, Iowa 51031

Pocahontas County
Court Square County Courthouse
Pocahontas, Iowa 50574

Polk County
500 Mulberry Street
Des Moines, Iowa 50309

Pottawattamie County
227 South 6th Street
Council Bluffs, Iowa 51501

Poweshiek County
302 East Main Street
Montezuma, Iowa 50171

Ringgold County
County Courthouse
Mount Ayr, Iowa 50854

Sac County
Post Office Box 368
Sac City, Iowa 50583

Scott County
416 West 4th Street
Davenport, Iowa 52801

Shelby County
Post Office Box 431
Harlan, Iowa 51537

Sioux County
210 Central Avenue Southwest
Orange City, Iowa 51041

Story County
900 6th Street
Nevada, Iowa 50201

Tama County
County Courthouse
Toledo, Iowa 52342

Taylor County
County Courthouse
Bedford, Iowa 50833

Union County
300 North Pine Street
Creston, Iowa 50801

Van Buren County
Post Office Box 475
Keosauqua, Iowa 52565

Wapello County
4th & Court Streets
Ottumwa, Iowa 52501

Warren County
Post Office Box 379
Indianola, Iowa 50125

Washington County
Post Office Box 391
Washington, Iowa 52353

Wayne County
Post Office Box 424
Corydon, Iowa 50060

Webster County
701 Central Avenue
Fort Dodge, Iowa 50501

Winnebago County
126 South Clark Street
Forest City, Iowa 50436

Winneshiuk County
201 West Main Street
Decorah, Iowa 52101

Woodbury County
101 Court Street
Sioux City, Iowa 51101

Worth County
1000 Central Avenue
Northwood, Iowa 50459

Wright County
Post Office Box 306
Clarion, Iowa 50525

KANSAS

Allen County
1st North Washington Street
Iola, Kansas 66749

Anderson County
100 East 4th Avenue
Garnett, Kansas 66032

Atchison County
5th & Parallel
Atchison, Kansas 66002

Barber County
120 East Washington Avenue
Medicine Lodge, Kansas 67104

Barton County
Post Office Box 1089
Great Bend, Kansas 67530

Bourbon County
210 South National Avenue
Fort Scott, Kansas 66701

Brown County
Courthouse Square
Hiawatha, Kansas 66434

Butler County
200 West Central Avenue
El Dorado, Kansas 67042

Chase County
Post Office Box 547
Cottonwood Falls, Kansas 66845

Chautauqua County
215 North Chautauqua Street
Sedan, Kansas 67361

Cherokee County
Post Office Box 14
Columbus, Kansas 66725

Cheyenne County
Post Office Box 985
Saint Francis, Kansas 67756

Clark County
Post Office Box 886
Ashland, Kansas 67831

Clay County
Post Office Box 98
Clay Center, Kansas 67432

Cloud County
811 Washington Street
Concordia, Kansas 66901

Coffey County
6th & Neosho
Burlington, Kansas 66839

Comanche County
Post Office Box 397
Coldwater, Kansas 67029

Cowley County
311 East 9th Avenue
Winfield, Kansas 67156

Crawford County
County Courthouse
Girard, Kansas 66743

Decatur County
194 South Penn Avenue
Oberlin, Kansas 67749

Dickinson County
Post Office Box 248
Abilene, Kansas 67410

Doniphan County
Main Street
Troy, Kansas 66087

Douglas County
111 East 11th Street
Lawrence, Kansas 66044

Edwards County
312 Massachusetts Avenue
Kinsley, Kansas 67547

Elk County
Post Office Box 606
Howard, Kansas 67349

Ellis County
1204 Fort Street
Hays, Kansas 67601

Ellsworth County
Post Office Box 396
Ellsworth, Kansas 67439

Finney County
Post Office Box M
Garden City, Kansas 67846

Ford County
Central & Spruce Streets
Dodge City, Kansas 67801

Franklin County
3rd & Main Streets
Ottawa, Kansas 66067

Geary County
8th & Franklin
Junction City, Kansas 66441

Gove County
Post Office Box 128
Gove, Kansas 67736

Graham County
410 North Pomeroy Street
Hill City, Kansas 67642

Grant County
108 South Glenn Street
Ulysses, Kansas 67880

Gray County
Post Office Box 487
Cimarron, Kansas 67835

Greeley County
Post Office Box 277
Tribune, Kansas 67879

Greenwood County
311 North Main Street
Eureka, Kansas 67045

Hamilton County
North Main Street
Syracuse, Kansas 67878

Harper County
County Courthouse
Anthony, Kansas 67003

Harvey County
Post Office Box 687
Newton, Kansas 67114

Haskell County
Post Office Box 518
Sublette, Kansas 67877

Hodgeman County
Post Office Box 247
Jetmore, Kansas 67854

Jackson County
Courthouse Square
Holton, Kansas 66436

Jefferson County
Post Office Box 321
Oskaloosa, Kansas 66066

Jewell County
307 North Commercial Street
Mankato, Kansas 66956

Johnson County
Santa Fe & Kansas Avenue
Olathe, Kansas 66061

Kearny County
305 North Main Street
Lakin, Kansas 67860

Kingman County
130 North Spruce Street
Kingman, Kansas 67068

Kiowa County
211 East Florida Avenue
Greensburg, Kansas 67054

Labelle County
Post Office Box 387
Oswego, Kansas 67356

Lane County
144 South Lane
Dighton, Kansas 67839

Leavenworth County
South 4th & Walnut Street
Leavenworth, Kansas 66048

Lincoln County
216 East Lincoln Avenue
Lincoln, Kansas 67455

Linn County
Post Office Box B
Mound City, Kansas 66056

Logan County
710 West 2nd Street
Oakley, Kansas 67748

Lyon County
402 Commercial Street
Emporia, Kansas 66801

Marion County
South 3rd Street Courthouse Square
Marion, Kansas 66861

Marshall County
1201 Broadway
Marysville, Kansas 66508

McPherson County
Kansas & Maple Streets
McPherson, Kansas 67460

Meade County
200 North Fowler Street
Meade, Kansas 67864

Miami County
120 South Pearl Street
Paola, Kansas 66071

Mitchell County
Post Office Box 190
Beloit, Kansas 67420

Montgomery County
Post Office Box 446
Independence, Kansas 67301

Morris County
501 West Main Street
Council Grove, Kansas 66846

Morton County
Post Office Box 1116
Elkhart, Kansas 67950

Nemaha County
607 Nemaha Street
Seneca, Kansas 66538

Neosho County
Post Office Box 138
Erie, Kansas 66733

Ness County
202 West Sycamore Street
Ness City, Kansas 67560

Norton County
Post Office Box 70
Norton, Kansas 67654

Osage County
Post Office Box 226
Lyndon, Kansas 66451

Osborne County
423 West Main Street
Osborne, Kansas 67473

Ottawa County
307 North Concord Street
Minneapolis, Kansas 67467

Pawnee County
715 Broadway
Larned, Kansas 67550

Phillips County
3rd & State Streets
Phillipsburg, Kansas 67661

Pottawatomie County
Post Office Box 187
Westmoreland, Kansas 66549

Pratt County
300 South Ninnescah Street
Pratt, Kansas 67124

Rawlins County
607 Main Street
Atwood, Kansas 67730

Reno County
206 West 1st Avenue
Hutchinson, Kansas 67501

Republic County
County Courthouse
Belleville, Kansas 66935

Rice County
101 West Commercial Street
Lyons, Kansas 67554

Riley County
110 Courthouse Plaza
Manhattan, Kansas 66502

Rooks County
115 North Walnut Street
Stockton, Kansas 67669

Rush County
Post Office Box 220
La Crosse, Kansas 67548

Russell County
Post Office Box 113
Russell, Kansas 67665

Saline County
300 West Ash Street
Salina, Kansas 67401

Scott County
303 Court Street
Scott City, Kansas 67871

Sedgwick County
525 North Main Street
Wichita, Kansas 67203

Seward County
415 North Washington Avenue
Liberal, Kansas 67901

Shawnee County
200 Southeast 7th Street
Topeka, Kansas 66603

Sheridan County
Post Office Box 899
Hoxie, Kansas 67740

Sherman County
813 Broadway
Goodland, Kansas 67735

Smith County
218 South Grant Street
Smith Center, Kansas 66967

Stafford County
209 North Broadway Street
Saint John, Kansas 67576

Stanton County
Post Office Box 190
Johnson, Kansas 67855

Stevens County
200 East 6th Street
Hugoton, Kansas 67951

Sumner County
500 North Washington Avenue
Wellington, Kansas 67152

Thomas County
300 North Court Avenue
Colby, Kansas 67701

Trego County
216 North Main Street
Wakeeney, Kansas 67672

Wabaunsee County
Post Office Box 278
Alma, Kansas 66401

Wallace County
313 Main Street
Sharon Springs, Kansas 67758

Washington County
214 C Street
Washington, Kansas 66968

Wichita County
Post Office Box 279
Leoti, Kansas 67861

Wilson County
615 Madison Street
Fredonia, Kansas 66736

Woodson County
105 West Rutledge Street
Yates Center, Kansas 66783

Wyandotte County
710 North 7th Street
Kansas City, Kansas 66101

KENTUCKY

Adair County
500 Public Square
Columbia, Kentucky 42728

Allen County
Post Office Box 336
Scottsville, Kentucky 42164

Anderson County
151 South Main Street
Lawrenceburg, Kentucky 40342

Ball County
County Courthouse
Pineville, Kentucky 40977

Ballard County
Post Office Box 145
Wicklitte, Kentucky 42087

Barren County
County Courthouse
Glasgow, Kentucky 42141

Bath County
Main Street
Owingsville, Kentucky 40360

Boone County
2950 East Washington Square
Burlington, Kentucky 41005

Bourbon County
Main Street
Paris, Kentucky 40361

Boyd County
2800 Louisa Street
Catlettsburg, Kentucky 41129

Boyle County
Main Street
Danville, Kentucky 40422

Bracken County
Locus Street
Brooksville, Kentucky 41004

Breathill County
1127 Main Street
Jackson, Kentucky 41339

Breckenridge County
Post Office Box 227
Hardinsburg, Kentucky 40143

Bullitt County
Buckman Street
Shepherdsville, Kentucky 40165

Butler County
Post Office Box 448
Morgantown, Kentucky 42261

Caldwell County
100 East Market Street
Princeton, Kentucky 42445

Calloway County
101 South 5th Street
Murray, Kentucky 42071

Campbell County
Post Office Box 340
Newport, Kentucky 41071

Carlisle County
Court Street
Bardwell, Kentucky 42023

Carroll County
Court Street County Courthouse
Carrollton, Kentucky 41008

Carter County
Courthouse
Grayson, Kentucky 41143

Casey County
Post Office Box 310
Liberty, Kentucky 42539

Christian County
511 South Main Street
Hopkinsville, Kentucky 42240

Clark County
34 South Main Street
Winchester, Kentucky 40391

Clay County
Post Office Box 463
Manchester, Kentucky 40962

Clinton County
County Courthouse
Albany, Kentucky 42602

Crittenden County
107 South Main Street
Marion, Kentucky 42064

Cumberland County
Post Office Box 275
Burkesville, Kentucky 42717

Davless County
Post Office Box 389
Owensboro, Kentucky 42302

Edmonson County
Main & Cross Street
Brownsville, Kentucky 42210

Elliott County
Post Office Box 225
Sandy Hook, Kentucky 41171

Estill County
130 Main Street
Irvine, Kentucky 40336

Fayette County
162 East Main Street
Lexington, Kentucky 40507

Fleming County
100 Court Square
Flemingsburg, Kentucky 41041

Floyd County
3rd Avenue
Prestonsburg, Kentucky 41653

Franklin County
Post Office Box 338
Frankfort, Kentucky 40602

Fulton County
Moulton & Wellington Streets
Hickman, Kentucky 42050

Gallatin County
Post Office Box 616
Warsaw, Kentucky 41095

Garrard County
Public Square
Lancaster, Kentucky 40444

Grant County
Post Office Box 469
Williamstown, Kentucky 41097

Graves County
Courthouse
Mayfield, Kentucky 42066

Grayson County
100 Court Square
Leitchfield, Kentucky 42754

Green County
203 West Court Street
Greensburg, Kentucky 42743

Greenup County
301 Main Street
Greenup, Kentucky 41144

Hancock County
County Administration Building
Hawesville, Kentucky 42348

Hardin County
14 Public Square
Elizabethtown, Kentucky 42701

Harlan County
Post Office Box 956
Harlan, Kentucky 40831

Harrison County
190 West Pike Street
Cynthiana, Kentucky 41031

Hart County
Post Office Box 277
Munfordville, Kentucky 42765

Henderson County
232 1st Street
Henderson, Kentucky 42420

Henry County
Post Office Box 202
New Castle, Kentucky 40050

Hickman County
Courthouse Square
Clinton, Kentucky 42031

Hopkins County
Main & Center
Madisonville, Kentucky 42431

Jackson County
Post Office Box 700
McKee, Kentucky 40447

Jefferson County
527 West Jefferson Street
Louisville, Kentucky 40202

Jessamine County
Post Office Box 38
Nicholasville, Kentucky 40356

Johnson County
Court Street
Paintsville, Kentucky 41240

Knott County
Post Office Box 446
Hindman, Kentucky 41822

Knox County
Post Office Box 105
Barbourville, Kentucky 40906

Konton County
3rd & Court Street, 1st Floor
Covington, Kentucky 41012

Laruo County
County Courthouse
Hodgenville, Kentucky 42748

Laurel County
County Courthouse
London, Kentucky 40741

Lawrence County
122 South Main Cross Street
Louisa, Kentucky 41230

Lee County
Post Office Box 551
Beattyville, Kentucky 41311

Leslin County
Post Office Box 916
Hyden, Kentucky 41749

Letcher County
Post Office Box 58
Whitesburg, Kentucky 41858

Lewis County
2nd Street
Vanceburg, Kentucky 41179

Lincoln County
County Courthouse
Stanford, Kentucky 40484

Livingston County
Post Office Box 400
Smithland, Kentucky 42081

Logan County
426 East 4th Street
Russellville, Kentucky 42276

Lyon County
Post Office Box 350
Eddyville, Kentucky 42038

Madison County
101 West Main Street
Richmond, Kentucky 40475

Magottin County
Court Street
Salyersville, Kentucky 41465

Marion County
Main Street
Lebanon, Kentucky 40033

Marshall County
1101 Main Street
Benton, Kentucky 42025

Martin County
Main Street
Inez, Kentucky 41224

Mason County
Post Office Box 234
Maysville, Kentucky 41056

McCracken County
Washington & 7th Streets
Paducah, Kentucky 42003

McCreary County
Main Street
Whitley City, Kentucky 42653

McLean County
Post Office Box 57
Calhoun, Kentucky 42327

Meade County
Post Office Box 614
Brandenburg, Kentucky 40108

Menilee County
County Courthouse
Frenchburg, Kentucky 40322

Mercer County
224 South Main Street
Harrodsburg, Kentucky 40330

Monroe County
Post Office Box 335
Tompkinsville, Kentucky 42167

Montgomery County
Court Street
Mount Sterling, Kentucky 40353

Morgan County
505 Prestonsburg Street
West Liberty, Kentucky 41472

Motcallo County
Post Office Box 850
Edmonton, Kentucky 42129

Muhlenberg County
Post Office Box 272
Greenville, Kentucky 42345

Nelson County
113 East Stephen Foster Avenue
Bardstown, Kentucky 40004

Nicholas County
Post Office Box 329
Carlisle, Kentucky 40311

Ohio County
Post Office Box 85
Hartford, Kentucky 42347

Oldham County
100 Main Street
La Grange, Kentucky 40031

Owen County
County Courthouse
Owenton, Kentucky 40359

Owsley County
154 Main Street
Booneville, Kentucky 41314

Pendleton County
County Courthouse Square
Falmouth, Kentucky 41040

Perry County
Post Office Box 150
Hazard, Kentucky 41702

Pike County
Post Office Box 631
Pikeville, Kentucky 41501

Powell County
Court Street
Stanton, Kentucky 40380

Pulaski County
Post Office Box 724
Somerset, Kentucky 42501

Robertson County
Post Office Box 95
Mount Olivet, Kentucky 41064

Rockcastle County
Post Office Box 365
Mount Vernon, Kentucky 40456

Rowan County
East Main Street, 2nd Floor
Morehead, Kentucky 40351

Russell County
Post Office Box 579
Jamestown, Kentucky 42629

Scott County
101 East Main Street
Georgetown, Kentucky 40324

Shelby County
501 Main Street
Shelbyville, Kentucky 40065

Simpson County
Post Office Box 268
Franklin, Kentucky 42134

Spencer County
Main Street
Taylorsville, Kentucky 40071

Taylor County
Court & Broadway
Campbellsville, Kentucky 42718

Todd County
Post Office Box 157
Elkton, Kentucky 42220

Trigg County
Post Office Box 1310
Cadiz, Kentucky 42211

Trimble County
Main Street & Highway 42
Bedford, Kentucky 40006

Union County
Post Office Box 119
Morganfield, Kentucky 42437

Warren County
429 East 10th Street
Bowling Green, Kentucky 42101

Washington County
Post Office Box 446
Springfield, Kentucky 40069

Wayne County
Post Office Box 565
Monticello, Kentucky 42633

Webster County
Post Office Box 155
Dixon, Kentucky 42409

Whitley County
111 Main Street
Williamsburg, Kentucky 40769

Wolfe County
Post Office Box 400
Campton, Kentucky 41301

Woodford County
County Courthouse
Versailles, Kentucky 40383

LOUISIANA

Acadia Parish
Post Office Box 922
Crowley, Louisiana 70527

Allen Parish
Post Office Box G
Oberlin, Louisiana 70655

Ascension Parish
Houmas Street
Donaldsonville, Louisiana 70346

Assumption Parish
Martin Luther King Drive & Highway 1
Napoleonville, Louisiana 70390

Avoyelles Parish
301 North Main Street
Marksville, Louisiana 71351

Beauregard Parish
Post Office Box 310
De Ridder, Louisiana 70634

Bienville Parish
300 Courthouse Square
Arcadia, Louisiana 71001

Bossier Parish
Post Office Box 369
Benton, Louisiana 71006

Caddo Parish
501 Texas Street
Shreveport, Louisiana 71101

Calcasleu Parish
Post Office Box 1030
Lake Charles, Louisiana 70602

Caldwell Parish
Main Street
Columbia, Louisiana 71418

Cameron Parish
Post Office Box 549
Cameron, Louisiana 70631

Catahoula Parish
Post Office Box 198
Harrisonburg, Louisiana 71340

Claiborne Parish
Courthouse Square
Homer, Louisiana 71040

Concordia Parish
Post Office Box 790
Vidalia, Louisiana 71373

Desoto Parish
Parish Courthouse
Mansfield, Louisiana 71052

East Baton Rouge Parish
222 Saint Louis Street
Baton Rouge, Louisiana 70802

East Countyarroll Parish
400 1st Street
Lake Providence, Louisiana 71254

East Feliciana Parish
Post Office Box 595
Clinton, Louisiana 70722

Evangeline Parish
Court Street, 2nd Floor
Ville Platte, Louisiana 70586

Franklin Parish
210 Main Street
Winnsboro, Louisiana 71295

Grant Parish
Main Street
Colfax, Louisiana 71417

Iberia Parish
300 Iberia Street
New Iberia, Louisiana 70560

Iberville Parish
Post Office Box 423
Plaquemine, Louisiana 70765

Jackson Parish
Post Office Box 737
Jonesboro, Louisiana 71251

Jefferson Davis Parish
Post Office Box 1409
Jennings, Louisiana 70546

Jefferson Parish
2nd & Derbigny
Gretna, Louisiana 70053

Lafayette Parish
Post Office Box 4508
Lafayette, Louisiana 70502

Lafourche Parish
209 Green Street
Thibodaux, Louisiana 70301

Lasalle Parish
Post Office Box 57
Jena, Louisiana 71342

Lincoln Parish
100 West Texas Avenue
Ruston, Louisiana 71270

Livingston Parish
Post Office Box 427
Livingston, Louisiana 70754

Madison Parish
100 North Cedar Street
Tallulah, Louisiana 71282

Morehouse Parish
125 East Madison Street
Bastrop, Louisiana 71221

Natchitoches Parish
Post Office Box 799
Natchitoches, Louisiana 71458

Orleans Parish
1300 Perdido Street
New Orleans, Louisiana 70112

Ouachita Parish
300 Saint John Street
Monroe, Louisiana 71201

Plaquemines Parish
Highway 39
Pointe A La Hache, Louisiana 70082

Pointe Countyoupee Parish
Post Office Box 86
New Roads, Louisiana 70760

Rapides Parish
700 Murray Street
Alexandria, Louisiana 71301

Red River Parish
615 East Carroll Street
Coushatta, Louisiana 71019

Richland Parish
108 Courthouse Square
Rayville, Louisiana 71269

Sabine Parish
Post Office Box 419
Many, Louisiana 71449

Saint Bernard Parish
8201 West Judge Perez Drive
Chalmette, Louisiana 70043

Saint Countyharles Parish
Post Office Box 302
Hahnville, Louisiana 70057

Saint Helena Parish
Court Square
Greensburg, Louisiana 70441

Saint James Parish
Post Office Box 106
Convent, Louisiana 70723

Saint John The Baptist Parish
1801 West Airline Highway
La Place, Louisiana 70068

Saint Landry Parish
Court & Landry Streets
Opelousas, Louisiana 70570

Saint Martin Parish
County Courthouse
Saint Martinville, Louisiana 70582

Saint Mary Parish
500 Main Street
Franklin, Louisiana 70538

Saint Tammany Parish
Post Office Box 1090
Covington, Louisiana 70434

Tangipahoa Parish
Post Office Box 215
Amite, Louisiana 70422

Tensas Parish
Courthouse Square
Saint Joseph, Louisiana 71366

Terrebonne Parish
301 Goode Street
Houma, Louisiana 70360

Union Parish
Main & Bayou Streets
Farmerville, Louisiana 71241

Vermilion Parish
Post Office Box 790
Abbeville, Louisiana 70511

Vernon Parish
201 South 3rd Street
Leesville, Louisiana 71446

Washington Parish
Washington & Main Street
Franklinton, Louisiana 70438

Webster Parish
Post Office Box 370
Minden, Louisiana 71058

West Baton Rouge Parish
Post Office Box 757
Port Allen, Louisiana 70767

West Countyarroll Parish
Post Office Box 630
Oak Grove, Louisiana 71263

West Feliciana Parish
Royal & Prosperity
Saint Francisville, Louisiana 70775

Winn Parish
Post Office Box 951
Winnfield, Louisiana 71483

MAINE

Androscoggin County
2 Turner Street
Auburn, Maine 04210

Arooslook County
Post Office Box 803
Houlton, Maine 04730

Cumberland County
142 Federal Street
Portland, Maine 04101

Franklin County
38 Main Street
Farmington, Maine 04938

Hancock County
60 State Street
Ellsworth, Maine 04605

Kennebee County
95 State Street
Augusta, Maine 04330

Knox County
Post Office Box 885
Rockland, Maine 04841

Lincoln County
High Street County Courthouse
Wiscassel, Maine 04578

Oxford County
Post Office Box 179
South Paris, Maine 04281

Penobscot County
97 Hammond Street
Bangor, Maine 04401

Piscataquis County
51 East Main Street
Dover-Foxcroft, Maine 04426

Sagadahoc County
Post Office Box 246
Bath, Maine 04530

Somerset County
County Courthouse
Skowhegan, Maine 04976

Waldo County
73 Church Street
Belfast, Maine 04915

Washington County
Post Office Box 297
Machias, Maine 04654

York County
Court Street
Alfred, Maine 04002

MARYLAND

Allegany County
3 Pershing Street
Cumberland, Maryland 21502

Anne Arundel County
44 Calvert Street
Annapolis, Maryland 21401

Baltimore County
100 North Holliday Street
Baltimore, Maryland 21202

Baltimore County
400 Washington Avenue
Towson, Maryland 21204

Calvert County
175 Main Street
Prince Frederick, Maryland 20678

Caroline County
Post Office Box 207
Denton, Maryland 21629

Carroll County
225 North Center Street
Westminster, Maryland 21157

Cecil County
East Main Street
Elkton, Maryland 21921

Charles County
Post Office Box B
La Plata, Maryland 20646

Dorchester County
Post Office Box 26
Cambridge, Maryland 21613

Frederick County
12 East Church Street
Frederick, Maryland 21701

Garrett County
203 South 4th Street
Oakland, Maryland 21550

Harford County
220 South Main Street
Bel Air, Maryland 21014

Howard County
3430 Court House Drive
Ellicott City, Maryland 21043

Kent County
230 North Cross Street
Chestertown, Maryland 21620

Montgomery County
100 Maryland Avenue
Rockville, Maryland 20850

Prince George's County
7911 Anchor Street
Landover, Maryland 20785

Queen Anne's County
208 North Commerce Street
Centreville, Maryland 21617

Saint Mary's County
Post Office Box 653
Leonardtown, Maryland 20650

Somerset County
21 Prince William Street
Princess Anne, Maryland 21853

Talbot County
Washington Street
Easton, Maryland 21601

Washington County
95 West Washington Street
Hagerstown, Maryland 21740

Wicomico County
Post Office Box 198
Salisbury, Maryland 21803

Worcester County
1 West Market Street
Snow Hill, Maryland 21863

MASSACHUSETTS

Barnstable County
Route 6-A
Barnstable, Massachusetts 02630

Berkshire County
76 East Street
Pittsfield, Massachusetts 01201

Bristol County
9 Court Street
Taunton, Massachusetts 02780

Dukes County
Post Office Box 190
Edgartown, Massachusetts 02539

Essex County
36 Federal Street
Salem, Massachusetts 01970

Franklin County
425 Main Street
Greenfield, Massachusetts 01301

Hampden County
50 State Street
Springfield, Massachusetts 01103

Hampshire County
99 Main Street
Northampton, Massachusetts 01060

Middlesex County
40 Thorndike Street
East Cambridge, Massachusetts 02141

Nantucket County
Town & County Building
Nantucket, Massachusetts 02554

Norfolk County
650 High Street
Dedham, Massachusetts 02026

Plymouth County
Post Office Box 3535
Plymouth, Massachusetts 02361

Suffolk County
55 Pemberton Square
Boston, Massachusetts 02108

Worcester County
2 Main Street
Worcester, Massachusetts 01608

MICHIGAN

Alcona County
106 5th Street
Harrisville, Michigan 48740

Alger County
101 Court Street
Munising, Michigan 49862

Allegan County
113 Chestnut Street
Allegan, Michigan 49010

Alpena County
720 West Chisholm Street
Alpena, Michigan 49707

Antrim County
Post Office Box 520
Bellaire, Michigan 49615

Arenac County
Post Office Box 747
Standish, Michigan 48658

Baraga County
12 South 3rd Street
L'Anse, Michigan 49946

Barry County
220 West State Street
Hastings, Michigan 49058

Bay County
515 Center Avenue
Bay City, Michigan 48708

Benzie County
224 Court Place
Beulah, Michigan 49617

Berrlen County
811 Port Street
Saint Joseph, Michigan 49085

Branch County
31 Division Street
Coldwater, Michigan 49036

Calhoun County
315 West Green Street
Marshall, Michigan 49068

Cass County
120 North Broadway Street
Cassopolis, Michigan 49031

Charlevoix County
301 State Street
Charlevoix, Michigan 49720

Cheboygan County
870 South Main Street
Cheboygan, Michigan 49721

Chippewa County
319 Court Street
Sault Sainte Marie, Michigan 49783

Clare County
Post Office Box 438
Harrison, Michigan 48625

Clinton County
100 East State Street
Saint Johns, Michigan 48879

Crawford County
200 West Michigan Avenue
Grayling, Michigan 49738

Delta County
310 Ludington Street
Escanaba, Michigan 49829

Dickinson County
Post Office Box 609
Iron Mountain, Michigan 49801

Eaton County
1045 Independence Drive
Charlotte, Michigan 48813

Emmet County
200 Division Street
Petoskey, Michigan 49770

Genesee County
900 South Saginaw Street
Flint, Michigan 48502

Gladwin County
401 West Cedar Avenue
Gladwin, Michigan 48624

Gogebic County
200 North Moore Street
Bessemer, Michigan 49911

Grand Traverse County
400 Boardman Avenue
Traverse City, Michigan 49684

Gratiot County
214 East Center Street
Ithaca, Michigan 48847

Hillsdale County
29 North Howell Street
Hillsdale, Michigan 49242

Houghton County
401 East Houghton Avenue
Houghton, Michigan 49931

Huron County
250 East Huron Avenue
Bad Axe, Michigan 48413

Ingham County
Post Office Box 179
Mason, Michigan 48854

Ionia County
Main Street
Ionia, Michigan 48846

Iosco County
Post Office Box 838
Tawas City, Michigan 48764

Iron County
2 South 6th Street
Crystal Falls, Michigan 49920

Isabella County
200 North Main Street
Mount Pleasant, Michigan 48858

Jackson County
120 West Michigan Avenue
Jackson, Michigan 49201

Kalamazoo County
201 West Kalamazoo Avenue
Kalamazoo, Michigan 49007

Kalkaska County
605 North Birch Street
Kalkaska, Michigan 49646

Kent County
300 Monroe Avenue Northwest
Grand Rapids, Michigan 49503

Kewoenaw County
4th Street County Courthouse
Eagle River, Michigan 49924

Lake County
800 10th Street
Baldwin, Michigan 49304

Lapeer County
255 Clay Street
Lapeer, Michigan 48446

Leelanau County
Post Office Box 467
Leland, Michigan 49654

Lenawee County
425 North Main Street
Adrian, Michigan 49221

Livingston County
200 East Grand River Avenue
Howell, Michigan 48843

Luce County
East Court Street
Newberry, Michigan 49868

Mackinac County
100 Marley Street
Saint Ignace, Michigan 49781

Macomb County
40 North Gratiot Avenue
Mount Clemens, Michigan 48043

Manistee County
415 3rd Street
Manistee, Michigan 49660

Marquette County
234 West Baraga Avenue
Marquette, Michigan 49855

Mason County
300 East Ludington Avenue
Ludington, Michigan 49431

Mecosta County
400 Elm Street
Big Rapids, Michigan 49307

Menominee County
839 10th Avenue
Menominee, Michigan 49858

Midland County
220 West Ellsworth Street
Midland, Michigan 48640

Missaukee County
Post Office Box J
Lake City, Michigan 49651

Monroe County
106 East 1st Street
Monroe, Michigan 48161

Montcalm County
211 West Main Street
Stanton, Michigan 48888

Montmorency County
County Courthouse
Atlanta, Michigan 49709

Muskegon County
990 Terrace Street
Muskegon, Michigan 49442

Newaygo County
Post Office Box 293
White Cloud, Michigan 49349

Oakland County
1200 North Telegraph Road
Pontiac, Michigan 48341

Oceana County
Post Office Box 153
Hart, Michigan 49420

Ogemaw County
Post Office Box 8
West Branch, Michigan 48661

Ontonagon County
725 Greenland Road
Ontonagon, Michigan 49953

Osceola County
301 West Upton Avenue
Reed City, Michigan 49677

Oscoda County
311 Morenci
Mio, Michigan 48647

Otsego County
225 West Main Street
Gaylord, Michigan 49735

Ottawa County
414 Washington Street
Grand Haven, Michigan 49417

Presque Isle County
151 East Huron Avenue
Rogers City, Michigan 49779

Roscommon County
Post Office Box 98
Roscommon, Michigan 48653

Saginaw County
111 South Michigan Avenue
Saginaw, Michigan 48602

Saint Clair County
201 McMorran Boulevard
Port Huron, Michigan 48060

Saint Joseph County
Post Office Box 189
Centreville, Michigan 49032

Sanilac County
60 West Sanilac Road
Sandusky, Michigan 48471

Schoolcraft County
300 Walnut Street
Manistique, Michigan 49854

Shlawassee County
208 North Shiawassee Street
Corunna, Michigan 48817

Tuscola County
440 North State Street
Caro, Michigan 48723

Van Buren County
212 East Paw Paw Street
Paw Paw, Michigan 49079

Washtenaw County
Post Office Box 8645
Ann Arbor, Michigan 48107

Wayne County
600 Randolph Street
Detroit, Michigan 48226

Wexford County
437 East Division Street
Cadillac, Michigan 49601

MINNESOTA

Aitkin County
209 2nd Street Northwest
Aitkin, Minnesota 56431

Anoka County
325 East Main Street
Anoka, Minnesota 55303

Becker County
Post Office Box 787
Detroit Lakes, Minnesota 56501

Beltrami County
619 Beltrami Avenue Northwest
Bemidji, Minnesota 56601

Benton County
531 Dewey Street
Foley, Minnesota 56329

Big Stone County
20 2nd Street Southeast
Ortonville, Minnesota 56278

Blue Earth County
204 South 5th Street
Mankato, Minnesota 56001

Brown County
Center & State Streets
New Ulm, Minnesota 56073

Carlton County
30 Maple Street
Carlton, Minnesota 55718

Carver County
600 East 4th Street
Chaska, Minnesota 55318

Cass County
Highway 371
Walker, Minnesota 56484

Chippewa County
11th Street & Highway 7
Montevideo, Minnesota 56265

Chisago County
County Courthouse
Center City, Minnesota 55012

Clay County
807 11th Street North
Moorhead, Minnesota 56560

Clearwater County
213 North Main Avenue
Bagley, Minnesota 56621

Cook County
Post Office Box 1048
Grand Marais, Minnesota 55604

Cottonwood County
900 3rd Avenue
Windom, Minnesota 56101

Crow Wing County
326 Laurel Street
Brainerd, Minnesota 56401

Dakota County
1560 Highway 55 West
Hastings, Minnesota 55033

Dodge County
Post Office Box 38
Mantorville, Minnesota 55955

Douglas County
305 8th Avenue West
Alexandria, Minnesota 56308

Faribault County
North Main Street
Blue Earth, Minnesota 56013

Fillmore County
Fillmore Street
Preston, Minnesota 55965

Freeborn County
411 South Broadway Avenue
Albert Lea, Minnesota 56007

Goodhue County
509 West 5th Street
Red Wing, Minnesota 55066

Grant County
County Courthouse
Elbow Lake, Minnesota 56531

Hennepin County
300 South 6th Street
Minneapolis, Minnesota 55487

Houston County
304 South Marshall Street
Caledonia, Minnesota 55921

Hubbard County
301 Court Street
Park Rapids, Minnesota 56470

Isantt County
237 2nd Avenue Southwest
Cambridge, Minnesota 55008

Itasca County
Courthouse
Grand Rapids, Minnesota 55744

Jackson County
413 4th Street
Jackson, Minnesota 56143

Kanabec County
18 Vine Street North
Mora, Minnesota 55051

Kandlyohl County
515 Becker Avenue Southwest
Willmar, Minnesota 56201

Killson County
410 South 5th Street
Hallock, Minnesota 56728

Koochiching County
4th Street & 6th Avenue
International Falls, Minnesota 56649

Lac Qui Parisharle County
600 6th Street
Madison, Minnesota 56256

Lake County
601 3rd Avenue
Two Harbors, Minnesota 55616

Lake Of The Woods County
206 Southeast 8th Avenue
Baudette, Minnesota 56623

Le Sueur County
88 South Parkway
Le Center, Minnesota 56057

Lincoln County
North Rebecca
Ivanhoe, Minnesota 56142

Lyon County
607 Main Street West
Marshall, Minnesota 56258

Mahnomen County
Post Office Box 379
Mahnomen, Minnesota 56557

Marshall County
208 East Colbin Avenue
Warren, Minnesota 56762

Martin County
201 Lake Avenue
Fairmont, Minnesota 56031

McLeod County
830 11th Street East
Glencoe, Minnesota 55336

Meeker County
325 North Sibley Avenue
Litchfield, Minnesota 55355

Mille Lacs County
635 2nd Street Southeast
Milaca, Minnesota 56353

Morrison County
County Courthouse
Little Falls, Minnesota 56345

Mower County
201 1st Street Northeast
Austin, Minnesota 55912

Murray County
2500 28th Street
Slayton, Minnesota 56172

Nicollet County
501 South Minnesota Avenue
Saint Peter, Minnesota 56082

Nobles County
10th Street
Worthington, Minnesota 56187

Norman County
163rd Avenue East
Ada, Minnesota 56510

Olmsted County
515 2nd Street Southwest
Rochester, Minnesota 55902

Otter Tail County
Junius Avenue County Courthouse
Fergus Falls, Minnesota 56537

Pennington County
Post Office Box 619
Thief River Falls, Minnesota 56701

Pine County
County Courthouse
Pine City, Minnesota 55063

Pipestone County
408 South Hiawatha Avenue
Pipestone, Minnesota 56164

Polk County
612 North Broadway
Crookston, Minnesota 56716

Pope County
130 Minnesota Avenue East
Glenwood, Minnesota 56334

Ramsey County
15 West Kellogg Boulevard
Saint Paul, Minnesota 55102

Red Lake County
100 Langavin Street
Red Lake Falls, Minnesota 56750

Redwood County
Post Office Box 130
Redwood Falls, Minnesota 56283

Renville County
500 Depue Avenue East
Olivia, Minnesota 56277

Rice County
218 3rd Street Northwest
Faribault, Minnesota 55021

Rock County
Post Office Box 245
Luverne, Minnesota 56156

Roseau County
216 Center Street West
Roseau, Minnesota 56751

Saint Louis County
100 North 5th Avenue West
Duluth, Minnesota 55802

Scott County
428 Holmes Street
Shakopee, Minnesota 55379

Sherburne County
13880 Highway 10
Elk River, Minnesota 55330

Sibley County
400 Court Street
Gaylord, Minnesota 55334

Stearns County
Post Office Box 1378
Saint Cloud, Minnesota 56302

Steele County
111 East Main Street
Owatonna, Minnesota 55060

Stevens County
Post Office Box 530
Morris, Minnesota 56267

Swift County
Post Office Box 110
Benson, Minnesota 56215

Todd County
215 1st Avenue South
Long Prairie, Minnesota 56347

Traverse County
County Courthouse
Wheaton, Minnesota 56296

Wabasha County
625 Jefferson Avenue
Wabasha, Minnesota 55981

Wadena County
Jefferson Street
Wadena, Minnesota 56482

Waseca County
307 North State Street
Waseca, Minnesota 56093

Washington County
14900 61st Street North
Stillwater, Minnesota 55082

Watonwan County
Post Office Box 518
Saint James, Minnesota 56081

Wilkin County
5th Street South
Breckenridge, Minnesota 56520

Winona County
171 West 3rd Street
Winona, Minnesota 55987

Wright County
10 2nd Street Northwest
Buffalo, Minnesota 55313

Yellow Medicine County
415 9th Avenue
Granite Falls, Minnesota 56241

MISSISSIPPI

Adams County
1 Court Street
Natchez, Mississippi 39120

Alcorn County
Post Office Box 112
Corinth, Mississippi 38834

Amite County
Post Office Box 680
Liberty, Mississippi 39645

Attala County
West Washington Street
Kosciusko, Mississippi 39090

Benton County
Main Street
Ashland, Mississippi 38603

Bolivar County
401 South Court Street
Cleveland, Mississippi 38732

Calhoun County
Post Office Box 8
Pittsboro, Mississippi 38951

Carroll County
Post Office Box 291
Carrollton, Mississippi 38917

Chickasaw County
County Courthouse
Houston, Mississippi 38851

Choctaw County
112 Quinn Street
Ackerman, Mississippi 39735

Claiborne County
Post Office Box 449
Port Gibson, Mississippi 39150

Clarke County
Post Office Box M
Quitman, Mississippi 39355

Clay County
Post Office Box 815
West Point, Mississippi 39773

Coahoma County
115 1st Street
Clarksdale, Mississippi 38614

Coplah County
Post Office Box 507
Hazlehurst, Mississippi 39083

Covington County
Post Office Box 1679
Collins, Mississippi 39428

De Soto County
2535 Highway 51
Hernando, Mississippi 38632

Forrest County
629 North Main Street
Hattiesburg, Mississippi 39401

Franklin County
Post Office Box 297
Meadville, Mississippi 39653

George County
Courthouse Square
Lucedale, Mississippi 39452

Greene County
Post Office Box 610
Leakesville, Mississippi 39451

Grenada County
Post Office Box 1208
Grenada, Mississippi 38901

Hancock County
242 Main Street
Bay Saint Louis, Mississippi 39520

Harrison County
1801 23rd Avenue
Gulfport, Mississippi 39501

Hinds County
Post Office Box 686
Jackson, Mississippi 39205

Holmes County
Post Office Box 239
Lexington, Mississippi 39095

Humphreys County
Post Office Box 547
Belzoni, Mississippi 39038

Issaquena County
Post Office Box 27
Mayersville, Mississippi 39113

Itawamba County
201 West Main Street
Fulton, Mississippi 38843

Jackson County
3109 Canty Street
Pascagoula, Mississippi 39567

Jasper County
Court Street
Bay Springs, Mississippi 39422

Jefferson County
307 Main Street
Fayette, Mississippi 39069

Jefferson Davis County
Post Office Box 1137
Prentiss, Mississippi 39474

Jones County
Post Office Box 1468
Laurel, Mississippi 39441

Kemper County
Post Office Box 188
De Kalb, Mississippi 39328

Lafayette County
Post Office Box 1240
Oxford, Mississippi 38655

Lamar County	**Monroe County**
Post Office Box 247	Post Office Box 578
Purvis, Mississippi 39475	Aberdeen, Mississippi 39730
Lauderdale County	**Montgomery County**
500 Constitution Avenue	Post Office Box 71
Meridian, Mississippi 39301	Winona, Mississippi 38967
Lawrence County	**Neshoba County**
Post Office Box 40	Post Office Box 67
Monticello, Mississippi 39654	Philadelphia, Mississippi 39350
Leake County	**Newton County**
Court Square	Post Office Box 68
Carthage, Mississippi 39051	Decatur, Mississippi 39327
Lee County	**Noxubee County**
300 West Main Street	Post Office Box 147
Tupelo, Mississippi 38801	Macon, Mississippi 39341
Leflore County	**Okibbeha County**
315 West Market Street	101 East Main Street
Greenwood, Mississippi 38930	Starkville, Mississippi 39759
Lincoln County	**Panola County**
300 South 1st Street	151 Public Square
Brookhaven, Mississippi 39601	Batesville, Mississippi 38606
Lowndes County	**Pearl River County**
Post Office Box 1364	Post Office Box 431
Columbus, Mississippi 39703	Poplarville, Mississippi 39470
Madison County	**Perry County**
Post Office Box 404	Post Office Box 198
Canton, Mississippi 39046	New Augusta, Mississippi 39462
Marion County	**Pike County**
502 Broad Street	Post Office Box 309
Columbia, Mississippi 39429	Magnolia, Mississippi 39652
Marshall County	**Pontotoc County**
Post Office Box 219	Post Office Box 209
Holly Springs, Mississippi 38635	Pontotoc, Mississippi 38863

Prentiss County
Post Office Box 477
Booneville, Mississippi 38829

Quitman County
Post Office Box 100
Marks, Mississippi 38646

Rankin County
221 North Timber Street
Brandon, Mississippi 39042

Scott County
Post Office Box 630
Forest, Mississippi 39074

Sharkey County
County Courthouse
Rolling Fork, Mississippi 39159

Simpson County
109 West Pine Avenue
Mendenhall, Mississippi 39114

Smith County
Main Street
Raleigh, Mississippi 39153

Stone County
Post Office Box 7
Wiggins, Mississippi 39577

Sunflower County
2nd Street
Indianola, Mississippi 38751

Tale County
201 South Ward Street
Senatobia, Mississippi 38668

Tallahatchie County
Post Office Box H
Charleston, Mississippi 38921

Tippah County
Post Office Box 99
Ripley, Mississippi 38663

Tishomingo County
1008 Highway 25 South
Luka, Mississippi 38852

Tunica County
Post Office Box 217
Tunica, Mississippi 38676

Union County
109 Main Street
New Albany, Mississippi 38652

Walthall County
Post Office Box 351
Tylertown, Mississippi 39667

Warren County
Post Office Box 351
Vicksburg, Mississippi 39181

Washington County
Post Office Box 309
Greenville, Mississippi 38702

Wayne County
Azalea Drive
Waynesboro, Mississippi 39367

Webster County
Main Street
Walthall, Mississippi 39771

Wilkinson County
Post Office Box 516
Woodville, Mississippi 39669

Winston County
115 South Court Avenue
Louisville, Mississippi 39339

Yalobusha County
Post Office Box 664
Water Valley, Mississippi 38965

Yazoo County
Post Office Box 68
Yazoo City, Mississippi 39194

MISSOURI

Adair County
County Courthouse
Kirksville, Missouri 63501

Andrew County
Post Office Box 206
Savannah, Missouri 64485

Atchison County
Post Office Box J
Rock Port, Missouri 64482

Audrain County
County Courthouse
Mexico, Missouri 65265

Barry County
County Courthouse
Cassville, Missouri 65625

Barton County
County Courthouse
Lamar, Missouri 64759

Batos County
County Courthouse
Butler, Missouri 64730

Benton County
Post Office Box 1238
Warsaw, Missouri 65355

Bollinger County
Post Office Box 46
Marble Hill, Missouri 63764

Boone County
8th & Walnut
Columbia, Missouri 65201

Buchanan County
5th & Jules Street
Saint Joseph, Missouri 64501

Butler County
County Courthouse
Poplar Bluff, Missouri 63901

Caldwell County
Post Office Box 67
Kingston, Missouri 64650

Callaway County
5 East 5th Street
Fulton, Missouri 65251

Camden County
1 Court Circle
Camdenton, Missouri 65020

Cape Girardeau County
1 Barton Square
Jackson, Missouri 63755

Carroll County
County Courthouse
Carrollton, Missouri 64633

Carter County
Post Office Box 517
Van Buren, Missouri 63965

Cass County
County Courthouse
Harrisonville, Missouri 64701

Cedar County
Post Office Box 126
Stockton, Missouri 65785

Charlton County
County Courthouse
Keytesville, Missouri 65261

Christian County
Post Office Box 549
Ozark, Missouri 65721

Clark County
111 East Court Street
Kahoka, Missouri 63445

Clay County
Administration Building Courthouse
  Square
Liberty, Missouri 64068

Clinton County
Post Office Box 245
Plattsburg, Missouri 64477

Cole County
301 East High Street
Jefferson City, Missouri 65101

Cooper County
Post Office Box 123
Boonville, Missouri 65233

Crawford County
201 Main Street
Steelville, Missouri 65565

Dade County
County Courthouse
Greenfield, Missouri 65661

Dallas County
Post Office Box 436
Buffalo, Missouri 65622

Daviess County
County Courthouse
Gallatin, Missouri 64640

De Kalb County
Post Office Box 248
Maysville, Missouri 64469

Dent County
County Courthouse
Salem, Missouri 65560

Douglas County
203 Southeast 2nd Avenue
Ava, Missouri 65608

Dunklin County
Post Office Box 188
Kennett, Missouri 63857

Franklin County
Post Office Box 311
Union, Missouri 63084

Gasconade County
Post Office Box 295
Hermann, Missouri 65041

Gentry County
County Courthouse
Albany, Missouri 64402

Greene County
940 North Boonville Avenue
Springfield, Missouri 65802

Grundy County
700 Main Street
Trenton, Missouri 64683

Harrison County
Post Office Box 27
Bethany, Missouri 64424

Henry County
Main & Franklin Streets
Clinton, Missouri 64735

Hickory County
Main & Polk Streets
Hermitage, Missouri 65668

Holt County
102 Nodaway Street
Oregon, Missouri 64473

Howard County
Post Office Box 551
Fayette, Missouri 65248

Howell County
County Courthouse Square
West Plains, Missouri 65775

Iron County
250 South Main Street
Ironton, Missouri 63650

Jackson County
415 East 12th Street
Kansas City, Missouri 64106

Jasper County
County Courthouse
Carthage, Missouri 64836

Jefferson County
Post Office Box 100
Hillsboro, Missouri 63050

Johnson County
County Courthouse
Warrensburg, Missouri 64093

Knox County
305 East Lafayette Street
Edina, Missouri 63537

Laclede County
2nd & Adam Streets
Lebanon, Missouri 65536

Lafayette County
Main Street
Lexington, Missouri 64067

Lawrence County
Post Office Box 309
Mount Vernon, Missouri 65712

Lewis County
100 East Lafayette Street
Monticello, Missouri 63457

Lincoln County
201 Main Street
Troy, Missouri 63379

Linn County
County Courthouse
Linneus, Missouri 64653

Livingston County
County Courthouse
Chillicothe, Missouri 64601

Macon County
Post Office Box 96
Macon, Missouri 63552

Madison County
1 Courthouse Square
Fredericktown, Missouri 63645

Maries County
Post Office Box 167
Vienna, Missouri 65582

Marion County
County Courthouse
Palmyra, Missouri 63461

McDonald County
Post Office Box 665
Pineville, Missouri 64856

Mercer County
County Courthouse
Princeton, Missouri 64673

Miller County
Courthouse Square
Tuscumbia, Missouri 65082

Mississippi County
Post Office Box 304
Charleston, Missouri 63834

Moniteau County
200 East Main Street
California, Missouri 65018

Monroe County
300 North Main Street
Paris, Missouri 65275

Montgomery County
211 East 3rd Street
Montgomery City, Missouri 63361

Morgan County
100 East Newton Street
Versailles, Missouri 65084

New Madrid County
Post Office Box 68
New Madrid, Missouri 63869

Newton County
Main & Wood Streets
Neosho, Missouri 64850

Nodaway County
Post Office Box 218
Maryville, Missouri 64468

Oregon County
Post Office Box 324
Alton, Missouri 65606

Osage County
Main Street
Linn, Missouri 65051

Ozark County
Post Office Box 416
Gainesville, Missouri 65655

Pemiscot County
Ward Avenue
Caruthersville, Missouri 63830

Perry County
15 West Sainte Marie Street
Perryville, Missouri 63775

Pettis County
415 South Ohio Avenue
Sedalia, Missouri 65301

Phelps County
3rd & Rolla Streets
Rolla, Missouri 65401

Pike County
115 West Main Street
Bowling Green, Missouri 63334

Platte County
Post Office Box 30
Platte City, Missouri 64079

Polk County
County Courthouse
Bolivar, Missouri 65613

Pulaski County
Waynesville Square
Waynesville, Missouri 65583

Putnam County
County Courthouse
Unionville, Missouri 63565

Ralls County
Main Street
New London, Missouri 63459

Randolph County
South Main Street
Huntsville, Missouri 65259

Ray County
Post Office Box 536
Richmond, Missouri 64085

Reynolds County
Courthouse Square
Centerville, Missouri 63633

Ripley County
County Courthouse
Doniphan, Missouri 63935

Saint Charles County
3rd & Jefferson Streets
Saint Charles, Missouri 63301

Saint Clair County
Post Office Box 405
Osceola, Missouri 64776

Saint Francis County
County Courthouse Square
Farmington, Missouri 63640

Saint Louis County
41 South Central Avenue
Clayton, Missouri 63105

Sainte Genevieve County
55 South 3rd Street
Sainte Genevieve, Missouri 63670

Saline County
County Courthouse
Marshall, Missouri 65340

Schuyler County
Post Office Box 187
Lancaster, Missouri 63548

Scotland County
County Courthouse
Memphis, Missouri 63555

Scott County
Post Office Box 188
Benton, Missouri 63736

Shannon County
County Courthouse
Eminence, Missouri 65466

Shelby County
1 Courthouse Square
Shelbyville, Missouri 63469

Stoddard County
Post Office Box H
Bloomfield, Missouri 63825

Stone County
Post Office Box 45
Galena, Missouri 65656

Sullivan County
2nd Street
Milan, Missouri 63556

Taney County
Post Office Box 156
Forsyth, Missouri 65653

Texas County
210 North Grand Avenue
Houston, Missouri 65483

Vernon County
102 West Cherry Street
Nevada, Missouri 64772

Warren County
105 South Market Street
Warrenton, Missouri 63383

Washington County
102 North Missouri Street
Potosi, Missouri 63664

Wayne County
County Courthouse
Greenville, Missouri 63944

Webster County
County Courthouse
Marshfield, Missouri 65706

Worth County
County Courthouse
Grant City, Missouri 64456

Wright County
Post Office Box 98
Hartville, Missouri 65667

MONTANA

Beaverhead County
2 South Pacific Cluster 3
Dillon, Montana 59725

Big Horn County
121 3rd Street West
Hardin, Montana 59034

Blaine County
Post Office Box 278
Chinook, Montana 59523

Broadwater County
Post Office Box 489
Townsend, Montana 59644

Carbon County
Post Office Box 887
Red Lodge, Montana 59068

Carter County
Courthouse Park Street
Ekalaka, Montana 59324

Cascade County
415 2nd Avenue North
Great Falls, Montana 59401

Chouteau County
1308 Franklin
Fort Benton, Montana 59442

Custer County
1010 Main Street
Miles City, Montana 59301

Daniel's County
Post Office Box 247
Scobey, Montana 59263

Dawson County
207 West Bell Street
Glendive, Montana 59330

Deer Lodge County
800 South Main Street
Anaconda, Montana 59711

Fallon County
10 West Fallon Avenue
Baker, Montana 59313

Fergus County
712 West Main Street
Lewistown, Montana 59457

Flathead County
800 South Main Street
Kalispell, Montana 59901

Gallatin County
311 West Main Street
Bozeman, Montana 59715

Garfield County
Post Office Box 7
Jordan, Montana 59337

Glacier County
502 East Main Street
Cut Bank, Montana 59427

Golden Valley County
Post Office Box 10
Ryegate, Montana 59074

Granite County
Sampson & Kearney Streets
Phillipsburg, Montana 59858

Hill County
315 4th Street County Courthouse
Havre, Montana 59501

Jefferson County
Post Office Box H
Boulder, Montana 59632

Judith Basin County
Courthouse
Stanford, Montana 59479

Lake County
106 4th Avenue East
Polson, Montana 59860

Lewis & Clark County
316 North Park Avenue
Helena, Montana 59624

Liberty County
101 1st Street East
Chester, Montana 59522

Lincoln County
512 California Avenue
Libby, Montana 59923

Madison County
110 West Wallace Street
Virginia City, Montana 59755

McCone County
206 2nd Avenue
Circle, Montana 59215

Meagher County
15 West Main Street
White Sulphur Spgs, Montana 59645

Mineral County
300 River Street
Superior, Montana 59872

Missoula County
200 West Broadway Street
Missoula, Montana 59802

Musselshell County
506 Main Street
Roundup, Montana 59072

Park County
414 East Callender Street
Livingston, Montana 59047

Petroleum County
201 East Main
Winnett, Montana 59087

Phillips County
County Courthouse
Malta, Montana 59538

Pondera County
204th Avenue Southwest
Conrad, Montana 59425

Powder River County
Courthouse Square
Broadus, Montana 59317

Powell County
409 Missouri Avenue
Deer Lodge, Montana 59722

Prairie County
County Courthouse
Terry, Montana 59349

Ravaill County
South 2nd & Bedford Streets
Hamilton, Montana 59840

Richland County
201 West Main Street
Sidney, Montana 59270

Roosevelt County
400 2nd Avenue South
Wolf Point, Montana 59201

Rosebud County
Post Office Box 47
Forsyth, Montana 59327

Sanders County
Main Street
Thompson Falls, Montana 59873

Sheridan County
100 West Laurel Avenue
Plentywood, Montana 59254

Silver Bow County
155 West Granite Street
Butte, Montana 59701

Stillwater County
Post Office Box 147
Columbus, Montana 59019

Sweet Grass County
Post Office Box 460
Big Timber, Montana 59011

Teton County
Post Office Box 610
Choteau, Montana 59422

Toole County
226 1st Street South
Shelby, Montana 59474

Treasure County
Post Office Box 392
Hysham, Montana 59038

Valley County
Post Office Box 311
Glasgow, Montana 59230

Wheatland County
Post Office Box C
Harlowton, Montana 59036

Wibaux County
200 South Wibaux
Wibaux, Montana 59353

Yellowstone County
Post Office Box 35001
Billings, Montana 59107

NEBRASKA

Adams County
4th & Denver Streets
Hastings, Nebraska 68901

Antelope County
501 Main Street
Neligh, Nebraska 68756

Arthur County
Main Street
Arthur, Nebraska 69121

Banner County
State Street
Harrisburg, Nebraska 69345

Blaine County
Lincoln Avenue
Brewster, Nebraska 68821

Boone County
222 South 4th Street
Albion, Nebraska 68620

Box Butte County
5th & Box Butte Streets
Alliance, Nebraska 69301

Boyd County
County Courthouse
Butte, Nebraska 68722

Brown County
148 West 4th Street
Ainsworth, Nebraska 69210

Buffalo County
16th & Central Avenue
Kearney, Nebraska 68848

Burl County
111 North 13th Street
Tekamah, Nebraska 68061

Butler County
451 5th Street
David City, Nebraska 68632

Cass County
4th & Main Streets
Plattsmouth, Nebraska 68048

Cedar County
101 South Broadway Avenue
Harlington, Nebraska 68739

Chase County
921 Broadway
Imperial, Nebraska 69033

Cherry County
Post Office Box 120
Valentine, Nebraska 69201

Cheyenne County
1000 10th Avenue
Sidney, Nebraska 69162

Clay County
111 West Fairfield Street
Clay Center, Nebraska 68933

Colfax County
411 East 11th Street
Schuyler, Nebraska 68661

Cuming County
Post Office Box 290
West Point, Nebraska 68788

Custer County
431 South 10th Avenue
Broken Bow, Nebraska 68822

Dakota County
Post Office Box 38
Dakota City, Nebraska 68731

Dawes County
451 Main Street
Chadron, Nebraska 69337

Dawson County
7th & Washington Streets
Lexington, Nebraska 68850

Deuel County
3rd & Vincent
Chappell, Nebraska 69129

Dixon County
302 3rd Street
Ponca, Nebraska 68770

Dodge County
435 North Park Avenue
Fremont, Nebraska 68025

Douglas County
1819 Farnam Street
Omaha, Nebraska 68183

Dundy County
Chief Street
Benkelman, Nebraska 69021

Fillmore County
900 G Street
Geneva, Nebraska 68361

Franklin County
405 15th Avenue
Franklin, Nebraska 68939

Frontier County
1 Wellington Street
Stockville, Nebraska 69042

Furnas County
Post Office Box 387
Beaver City, Nebraska 68926

Gage County
Post Office Box 429
Beatrice, Nebraska 68310

Garden County
Main Street
Oshkosh, Nebraska 69154

Garfield County
Post Office Box 218
Burwell, Nebraska 68923

Gosper County
Post Office Box 136
Elwood, Nebraska 68937

Grant County
Post Office Box 139
Hyannis, Nebraska 69350

Greeley County
28th & Kildare Streets
Greeley, Nebraska 68842

Hall County
121 South Pine Street
Grand Island, Nebraska 68801

Hamilton County
County Courthouse
Aurora, Nebraska 68818

Harlan County
Post Office Box 379
Alma, Nebraska 68920

Hayes County
Troth Street
Hayes Center, Nebraska 69032

Hitchcock County
229 East D Street
Trenton, Nebraska 69044

Holt County
Post Office Box 329
O'Neill, Nebraska 68763

Hooker County
Post Office Box 184
Mullen, Nebraska 69152

Howard County
612 Indian Street
Saint Paul, Nebraska 68873

Jefferson County
411 4th Street
Fairbury, Nebraska 68352

Johnson County
Post Office Box 416
Tecumseh, Nebraska 68450

Kearney County
Post Office Box 339
Minden, Nebraska 68959

Keith County
Post Office Box 149
Ogallala, Nebraska 69153

Keya Parishaha County
Post Office Box 349
Springview, Nebraska 68778

Kimball County
114 East 3rd Street
Kimball, Nebraska 69145

Knox County
Main Street
Center, Nebraska 68724

Lancaster County
555 South 10th Street
Lincoln, Nebraska 68508

Lincoln County
County Square
North Platte, Nebraska 69101

Logan County
Post Office Box 8
Stapleton, Nebraska 69163

Loup County
4th Street
Taylor, Nebraska 68879

Madison County
Post Office Box 290
Madison, Nebraska 68748

McPherson County
Post Office Box 122
Tryon, Nebraska 69167

Merrick County
Post Office Box 27
Central City, Nebraska 68826

Morrill County
Post Office Box 610
Bridgeport, Nebraska 69336

Nance County
Post Office Box 338
Fullerton, Nebraska 68638

Nemaha County
1824 North Street
Auburn, Nebraska 68305

Nuckolls County
150 South Main Street
Nelson, Nebraska 68961

Otoe County
Post Office Box 249
Nebraska City, Nebraska 68410

Pawnee County
County Courthouse
Pawnee City, Nebraska 68420

Perkins County
Post Office Box 156
Grant, Nebraska 69140

Phelps County
715 5th Avenue
Holdrege, Nebraska 68949

Pierce County
111 West Court Street
Pierce, Nebraska 68767

Platte County
2610 14th Street
Columbus, Nebraska 68601

Polk County
County Courthouse
Osceola, Nebraska 68651

Red Willow County
500 Norris Avenue
McCook, Nebraska 69001

Richardson County
1701 Stone Street
Falls City, Nebraska 68355

Rock County
400 State Street
Bassett, Nebraska 68714

Saline County
215 Court Street
Wilber, Nebraska 68465

Sarpy County
1208 Golden Gate Drive
Omaha, Nebraska 68046

Saunders County
Chestnut Street Courthouse
Wahoo, Nebraska 68066

Scotts Bluff County
1825 10th Street
Gering, Nebraska 69341

Seward County
County Courthouse
Seward, Nebraska 68434

Sheridan County
301 East 2nd Street
Rushville, Nebraska 69360

Sherman County
Post Office Box 456
Loup City, Nebraska 68853

Sioux County
Main Street
Harrison, Nebraska 69346

Stanton County
804 Ivy Street
Stanton, Nebraska 68779

Thayer County
235 North 4th Street
Hebron, Nebraska 68370

Thomas County
Post Office Box 226
Thedford, Nebraska 69166

Thurston County
106 South 5th Street
Pender, Nebraska 68047

Valley County
125 South 15th Street
Ord, Nebraska 68862

Washington County
Post Office Box 466
Blair, Nebraska 68008

Wayne County
510 North Pearl Street
Wayne, Nebraska 68787

Webster County
621 North Cedar Street
Red Cloud, Nebraska 68970

Wheeler County
County Courthouse
Bartlett, Nebraska 68622

York County
510 Lincoln Avenue
York, Nebraska 68467

NEVADA

Carson City County
2621 Northgate Lane
Carson City, Nevada 89706

Churchill County
10 West Williams Avenue
Fallon, Nevada 89406

Clark County
200 South 3rd Street
Las Vegas, Nevada 89155

Douglas County
Post Office Box 218
Minden, Nevada 89423

Elko County
571 Idaho Street
Elko, Nevada 89801

Esmeralda County
Post Office Box 547
Goldfield, Nevada 89013

Eureka County
Post Office Box 677
Eureka, Nevada 89316

Humboldt County
Bridge & 5th Streets
Winnemucca, Nevada 89445

Lander County
315 South Humboldt
Battle Mountain, Nevada 89820

Lincoln County
1 Main Street
Pioche, Nevada 89043

Lyon County
31 South Main Street
Yerington, Nevada 89447

Mineral County
Post Office Box 1450
Hawthorne, Nevada 89415

Nye County
Post Office Box 1031
Tonopah, Nevada 89049

Pershing County
Post Office Box 820
Lovelock, Nevada 89419

Storey County
Post Office Box D
Virginia City, Nevada 89440

Washoe County
Post Office Box 11130
Reno, Nevada 89520

White Parishine County
Post Office Box 1002
Ely, Nevada 89301

NEW HAMPSHIRE

Belknap County
64 Court Street
Laconia, New Hampshire 03246

Carroll County
Route 171
Ossipee, New Hampshire 03864

Cheshire County
33 West Street
Keene, New Hampshire 03431

Coos County
Post Office Box 309
Lancaster, New Hampshire 03584

Grafton County
Post Office Box 108
Woodsville, New Hampshire 03785

Hillsborough County
19 Temple Street
Nashua, New Hampshire 03060

Merrimack County
163 North Main Street
Concord, New Hampshire 03301

Rockingham County
North Road
Brentwood, New Hampshire 03042

Stratford County
County Farm Road
Dover, New Hampshire 03820

Sullivan County
Post Office Box 45
Newport, New Hampshire 03773

NEW JERSEY

Atlantic County
2 Main Street West
Mays Landing, New Jersey 08330

Bergen County
21 Main Street
Hackensack, New Jersey 07601

Burlington County
49 Rancocas Road
Mount Holly, New Jersey 08060

Camden County
5th & Mickle Boulevard
Camden, New Jersey 08103

Cape May County
7 North Main Street
Cape May, New Jersey 08210

Cumberland County
Broad & Fayette Street
Bridgeton, New Jersey 08302

Essex County
469 King Boulevard
Newark, New Jersey 07102

Gloucester County
1 North Broad Street
Woodbury, New Jersey 08096

Hudson County
595 Newark Avenue
Jersey City, New Jersey 07306

Hunterdon County
71 Main Street
Flemington, New Jersey 08822

Mercer County
Post Office Box 8068
Trenton, New Jersey 08650

Middlesex County
1 John F. Kennedy Square
New Brunswick, New Jersey 08901

Monmouth County
Main Street
Freehold, New Jersey 07728

Morris County
Post Office Box 900
Morristown, New Jersey 07963

Ocean County
Post Office Box Cn 2191
Toms River, New Jersey 08754

Passaic County
77 Hamilton Street
Paterson, New Jersey 07505

Salem County
92 Market Street
Salem, New Jersey 08079

Somerset County
Post Office Box 3000
Somerville, New Jersey 08876

Sussex County
Post Office Box 709
Newton, New Jersey 07860

Union County
2 Broad Street
Elizabeth, New Jersey 07201

Warren County
Route 519 Wayne Dumont, Jr.
Belvidere, New Jersey 07823

NEW MEXICO

Bernalitto County
1 Civic Plaza
Albuquerque, New Mexico 87102

Catron County
Post Office Box 507
Reserve, New Mexico 87830

Chaves County
401 North Main Street
Roswell, New Mexico 88201

Cibola County
515 West High Avenue
Grants, New Mexico 87020

Colfax County
Post Office Box 1498
Raton, New Mexico 87740

Curry County
700 North Main Street
Clovis, New Mexico 88101

De Baca County
Post Office Box 347
Fort Sumner, New Mexico 88119

Dona Ana County
251 West Amador Avenue
Las Cruces, New Mexico 88005

Eddy County
Post Office Box 1139
Carlsbad, New Mexico 88221

Grant County
Post Office Box 898
Silver City, New Mexico 88062

Guadalupe County
420 Park Avenue
Santa Rosa, New Mexico 88435

Harding County
Post Office Box 1002
Mosquero, New Mexico 87733

Hidalgo County
300 South Shakespeare Street
Lordsburg, New Mexico 88045

Lea County
Post Office Box 4C
Lovington, New Mexico 88260

Lincoln County
300 Central Avenue
Carrizozo, New Mexico 88301

Los Alamos County
2300 Trinity Drive
Los Alamos, New Mexico 87544

Luna County
700 South Silver Avenue
Deming, New Mexico 88030

McKinley County
200 West Hill Avenue
Gallup, New Mexico 87301

Mora County
Highway 518
Mora, New Mexico 87732

Otero County
Post Office Box 1749
Alamogordo, New Mexico 88311

Quay County
300 South 3rd Street
Tucumcari, New Mexico 88401

Rio Arriba County
County Courthouse
Tierra Amarilla, New Mexico 87575

Roosevelt County
County Courthouse
Portales, New Mexico 88130

San Juan County
Post Office Box 550
Aztec, New Mexico 87410

San Miguel County
County Courthouse
Las Vegas, New Mexico 87701

Sandoval County
Post Office Box 40
Bernalitto, New Mexico 87004

Santa Fe County
Post Office Box 1985
Santa Fe, New Mexico 87504

Sierra County
300 Dale Street
Truth Or Consequence, New Mexico 87901

Socorro County
131 Court Street
Socorro, New Mexico 87801

Taos County
Post Office Box 676
Taos, New Mexico 87571

Torrance County
9th & Allen
Estancia, New Mexico 87016

Union County
200 Court Street
Clayton, New Mexico 88415

Valencia County
Post Office Box 1119
Los Lunas, New Mexico 87031

NEW YORK

Albany County
16 Eagle Street
Albany, New York 12207

Allegany County
Court Street
Belmont, New York 14813

Bronx County
851 Grand Concourse
Bronx, New York 10451

Broome County
44 Hawley Street
Binghamton, New York 13901

Cattaraugus County
303 Court Street
Little Valley, New York 14755

Cayuga County
160 Genesee Street
Auburn, New York 13021

Chautauqua County
Gerace Office Building
Mayville, New York 14757

Chemung County
425 Pennsylvania Avenue
Elmira, New York 14904

Chenango County
5 Court Street
Norwich, New York 13815

Clinton County
137 Margaret Street
Plattsburgh, New York 12901

Columbia County
Allen & Union Streets
Hudson, New York 12534

Cortland County
60 Central Avenue
Cortland, New York 13045

Delaware County
4 Court Street
Delhi, New York 13753

Dutchess County
22 Market Street
Poughkeepsie, New York 12601

Erie County
95 Franklin Street
Buffalo, New York 14202

Essex County
Court Street
Elizabethtown, New York 12932

Franklin County
63 West Main Street
Malone, New York 12953

Fulton County
223 West Main Street
Johnstown, New York 12095

Genesee County
Main & Court Streets
Batavia, New York 14020

Greene County
388 Main Street
Catskill, New York 12414

Hamilton County
Route 8
Lake Pleasant, New York 12108

Herkimer County
109 Mary Street
Herkimer, New York 13350

Jefferson County
175 Arsenal Street
Watertown, New York 13601

Kings County
360 Adams Street
Brooklyn, New York 11201

Lewis County
7660 North State Street
Lowville, New York 13367

Livingston County
2 Court Street
Geneseo, New York 14454

Madison County
North Court Street
Wampsville, New York 13163

Monroe County
39 West Main Street
Rochester, New York 14614

Montgomery County
Broadway
Fonda, New York 12068

Nassau County
240 Old Country Road
Mineola, New York 11501

New York County
60 Centre Street
New York, New York 10007

Niagara County
Post Office Box 461
Lockport, New York 14095

Oneida County
800 Park Avenue
Utica, New York 13501

Onondaga County
421 Montgomery Street
Syracuse, New York 13202

Ontario County
27 North Main Street
Canandaigua, New York 14424

Orange County
255-275 Main Street
Goshen, New York 10924

Orleans County
Courthouse Square
Albion, New York 14411

Oswego County
46 East Bridge Street
Oswego, New York 13126

Otsego County
197 Main Street
Cooperstown, New York 13326

Putnam County
2 County Center
Carmel, New York 10512

Queens County
83-11 Sutphin Boulevard
Jamaica, New York 11435

Rensselaer County
1600 7th Avenue
Troy, New York 12180

Richmond County
18 Richmond Terrace
Staten Island, New York 10301

Rockland County
11 New Hempstead Road
New City, New York 10956

Saint Lawrence County
48 Court Street
Canton, New York 13617

Saratoga County
40 McMasters Street
Ballston Spa, New York 12020

Schenectady County
620 State Street
Schenectady, New York 12305

Schoharie County
Post Office Box 549
Schoharie, New York 12157

Schuyler County
105 9th Street
Watkins Glen, New York 14891

Seneca County
1 Dipronio Drive
Waterloo, New York 13165

Steuben County
3 Pulteney Square
Bath, New York 14810

Suffolk County
County Center
Riverhead, New York 11901

Sullivan County
100 North Street
Monticello, New York 12701

Tioga County
16 Court Street
Owego, New York 13827

Tompkins County
320 North Tioga Street
Ithaca, New York 14850

Ulster County
285 Wall Street
Kingston, New York 12401

Warren County
Route 9
Lake George, New York 12845

Washington County
Upper Broadway
Fort Edward, New York 12828

Wayne County
26 Church Street
Lyons, New York 14489

Westchester County
110 Grove Street
White Plains, New York 10601

Wyoming County
143 North Main Street
Warsaw, New York 14569

Yates County
110 Court Street
Penn Yan, New York 14527

NORTH CAROLINA

Alamance County
124 West Elm Street
Graham, North Carolina 27253

Alexander County
100 1st Street Southwest
Taylorsville, North Carolina 28681

Alleghany County
Main Street
Sparta, North Carolina 28675

Anson County
North Green Street
Wadesboro, North Carolina 28170

Ashe County
Court Street
Jefferson, North Carolina 28640

Avery County
Main Street
Newland, North Carolina 28657

Beaufort County
112 West 2nd Street
Washington, North Carolina 27889

Bertie County
106 West Dundee Street
Windsor, North Carolina 27983

Bladen County
Courthouse Drive
Elizabethtown, North Carolina 28337

Brunswick County
Post Office Box 249
Bolivia, North Carolina 28422

Bunconiho County
60 Courthouse Plaza
Asheville, North Carolina 28801

Burke County
Post Office Box 796
Morganton, North Carolina 28655

Cabarrus County
Post Office Box 70
Concord, North Carolina 28026

Caldwell County
Post Office Box 1376
Lenoir, North Carolina 28645

Camden County
Highway 343
Camden, North Carolina 27921

Carteret County
Courthouse Square
Beaufort, North Carolina 28516

Caswell County
East Church Street & North Avenue
Yanceyville, North Carolina 27379

Catawba County
Post Office Box 389
Newton, North Carolina 28658

Chatham County
Courthouse Square
Pittsboro, North Carolina 27312

Cherokee County
201 Peachtree Street
Murphy, North Carolina 28906

Chowan County
South Broad.Street
Edenton, North Carolina 27932

Clay County
Post Office Box 118
Hayesville, North Carolina 28904

Cleveland County
Post Office Box 1210
Shelby, North Carolina 28150

Columbus County
111 Washington Street
Whiteville, North Carolina 28472

Craven County
302 Broad Street
New Bern, North Carolina 28560

Cumberland County
113 Dick Street
Fayetteville, North Carolina 28301

Currituck County
Post Office Box 39
Curntuck, North Carolina 27929

Dare County
Budleigh Street
Manteo, North Carolina 27954

Davidson County
Post Office Box 1067
Lexington, North Carolina 27292

Davie County
123 South Main Street
Mocksville, North Carolina 27028

Duplin County
Courthouse Plaza
Kenansville, North Carolina 28349

Durham County
201 East Main Street
Durham, North Carolina 27701

Edgecombe County
301 Saint Andrews Street
Tarboro, North Carolina 27886

Forsyth County
Hall Of Justice
Winston-Salem, North Carolina 27101

Franklin County
215 East Nash Street
Louisburg, North Carolina 27549

Gaston County
151 South South Street
Gastonia, North Carolina 28052

Gates County
Post Office Box 141
Gatesville, North Carolina 27938

Graham County
Post Office Box 575
Robbinsville, North Carolina 28771

Granville County
141 Williamsboro Street
Oxford, North Carolina 27565

Greene County
2nd & Greene
Snow Hill, North Carolina 28580

Guilford County
301 Market Street
Greensboro, North Carolina 27402

Halifax County
28 South King Street
Halifax, North Carolina 27839

Harnett County
729 South Main Street
Lillington, North Carolina 27546

Haywood County
County Courthouse Annex
Waynesville, North Carolina 28786

Henderson County
100 North King Street
Hendersonville, North Carolina 28792

Hertford County
King Street
Winton, North Carolina 27986

Hoke County
227 North Main Street
Raeford, North Carolina 28376

Hyde County
264 Business Highway
Swanquarter, North Carolina 27885

Iredell County
Post Office Box 788
Statesville, North Carolina 28677

Jackson County
50 Keener Street
Sylva, North Carolina 28779

Johnston County
207 East Johnston Street
Smithfield, North Carolina 27577

Jones County
Post Office Box 266
Trenton, North Carolina 28585

Lee County
Post Office Box 1968
Sanford, North Carolina 27331

Lenoir County
Post Office Box 3289
Kinston, North Carolina 28502

Lincoln County
115 West Main Street
Lincolnton, North Carolina 28092

Macon County
5 West Main Street
Franklin, North Carolina 28734

Madison County
Post Office Box 684
Marshall, North Carolina 28753

Martin County
Post Office Box 668
Williamston, North Carolina 27892

McDowell County
10 East Court Street
Marion, North Carolina 28752

Mecklenburg County
600 East 4th Street
Charlotte, North Carolina 28202

Mitchell County
Crimson Laurel Way
Bakersville, North Carolina 28705

Montgomery County
Post Office Box 637
Troy, North Carolina 27371

Moore County
Post Office Box 936
Carthage, North Carolina 26327

New Hanover County
320 Chestnut Street
Wilmington, North Carolina 28401

Northampton County
Jefferson Street
Jackson, North Carolina 27845

Onslow County
521 Mill Avenue
Jacksonville, North Carolina 28540

Orange County
106 East Margaret Lane
Hillsborough, North Carolina 27278

Pamlico County
Post Office Box 776
Bayboro, North Carolina 28515

Pasquotank County
Post Office Box 39
Elizabeth City, North Carolina 27907

Pender County
Post Office Box 5
Burgaw, North Carolina 28425

Perquimans County
Post Office Box 45
Hertford, North Carolina 27944

Person County
County Courthouse
Roxboro, North Carolina 27573

Pitt County
1717 West 5th Street
Greenville, North Carolina 27834

Polk County
Post Office Box 308
Columbus, North Carolina 28722

Randolph County
145 Worth Street
Asheboro, North Carolina 27203

Robeson County
500 North Elm Street
Lumberton, North Carolina 28358

Rockingham County
Post Office Box 26
Wentworth, North Carolina 27375

Rowan County
202 North Main Street
Salisbury, North Carolina 28144

Rutherford County
Post Office Box 630
Rutherfordton, North Carolina 28139

Sampson County
313 Rowan Road
Clinton, North Carolina 28328

Scotland County
1405 West Boulevard
Canonburg, North Carolina 28352

Stanley County
201 South 2nd Street
Albemarle, North Carolina 28001

Stokes County
Highway 89
Danbury, North Carolina 27016

Surry County
Post Office Box 345
Dobson, North Carolina 27017

Swain County
Mitchell Street
Bryson City, North Carolina 28713

Transylvania County
28 East Main Street
Brevard, North Carolina 28712

Tyrrell County
Water Street
Columbia, North Carolina 27925

Union County
500 North Main Street
Monroe, North Carolina 28112

Vance County
122 Young Street
Henderson, North Carolina 27536

Wake County
336 Fayetteville Street Mall
Raleigh, North Carolina 27601

Warren County
Post Office Box 709
Warrenton, North Carolina 27589

Washington County
120 Adams Street
Plymouth, North Carolina 27962

Watauga County
403 West King Street
Boone, North Carolina 28607

Wayne County
215 South William Street
Goldsboro, North Carolina 27530

Wilkes County
110 North Street
Wilkesboro, North Carolina 28697

Wilson County
Post Office Box 1728
Wilson, North Carolina 27894

Yadkin County
Post Office Box 146
Yadkinville, North Carolina 27055

Yancey County
County Courthouse
Burnsville, North Carolina 28714

NORTH DAKOTA

Adams County
County Courthouse
Hettinger, North Dakota 58639

Barnes County
Post Office Box 774
Valley City, North Dakota 58072

Benson County
311 B Avenue South
Minnewaukan, North Dakota 58351

Billings County
Post Office Box 138
Medora, North Dakota 58645

Bottineau County
315 West 5th Street
Bottineau, North Dakota 58318

Bowman County
104 West 1st
Bowman, North Dakota 58623

Burke County
Post Office Box 219
Bowbells, North Dakota 58721

Burleigh County
514 East Thayer Avenue
Bismarck, North Dakota 58501

Cass County
207 9th Street South
Fargo, North Dakota 58103

Cavalier County
901 3rd Street
Langdon, North Dakota 58249

Dickey County
309 North 2nd Street
Ellendale, North Dakota 58436

Divide County
300 North Main Street
Crosby, North Dakota 58730

Dunn County
County Courthouse
Manning, North Dakota 58642

Eddy County
524 Central Avenue
New Rockford, North Dakota 58356

Emmons County
Post Office Box 87
Linton, North Dakota 58552

McIntosh County
112 Northeast 1st Street
Ashley, North Dakota 58413

Foster County
1000 5th Street North
Carrington, North Dakota 58421

McKenzie County
Post Office Box 523
Watford City, North Dakota 58854

Golden Valley County
Post Office Box 596
Beach, North Dakota 58621

McLean County
712 5th Avenue
Washburn, North Dakota 58577

Grand Forks County
Post Office Box 1477
Grand Forks, North Dakota 58206

Mercer County
Post Office Box 39
Stanton, North Dakota 58571

Grant County
County Courthouse
Carson, North Dakota 58529

Morton County
210 2nd Avenue Northwest
Mandan, North Dakota 58554

Griggs County
Post Office Box 326
Cooperstown, North Dakota 58425

Mountrail County
Post Office Box 69
Stanley, North Dakota 58784

Hettinger County
336 Pacific Avenue
Mott, North Dakota 58646

Nelson County
Post Office Box 565
Lakota, North Dakota 58344

Kidder County
Post Office Box 110
Steele, North Dakota 58482

Oliver County
Post Office Box 166
Center, North Dakota 58530

La Moure County
202 4th Avenue Northeast
La Moure, North Dakota 58458

Pembina County
Post Office Box 357
Cavalier, North Dakota 58220

Logan County
301 Main Street
Napoleon, North Dakota 58561

Pierce County
240 2nd Street Southeast
Rugby, North Dakota 58368

McHenry County
407 Main Street South
Towner, North Dakota 58788

Ramsey County
6th & 4th Street
Devils Lake, North Dakota 58301

Renville County
Post Office Box 68
Mohall, North Dakota 58761

Richland County
Post Office Box 966
Wahpeton, North Dakota 58074

Rolette County
Post Office Box 460
Rolla, North Dakota 58367

Sargent County
Post Office Box 98
Forman, North Dakota 58032

Sheridan County
Post Office Box 636
McClusky, North Dakota 58463

Siope County
Post Office Box J
Amidon, North Dakota 58620

Sioux County
Post Office Box L
Fort Yates, North Dakota 58538

Stark County
Post Office Box 130
Dickinson, North Dakota 58602

Steele County
County Courthouse
Finley, North Dakota 58230

Stutsman County
511 2nd Avenue Southeast
Jamestown, North Dakota 58401

Towner County
Post Office Box 517
Cando, North Dakota 58324

Trail County
County Courthouse
Hillsboro, North Dakota 58045

Walsh County
600 Cooper Avenue
Grafton, North Dakota 58237

Ward County
3rd Street Southeast
Minot, North Dakota 58701

Wells County
Post Office Box 596
Fessenden, North Dakota 58438

Williams County
205 East Broadway
Williston, North Dakota 58801

OHIO

Adams County
110 West Main Street
West Union, Ohio 45693

Allen County
301 North Main Street
Lima, Ohio 45801

Ashland County
110 West 2nd Street
Ashland, Ohio 44805

Ashtabula County
25 West Jefferson Street
Jefferson, Ohio 44047

Athens County
Court & Washington Streets
Athens, Ohio 45701

Auglaize County
36 East Auglaize Street
Wapakoneta, Ohio 45895

Belmont County
100 West Main Street
Saint Clairsville, Ohio 43950

Brown County
Danny L. Pride Courthouse
Georgetown, Ohio 45121

Butler County
130 High Street
Hamilton, Ohio 45011

Carroll County
119 Public Square
Carrollton, Ohio 44615

Champaign County
Main & Court Street
Urbana, Ohio 43078

Clark County
101 North Limestone Street
Springfield, Ohio 45502

Clermont County
76 South Riverside Drive
Batavia, Ohio 45103

Clinton County
46 South South Street
Wilmington, Ohio 45177

Columbiana County
105 South Market Street
Lisbon, Ohio 44432

Coshocton County
349 Main Street
Coshocton, Ohio 43812

Crawford County
112 East Mansfield Street
Bucyrus, Ohio 44820

Cuyahoga County
1200 Ontario Street
Cleveland, Ohio 44113

Darke County
4th & Broadway
Greenville, Ohio 45331

Delaware County
91 North Sandusky Street
Delaware, Ohio 43015

Defiance County
500 Court Street
Defiance, Ohio 43512

Erie County
323 Columbus Avenue
Sandusky, Ohio 44870

Fairfield County
224 East Main Street
Lancaster, Ohio 43130

Fayette County
110 East Court Street
Washington, Ohio 43160

Franklin County
410 South High Street
Columbus, Ohio 43215

Fulton County
210 South Fulton Street
Wauseon, Ohio 43567

Gallia County
18 Locust Street
Gallipolis, Ohio 45631

Genuga County
231 Main Street
Chardon, Ohio 44024

Greene County
45 North Detroit Street
Xena, Ohio 45385

Guernsey County
836 Steubenville Avenue
Cambridge, Ohio 43725

Hamilton County
1000 Main Street
Cincinnati, Ohio 45202

Hancock County
300 South Main Street
Findlay, Ohio 45840

Hardin County
Public Square
Kenton, Ohio 43326

Harrison County
100 West Market Street
Cadiz, Ohio 43907

Henry County
Post Office Box 546
Napoleon, Ohio 43545

Highland County
114 Governor Foraker Place
Hillsboro, Ohio 45133

Hocking County
1 East Main Street
Logan, Ohio 43138

Holmes County
10 East Jackson Street
Millersburg, Ohio 44654

Huron County
2 East Main Street
Norwalk, Ohio 44857

Jackson County
226 Main Street
Jackson, Ohio 45640

Jefferson County
301 Market Street
Steubenville, Ohio 43952

Knox County
106 East High Street
Mount Vernon, Ohio 43050

Lake County
105 Main Street
Painesville, Ohio 44077

Lawrence County
5th & Park Avenue
Ironton, Ohio 45638

Licking County
20 South 2nd Street
Newark, Ohio 43055

Logan County
Main & East Columbus 2nd Floor
Bellefontaine, Ohio 43311

Lorain County
Post Office Box 749
Elyria, Ohio 44036

Lucus County
1 Government Center
Toledo, Ohio 43604

Madison County
County Courthouse
London, Ohio 43140

Mahoning County
120 Market Street
Youngstown, Ohio 44503

Marion County
114 North Main Street
Marion, Ohio 43302

Medina County
93 Public Square
Medina, Ohio 44256

Meigs County
2nd Street
Pomeroy, Ohio 45769

Mercer County
101 North Main Street
Celina, Ohio 45822

Miami County
201 West Main Street
Troy, Ohio 45373

Monroe County
Post Office Box 574
Woodsfield, Ohio 43793

Montgomery County
451 West 3rd Street
Dayton, Ohio 45422

Morgan County
19 East Main Street
McConnelsville, Ohio 43756

Morrow County
48 East High Street
Mount Gilead, Ohio 43338

Muskingum County
Post Office Box 268
Zanesville, Ohio 43702

Noble County
County Courthouse
Caldwell, Ohio 43724

Ottawa County
315 Madison South
Port Clinton, Ohio 43452

Paulding County
County Courthouse
Paulding, Ohio 45879

Perry County
121 West Brown Street
New Lexington, Ohio 43764

Pickaway County
207 South Court Street
Circleville, Ohio 43113

Pike County
100 East 2nd Street
Waverly, Ohio 45690

Portage County
Post Office Box 1035
Ravenna, Ohio 44266

Preble County
100 Main Street
Eaton, Ohio 45320

Putnam County
245 East Main Street
Ottawa, Ohio 45875

Richland County
50 Park Avenue East
Mansfield, Ohio 44902

Ross County
North Paint Street
Chillicothe, Ohio 45601

Sandusky County
100 North Park Avenue
Fremont, Ohio 43420

Sciolo County
602 7th Street
Portsmouth, Ohio 45662

Seneca County
81 Jefferson Street
Tiffin, Ohio 44883

Shelby County
129 East Court Street
Sidney, Ohio 45365

Stark County
209 Tuscarawas Street West
Canton, Ohio 44702

Summit County
175 South Main Street
Akron, Ohio 44308

Trumbull County
160 High Street Northwest
Warren, Ohio 44481

Tuscarawas County
Public Square
New Philadelphia, Ohio 44663

Union County
5th & Court Street
Marysville, Ohio 43040

Van Wert County
121 East Main Street
Van Wert, Ohio 45891

Vinton County
Vinton County Courthouse
McArthur, Ohio 45651

Warren County
320 East Silver Street
Lebanon, Ohio 45036

Washington County
205 Putnam Street
Marietta, Ohio 45750

Wayne County
107 West Liberty Street
Wooster, Ohio 44691

Williams County
County Courthouse Square
Bryan, Ohio 43506

Wood County
1 Courthouse Square
Bowling Green, Ohio 43402

Wyandot County
County Courthouse
Upper Sandusky, Ohio 43351

OKLAHOMA

Adair County
Post Office Box 169
Stilwell, Oklahoma 74960

Altalla County
300 South Grand Avenue
 County Courthouse
Cherokee, Oklahoma 73728

Atoka County
201 East Court Street
Atoka, Oklahoma 74525

Beaver County
111 West 2nd Street
Beaver, Oklahoma 73932

Beckham County
Post Office Box 67
Sayre, Oklahoma 73662

Blaine County
212 North Weigle Avenue
Watonga, Oklahoma 73772

Bryan County
402 West Evergreen Street
Durant, Oklahoma 74701

Caddo County
Post Office Box 1427
Anadarko, Oklahoma 73005

Canadian County
301 North Choctaw Avenue
El Reno, Oklahoma 73036

Carter County
1st & B Street Southwest
Ardmore, Oklahoma 73401

Cherokee County
213 West Delaware Street
Tahlequah, Oklahoma 74464

Choctaw County
County Courthouse
Hugo, Oklahoma 74743

Cimarron County
Post Office Box 145
Boise City, Oklahoma 73933

Cleveland County
201 South Jones Avenue
Norman, Oklahoma 73069

Coal County
3 North Main Street
Coalgate, Oklahoma 74538

Comanche County
Post Office Box 9026
Lawton, Oklahoma 73501

Cotton County
301 North Broadway Street
Walters, Oklahoma 73572

Craig County
301 West Canadian Avenue
Vinita, Oklahoma 74301

Creek County
Post Office Box 129
Sapulpa, Oklahoma 74067

Custer County
675 West B Street
Arapaho, Oklahoma 73620

Delaware County
Krouse Street
Jay, Oklahoma 74346

Dewey County
Post Office Box 368
Taloga, Oklahoma 73667

Ellis County
100 South Washington Courthouse
Sqarnett, Oklahoma 73832,

Garfield County
County Courthouse
Enid, Oklahoma 73701

Garvin County
Walnut & Grant
Pauls Valley, Oklahoma 73075

Grady County
Post Office Box 459
Chickasha, Oklahoma 73023

Grant County
County Courthouse
Medford, Oklahoma 73759

Greer County
Courthouse
Mangum, Oklahoma 73554

Harmon County
114 West Hollis County Courthouse
Hollis, Oklahoma 73550

Harper County
311 Southeast 1st
Buffalo, Oklahoma 73834

Haskell County
202 East Main Street
Stigler, Oklahoma 74462

Hughes County
Post Office Box 914
Holdenville, Oklahoma 74848

Jackson County
101 West Broadway Street
Altus, Oklahoma 73521

Jefferson County
220 North Main Street
Waurika, Oklahoma 73573

Johnston County
Post Office Box 338
Tishomingo, Oklahoma 73460

Kay County
Post Office Box 450
Newkirk, Oklahoma 74647

Kingfisher County
Post Office Box 118
Kingfisher, Oklahoma 73750

Kiowa County
County Courthouse
Hobart, Oklahoma 73651

Latimer County
109 North Central Street
Wilburton, Oklahoma 74578

Le Flore County
Post Office Box 607
Poteau, Oklahoma 74953

Lincoln County
Post Office Box 126
Chandler, Oklahoma 74834

Logan County
301 East Harrison Avenue
Guthrie, Oklahoma 73044

Love County
405 West Main Street
Marietta, Oklahoma 73448

Major County
Post Office Box 379
Fairview, Oklahoma 73737

Marshall County
County Courthouse
Madill, Oklahoma 73446

Mayes County
Post Office Box 95
Pryor, Oklahoma 74362

McClain County
Post Office Box 629
Purcell, Oklahoma 73080

McCurtain County
108 North Central Avenue
Idabel, Oklahoma 74745

McIntosh County
110 North 1st Street
Eufaula, Oklahoma 74432

Murray County
Post Office Box 240
Sulphur, Oklahoma 73086

Muskogee County
Post Office Box 2307
Muskogee, Oklahoma 74402

Noble County
Post Office Box 409
Perry, Oklahoma 73077

Nowala County
229 North Maple Street
Nowala, Oklahoma 74048

Oklahoma County
321 Park Avenue
Oklahoma City, Oklahoma 73102

Okluskee County
Post Office Box 26
Okemah, Oklahoma 74859

Okmulgee County
314 West 7th Street
Okmulgee, Oklahoma 74447

Osage County
Post Office Box 87
Pawhuska, Oklahoma 74056

Ottawa County
County Courthouse
Miami, Oklahoma 74354

Pawnee County
County Courthouse
Pawnee, Oklahoma 74058

Payne County
606 South Husband Street
Stillwater, Oklahoma 74074

Pittsburg County
2nd & Carl Albert
McAlester, Oklahoma 74501

Pontotoc County
13th & Broadway
Ada, Oklahoma 74820

Pottawatomie County
325 North Broadway Street
Shawnee, Oklahoma 74801

Pushmataha County
203 Southwest 3rd Street
Antlers, Oklahoma 74523

Roger Mills County
Post Office Box 708
Cheyenne, Oklahoma 73628

Rogers County
219 South Missouri Avenue
Claremore, Oklahoma 74017

Seminole County
Post Office Box 457
Wewoka, Oklahoma 74884

Sequoyah County
120 East Chickasaw Avenue
Sallisaw, Oklahoma 74955

Stephens County
3 County Courthouse
Duncan, Oklahoma 73533

Texas County
319 North Main Street
Guymon, Oklahoma 73942

Tillman County
Post Office Box 992
Frederick, Oklahoma 73542

Tulsa County
500 South Denver Avenue
Tulsa, Oklahoma 74103

Wagoner County
307 East Cherokee Street
Wagoner, Oklahoma 74467

Washington County
420 South Johnstone Avenue
Bartlesville, Oklahoma 74003

Washita County
Post Office Box 380
Cordell, Oklahoma 73632

Woods County
Post Office Box 386
Alva, Oklahoma 73717

Woodward County
1600 Main Street
Woodward, Oklahoma 73801

OREGON

Baker County
1995 3rd Street
Baker, Oregon 97814

Benton County
180 Northwest 5th Street
Corvallis, Oregon 97330

Clackamas County
906 Main Street
Oregon City, Oregon 97045

Clatsop County
Post Office Box 179
Astoria, Oregon 97103

Columbia County
County Courthouse
Saint Helens, Oregon 97051

Coos County
250 North Baxter Street
Coquille, Oregon 97423

Crook County
300 East 3rd Street
Prineville, Oregon 97754

Curry County
Post Office Box 746
Gold Beach, Oregon 97444

Deschutes County
1130 Northwest Harriman Street
Bend, Oregon 97701

Douglas County
1036 Southeast Douglas Avenue
Roseburg, Oregon 97470

Gilliam County
221 South Oregon Street
Condon, Oregon 97823

Grant County
200 South Canyon Boulevard
Canyon City, Oregon 97820

Harney County
450 North Buena Vista Avenue
Burns, Oregon 97720

Hood River County
309 State Street
Hood River, Oregon 97031

Jackson County
10 South Oakdale Avenue
Medford, Oregon 97501

Jefferson County
657 C Street
Madras, Oregon 97741

Josephine County
County Courthouse
Grants Pass, Oregon 97526

Klamath County
316 Main Street
Klamath Falls, Oregon 97601

Lake County
513 Center Street
Lakeview, Oregon 97630

Lane County
125 East 8th Avenue
Eugene, Oregon 97401

Lincoln County
225 West Olive Street
Newport, Oregon 97365

Linn County
Post Office Box 100
Albany, Oregon 97321

Malheur County
Post Office Box 4
Vale, Oregon 97918

Marion County
100 Hugh Street Northeast
Salem, Oregon 97301

Morrow County
Post Office Box 338
Heppner, Oregon 97836

Mullnomah County
1021 Southwest 4th Avenue
Portland, Oregon 97204

Polk County
850 Main Street, Room 201
Dallas, Oregon 97338

Sherman County
Post Office Box 365
Moro, Oregon 97039

Tillamook County
201 Laurel Avenue
Tillamook, Oregon 97141

Umatilla County
216 Southeast 4th Street
Pendleton, Oregon 97801

Union County
1106 K Avenue
La Grande, Oregon 97850

Wallowa County
101 South River Street
Enterprise, Oregon 97828

Wasco County
5th & Washington
The Dalles, Oregon 97058

Washington County
155 North 1st Avenue
Hillsboro, Oregon 97124

Wheeler County
Post Office Box 327
Fossil, Oregon 97830

Yamhill County
535 East 5th Street
McMinnville, Oregon 97128

PENNSYLVANIA

Adams County
111 Baltimore Street
Gettysburg, Pennsylvania 17325

Allegheny County
436 Grant Street
Pittsburgh, Pennsylvania 15219

Armstrong County
Market Street
Kittanning, Pennsylvania 16201

Beaver County
3rd & Turnpike Street
Beaver, Pennsylvania 15009

Bedford County
230 South Juliana Street
Bedford, Pennsylvania 15522

Berks County
33 North 6th Street
Reading, Pennsylvania 19601

Blair County
423 Allegheny Street
Hollidaysburg, Pennsylvania 16648

Bradford County
301 Main Street
Towanda, Pennsylvania 18848

Bucks County
Main & Court Streets
Doylestown, Pennsylvania 18901

Butler County
Main Street
Butler, Pennsylvania 16001

Cambria County
200 South Center Street
Ebensburg, Pennsylvania 15931

Cameron County
20 East 5th Street
Emporium, Pennsylvania 15834

Carbon County
Broadway Lock Box 129
Jim Thorpe, Pennsylvania 18229

Centre County
County Courthouse
Bellefonte, Pennsylvania 16823

Chester County
Market & High Streets
West Chester, Pennsylvania 19380

Clarion County
421 Main Street
Clarion, Pennsylvania 16214

Clearfield County
North 2nd & Market Streets
Clearfield, Pennsylvania 16830

Clinton County
County Courthouse
Lock Haven, Pennsylvania 17745

Columbia County
Post Office Box 380
Bloomsburg, Pennsylvania 17815

Crawford County
360 Center Street
Meadville, Pennsylvania 16335

Cumberland County
Hanover & High Streets
Carlisle, Pennsylvania 17013

Dauphin County
Front & Market Streets
Harrisburg, Pennsylvania 17101

Delaware County
West Front Street
Media, Pennsylvania 19063

Elk County
Main Street
Ridgway, Pennsylvania 15853

Erie County
140 West 6th Street
Erie, Pennsylvania 16501

Fayette County
61 East Main Street
Uniontown, Pennsylvania 15401

Forest County
526 Elm Street
Tionesta, Pennsylvania 16353

Franklin County
157 Lincoln Way East
Chambersburg, Pennsylvania 17201

Fulton County
North 2nd Street
McConnellsburg, Pennsylvania 17233

Greene County
93 East High Street County Office
Blgwaynesburg, Pennsylvania 15370,

Huntingdon County
223 Penn Street
Huntingdon, Pennsylvania 16652

Indiana County
825 Philadelphia Street
Indiana, Pennsylvania 15701

Jefferson County
200 Main Street
Brookville, Pennsylvania 15825

Juniata County
Post Office Box 68
Mifflintown, Pennsylvania 17059

Lackawanna County
Post Office Box 133
Scranton, Pennsylvania 18503

Lancaster County
50 North Duke Street
Lancaster, Pennsylvania 17602

Lawrence County
433 Court Street
New Castle, Pennsylvania 16101

Lebanon County
400 South 8th Street
Lebanon, Pennsylvania 17042

Lehigh County
455 Hamilton Street
Allentown, Pennsylvania 18101

Luzerne County
211 North River Street
Wilkes-Barre, Pennsylvania 18704

Lycoming County
48 West 3rd Street
Williamsport, Pennsylvania 17701

McKean County
500 West Main Street
Smethport, Pennsylvania 16749

Mercer County
138 South Diamond Street
Mercer, Pennsylvania 16137

Mifflin County
20 North Wayne Street
Lewistown, Pennsylvania 17044

Monroe County
County Courthouse Square
Stroudsburg, Pennsylvania 18360

Montgomery County
Swede & Airy Streets
Norristown, Pennsylvania 19404

Montour County
29 Mill Street
Danville, Pennsylvania 17821

Northampton County
7th & Washington Streets
Easton, Pennsylvania 18042

Northumberland County
2nd & Market Streets
Sunbury, Pennsylvania 17801

Perry County
Post Office Box 37
New Bloomfield, Pennsylvania 17068

Philadelphia County
Broad & Market Streets
Philadelphia, Pennsylvania 19107

Pike County
506 Broad Street
Milford, Pennsylvania 18337

Potter County
227 North Main Street
Coudersport, Pennsylvania 16915

Schuylkill County
North 2nd Street & Laurel Boulevard
Pottsville, Pennsylvania 17901

Snyder County
11 West Market Street
Middleburg, Pennsylvania 17842

Somerset County
111 East Union Street
Somerset, Pennsylvania 15501

Sullivan County
Main & Muncy
Laporte, Pennsylvania 18626

Susquehanna County
County Courthouse
Montrose, Pennsylvania 18801

Tioga County
116-118 Main Street
Wellsboro, Pennsylvania 16901

Union County
103 South 2nd Street
Lewisburg, Pennsylvania 17837

Venango County
Liberty & 12th Streets
Franklin, Pennsylvania 16323

Warren County
204 4th Avenue
Warren, Pennsylvania 16365

Washington County
100 West Beau Street
Washington, Pennsylvania 15301

Wayne County
925 Court Street
Honesdale, Pennsylvania 18431

Westmoreland County
2 North Main Street
Greensburg, Pennsylvania 15601

Wyoming County
Court House Square
Tunkhannock, Pennsylvania 18657

York County
28 East Market Street
York, Pennsylvania 17401

RHODE ISLAND

Bristol County
516 Main Street
Warren, Rhode Island 02885

Kent County
222 Quaker Lane
West Warwick, Rhode Island 02893

Newport County
8 Washington Square
Newport, Rhode Island 02840

Providence County
250 Benefit Street
Providence, Rhode Island 02903

Washington County
4800 Tower Hill Road
Wakefield, Rhode Island 02879

SOUTH CAROLINA

Abbeville County
Post Office Box 99
Abbeville, South Carolina 29620

Aiken County
828 Richland Avenue West
Aiken, South Carolina 29801

Allendale County
Post Office Box 126
Allendale, South Carolina 29810

Anderson County
Post Office Box 1656
Anderson, South Carolina 29622

Bamberg County
Post Office Box 150
Bamberg, South Carolina 29003

Barnwell County
Post Office Box 723
Barnwell, South Carolina 29812

Beaufort County
Post Office Box 1128
Beaufort, South Carolina 29901

Berkeley County
223 North Live Oak Drive
Moncks Corner, South Carolina 29461

Calhoun County
302 South Railroad Avenue
Saint Matthews, South Carolina 29135

Charleston County
Post Office Box 70219
North Charleston, South Carolina 29415

Cherokee County
Post Office Box 866
Gaffney, South Carolina 29342

Chester County
Main Street
Chester, South Carolina 29706

Chesterfield County
200 West Main Street
Chesterfield, South Carolina 29709

Clarendon County
Post Office Box East
Manning, South Carolina 29102

Colleton County
Post Office Box 620
Walterboro, South Carolina 29488

Darlington County
Courthouse Public Square
Darlington, South Carolina 29532

Dillon County
Post Office Box 449
Dillon, South Carolina 29536

Dorchester County
Post Office Box 613
Saint George, South Carolina 29477

Edgefield County
Post Office Box 663
Edgefield, South Carolina 29824

Fairfield County
115 South Congress Street
Winnsboro, South Carolina 29180

Florence County
180 North Irby Street
Florence, South Carolina 29501

Georgetown County
715 Prince Street
Georgetown, South Carolina 29440

Greenville County
301 University Ridge
Greenville, South Carolina 29601

Greenwood County
528 Monument Street
Greenwood, South Carolina 29646

Hampton County
Post Office Box 7
Hampton, South Carolina 29924

Horry County
Post Office Box 677
Conway, South Carolina 29526

Jasper County
Post Office Box 248
Ridgeland, South Carolina 29936

Kershaw County
1121 Broad Street
Camden, South Carolina 29020

Lancaster County
Post Office Box 1809
Lancaster, South Carolina 29720

Laurens County
Post Office Box 445
Laurens, South Carolina 29360

Lee County
Post Office Box 309
Bishopville, South Carolina 29010

Lexington County
139 East Main Street
Lexington, South Carolina 29072

Marion County
Post Office Box 183
Marion, South Carolina 29571

Marlboro County
Post Office Box 996
Bennettsville, South Carolina 29512

McCormick County
Post Office Box 86
McCormick, South Carolina 29835

Newberry County
Post Office Box 278
Newberry, South Carolina 29108

Oconee County
West Main Street
Walhalla, South Carolina 29691

Orangeburg County
190 Sunnyside Street Northeast
Orangeburg, South Carolina 29115

Pickens County
Post Office Box 215
Pickens, South Carolina 29671

Richland County
1701 Main Street
Columbia, South Carolina 29201

Saluda County
101 South 9th Street
Saluda, South Carolina 29138

Spartanburg County
180 Magnolia Street
Spartanburg, South Carolina 29301

Sumter County
141 North Main Street
Sumter, South Carolina 29150

Union County
Post Office Box G
Union, South Carolina 29379

Williamsburg County
125 West Main Street
Kingstree, South Carolina 29556

York County
2 Congress Street
York, South Carolina 29745

SOUTH DAKOTA

Aurora County
Post Office Box 366
Plankinton, South Dakota 57368

Beadle County
450 3rd Street Southwest
Huron, South Dakota 57350

Bennell County
Post Office Box 281
Martin, South Dakota 57551

Bon Homme County
Post Office Box 6
Tyndall, South Dakota 57066

Brookings County
314 6th Avenue
Brookings, South Dakota 57006

Brown County
101 1st Avenue Southeast
Aberdeen, South Dakota 57401

Brule County
300 South Courtland Street
Chamberlain, South Dakota 57325

Buffalo County
Post Office Box 148
Gannvalley, South Dakota 57341

Butte County
839 5th Avenue
Belle Fourche, South Dakota 57717

Campbell County
Post Office Box 37
Mound City, South Dakota 57646

Carson County
Post Office Box 175
McIntosh, South Dakota 57641

Charles Mix County
Post Office Box 640
Lake Andes, South Dakota 57356

Clark County
Post Office Box 294
Clark, South Dakota 57225

Clay County
211 West Main Street
Vermillion, South Dakota 57069

Codington County
14 1st Avenue Southeast
Watertown, South Dakota 57201

Custer County
420 Mount Rushmore Road
Custer, South Dakota 57730

Davison County
200 East 4th Avenue
Mitchell, South Dakota 57301

Day County
710 West 1st Street
Webster, South Dakota 57274

Deuel County
Post Office Box 125
Clear Lake, South Dakota 57226

Dewey County
County Courthouse
Timber Lake, South Dakota 57656

Douglas County
Post Office Box 36
Armour, South Dakota 57313

Edmunds County
2nd Street
Ipswich, South Dakota 57451

Fall River County
906 North River Street
Hot Springs, South Dakota 57747

Faulk County
Post Office Box 309
Faulkton, South Dakota 57438

Grant County
210 East 5th Avenue
Milbank, South Dakota 57252

Gregory County
Post Office Box 430
Burke, South Dakota 57523

Haakon County
Post Office Box 70
Philip, South Dakota 57567

Hamlin County
Post Office Box 256
Hayti, South Dakota 57241

Hand County
415 West 1st Avenue
Miller, South Dakota 57362

Hanson County
Post Office Box 127
Alexandria, South Dakota 57311

Harding County
901 Ramsland Street
Buffalo, South Dakota 57720

Hughes County
104 East Capitol Avenue
Pierre, South Dakota 57501

Hutchinson County
Post Office Box 7
Olivet, South Dakota 57052

Hyde County
Post Office Box 306
Highmore, South Dakota 57345

Jackson County
1 Main Street
Kadoka, South Dakota 57543

Jerauld County
Post Office Box 435
Wessington Springs, South Dakota 57382

Jones County
Post Office Box 448
Murdo, South Dakota 57559

Kingsbury County
101 2nd Street Southeast
De Smet, South Dakota 57231

Lake County
200 East Center
Madison, South Dakota 57042

Lawrence County
County Courthouse
Deadwood, South Dakota 57732

Lincoln County
100 East 5th Street
Canton, South Dakota 57013

Lyman County
County Courthouse
Kennebec, South Dakota 57544

Marshall County
County Courthouse
Britton, South Dakota 57430

McCook County
130 West Essex Avenue
Salem, South Dakota 57058

McPherson County
County Courthouse
Leola, South Dakota 57456

Meade County
Post Office Box 939
Sturgis, South Dakota 57785

Mellette County
South 1st Street
White River, South Dakota 57579

Miner County
North Main Street
Howard, South Dakota 57349

Minnehaha County
415 North Dakota Avenue
Sioux Falls, South Dakota 57102

Moody County
101 East Pipestone Avenue
Flandreau, South Dakota 57028

Pennington County
Post Office Box 230
Rapid City, South Dakota 57709

Perkins County
Post Office Box 27
Bison, South Dakota 57620

Potter County
201 South Exene Street
Gettysburg, South Dakota 57442

Roberts County
411 2nd Avenue East
Sisseton, South Dakota 57262

Sanborn County
Post Office Box 56
Woonsocket, South Dakota 57385

Shannon County
906 North River Street
Hot Springs, South Dakota 57747

Spink County
210 East 7th Avenue
Bedfield, South Dakota 57469

Stanley County
Post Office Box 595
Fort Pierre, South Dakota 57532

Sully County
Main Street
Onida, South Dakota 57564

Todd County
200 East 3rd Street
Winner, South Dakota 57580

Tripp County
200 East 3rd Street
Winner, South Dakota 57580

Turner County
Post Office Box 446
Parker, South Dakota 57053

Union County
Post Office Box 757
Elk Point, South Dakota 57025

Walworth County
Post Office Box 199
Selby, South Dakota 57472

Yankton County
410 Walnut Street
Yankton, South Dakota 57078

Ziebach County
Post Office Box 68
Dupree, South Dakota 57623

TENNESSEE

Anderson County
100 North Main Street
Clinton, Tennessee 37716

Bedford County
1 Public Square
Shelbyville, Tennessee 37160

Benton County
Court Square
Camden, Tennessee 38320

Bledsoe County
Post Office Box 212
Pikeville, Tennessee 37367

Blount County
301 Court Street
Maryville, Tennessee 37801

Bradley County
Post Office Box 46
Cleveland, Tennessee 37364

Camdon County
County Courthouse
Woodbury, Tennessee 37190

Campbell County
Post Office Box 13
Jacksboro, Tennessee 37757

Carroll County
Post Office Box 110
Huntingdon, Tennessee 38344

Carter County
Main Street
Elizabethton, Tennessee 37643

Cheatham County
100 Public Square
Ashland City, Tennessee 37015

Chester County
Post Office Box 205
Henderson, Tennessee 38340

Claiborne County
Post Office Box 173
Tazewell, Tennessee 37879

Clay County
Post Office Box 218
Celina, Tennessee 38551

Cocke County
Court Avenue
Newport, Tennessee 37821

Coffee County
300 Hillsboro Boulevard
Manchester, Tennessee 37355

Crockett County
County Courthouse
Alamo, Tennessee 38001

Cumberland County
Main Street
Crossville, Tennessee 38555

Davidson County
700 2nd Avenue South
Nashville, Tennessee 37210

Decatur County
Post Office Box 488
Decaturville, Tennessee 38329

Dekalb County
County Courthouse
Smithville, Tennessee 37166

Dickson County
Court Square
Charlotte, Tennessee 37036

Dyer County
Post Office Box 1360
Dyersburg, Tennessee 38025

Fayette County
Court Square
Somerville, Tennessee 38068

Fentress County
Post Office Box C
Jamestown, Tennessee 38556

Franklin County
Public Square
Winchester, Tennessee 37398

Gibson County
County Courthouse
Trenton, Tennessee 38382

Giles County
Post Office Box 678
Pulaski, Tennessee 38478

Grainger County
County Courthouse
Rutledge, Tennessee 37861

Greene County
101 South Main Street
Greeneville, Tennessee 37743

Grundy County
Post Office Box 215
Altamont, Tennessee 37301

Hamblen County
511 West 2nd North Street
Morristown, Tennessee 37814

Hamilton County
County Courthouse
Chattanooga, Tennessee 37402

Hancock County
Main Street
Sneedville, Tennessee 37869

Hardeman County
100 North Main Street
Bolivar, Tennessee 38008

Hardin County
601 Main Street
Savannah, Tennessee 38372

Hawkins County
1121 East Main Street
Rogersville, Tennessee 37857

Haywood County
1 North Washington Street
Brownsville, Tennessee 38012

Henderson County
Church & Main Streets
Lexington, Tennessee 38351

Henry County
County Courthouse
Paris, Tennessee 38242

Hickman County
Public Square
Centerville, Tennessee 37033

Houston County
Post Office Box 388
Erin, Tennessee 37061

Humphreys County
102 Thompson Street
Waverly, Tennessee 37185

Jackson County
Post Office Box 346
Gainesboro, Tennessee 38562

Jefferson County
Post Office Box 710
Dandridge, Tennessee 37725

Johnson County
222 Main Street
Mountain City, Tennessee 37683

Knox County
300 West Main Avenue
Knoxville, Tennessee 37902

Lake County
229 Church Street
Tiptonville, Tennessee 38079

Lauderdale County
County Courthouse
Ripley, Tennessee 38063

Lawrence County
Post Office Box 2
Lawrenceburg, Tennessee 38464

Lewis County
County Courthouse
Hohenwald, Tennessee 38462

Lincoln County
Post Office Box 577
Fayetteville, Tennessee 37334

Loudon County
Grove Street
Loudon, Tennessee 37774

Macon County
Public Square Courthouse
Lafayette, Tennessee 37083

Madison County
County Courthouse
Jackson, Tennessee 38301

Marion County
County Courthouse Square
Jasper, Tennessee 37347

Marshall County
Public Square
Lewisburg, Tennessee 37091

Maury County
Post Office Box 1615
Columbia, Tennessee 38402

McMinn County
6 East Madison Avenue
Athens, Tennessee 37303

McNairy County
County Courthouse
Selmer, Tennessee 38375

Meigs County
Main Street
Decatur, Tennessee 37322

Monroe County
105 College Street
Madisonville, Tennessee 37354

Montgomery County
Post Office Box 687
Clarksville, Tennessee 37041

Moore County
County Courthouse
Lynchburg, Tennessee 37352

Morgan County
Main Street
Wartburg, Tennessee 37887

Obion County
County Courthouse
Union City, Tennessee 38261

Overton County
County Courthouse Anex University
Stlivingston, Tennessee 38570

Perry County
Post Office Box 16
Linden, Tennessee 37096

Pickett County
County Courthouse
Byrdstown, Tennessee 38549

Polk County
Post Office Box 128
Benton, Tennessee 37307

Putnam County
County Courthouse
Cookeville, Tennessee 38501

Rhea County
301 North Market Street
Dayton, Tennessee 37321

Roane County
Post Office Box 546
Kingston, Tennessee 37763

Robertson County
County Courthouse
Springfield, Tennessee 37172

Rutherford County
26 Public Square
Murfreesboro, Tennessee 37130

Scott County
Post Office Box 87
Huntsville, Tennessee 37756

Sequatchie County
Cherry Street
Dunlap, Tennessee 37327

Sevier County
125 Court Avenue
Sevierville, Tennessee 37862

Shelby County
160 North Mid-America Mall
Memphis, Tennessee 38103

Smith County
218 Main Street
Carthage, Tennessee 37030

Stewart County
Main Street
Dover, Tennessee 37058

Sullivan County
Post Office Box 530
Blountville, Tennessee 37617

Sumner County
County Courthouse
Gallatin, Tennessee 37066

Tipton County
Post Office Box 528
Covington, Tennessee 38019

Trousdale County
Main Street & Court Square
Hartsville, Tennessee 37074

Unicol County
Courthouse Post Office Box 340
Erwin, Tennessee 37650

Union County
Post Office Box 395
Maynardville, Tennessee 37807

Van Buren County
Courthouse Square
Spencer, Tennessee 38585

Warren County
Post Office Box 231
McMinnville, Tennessee 37110

Washington County
Post Office Box 218
Jonesborough, Tennessee 37659

Wayne County
Post Office Box 206
Waynesboro, Tennessee 38485

Weakley County
County Courthouse
Dresden, Tennessee 38225

White County
County Courthouse
Sparta, Tennessee 38583

Williamson County
1320 West Main Street
Franklin, Tennessee 37064

Wilson County
Post Office Box 918
Lebanon, Tennessee 37088

TEXAS

Anderson County
500 North Church Street
Palestine, Texas 75801

Andrews County
Post Office Box 727
Andrews, Texas 79714

Angelina County
215 East Lufkin Avenue
Lufkin, Texas 75901

Aransas County
301 North Live Oak Street
Rockport, Texas 78382

Archer County
Post Office Box 815
Archer City, Texas 76351

Armstrong County
Post Office Box 189
Claude, Texas 79019

Atascosa County
Circle Drive
Jourdanton, Texas 78026

Austin County
1 East Main Street
Bellville, Texas 77418

Bailey County
300 South 1st Street
Muleshoe, Texas 79347

Bandera County
500 Main Street
Bandera, Texas 78003

Bastrop County
803 Pine Street
Bastrop, Texas 78602

Baylor County
Post Office Box 689
Seymour, Texas 76380

Bee County
105 West Corpus Christi Street
Beeville, Texas 78102

Bell County
Main & Central Streets
Belton, Texas 76513

Bexar County
100 Dolorosa Street
San Antonio, Texas 78205

Blanco County
Post Office Box 65
Johnson City, Texas 78636

Borden County
101 Main Street
Gail, Texas 79738

Bosque County
Morgan & Main Streets
Meridan, Texas 76665

Bowie County
Post Office Box 248
New Boston, Texas 75570

Brazoria County
111 East Locust Street
Angleton, Texas 77515

Brazos County
300 East 26th Street
Bryan, Texas 77803

Brewster County
201 West Avenue
Alpine, Texas 79830

Briscoe County
415 Main Street
Silverton, Texas 79257

Brooks County
County Courthouse
Falfurrias, Texas 78355

Brown County
200 South Broadway Street
Brownwood, Texas 76801

Burleson County
205 West Buck Street
Caldwell, Texas 77836

Burnet County
220 South Pierce Street
Burnet, Texas 78611

Caldwell County
Main Street
Lockhart, Texas 78644

Calhoun County
211 South Ann Street
Port Lavaca, Texas 77979

Callahan County
400 Market Street
Baird, Texas 79504

Cameron County
964 East Harrison Street
Brownsville, Texas 78520

Camp County
126 Church Street
Pittsburg, Texas 75686

Carson County
501 Main Street
Panhandle, Texas 79068

Cass County
Post Office Box 468
Linden, Texas 75563

Castro County
100 East Bedford Street
Dimmitt, Texas 79027

Chambers County
404 Washington
Anahuac, Texas 77514

Cherokee County
6th Street
Rusk, Texas 75785

Childress County
100 Avenue East Northwest
Childress, Texas 79201

Clay County
100 North Bridge Street
Henrietta, Texas 76365

Cochran County
100 North Main Street
Morton, Texas 79346

Coke County
13 East 7th Street
Robert Lee, Texas 76945

Coleman County
Post Office Box 591
Coleman, Texas 76834

Collin County
210 South McDonald Street
McKinney, Texas 75069

Collingsworth County
County Courthouse
Wellington, Texas 79095

Colorado County
400 Spring Street
Columbus, Texas 78934

Comal County
100 Main Plaza
New Braunfels, Texas 78130

Comanche County
County Courthouse
Comanche, Texas 76442

Concho County
Post Office Box 98
Paint Rock, Texas 76866

Cooke County
Dixon Street County Courthouse
Gainesville, Texas 76240

Coryell County
Post Office Box 237
Gatesville, Texas 76528

Cottle County
Post Office Box 717
Paducah, Texas 79248

Crane County
Post Office Box 578
Crane, Texas 79731

Crockett County
907 Avenue D
Ozona, Texas 76943

Crosby County
Post Office Box 218
Crosbyton, Texas 79322

Culberson County
Post Office Box 158
Van Horn, Texas 79855

Dallam County
101 East 5th Street
Dalhart, Texas 79022

Dallas County
500 Main Street
Dallas, Texas 75202

Dawson County
North 1st & Main Streets
Lamesa, Texas 79331

Deal Smith County
243 East 3rd County Courthouse
Hereford, Texas 79045

Della County
Post Office Box 455
Cooper, Texas 75432

Denton County
401 West Hickory Street
Denton, Texas 76201

Dewitt County
307 North Gonzales Street
Cuero, Texas 77954

Dickens County
Post Office Box 120
Dickens, Texas 79229

Dimmit County
103 North 5th Street
Carrizo Springs, Texas 78834

Donley County
Post Office Box U
Clarendon, Texas 79226

Duval County
400 East Gravis Street
San Diego, Texas 78384

Eastland County
Post Office Box 110
Eastland, Texas 76448

Ector County
300 North Grant Avenue
Odessa, Texas 79761

Edwards County
Post Office Box 184
Rocksprings, Texas 78880

El Parishaso County
500 East San Antonio Avenue
El Paso, Texas 79901

Ellis County
Post Office Box 250
Waxahachie, Texas 75165

Erath County
County Courthouse Square
Stephenville, Texas 76401

Falls County
Post Office Box 458
Marlin, Texas 76661

Fannin County
County Courthouse
Bonham, Texas 75418

Fayette County
151 North Washington Street
La Grange, Texas 78945

Fisher County
Post Office Box 368
Roby, Texas 79543

Floyd County
100 Main Street
Floydada, Texas 79235

Foard County
Post Office Box 539
Crowell, Texas 79227

Fort Bend County
Post Office Box 520
Richmond, Texas 77469

Franklin County
Dallas & Kaufman Streets
Mount Vernon, Texas 75457

Freestone County
Main & Mount Streets
Fairfield, Texas 75840

Frio County
Post Office Box X
Pearsall, Texas 78061

Gaines County
100 South Main Street
Seminole, Texas 79360

Galveston County
722 Moody Avenue
Galveston, Texas 77550

Garza County
County Courthouse
Post, Texas 79356

Gillespie County
Post Office Box 351
Fredericksburg, Texas 78624

Glasscock County
Post Office Box 190
Garden City, Texas 79739

Goliad County
Post Office Box 5
Goliad, Texas 77963

Gonzales County
414 North Saint Joseph Street
Gonzales, Texas 78629

Gray County
205 North Russell Street
Pampa, Texas 79065

Grayson County
Houston & Lamar Streets
Sherman, Texas 75090

Gregg County
Post Office Box 3049
Longview, Texas 75606

Grimes County
Main Street
Anderson, Texas 77830

Guadalupe County
101 East Court Street
Seguin, Texas 78155

Hale County
500 Broadway Street
Plainview, Texas 79072

Hall County
County Courthouse
Memphis, Texas 79245

Hamilton County
County Courthouse
Hamilton, Texas 76531

Hansford County
1 Northwest Court Street
Spearman, Texas 79081

Hardeman County
Post Office Box 30
Quanah, Texas 79252

Hardin County
Highway 326 & Courthouse Square
Kountze, Texas 77625

Harris County
1001 Preston Street
Houston, Texas 77002

Harrison County
Houston & Wellington Streets
Marshall, Texas 75670

Hartley County
Post Office Box T
Channing, Texas 79018

Haskell County
Post Office Box 725
Haskell, Texas 79521

Hays County
County Courthouse
San Marcos, Texas 78666

Hemphill County
Post Office Box 867
Canadian, Texas 79014

Henderson County
Courthouse Square
Athens, Texas 75751

Hidalgo County
100 North Closner Boulevard
Edinburg, Texas 78539

Hill County
Post Office Box 398
Hillsboro, Texas 76645

Hockley County
800 Houston Street Courthouse
Levelland, Texas 79336

Hood County
101 East Pearl Street
Granbury, Texas 76048

Hopkins County
Post Office Box 288
Sulphur Springs, Texas 75482

Houston County
Post Office Box 370
Crockett, Texas 75835

Howard County
300 Main Street
Big Spring, Texas 79720

Hudspeth County
Post Office Box A
Sierra Blanca, Texas 79851

Hunt County
2500 Lee Street
Greenville, Texas 75401

Hutchinson County
Post Office Box F
Stinnett, Texas 79083

Irion County
County Courthouse
Mertzon, Texas 76941

Jack County
100 North Main Street
Jacksboro, Texas 76458

Jackson County
115 West Main Street
Edna, Texas 77957

Jasper County
Main & Lamar Street
Jasper, Texas 75951

Jeff Davis County
Post Office Box 398
Fort Davis, Texas 79734

Jefferson County
1149 Pearl Street
Beaumont, Texas 77701

Jim Hogg County
Post Office Box 729
Hebbronville, Texas 78361

Jim Wells County
Post Office Box 1459
Alice, Texas 78333

Johnson County
Post Office Box 662
Cleburne, Texas 76033

Jones County
Post Office Box 552
Anson, Texas 79501

Karnes County
101 North Panna Maria Avenue
Karnes City, Texas 78118

Kaufman County
Washington Street
Kaufman, Texas 75142

Kendall County
204 East San Antonio Street
Boerne, Texas 78006

Kenedy County
Post Office Box 7
Santa, Texas 78385

Kent County
Main Street
Jayton, Texas 79528

Kerr County
700 Main Street
Kerrville, Texas 78028

Kimble County
501 Main Street
Junction, Texas 76840

King County
County Courthouse
Guthrie, Texas 79236

Kinney County
Ann & James Streets
Brackettville, Texas 78832ʻ

Kleberg County
Post Office Box 1327
Kingsville, Texas 78364

Knox County
Post Office Box 196
Benjamin, Texas 79505

Lamar County
119 North Main Street
Paris, Texas 75460

Lamb County
100 6th Street
Littlefield, Texas 79339

Lampasas County
Post Office Box 231
Lampasas, Texas 76550

Lasalle County
Post Office Box 340
Cotulla, Texas 78014

Lavaca County
Post Office Box 326
Hallettsville, Texas 77964

Lee County
Main & Hempstead Streets
Giddings, Texas 78942

Leon County
Post Office Box 98
Centerville, Texas 75833

Liberty County
1923 Sam Houston Street
Liberty, Texas 77575

Limestone County
Post Office Box 350
Groesbeck, Texas 76642

Lipscomb County
Post Office Box 175
Lipscomb, Texas 79056

Live Oak County
Post Office Box 280
George West, Texas 78022

Llano County
801 Ford Street
Llano, Texas 78643

Loving County
Highway 302
Mentone, Texas 79754

Lubbock County
904 Broadway Street
Lubbock, Texas 79401

Lynn County
Post Office Box 937
Tahoka, Texas 79373

Madison County
101 West Main Street
Madisonville, Texas 77864

Malagorda County
1700 7th Street
Bay City, Texas 77414

Marion County
Post Office Box F
Jefferson, Texas 75657

Martin County
Post Office Box 906
Stanton, Texas 79782

Mason County
Westmoreland Street & Post Hill
Mason, Texas 76856

Maverick County
Post Office Box 4050
Eagle Pass, Texas 78853

McCulloch County
County Courthouse
Brady, Texas 76825

McLennan County
5th & Washington
Waco, Texas 76701

McMullen County
River & Elm Streets
Tilden, Texas 78072

Medina County
County Courthouse
Hondo, Texas 78661

Menard County
Post Office Box 1028
Menard, Texas 76859

Midland County
200 West Wall Street
Midland, Texas 79701

Milam County
100 South Fannin Avenue
Cameron, Texas 76520

Mills County
Post Office Box 646
Goldthwaite, Texas 76844

Mitchell County
301 Oak Street
Colorado City, Texas 79512

Molley County
Main Street
Matador, Texas 79244

Montague County
Post Office Box 77
Montague, Texas 76251

Montgomery County
300 North Main Street
Conroe, Texas 77301

Moore County
Post Office Box 396
Dumas, Texas 79029

Morris County
500 Broadnax Street
Daingerfield, Texas 75638

Nacogdoches County
101 West Main Street
Nacogdoches, Texas 75961

Navarro County
300 West 3rd Avenue
Corsicana, Texas 75110

Newton County
Courthouse Square Highway 190
Newton, Texas 75966

Nolan County
102 East 3rd Street
Sweetwater, Texas 79556

Nucces County
901 Leopard Street
Corpus Christi, Texas 78401

Ochiltree County
511 South Main Street
Perryton, Texas 79070

Oldham County
Post Office Box 469
Vega, Texas 79092

Orange County
Post Office Box 1536
Orange, Texas 77631

Palo Parishinto County
Post Office Box 8
Palo Pinto, Texas 76072

Panola County
Sabine & Sycamore Streets
Carthage, Texas 75633

Parker County
Post Office Box 819
Weatherford, Texas 76086

Parmer County
401 3rd Street
Farwell, Texas 79325

Pecos County
103 West Callaghan Street
Fort Stockton, Texas 79735

Polk County
101 West Church Street
Livingston, Texas 77351

Potter County
511 South Taylor Street
Amarillo, Texas 79101

Presidio County
320 North Highland Street
Marta, Texas 79843

Rains County
Post Office Box 187
Emory, Texas 75440

Randall County
401 15th Street
Canyon, Texas 79015

Reagan County
Post Office Box 100
Big Lake, Texas 76932

Real County
Post Office Box 656
Leakey, Texas 78873

Red River County
400 North Walnut Street
Clarksville, Texas 75426

Reeves County
Post Office Box 867
Pecos, Texas 79772

Refugio County
Post Office Box 704
Refugio, Texas 78377

Roberts County
Kiowa & Commercial Streets
Miami, Texas 79059

Robertson County
Center Street
Franklin, Texas 77856

Rockwall County
Highway 66 & Goliad
Rockwall, Texas 75087

Runnels County
Hutchings & Broadway
Ballinger, Texas 76821

Rusk County
115 North Main Street
Henderson, Texas 75652

Sabine County
Oak Street
Hemphill, Texas 75948

San Augustine County
106 Courthouse
San Augustine, Texas 75972

San Jacinto County
Church & Bird Streets
Coldspring, Texas 77331

San Parishatricio County
Post Office Box 578
Sinton, Texas 78387

San Saha County
518 East Wallace Street
San Saha, Texas 76877

Schleichur County
Highway 277
Eldorado, Texas 76936

Scurry County
County Courthouse
Snyder, Texas 79549

Shackelford County
Post Office Box 247
Albany, Texas 76430

Shelby County
Courthouse
Center, Texas 75935

Sherman County
701 North 3rd Street
Stratford, Texas 79084

Smith County
Post Office Box 1018
Tyler, Texas 75710

Somervell County
Post Office Box 1098
Glen Rose, Texas 76043

Starr County
Britton Avenue
Rio Grande City, Texas 78582

Stephens County
County Courthouse
Breckenridge, Texas 76024

Sterling County
Post Office Box 55
Sterling City, Texas 76951

Stonewall County
Post Office Box P
Aspermont, Texas 79502

Sutton County
300 East Oak Street
Sonora, Texas 76950

Swisher County
County Courthouse
Tulia, Texas 79088

Tarrant County
100 West Weatherford
Fort Worth, Texas 76196

Taylor County
300 Oak Street
Abilene, Texas 79602

Terrell County
Post Office Box 410
Sanderson, Texas 79848

Terry County
5th & Main
Brownfield, Texas 79316

Throckmorton County
Post Office Box 309
Throckmorton, Texas 76083

Titus County
Courthouse Square
Mount Pleasant, Texas 75455

Tom Green County
112 West Beauregard Avenue
San Angelo, Texas 76903

Travis County
1000 Guadalupe Street
Austin, Texas 78701

Trinity County
Highways 94 & 287
Groveton, Texas 75845

Tyler County
100 Courthouse
Woodville, Texas 75979

Upshur County
Highway 154 & Simpson Street
Gilmer, Texas 75644

Upton County
Post Office Box 465
Rankin, Texas 79778

Uvalde County
Post Office Box 284
Uvalde, Texas 78802

Val Verdo County
400 Pecan Street
Del Rio, Texas 78840

Van Zandt County
Post Office Box 515
Canton, Texas 75103

Victoria County
115 North Bridge Street
Victoria, Texas 77901

Walker County
1100 University Avenue
Huntsville, Texas 77840

Walter County
836 Austin Street
Hempstead, Texas 77445

Ward County
County Courthouse
Monahans, Texas 79756

Washington County
105 East Main Street
Brenham, Texas 77833

Webb County
1000 Houston Street
Laredo, Texas 78040

Wharton County
101 Milam Street
Wharton, Texas 77488

Wheeler County
Post Office Box 465
Wheeler, Texas 79096

Wichita County
900 7th Street
Wichita Falls, Texas 76301

Wilbarger County
1700 Wilbarger Street
Vernon, Texas 76384

Willacy County
Hidalgo & 3rd Street
Raymondville, Texas 78580

Williamson County
Post Office Box 16
Georgetown, Texas 78627

Wilson County
1420 3rd Street
Floresville, Texas 78114

Winkler County
100 East Winkler Street
Kermit, Texas 79745

Wise County
Post Office Box 359
Decatur, Texas 76234

Wood County
Post Office Box 338
Quitman, Texas 75783

Yoakum County
Post Office Box 309
Plains, Texas 79355

Young County
Post Office Box 218
Graham, Texas 76046

Zapata County
7th Avenue & Hidalgo
Zapata, Texas 78076

Zavata County
County Courthouse
Crystal City, Texas 78839

UTAH

Beaver County
Post Office Box 392
Beaver, Utah 84713

Box Elder County
1 South Main Street
Brigham City, Utah 84302

Cache County
170 North Main Street
Logan, Utah 84321

Carbon County
120 East Main Street
Price, Utah 84501

Daggett County
Post Office Box 218
Manila, Utah 84046

Davis County
Post Office Box 618
Farmington, Utah 84025

Duchesne County
Post Office Box 270
Duchesne, Utah 84021

Emery County
Post Office Box 907
Castle Dale, Utah 84513

Garfield County
Post Office Box 77
Panoutch, Utah 84759

Grand County
125 East Center Street
Moab, Utah 84532

Iron County
Post Office Box 429
Parowan, Utah 84761

Juab County
160 North Main Street
Nephi, Utah 84648

Kane County
76 North Main Street
Kanab, Utah 84741

Millard County
Post Office Box 226
Fillmore, Utah 84631

Morgan County
48th West Young Street
Morgan, Utah 84050

Piute County
21 North Main
Junction, Utah 84740

Rich County
Post Office Box 218
Randolph, Utah 84064

Salt Lake County
2001 State Street
Salt Lake City, Utah 84190

San Juan County
Post Office Box 338
Monticello, Utah 84535

Sanpete County
160 North Main Street
Manti, Utah 84642

Sevier County
250 North Main Street
Richfield, Utah 84701

Summit County
Post Office Box 128
Coalville, Utah 84017

Tooele County
47 South Main Street
Tooele, Utah 84074

Uintah County
152 East 100 North
Vernal, Utah 84078

Utah County
51 South University Avenue
Provo, Utah 84601

Wasatch County
25 North Main Street
Heber City, Utah 84032

Washington County
197 East Tabernacle Street
Saint George, Utah 84770

Wayne County
18 South Main
Loa, Utah 84747

Weber County
2549 Washington Boulevard
Ogden, Utah 84401

VERMONT

Addison County
5 Court Street
Middlebury, Vermont 05753

Bennington County
207 South Street
Bennington, Vermont 05201

Caledonia County
Post Office Box 404
Saint Johnsbury, Vermont 05819

Chittenden County
175 Main Street
Burlington, Vermont 05401

Essex County
Post Office Box 75
Guildhall, Vermont 05905

Franklin County
Post Office Box 808
Saint Albans, Vermont 05478

Grand Isle County
Route 2
North Hero, Vermont 05474

Lamoille County
Post Office Box 303
Hyde Park, Vermont 05655

Orange County
Post Office Box 95
Chelsea, Vermont 05038

Orleans County
Post Office Box 787
Newport, Vermont 05855

Rutland County
83 Center Street
Rutland, Vermont 05701

Washington County
Post Office Box 426
Montpelier, Vermont 05602

Windham County
Post Office Box 207
Newfane, Vermont 05345

Windsor County
12 The Green
Woodstock, Vermont 05091

VIRGINIA

Accomack County
County Courthouse
Accomac, Virginia 23301

Albemarle County
401 McIntire Road
Charlottesville, Virginia 22901

Alexandria County
301 King Street
The Courthouse
Alexandria, Virginia 22314

Alleghany County
266 West Main Street
Covington, Virginia 24426

Amelia County
Post Office Box A
Amelia, Virginia 23002

Amherst County
100 East Court Street
The Courthouse
Amherst, Virginia 24521

Appomattox County
Post Office Box 672
Appomattox, Virginia 24522

Arlington County
2100 Clarendon Boulevard
Arlington, Virginia 22201

Augusta County
6 East Johnson Street
Staunton, Virginia 24401

Bath County
Post Office Box 180
The Courthouse
Warm Springs, Virginia 24484

Bedford County
129 East Main Street
The Courthouse
Bedford, Virginia 24523

Bland County
Post Office Box 295
Bland, Virginia 24315

Botelourt County
1 West Main Street
Fincastle, Virginia 24090

Bristol County
497 Cumberland Street
Bristol, Virginia 24201

Brunswick County
102 Tobacco Street
Lawrenceville, Virginia 23868

Buchanan County
Post Office Box 950
Grundy, Virginia 24614

Buckingham County
Post Office Box 252
Buckingham, Virginia 23921

Buena Vista County
2039 Sycamore Avenue
Buena Vista, Virginia 24416

Campbell County
Post Office Box 7
Rustburg, Virginia 24588

Caroline County
Post Office Box 309
Bowling Green, Virginia 22427

Carroll County
Post Office Box 515
Hillsville, Virginia 24343

Charles City County
Post Office Box 128
Charles City, Virginia 23030

Charlotte County
Post Office Box 38
Charlotte, Virginia 23923

Charlottesville County
605 East Main Street
Charlottesville, Virginia 22901

Chesapeake County
306 Cedar Road
Chesapeake, Virginia 23320

Chesterfield County
9901 Lon Road
Chesterfield, Virginia 23832

Clarke County
102 North Church Street
Berryville, Virginia 22611

Clifton Forge County
Post Office Box 631
Clifton Forge, Virginia 24422

Colonial Heights County
1507 Boulevard
Colonial Heights, Virginia 23834

Covington County
158 North Court Avenue
Covington, Virginia 24426

Craig County
Post Office Box 185
New Castle, Virginia 24127

Culpeper County
135 West Cameron Street
Culpeper, Virginia 22701

Cumberland County
County Courthouse
Cumberland, Virginia 23040

Danville County
212 Lynn Street
Danville, Virginia 24541

Dickenson County
Post Office Box 190
Clintwood, Virginia 24228

Dinwiddie County
Post Office Box 280
Dinwiddie, Virginia 23841

Emporia County
201 North Main Street
Emporia, Virginia 23817

Essex County
Post Office Box 445
Tappahannock, Virginia 22560

Fairfax County
10455 Armstrong Street
Fairfax, Virginia 22030

Fairfax County
4110 Chain Bridge Road
Fairfax, Virginia 22030

Falls Church County
300 Park Avenue
Falls Church, Virginia 22046

Fauquier County
40 Culpeper Street
Warrenton, Virginia 22186

Floyd County
100 East Main Street
Floyd, Virginia 24091

Fluvanna County
Post Office Box 299
Palmyra, Virginia 22963

Franklin County
207 2nd Avenue West
Franklin, Virginia 23851

Franklin County
Main Street
The Courthouse
Rocky Mount, Virginia 24151

Frederick County
9 Court Square
Winchester, Virginia 22601

Fredericksburg County
Post Office Box 7447
Fredericksburg, Virginia 22404

Giles County
Post Office Box 502
Pearisburg, Virginia 24134

Gloucester County
Post Office Box 329
The Courthouse
Gloucester, Virginia 23061

Goochland County
2938 River Road West
The Courthouse
Goochland, Virginia 23063

Grayson County
129 Davis Street
The Courthouse
Independence, Virginia 24348

Greene County
Court Square
Slanardsville, Virginia 22973

Greensville County
337 South Main Street
Emporia, Virginia 23847

Halifax County
Main Street Courthouse Square
Halifax, Virginia 24558

Hampton County
22 Lincoln Street
Hampton, Virginia 23669

Hanover County
Post Office Box 470
Hanover, Virginia 23069

Harrisonburg County
345 South Main Street
Harrisonburg, Virginia 22801

Henrico County
4301 East Parham Road
Richmond, Virginia 23228

Henry County
Post Office Box 1049
Martinsville, Virginia 24114

Highland County
Main Street
Monterey, Virginia 24465

Hopewell County
300 North Main Street
Hopewell, Virginia 23860

Isle Of Wight County
Highway 258
Isle Of Wight, Virginia 23397

James City County
321-45 Court Street West
Williamsburg, Virginia 23185

King & Queen County
County Courthouse
King & Queen Crthse Virginia 23085,

King George County
Post Office Box 105
King George, Virginia 22485

King William County
Post Office Box 215
King William, Virginia 23086

Lancaster County
Post Office Box 125
Lancaster, Virginia 22503

Lee County
Post Office Box 326
Jonesville, Virginia 24263

Lexington County
Post Office Box 922
Lexington, Virginia 24450

Loudoun County
18 North King Street
Leesburg, Virginia 22075

Louisa County
Post Office Box 160
Louisa, Virginia 23093

Lunenburg County
County Courthouse
Lunenburg, Virginia 23952

Lynchburg County
900 Church Street
Lynchburg, Virginia 24504

Madison County
Post Office Box 220
Madison, Virginia 22727

Manassas Parishark County
1 Park Center Place
Manassas Park, Virginia 22111

Martinsville County
Post Office Box 1112
Martinsville, Virginia 24114

Mathews County
Post Office Box 463
Mathews, Virginia 23109

Mecklenburg County
Washington Street
Boydton, Virginia 23917

Middlesex County
Rts 17 & 33
Saluda, Virginia 23149

Montgomery County
1 East Main Street
Christiansburg, Virginia 24073

Nelson County
Post Office Box 55
Lovingston, Virginia 22949

New Kent County
Post Office Box 98
New Kent, Virginia 23124

Newport News County
2400 Washington Avenue
Newport News, Virginia 23607

Norfolk County
810 Union Street
Norfolk, Virginia 23510

Northampton County
Business Route 13
Eastville, Virginia 23347

Northumberland County
Post Office Box 217
Heathsville, Virginia 22473

Norton County
Post Office Box 618
Norton, Virginia 24273

Nottoway County
Highway 625
Nottoway, Virginia 23955

Orange County
109-A West Main Street
Orange, Virginia 22960

Page County
108 South Court Street
Luray, Virginia 22835

Patrick County
Post Office Box 148
Stuart, Virginia 24171

Petersburg County
Courthouse Hill
Petersburg, Virginia 23803

Pittsylvania County
1 South Main Street
Chatham, Virginia 24531

Poquoson County
830 Poquoson Avenue
Poquoson, Virginia 23662

Portsmouth County
Post Office Box 820
Portsmouth, Virginia 23705

Powhatan County
3834 Old Buckingham Road
Powhatan, Virginia 23139

Prince Edward County
Post Office Box 304
Farmville, Virginia 23901

Prince George County
6400 Courthouse Road
Prince George, Virginia 23875

Prince William County
9311 Lee Avenue
Manassas, Virginia 22110

Pulaski County
45 3rd Street Northwest
Pulaski, Virginia 24301

Radford County
619 2nd Street
Radford, Virginia 24141

Rappahannock County
Post Office Box 517
Washington, Virginia 22747

Richmond County
900 East Broad Street
Richmond, Virginia 23219

Richmond County
10 Court Street
Warsaw, Virginia 22572

Roanoke County
315 Church Avenue Southwest
Roanoke, Virginia 24016

Rockbridge County
2 South Main Street
Lexington, Virginia 24450

Rockingham County
Circuit Court
Harrisonburg, Virginia 22801

Russell County
Post Office Box 435
Lebanon, Virginia 24266

Salem County
114 North Broad Street
Salem, Virginia 24153

Scott County
104 East Jackson Street
Gate City, Virginia 24251

Shenandoah County
112 South Main Street
Woodstock, Virginia 22664

Smyth County
Post Office Box 1025
Marion, Virginia 24354

South Boston County
455 Ferry Street
South Boston, Virginia 24592

Southampton County
County Courthouse
Courtland, Virginia 23837

Spotsylvania County
Post Office Box 99
Spotsylvania, Virginia 22553

Stafford County
Post Office Box 339
Stafford, Virginia 22554

Staunton County
113 East Beverly Street
Staunton, Virginia 24401

Suffolk County
441 Market Street
Suffolk, Virginia 23434

Surry County
Highway 10 & School Street
Surry, Virginia 23883

Sussex County
Route 735
Sussex, Virginia 23884

Tazewell County
315 School Street
Tazewell, Virginia 24651

Virginia Beach County
Municipal Center
Virginia Beach, Virginia 23456

Warren County
22 South Royal Avenue
Front Royal, Virginia 22630

Washington County
216 Park Street Southeast
Abingdon, Virginia 24210

Waynesboro County
250 South Wayne Avenue
Waynesboro, Virginia 22980

Westmoreland County
Polk Street
Montross, Virginia 22520

Williamsburg County
401 Lafayette Street
Williamsburg, Virginia 23185

Winchester County
North Kent Street
Winchester, Virginia 22601

Wise County
108 Main Street
Wise, Virginia 24293

Wythe County
225 South 4th Street
Wytheville, Virginia 24382

York County
Post Office Box 532
Yorktown, Virginia 23690

WASHINGTON

Adams County
210 West Broadway Avenue
Ritzville, Washington 99169

Asotin County
Post Office Box 159
Asotin, Washington 99402

Benton County
Post Office Box 190
Prosser, Washington 99350

Chelan County
Post Office Box 3025
Wenatchee, Washington 98807

Clallam County
223 East 4th Street
Port Angeles, Washington 98362

Clark County
Post Office Box 5000
Vancouver, Washington 98668

Columbia County
341 East Main Street
Dayton, Washington 99328

Cowlitz County
312 Southwest 1st Avenue
Kelso, Washington 98626

Douglas County
Post Office Box 516
Waterville, Washington 98858

Ferry County
Post Office Box 302
Republic, Washington 99166

Franklin County
1016 North 4th Avenue
Pasco, Washington 99301

Garfield County
Post Office Box 915
Pomeroy, Washington 99347

Grant County
Post Office Box 37
Ephrata, Washington 98823

Grays Harbor County
Post Office Box 711
Montesano, Washington 98563

Island County
Post Office Box 5000
Coupeville, Washington 98239

Jefferson County
Post Office Box 1220
Port Townsend, Washington 98368

King County
516 3rd Avenue
Seattle, Washington 98104

Kitsap County
614 Division Street
Port Orchard, Washington 98366

Kittitas County
205 West 5th Avenue
Ellensburg, Washington 98926

Klickitat County
205 South Columbus Avenue
Goldendale, Washington 98620

Lewis County
351 Northwest North Street
Chehalis, Washington 98532

Lincoln County
Post Office Box 369
Davenport, Washington 99122

Mason County
Post Office Box 186
Shelton, Washington 98584

Okanogan County
Post Office Box 72
Okanogan, Washington 98840

Pacific County
Post Office Box 67
South Bend, Washington 98586

Pend Oreille County
Post Office Box 5000
Newport, Washington 99156

Pierce County
930 Tacoma Avenue South
Tacoma, Washington 98402

San Juan County
Post Office Box 1249
Friday Harbor, Washington 98250

Skagit County
Post Office Box 837
Mount Vernon, Washington 98273

Skamanla County
Post Office Box 790
Stevenson, Washington 98648

Snohomish County
3000 Rockefeller Avenue
Everett, Washington 98201

Spokane County
1116 West Broadway Avenue
Spokane, Washington 99260

Stevens County
Post Office Box 191
Colville, Washington 99114

Thurston County
2000 Lakeridge Drive Southwest
Olympia, Washington 98502

Wahkiakum County
Post Office Box 116
Cathlamet, Washington 98612

Walla Walla County
Post Office Box 836
Walla Walla, Washington 99362

Whalcom County
Post Office Box 1144
Bellingham, Washington 98227

Whitman County
400 North Main Street
Colfax, Washington 99111

Yakima County
2nd & B Streets
Yakima, Washington 98901

WEST VIRGINIA

Barbour County
Post Office Box 310
Philippi, West Virginia 26416

Berkeley County
119 West King Street
Martinsburg, West Virginia 25401

Boone County
200 State Street
Madison, West Virginia 25130

Braxton County
Post Office Box 486
Sutton, West Virginia 26601

Brooke County
Main & 7th Streets
Wellsburg, West Virginia 26070

Cabell County
8th Street & 4th Avenue
Huntington, West Virginia 25701

Calhoun County
Main Street
Grantsville, West Virginia 26147

Clay County
Main Street
Clay, West Virginia 25043

Doddridge County
118 East Court Street
West Union, West Virginia 26456

Fayette County
Court Street
Fayetteville, West Virginia 25840

Gilmer County
10 Howard Street
Glenville, West Virginia 26351

Grant County
5 Highland Avenue
Petersburg, West Virginia 26847

Greenbrier County
Post Office Box 506
Lewisburg, West Virginia 24901

Hampshire County
153 West Main Street
Romney, West Virginia 26757

Hancock County
Post Office Box 367
New Cumberland, West Virginia 26047

Hardy County
Washington Street
Moorefield, West Virginia 26836

Harrison County
301 West Main Street
Clarksburg, West Virginia 26301

Jackson County
Court Street
Ripley, West Virginia 25271

Jefferson County
George & Washington Streets
Charles Town, West Virginia 25414

Kanawha County
Post Office Box 3627
Charleston, West Virginia 25336

Lewis County
110 Center Avenue
Weston, West Virginia 26452

Lincoln County
8000 Court Avenue
Hamlin, West Virginia 25523

Logan County
Main & Stratton Streets
Logan, West Virginia 25601

Marion County
211 Adams Street
Fairmont, West Virginia 26554

Marshall County
7th Street
Moundsville, West Virginia 26041

Mason County
6th & Main Street
Point Pleasant, West Virginia 25550

McDowell County
Post Office Box 447
Welch, West Virginia 24801

Mercer County
County Courthouse Square
Princeton, West Virginia 24740

Mineral County
150 Armstrong Street
Keyser, West Virginia 26726

Mingo County
Post Office Box 1197
Williamson, West Virginia 25661

Monongalia County
243 High Street
Morgantown, West Virginia 26505

Monroe County
Main Street
Union, West Virginia 24983

Morgan County
202 Fairfax Street
Berkeley Springs, West Virginia 25411

Nicholas County
700 Main Street
Summersville, West Virginia 26651

Ohio County
205 City County Building
Wheeling, West Virginia 26003

Pendleton County
Post Office Box 89
Franklin, West Virginia 26807

Pleasants County
County Courthouse
Saint Marys, West Virginia 26170

Pocahontas County
900C 10th Avenue
Marlinton, West Virginia 24954

Preston County
101 West Main Street
Kingwood, West Virginia 26537

Putnam County
County Courthouse
Winfield, West Virginia 25213

Raleigh County
215 Main Street
Beckley, West Virginia 25801

Randolph County
2 Randolph Avenue
Elkins, West Virginia 26241

Ritchie County
115 East Main Street
Harrisville, West Virginia 26362

Roane County
200 Main Street
Spencer, West Virginia 25276

Summers County
Ballengee Street
Hinton, West Virginia 25951

Taylor County
214 West Main Street
Grafton, West Virginia 26354

Tucker County
1st & Walnut Streets
Parsons, West Virginia 26287

Tyler County
Post Office Box 66
Middlebourne, West Virginia 26149

Upshur County
Main Street
Buckhannon, West Virginia 26201

Wayne County
Hendricks Street
Wayne, West Virginia 25570

Webster County
Post Office Box 32
Webster Springs, West Virginia 26288

Wetzel County
Post Office Box 156
New Martinsville, West Virginia 26155

Wirl County
Post Office Box 53
Elizabeth, West Virginia 26143

Wood County
Post Office Box 1474
Parkersburg, West Virginia 26102

Wyoming County
Bank Street
Pineville, West Virginia 24874

WISCONSIN

Adams County
Post Office Box 278
Friendship, Wisconsin 53934

Ashland County
201 2nd Street West
Ashland, Wisconsin 54806

Barron County
330 East La Salle Avenue
Barron, Wisconsin 54812

Bayfield County
117 East 5th Street
Washburn, Wisconsin 54891

Brown County
Post Office Box 1600
Green Bay, Wisconsin 54305

Buffalo County
407 North 2nd Street
Alma, Wisconsin 54610

Burnett County
7410 County Road
Siren, Wisconsin 54872

Calumet County
206 Court Street
Chilton, Wisconsin 53014

Chippewa County
711 North Bridge Street
Chippewa Falls, Wisconsin 54729

Clark County
517 Court Street
Neillsville, Wisconsin 54456

Columbia County
Post Office Box 177
Portage, Wisconsin 53901

Crawford County
220 North Beaumont Road
Prairie Du Chien, Wisconsin 53821

Dane County
210 Martin Luther King Jr Boulevard
Madison, Wisconsin 53709

Dodge County
County Courthouse
Juneau, Wisconsin 53039

Door County
138 South 4th Avenue
Sturgeon Bay, Wisconsin 54235

Douglas County
1313 Belknap Street
Superior, Wisconsin 54880

Dunn County
800 Wilson Avenue
Menomonie, Wisconsin 54751

Eau Claire County
721 Oxford Avenue
Eau Claire, Wisconsin 54703

Florence County
Post Office Box 410
Florence, Wisconsin 54121

Fond Du Lac County
160 South Macy Street
Fond Du Lac, Wisconsin 54935

Forest County
County Courthouse
Crandon, Wisconsin 54520

Grant County
130 West Maple Street
Lancaster, Wisconsin 53813

Green County
County Courthouse
Monroe, Wisconsin 53566

Green Lake County
570 South Street
Green Lake, Wisconsin 54941

Iowa County
222 North Iowa Street
Dodgeville, Wisconsin 53533

Iron County
300 Taconite Street
Hurley, Wisconsin 54534

Jackson County
307 Main Street
Black River Falls, Wisconsin 54615

Jefferson County
320 South Main Street
Jefferson, Wisconsin 53549

Juneau County
220 East State Street
Mauston, Wisconsin 53948

Kenosha County
912 56th Street
Kenosha, Wisconsin 53140

Kewaunee County
613 Dodge Street
Kewaunee, Wisconsin 54216

La Crosse County
400 4th Street North
La Crosse, Wisconsin 54601

Lafayette County
626 Main Street
Darlington, Wisconsin 53530

Langlade County
800 Clermont Street
Antigo, Wisconsin 54409

Lincoln County
1110 East Main Street
Merrill, Wisconsin 54452

Manitowoc County
1010 South 8th Street
Manitowoc, Wisconsin 54220

Marathon County
500 Forest Street
Wausau, Wisconsin 54401

Marinette County
1926 Hall Avenue
Marinette, Wisconsin 54143

Marquette County
77 West Park Street
Montello, Wisconsin 53949

Menominee County
County Courthouse
Keshena, Wisconsin 54135

Milwaukee County
901 North 9th Street
Milwaukee, Wisconsin 53233

Monroe County
112 South Court Street
Sparta, Wisconsin 54656

Oconto County
300 Washington Street
Oconto, Wisconsin 54153

Oneida County
Post Office Box 400
Rhinelander, Wisconsin 54501

Outagamie County
410 South Walnut Street
Appleton, Wisconsin 54911

Ozaukee County
121 West Main Street
Port Washington, Wisconsin 53074

Pepin County
740 7th Avenue West
Durand, Wisconsin 54736

Pierce County
Post Office Box 119
Ellsworth, Wisconsin 54011

Polk County
914 1st Avenue North
Balsam Lake, Wisconsin 54810

Portage County
1516 Church Street
Stevens Point, Wisconsin 54481

Price County
100 North Lake Avenue
Phillips, Wisconsin 54555

Racine County
730 Wisconsin Avenue
Racine, Wisconsin 53403

Richland County
Seminary & Central Streets
Richland Center, Wisconsin 53581

Rock County
51 South Main Street
Janesville, Wisconsin 53545

Rusk County
311 Miner Avenue East
Ladysmith, Wisconsin 54848

Saint Croix County
911 4th Street
Hudson, Wisconsin 54016

Sauk County
515 Oak Street
Baraboo, Wisconsin 53913

Sawyer County
Post Office Box 273
Hayward, Wisconsin 54843

Shawano County
311 North Main Street
Shawano, Wisconsin 54166

Sheboygan County
615 North 6th Street
Sheboygan, Wisconsin 53081

Taylor County
224 South 2nd Street
Medford, Wisconsin 54451

Trempealeau County
Post Office Box 67
Whitehall, Wisconsin 54773

Vernon County
West Decker
Viroqua, Wisconsin 54665

Vilas County
Post Office Box 369
Eagle River, Wisconsin 54521

Walworth County
Post Office Box 1001
Elkhorn, Wisconsin 53121

Washburn County
110 West 4th Avenue
Shell Lake, Wisconsin 54871

Washington County
432 East Washington Street
West Bend, Wisconsin 53095

Waukesha County
515 West Moreland Boulevard
Waukesha, Wisconsin 53168

Waupaca County
811 Harding Street
Waupaca, Wisconsin 54981

Waushara County
209 South Saint Marie Street
Wautoma, Wisconsin 54982

Winnebago County
415 Jackson Street
Oshkosh, Wisconsin 54901

Wood County
400 Market Street
Wisconsin Rapids, Wisconsin 54494

WYOMING

Albany County
County Courthouse
Laramie, Wyoming 82070

Big Horn County
Post Office Box 31
Basin, Wyoming 82410

Campbell County
500 South Gillette Avenue
Gillette, Wyoming 82716

Carbon County
Post Office Box 6
Rawlins, Wyoming 82301

Converse County
Post Office Box 990
Douglas, Wyoming 82633

Crook County
Post Office Box 37
Sundance, Wyoming 82729

Fremont County
Post Office Box C
Lander, Wyoming 82520

Goshen County
Post Office Box 160
Torrington, Wyoming 82240

Hot Springs County
415 Arapahoe Street
Thermopolis, Wyoming 82443

Johnson County
76 North Main Street
Buffalo, Wyoming 82834

Laramie County
19th Street & Cary Avenue
Cheyenne, Wyoming 82001

Lincoln County
Post Office Box 670
Kemmerer, Wyoming 83101

Natrona County
200 North Center Street
Casper, Wyoming 82601

Niobrara County
Post Office Box 420
Lusk, Wyoming 82225

Park County
1002 Sheridan Avenue
Cody, Wyoming 82414

Platto County
Post Office Box 728
Wheatland, Wyoming 82201

Telon County
Post Office Box 1727
Jackson, Wyoming 83001

Sheridan County
224 South Main Street
Sheridan, Wyoming 82801

Uinta County
225 9th Street
Evanston, Wyoming 82930

Sublette County
Post Office Box 250
Pinedale, Wyoming 82941

Washakie County
10th Street & Big Horn Avenue
Worland, Wyoming 82401

Sweetwater County
50 West Flaming Gorge Way
Green River, Wyoming 82935

Weston County
1 West Main Street
Newcastle, Wyoming 82701

VOTER'S REGISTRATION

Voter's registration information is available upon written request. Write to the county you believe your subject may have been or is registered in.

The example shown will clearly illustrate how easy it is to ascertain the subject's date of birth and home address. In this case, the only information I had was that the subject named Lub lived in Baldwin, New York, at one time. I was not supplied a first name. I wrote to the Board of Elections of the county of jurisdiction for Baldwin. I sent a nominal fee of $3.00 because this is the average cost of requesting a voter's registration record.

I requested that I be sent the voter's registration information of every person named Lub in Baldwin. In this case I was fortunate that my request was for an unusual name.

The response I was sent stated that the potential subject, Lub, did not live in Baldwin and had moved in 1985. The potential subject's new address was 140 Larch Street, Wantagh, New York and included the date of birth of the potential subject. Since I was aware that my subject had been in a serious accident on a certain date and at a certain location, I ordered this potential subject's driving record. The accident date and location that I had been supplied with matched with what was listed on the driving record.

To be able to write one letter and be provided with a full name for the subject makes this one of the best searching techniques.

OFFICIAL RECEIPT

BOARD OF ELECTIONS 19308
18326

COUNTY OF NASSAU
MINEOLA, NEW YORK 11501

July 25 19 91

$ 3 00

Received of _____

_____ three _____ Dollars

For _____ research request _____

COMMISSIONERS OF ELECTIONS

By _L. Talosky_

Clerk

Sinita Walker, President
Republican Commissioner

John W. Matthews, Secretary
Democratic Commissioner

BOARD OF ELECTIONS
ADMINISTRATION BUILDING
400 COUNTY SEAT DRIVE
MINEOLA, L.I., NEW YORK 11501
(516) 535-2411

July 24, 1991

RE: Lub

To Whom It May Concern:

A letter was received in this office requesting information on the above mentioned, possibly residing in Baldwin, New York.

A search of our official records shows that there was a Kathleen J. Lub who moved out of Baldwin in 1985 and now resides from 140 Larch Street, Wantagh, New York.

Her date of birth is 9/30/56.

Enclosed, is your receipt for research fee. Thank you.

Very truly yours,

Edward ~~~~~~~~~~ Rep. Member

Norbert ~~~~~~~~~~ Dem. Member
Record Access Officers

EH/NAS: lt
enc.

The following are some other records that may assist you in learning more about your subject, thus making the search for the subject's location easier.

OCCUPATIONAL LICENSES

Many counties require that a person who has any type of independent business apply for an occupational or vendor's license. These records are usually filed three ways:

> By name
> By address
> By company name

You may want to request a search be done by address or company name if you have this information. The subject may not be listed if you order the search to be conducted by name because the subject could have changed their name by just a few letters or assumed a whole new identity. When accessing by address or company name, you will be able to evaluate if any of the principles of the company fit the profile of whom you believe your subject to be.

PET LICENSES

Persons that arrange many details of their lives to avoid being found will overlook the fact that the license they had issued for their pet is public record. Write to the county you believe your subject resides in for a list of all pet licenses issued in your subject's name or a spouse.

TAX COLLECTOR/PROPERTY APPRAISER

The tax collector will have an alphabetical listing of all persons that paid property tax. Request that a search be conducted and specify the years. The tax collector maintains records that go back in time longer than any other record. The necessity of title companies to trace a complete history of property ownership is the reason these records are maintained for perpetuity.

Property may be owned by your subject and a review of the tax bill may show that the address it is being sent to is out of state or in another country.

You may want to question the present owners of any property your subject had owned at one time. Your subject may hold a mortgage on the property and there may be constant contact between the present owners and your subject.

SMALL CLAIMS COURT

If a search of county records reveals that your subject had a case filed in small claims court, you will want to order the complete file. The file will contain the address of the subject, any witnesses the subject subpoenaed to court, and details about the court case. You may want to review the subpoena the subject was served if the subject had been a defendant in the case. The subpoena will have noted the address the subject had been served at. If the subject had been trying to conceal their whereabouts, but was found by a process server, then you will want to pay special attention to this address because it may be different than the listed home address.

When an individual or company has a case decided in their favor in Small Claims Court, they are entitled to file a lien against any property that the defendant owns, if the damages awarded are not paid.

The plaintiff, in many instances, is made aware of the ownership of property by the defendant through a questionnaire that the judge, at the request of the plaintiff, ordered the defendant to answer. The questions ask about property ownership, stocks, bank account locations, etc. You may review this question-naire, which is part of the court file. You will be able to glean a location of your subject by checking the current address from the aforementioned.

FICTITIOUS NAMES

Your subject may own a business but did not want to incorporate. Your subject would be required to apply for a fictitious name if they wanted to open a business account at a bank. Your subject could have a house painting, landscaping, accounting, hot-dog vending cart or any type of business and they will have filed a fictitious name with the county. The application on file will provide you with home and business addresses.

Write to the county asking that a search be conducted. Provide the subject's full name and the years you want searched.

APPLICATION FOR
REGISTRATION OF FICTITIOUS NAME

Section 1

1. Investments Unlimited
   Fictitious Name to be Registered

2. 5686 36th Street
   Mailing Address of Business
   White Plains,   32801

3. County of Westchester

4. City of White Plains, Florida 32801

5. FEI Number: _____ Zip Code

This space for office use only

Section 2

A. Owner(s) of Fictitious Name If Individual(s) (use additional sheets if necessary):

1. Rogers, Harold
   Last   First   M.I.
   15672 Emeet Street
   Address
   Orlando, Florida 32801
   City   State   Zip Code
   SS# 251-28-2982

2. Hadesty, Nancy
   Last   First   M.I.
   15672 Emeet Street
   Address
   Orlando, Florida 32801
   City   State   Zip Code
   SS# 325-78-2789

B. Owner(s) of Fictitious Name If Corporation(s) (use additional sheets if necessary):

1. N/A
   Corporate Name
   _____
   Address
   _____
   City   State   Zip Code
   Corporate Document Number: _____
   FEI Number: _____
   ☐ Applied for   ☐ Not Applicable

2. N/A
   Corporate Name
   _____
   Address
   _____
   City   State   Zip Code
   Corporate Document Number: _____
   FEI Number: _____
   ☐ Applied for   ☐ Not Applicable

Section 3

I (we) the undersigned, being the sole (all the) party(ies) owning interest in the above fictitious name, certify that the information indicated on this form is true and accurate. I (we) further certify that the fictitious name shown in Section 1 of this form has been advertised at least once in a newspaper as defined in chapter 50, Florida Statutes, in the county where the applicant's principal place of business is located. I (we) understand that the signature(s) below shall have the same legal effect as if made under oath. (At Least One Signature Required)

Harold H. R___
Signature of Owner   Date
Phone Number: 407-982-9276

Nancy Hardesty
Signature of Owner   Date
Phone Number: 407-982-9276

PENDING LITIGATION

If you have information that your subject had been at fault in an automobile accident, then you will want to find out in what county the accident occurred. Write to that county once a month and eventually a suit may be filed, naming your subject as the defendant. If an action is filed, you will want to order the file. As noted previously, check the file for the address that your subject was served at. Paternity suits, judgments, tax liens and foreclosures are some actions that may not be listed now but are public records you may be able to anticipate the filing of.

POWER OF ATTORNEY

Pay special attention to any filing that involves your subject that is listed as Power of Attorney. You will want to know the person's name that your subject gave Power of Attorney to. If you are having difficulty in finding anything under your subject's name, this may be the reason why. Persons that are trying to avoid detection will often give Power of Attorney to a family member or close friend. That person will then conduct all business transactions on behalf of your subject thus giving the subject the benefit of not having their name listed in public records.

ASSET CHECKS

If you have a judgment against an individual or a business then you may wish to conduct an asset check to determine if any property exists that can be attached by lien. You may use the addresses in this manual to check for ownership of automobiles, trucks, motorcycles, recreational vehicles, boats, aircrafts, real estate, etc.

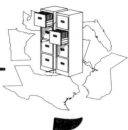

5

State Records

The State licenses many professions, trades and crafts. Write to the Secretary of State (see addresses in Chapter Eight) and submit your subject's name to be searched for any licensure by the state. The following are some occupations that may require licensing.

Aircraft Mechanics	Bill Collectors
Airports	Builders/Carpenters
Alarm Contractor	Building Contractors
Alarm Installers	Building Wreckers
Auctioneers	Carpet Cleaners
Auto Inspectors	Certified Public Accountants
Auto Wreckers	Embalmers
Bankers	Investigators
Barbers	Notary Public

Pawnbrokers	Security Guards
Pest Controllers	Stock Brokers
Pet Groomers	Surveyors
Pharmacists	Talent Agents
Pilots	Teachers
Real Estate Agents and Brokers	Therapists
Scrap Dealers	Veterinarians
Security Dealers	X-Ray Technicians

If your subject is licensed by the state for any of the above occupations or any others not listed, then you will be able to receive, at least, the following information from the licensing board: work and home address, length of time the subject has been licensed, the schools attended to be certified if applicable, date of birth and any complaints lodged against the subject.

Of course the most important information will be the addresses that you are given but you may want to take special note of any complaints filed. If the addresses listed do not prove to be valid, you will want to review the complaint file. A court or hearing date may be scheduled in the near future and the exact date and location will be listed. You can then meet your subject when he/she appears for the complaint hearing.

The employer of the subject will be part of the information the licensing department will be giving you. You now have a location that you can write to or visit.

COLLEGES AND UNIVERSITIES

There are over 3,500 colleges and universities in the United States. If you are aware of the institution of higher learning that your subject had attended, then inquiring about "directory information" may yield much information. The term "directory information" is used to describe the information that the school will release to the public about the student.

The following is a quote from Florida State University regarding the school's "directory information" policy:

> "*Prior consent of the student is **not required*** for disclosure of portions of the educational record defined by the institution as DIRECTORY INFORMATION, which can be released via official media of the University:
>
> **Name, date, and place of birth**
> **Local address**
> **Permanent address**
> **Telephone listing**
> **Classification**
> **Major field of study**
> **Participation in official University activities and sports**
> **Weight and height of members of athletic teams**
> **Dates of attendance at the University**
> **Degrees, honors, and awards received**
> **The most recently attended educational institution.**"

Stanford University's "directory information" policy is quoted as follows:

> "The University regards the following items of information as 'directory information,' i.e., information **available to any person** upon specific request:
>
> **Student name**
> **Sex**
> **Class status**
> **Major**
> **Local address and/or Stanford Post Office Box number**
> **Local phone number**
> **Permanent or legal address**
> **Summer address**
> **Summer phone number**

Residence assignment and room or apartment number
Stanford student identification number
Specific quarters or semesters of registration at Stanford
Stanford degree(s) awarded and date(s), degree major(s)
University degree honors
Institution attended immediately prior to Stanford"

The above information that is released is obviously about currently enrolled students. You may contact the alumni association and you will receive the same information regarding former students.

Even though the permanent address listed may be years old, you may want to check the owner of record with the tax collector to see if the family of your subject is still the owner. Also, do not overlook the summer residence that is listed. The address will, in many instances, prove to be a vacation home that the subject's family still owns.

The date of birth and place of birth is of obvious value. You now have an exact date of birth that can be utilized to access the driving record of the subject. Even though years have passed, you may want to try calling the telephone numbers listed. In many instances, these numbers will still be good numbers that will enable you to contact the family.

HUNTING AND FISHING LICENSES

Even if your subject is trying to avoid detection, the subject will still want to be issued a license for hunting or fishing, if this is their sport. The reason the subject will want to have a current license is to avoid being arrested by a game warden or other law enforcement official when enjoying their sport. Write to the state and submit a request asking that an alpha search be conducted on your subject so that you may ascertain if they do have a hunting or fishing license.

If you are successful with your inquiry, you will receive the subject's current address, date of birth and the current status of the license. If the license has been expired for some time, then you will want to use the date of birth that you received and order the subject's driving record.

HUNTING & FISHING LICENSES

ALABAMA

Hunting and Fishing Licenses
Department of Conservation
State of Alabama
State Administrative Building
Montgomery, Alabama 36130

ALASKA

Hunting and Fishing Licenses
State of Alaska
Post Office Box 6188 Annex
Anchorage, Alaska 99502

ARIZONA

Hunting and Fishing Licenses
Game and Fish Department
State of Arizona
2221 West Greenway Road
Phoenix, Arizona 85023

ARKANSAS

Hunting and Fishing Licenses
State of Arkansas
2 Natural Resources Drive
Little Rock, Arkansas 72205

CALIFORNIA

Hunting and Fishing Licenses
State of California
Post Office Box 11319
Sacramento, California 95853

COLORADO

Hunting and Fishing Licenses
Division of Parks & Outdoor Recreation
State of Colorado
13787 South Highway 85
Littleton, Colorado 80125

CONNECTICUT

Hunting and Fishing Licenses
State of Connecticut
165 Capitol Avenue
Hartford, Connecticut 06106

DELAWARE

Hunting and Fishing Licenses
Division of Fish and Wildlife
State of Delaware
Post Office Box 1401
Dover, Delaware 19903

DISTRICT OF COLUMBIA

Hunting and Fishing Licenses
District of Columbia
550 Water Street, S.W.
Washington, D.C. 20024

FLORIDA

Hunting and Fishing Licenses
Department of Natural Resources
State of Florida
3900 Commonwealth Boulevard
Tallahassee, Florida 32399

GEORGIA

Hunting and Fishing Licenses
Department of Natural Resources
State of Georgia
270 Washington Street, S.W.
Atlanta, Georgia 30034

HAWAII

Hunting and Fishing Licenses
State of Hawaii
79 South Nimitz Highway
Honolulu, Hawaii 96813

IDAHO

Hunting and Fishing Licenses
State of Idaho
2177 Warm Springs Avenue
Boise, Idaho 83720

ILLINOIS

Hunting and Fishing Licenses
Conservation Department
State of Illinois
524 South Second Street
Springfield, Illinois 62701

INDIANA

Hunting and Fishing Licenses
Department of Natural Resources
State of Indiana
402 West Washington St.
Indianapolis, Indiana 46204

IOWA

Hunting and Fishing Licenses
State Conservation Commission
State of Iowa
Wallace Building
Des Moines, Iowa 50319

KANSAS

Hunting and Fishing Licenses
Kansas Department of Wildlife
R. R. No. 2, Box 54A
Pratt, Kansas 67124

KENTUCKY

Hunting and Fishing Licenses
Department of Natural Resources
1 Game Farm Road
Frankfort, Kentucky 40601

LOUISIANA

Hunting and Fishing Licenses
Department of Wildlife and Fisheries
State of Louisiana
Post Office Box 14796
Baton Rouge, Louisiana 70898

MAINE

Hunting and Fishing Licenses
Department of Fisheries and Wildlife
State of Maine
284 State Street
Augusta, Maine 04333

MARYLAND

Hunting and Fishing Licenses
Department of Natural Resources
State of Maryland
Post Office Box 1869
Annapolis, Maryland 21404-1869

MASSACHUSETTS

Hunting and Fishing Licenses
Commonwealth of Massachusetts
100 Nashua Street
Boston, Massachusetts 02114

MICHIGAN

Hunting and Fishing Licenses
State of Michigan
7064 Crowner Drive
Lansing, Michigan 48918

MINNESOTA

Hunting and Fishing Licenses
Department of Natural Resources
State of Minnesota
500 Lafayette Road
Saint Paul, Minnesota 55146

MISSISSIPPI

Hunting and Fishing Licenses
Department of Wildlife Conservation
Post Office Box 451
Jackson, Mississippi 39205

MISSOURI

Hunting and Fishing Licenses
Department of Conservation
State of Missouri
2901 West Truman Boulevard
Jefferson City, Missouri 65102

MONTANA

Hunting and Fishing Licenses
State of Montana
1420 East Sixth Avenue
Helena, Montana 59620

NEBRASKA

Hunting and Fishing Licenses
State Game and Parks Commission
State of Nebraska
2200 North 33rd Street
Lincoln, Nebraska 68503

NEVADA

Hunting and Fishing Licenses
Department of Wildlife
State of Nevada
Post Office Box 10678
Reno, Nevada 89520

NEW HAMPSHIRE

Hunting and Fishing Licenses
State of New Hampshire
10 Hazen Drive
Concord, New Hampshire 03305

NEW JERSEY

Hunting and Fishing Licenses
State of New Jersey
Post Office Box 7068
West Trenton, New Jersey 08625

NEW MEXICO

Hunting and Fishing Licenses
Natural Resources Department
State of New Mexico
Post Office Box 1147
Santa Fe, New Mexico 87504

NEW YORK

Hunting and Fishing Licenses
State of New York
Empire State Plaza
Albany, New York 12238

NORTH CAROLINA

Hunting and Fishing Licenses
Wildlife Resources Commission
State of North Carolina
512 North Salisbury Street
Raleigh, North Carolina 27604

NORTH DAKOTA

Hunting and Fishing Licenses
State Game and Fish Department
State of North Dakota
2121 Lovett Avenue
Bismarck, North Dakota 58505

OHIO

Hunting and Fishing Licenses
Department of Natural Resources
State of Ohio
Fountain Square
Columbus, Ohio 43224

OKLAHOMA

Hunting and Fishing Licenses
State of Oklahoma
2501 North Lincoln
Oklahoma City, Oklahoma 73194

OREGON

Hunting and Fishing Licenses
State of Oregon
3000 Market Street, N.E.
Salem, Oregon 97310

PENNSYLVANIA

Hunting and Fishing Licenses
Commonwealth of Pennsylvania
3532 Walnut Street
Harrisburg, Pennsylvania 17105

PUERTO RICO

Hunting and Fishing Licenses
Commonwealth of Puerto Rico
GPO Box 2829
San Juan, Puerto Rico 00936

RHODE ISLAND
Hunting and Fishing Licenses
State of Rhode Island
22 Hayes Street
Providence, Rhode Island 02903

SOUTH CAROLINA
Hunting and Fishing Licenses
State of South Carolina
Post Office Box 11710
Columbia, South Carolina 29211

SOUTH DAKOTA
Hunting and Fishing Licenses
State of South Dakota
412 West Missouri Street
Pierre, South Dakota 57501

TENNESSEE
Hunting and Fishing Licenses
Tennessee Wildlife Resources Agency
Ellington Agriculture Center
Nashville, Tennessee 37204

TEXAS
Hunting and Fishing Licenses
State of Texas
4200 Smith School Road
Austin, Texas 78744

UTAH
Hunting and Fishing Licenses
State of Utah
1095 Motor Avenue
Salt Lake City, Utah 84116

VERMONT
Hunting and Fishing Licenses
State of Vermont
103 Main Street
Waterbury, Vermont 05676

VIRGINIA
Hunting and Fishing Licenses
Commission of Game & Inland Fisheries
State of Virginia
Post Office Box 11104
Richmond, Virginia 23230

VIRGIN ISLANDS
Hunting and Fishing Licenses
Department of Natural Resources
State of Virgin Islands
Nisky Center, Suite 231
St. Thomas, U.S. Virgin Islands 00803

WASHINGTON
Hunting and Fishing Licenses
Department of Natural Resources
State of Washington
Post Office Box 43135
Olympia, Washington 98504

WEST VIRGINIA
Hunting and Fishing Licenses
Department of Natural Resources
State of West Virginia
1800 Washington Street, East
Charleston, West Virginia 25305

WISCONSIN
Hunting and Fishing Licenses
Department of Natural Resources
State of Wisconsin
Post Office Box 7921
Madison, Wisconsin 53707

WYOMING
Hunting and Fishing Licenses
Game and Fish Department
State of Wyoming
5400 Bishop Boulevard
Cheyenne, Wyoming 82002

DEPARTMENT OF GAME, FISH AND PARKS
Licensing Office
412 West Missouri
Pierre, South Dakota 57501
(605) 773-3393

March 2, 1993

Dear Joseph:

We find no record in our current files of a Robert K. Pavella having any kind of South Dakota hunting or fishing license.

Sincerely,

Chuck Schlueter
Administrative Asst.

NOTES

Federal Records

MILITARY RECORDS

Under the Freedom of Information Act, you are permitted access to the following information about military personnel:

> **Full name**
> **Rank**
> **Gross salary**
> **Past duty assignments**
> **Present duty assignments**
> **Office or duty telephone number**
> **Awards and decorations**
> **Attendance at military schools**

The most important information from the above list is, of course, the present duty assignment of your subject. If your subject has a close relative in the Armed

Forces, then you will want to order their records. This relative can turn out to be an excellent source and may give you the location of your subject.

Army:
Chief, Information Access Section
HQ USAISC (ASQNS-OP-F)
Hoffman I, Room 1146
2461 Eisenhower Avenue
Alexandria, Virginia 22331-0301

Air Force:
Secretary of the Air Force
Freedom of Information Manager
SAF/AADS (FOIA)
Pentagon, Room 4A1088C
Washington, D.C. 20330-1000

Navy:
Director, OPNAV Services and Security Division
OP-09B30
Pentagon, Room 5E521
Washington, D.C. 20350-2000

Marine Corps:
Freedom of Information and Privacy Act
Office (Code MI-3)
Headquarters, U.S. Marine Corps, Room 4327
Washington, D.C. 20380-0001

Coast Guard:
Freedom of Information Act
Commandant of the Coast Guard
2100 Second Street, Southwest
Washington, D.C. 20593-0201

MILITARY LOCATOR SERVICES

The military will supply you with the current unit number and installation to which a person on active duty is assigned. If the person is retired, a letter will be forwarded to them.

ARMY

Active Duty

Army Locator
Fort Benjamin, Indiana 46249

Retired

Army Personnel Center
Attention: DARP—PAS
9700 Page Boulevard
Saint Louis, Missouri 63132

AIR FORCE

Active Duty

Air Force Locator Service
Air Force Military Personnel Center
Randolph Air Force Base, Texas 78150

Retired

Retired Personnel Command
Air Force Military Personnel Center
Randolph Air Force Base, Texas 78150

NAVY

Active Duty

Naval Personnel Command Locator Service
NMC–21
Washington, D.C. 20307

Retired

Retired Personnel Command Locator Service
4400 Dauphin Street
New Orleans, Louisiana 70149

MARINE CORPS

Active Duty

Marine Corps Locator Service
MMRD–10
Commandant of the Marine Corps
Washington, D.C. 20380

Retired

Marine Corps Retired Locator Service
MMRD–06
Commandant of the Marine Corps
Washington, D.C. 20380

COAST GUARD

Active Duty

United States Coast Guard Locator Service
Commandant – G-PIM
2100 Second Street, Southwest
Washington, D.C. 20593

Retired

United States Coast Guard
Retired Locator Service
G–PS–5
2100 Second Street, Southwest
Washington, D.C. 20593

DEPARTMENT OF VETERANS AFFAIRS

The Department of Veterans Affairs will also forward a letter from you to a veteran. There is no charge for this service.

Department of Veterans Affairs
Veterans Benefits Administration
Administrative Support Staff (20A52)
810 Vermont Avenue, Northwest
Washington, D.C. 20420

THE SALVATION ARMY

I am including the Salvation Army in this chapter even though it is not a federal agency.

The Salvation Army has a very competent and experienced missing persons bureau. They will conduct a search for you to find a father, mother, brother, sister, son or daughter. **The fee is just ten dollars**. Contact the local Salvation Army listed in the white pages of your telephone book.

PATERNITY AND CHILD SUPPORT LOCATOR SERVICE

If you want to contact your subject because of a paternity or child support matter then you may use the following address. This center will locate your subject and then guide you on what procedures to follow.

Armed Services Community and Family Support
Attention: TAPC–PDO–IP
200 Stovall Street
Alexandria, Virginia   22331

CIVIL AIR PATROL LOCATOR SERVICE
Active Duty and Retired
Civil Air Patrol Locator Service
G–10
Maxwell Air Force Base, Alabama   36112

UNITED STATES CIVIL SERVICE

If your subject is a current or retired civil servant then you will want to write to the Office of Personnel Management. They will give you the work site address of a current employee or, if the subject is retired, forward a letter from you.

United States Office of Personnel Management
1900 East E Street
Washington, D.C.   20415

RAILROAD RETIREMENT BOARD

The Railroad Retirement Board administers the retirement and survivor benefit programs provided the nation's railroad workers and their families. If your subject was a railroad worker and you believe that they may be collecting benefits then write to the Board and request that they forward a letter to the subject from you.

> Railroad Retirement Board
> 844 Rush Street
> Chicago, Illinois 60611

UNITED STATES PUBLIC HEALTH PERSONNEL

You may write to the following address if your subject has ever been employed by the United States Public Health Service. They will forward a letter from you if the person is retired. If your subject is currently employed, you will be supplied with their grade and salary information, employment address and date that employment started.

> United States Public Health Service
> Department of Health and Human Services
> PHS/O5G/DCP
> 5600 Fishers Lane
> Parklawn Building, Room 4-35
> Rockville, Maryland 20857

PEACE CORPS

If you have reason to believe that your subject has or is now serving in the Peace Corps, you will want to write requesting that a letter be forwarded to the subject at the last known address. Also request that you be supplied with the dates of service and duty locations of the subject.

If you are unable to secure any driving records, vehicle registrations or other public record information regarding the subject, then this may indicate that they may have returned to a location of duty to reside. Look at this avenue closely if your subject does not respond to a forwarded letter.

> Peace Corps
> 1990 K Street, Northwest
> Washington, D.C. 20526

UNITED STATES SOLDIERS' AND AIRMENS' HOME

The United States Soldiers' and Airmen's Home is a fine source to contact if your subject is a person that has been missing for many years and was a member of the Armed Forces. Inquire by name and the Home will inform you if your subject now resides there.

This is a good source to use if you believe that the subject's father resides at the home. You may be able to receive information from the father that will lead to the location of your subject.

> United States Soldiers' and Airmens' Home
> 3700 North Capitol Street, Northwest
> Washington, D.C. 20317

FEDERAL AVIATION ADMINISTRATION

If your subject is a pilot or owns an aircraft, you may write to the Federal Aviation Administration. A search will be conducted by name. The subject's address, date of birth, pilot rating and even the date of the last medical exam will be furnished to you if the subject has a pilot's license.

You may wish to order a list of any aircraft your subject may own. The request for a search can be conducted by your subject's name or by the name of the company he owns. If there is a listing of an aircraft, you will be given the address that the aircraft is registered to, the year and make of the aircraft, the name of pilots that will utilize the aircraft and the name of the insurance carrier.

Once you have the registration number for an aircraft, the name of all the previous owners may be retrieved. These former owners may have a personal knowledge of the habits and personal details of the life of your subject. Order a copy of the bill of sale of the aircraft that your subject owns. This document will contain much information including witnesses to the signing of the bill of sale and their addresses, the name of the financial institution that may have a lien on the aircraft and the names and addresses of any other owners. The aforementioned sources may be able to direct you to the location of your subject if your subject cannot be located at the address listed on the registration.

> Federal Aviation Administration
> Post Office Box 25504
> Oklahoma City, Oklahoma 73125

INTERSTATE COMMERCE COMMISSION

If your subject is in any form of the transportation business that crosses state lines, there will be records with important information on file. The Interstate Commerce Commission regulates moving companies, trucking firms and many other entities that use the nation's interstate highway system.

> Interstate Commerce Commission
> 12th Street and Constitution Avenue
> Washington, D.C. 20423

PASSPORT RECORDS

If you are searching for a subject that may have been a minor when they were taken and hidden by an adult years ago, you may want to explore passport records. If, for instance, you discover that the person who had absconded with the minor has died but you do not have the whereabouts of the subject, write for the passport records of the deceased.

These records will contain the information that was on the passport application. This information will, of course, list much personal data about the deceased including addresses, references, etc. that will, perhaps, give you new information that may lead to the location of your subject. Many times the person and address listed by the applicant to contact in case of emergency may be the person that now has possession of your subject.

Third party requestors may request the release of documents in the custody of the Department of State, under provisions of the Freedom of Information Act (5 USC 552). Write to:

> Department of State
> Office of Freedom of Information (IM/IS/FPC)
> 2201 C Street, Northwest
> Washington, D.C. 20520-1239

While on the subject of passports, you may need to obtain one if your search indicates that your subject is abroad. The following is a complete list of all United States Passport Agencies. You may also apply for a Passport at many larger Post Offices and at certain state and federal courts.

PASSPORT AGENCIES

Boston Passport Agency
Thomas P. O'Neill Federal Building
10 Causeway Street
Boston, Massachusetts 02222
*Recording: (617) 565-6998
**Public Inquiries: (617) 565-6990

Chicago Passport Agency
Kluczynski Federal Building
230 South Dearborn Street
Chicago, Illinois 60604
*Recording: (342) 353-5426
**Public Inquiries: (342) 353-7155

Honolulu Passport Agency
New Federal Building
300 Ala Moana Boulevard
Honolulu, Hawaii 96850
*Recording: (808) 541-1919
**Public Inquiries: (808) 541-1918

Houston Passport Agency
Concord Towers
1919 Smith Street
Houston, Texas 77002
*Recording: (713) 653-3159
**Public Inquiries: (713) 229-3600

Los Angeles Passport Agency
11000 Wilshire Boulevard
Los Angeles, California 90024
*Recording: (213) 209-7070
**Public Inquiries: (213) 209-7075

Miami Passport Agency
Federal Office Building
51 Southwest First Avenue
Miami, Florida 33130
*Recording: (305) 536-5395 (English)
                536-4448 (Spanish)
**Public Inquiries: (305) 536-4681

New Orleans Passport Agency
Postal Services Building
Room T—12005
701 Loyola Avenue
New Orleans, Louisiana 70113
*Recording: (504) 589-6728
**Public Inquiries: (504) 589-6161

New York Passport Agency
Rockefeller Center
630 Fifth Avenue
New York, New York 10111
*Recording: (212) 541-7700
**Public Inquiries: (212) 541-7710

Philadelphia Passport Agency
Federal Building
600 Arch Street
Philadelphia, Pennsylvania 19106
*Recording: (215) 597-7482
**Public Inquiries: (215) 597-7480, 7481

San Francisco Passport Agency
525 Market Street
San Francisco, California 94105
*Recording: (415) 974-7972
**Public Inquiries: (415) 974-9941, 9948

Seattle Passport Agency
Federal Office Building
915 Second Avenue
Seattle, Washington 98174
*Recording: (206) 442-7941
**Public Inquiries: (206) 442-7945

Stamford Passport Agency
One Landmark Square
Street Level
Stamford, Connecticut 06901
*Recording: (203) 325-4401
**Public Inquiries: (203) 325-3538, 3539

UNITED STATES COURT OF MILITARY APPEALS

The United States Court of Military Appeals was created by Congress in 1950 and is composed of three civilian judges. Even though this court operates as part of the Department of Defense for administrative purposes, it is independent of any influence from the military. The court's function is to be an impartial final appeal board for members of the military that have been convicted of crimes.

You will want to order a photocopy of your subject's complete court file if they have ever availed themselves of this avenue of redress. The file will contain information you will need to start a current search for your subject. The date of birth, Social Security Number, grade and rank information, addresses and the details of the court case will be part of the file.

United States Court of Military Appeals
450 E Street, Northwest
Washington, D.C. 20442

UNITED STATES COURT OF VETERANS APPEALS

Your subject may be a veteran of the Armed Forces that had made an appeal to the United States Court of Veterans Appeals. Cases are filed, in some cases, decades after the veteran had been separated from the service.

Much information such as Social Security Number, date of birth and home address will be in this public record. Spouse and dependent information will be included if applicable and they may be easier to contact than the subject and can be of assistance in locating your subject.

United States Court of Veterans Appeal
625 Indiana Avenue
Washington, D.C. 20004

THE UNITED STATES CLAIMS COURT

The United States Claims Court may have been used by your subject to make a claim against the Federal Government. If you had heard that at one time your subject had filed suit then you can write and order a photocopy of the court file. You will be able to learn such information as the Social Security Number, date of birth, home and business address and the spouse information of the subject.

The amount of any award of damages will be listed. If the address of the subject contained in the file is no longer valid then you will be able to use the other listed personal information to continue your search.

United States Claims Court
717 Madison Place, Northwest
Washington, D.C. 20005

UNITED STATES TAX COURT

Congress created the United States Tax Court to provide a forum where a taxpayer may dispute a deficiency in taxes claimed by the Internal Revenue Service. The court allows only cases where the amount disputed is $10,000 or less.

Write to the tax court for a photocopy of the court file if you believe your subject may have had a case heard in this arena. The file will contain much information that will be of a personal nature such as Social Security Number, home and business address, name of spouse and nature of the tax dispute.

If you have reason to believe a parent or close relative may have had a case in this court and you do not know where this person can be found at the present time then you may order that person's file. The information supplied will enable you to contact the relative and query them on the whereabouts of your subject.

United States Tax Court
400 Second Street, Northwest
Washington, D.C. 20217

GENERAL SERVICES ADMINISTRATION

The General Services Administration's function is to evaluate and award contracts to firms so that they may supply products or services to branches of the Federal Government. If your subject is a business person and you have reason to believe that he may have conducted business with the Federal Government, then you will want to request photocopies of the files containing the contracts that have been or presently are in force.

The contracts will have the business and, in many instances, home address, the Social Security Number, personal references, business and bank references, former addresses and other important information regarding the subject that will assist you in your search for the subject.

General Services Administration
CAIR/Room 3016
18th & F Street, Northwest
Washington, D.C. 20405

Many times I will need the telephone number and address of an agency of the Federal Government that I believe a subject may be employed by. I will want to check employment status with the least amount of delay. The following toll-free telephone numbers are of great assistance. The operators that staff these centers have access to every telephone number and address in the Federal Government so even if the agency is obscure, this number will be able to satisfy your inquiry.

ALABAMA
(800) 366-2998

ALASKA
(800) 729-8003

ARIZONA
(800) 359-3997

ARKANSAS
(800) 366-2998

CALIFORNIA
Los Angeles, San Diego, San Francisco, Santa Ana
(800) 726-4995
Sacramento
(916) 973-1695

COLORADO
(800) 359-3997

CONNECTICUT
(800) 347-1997

FLORIDA
(800) 347-1997

GEORGIA
(800) 347-1997

HAWAII
(800) 733-5996

ILLINOIS
(800) 366-2998

INDIANA
Gary
(800) 366-2998
Indianapolis
(800) 347-1997

IOWA
(800) 735-8004

KANSAS
(800) 735-8004

KENTUCKY
(800) 347-1997

LOUISIANA
(800) 366-2998

MARYLAND
(800) 347-1997

MASSACHUSETTS
(800) 347-1997

MICHIGAN
(800) 347-1997

MINNESOTA
(800) 366-2998

MISSOURI
St. Louis
(800) 366-2998
All other locations
(800) 735-8004

NEBRASKA
Omaha
(800) 366-2998
All other locations
(800) 735-8004

NEW JERSEY
(800) 347-1997

NEW MEXICO
(800) 359-3997

NEW YORK
(800) 347-1997

NORTH CAROLINA
(800) 347-1997

OHIO
(800) 347-1997

OKLAHOMA
(800) 366-2998

OREGON
(800) 726-4995

PENNSYLVANIA
(800) 347-1997

TENNESSEE	**VIRGINIA**
(800) 366-2998	(800) 347-1997
TEXAS	**WASHINGTON**
(800) 366-2998	(800) 726-4995
UTAH	**WISCONSIN**
(800) 359-3997	(800) 366-2998

Call (301) 722-9098 if your state is not listed or one of the above telephone numbers is inoperable.

UNITED STATES POST OFFICE

The Postal Service will not provide you with a street address for a person who uses a Post Office Box for personal mail. But if your subject is conducting business using a Post Office Box for business purposes, the Post Office is required by law to furnish you with the street address. The street address may be of significant importance because this may actually be the residence of your subject. You may wish to check with the property appraiser's office to see who owns property.

UNITED STATES GOVERNMENT DEPOSITORY LIBRARIES

Libraries that are considered complete and well-rounded are selected by the Superintendent of Documents to participate in the Depository Library Program. These libraries will receive all Federal Government publications free of charge if they pledge to make available free access to their facilities for all library patrons.

The libraries selected to be United States Government Depository Libraries must maintain a high standard of responsiveness, inventory and access. This is a quote from the congressional edict that will clearly demonstrate that the government is serious about the accountability of the Depository Libraries:

"The Superintendent of Documents shall make firsthand investigation of conditions for which need is indicated and include the results of investigations in his annual report. When he ascertains that the number of books in a depository library is below ten thousand, other than

Government publications, or it has ceased to be maintained so as to be **accessible to the public**, or that the Government publications which have been furnished the library have not been properly maintained, he shall delete the library from the list of depository libraries if the library fails to correct the unsatisfactory conditions within six months."

I use these particular libraries because they provide a level of service and availability of different publications that I require for research. These libraries, for instance, have on hand criss-cross directories. These directories can be accessed two ways:

1. **The listings are by telephone number.** Look for a telephone number in the numerical listing and, if the number is a published number, it will show the name and address of the person with that telephone number.

2. **The listings are by address.** You may look up a street address and you will be shown the name of the occupant and the telephone number corresponding to the address. All of the information on the neighbors will, of course, also be in the sequence.

The library will have the books for the locale you are in and, in many instances, the books for the surrounding cities will be available. The libraries also keep the previous issues of the criss-cross directories for several years. The importance of these publications is obvious. You may have retrieved a telephone number in your search but no address. Now you have the means to find the address. Or you may have an address, but no telephone number.

If the information operator is not of any assistance because your subject does not have the telephone number listed under his name, use the criss-cross directory. Retrieval of the telephone number at the subject's address is possible because the telephone listing is by address, not name. From these books you now have the names, addresses, and telephone numbers of all the neighbors of your subject.

The library will have a publication called "Directory of United States Public and Private Companies". You will want to review this reference if you believe your subject to be an owner of a business. The list of over 107,000 businesses (of which 90% are privately held) includes the names of the principals in the business, address, regular and fax telephone numbers, financial information and corporate structure information. Search for the company name you feel the subject may be using. Many persons will move to another state and use basically the same company name that they had used previously.

You may want to refer to the publication that is called the "Congressional Directory." Not only does this book list the names, addresses and telephone numbers of members of Congress, but it contains the names, addresses and telephone numbers of every Freedom of Information officer in every agency of the Federal Government. You are permitted to ask if your subject is an employee of any department of government by just directing your inquiry to the appropriate Freedom of Information Officer.

If your subject was or is a member of any union, trade organization, hobby group or club, then you will be able to access the address and telephone number of the desired organization. Ask for the Gale Research edition of organizations and you will have over 47,000 entries to assist you in locating the correct information. The international edition lists over 10,300 entries. Write to the above noted sources and ask if your subject is a member and, if so, what local chapter or unit he belongs to. This will give you a defined geographical location to start or continue your search in. This is an excellent technique to use because just about everyone will belong to some type of organization. Even if your subject does not want to be found, he probably will still maintain a membership in a local group of the organization that he belonged to when he was in the mainstream.

UNITED STATES DEPOSITORY LIBRARIES

ALABAMA

Auburn University
Ralph Brown Draughon Library
Microforms & Documents Department
Mell Street
Auburn, Alabama 36849

Birmingham Public Library
Government Documents Department
2100 Park Place
Birmingham, Alabama 35203

University of Alabama in Huntsville
Library
Government Documents
Post Office Box 2600
Huntsville, Alabama 35899

Mobile Public Library
Government Documents Collection
701 Government Street
Mobile, Alabama 36602

University of Alabama
Amelia Gayle Gorgas Library
Government Documents
Box 870266
Tuscaloosa, Alabama 35487

ALASKA

United States Alaska Resources Library
Bureau of Land Management
222 West 7th Avenue, Box 36
Anchorage, Alaska 99513

Alaska State Library
Federal Documents Collection
Post Office Box G
Juneau, Alaska 99811

ARIZONA

Northern Arizona University
Cline Library
Government Documents Department
Box 6022
Flagstaff, Arizona 86011

Department of Library Archives, and
Public Records
Federal Documents
Third Floor State Capitol
1700 West Washington
Phoenix, Arizona 85007

Arizona State University
College of Law Library
Government Documents Department
Tempe, Arizona 85287

University of Arizona Library
Government Documents Department
Main Library
Tucson, Arizona 85721

ARKANSAS

University of Arkansas
Mullins Library
Government Documents Department
Fayetteville, Arkansas 72701

Arkansas Supreme Court Library
Justice Building
625 Marshall Street
Little Rock, Arkansas 72201

Southern Arkansas University
Magale Library
Government Documents
Post Office Box 1228
Magnolia, Arkansas 71753

Harding University
Brackett Library
Government Documents Department
Station A, Box 928
900 East Center Avenue
Searcy, Arkansas 72143

CALIFORNIA

University of California
General Library
Government Documents Department
Berkeley, California 94720

University of California
Shields Library
Government Documents Department
Davis, California 95616

University of California at Irvine
Main Library
Government Publications
Post Office Box 19557
Irvine, California 92713

Angelo Iacoboni Public Library
Government Publications Collection
4990 Clark Avenue
Lakewood, California 90712

California State University at Long Beach
Library
Government Documents
1250 Bellflower Boulevard
Long Beach, California 90840

California State University, Los Angeles
University Library
Government Publications Section
5151 State University Drive
Los Angeles, California 90032

Pepperdine University
Payson Library
24255 Pacific Coast Highway
Malibu, California 90263

California State Library
Government Publications Section
914 Capitol Mall
Post Office Box 942837
Sacramento, California 94237

San Diego State University Library
Government Publications Division
San Diego, California 92182

San Francisco Public Library
Government Documents Department
Civic Center
San Francisco, California 94102

University of California at Santa Barbara
Library
Government Publications Department
Santa Barbara, California 93106

Mount San Antonio College Library
Documents Section
1100 North Grand Avenue
Walnut, California 91789

COLORADO

University of Colorado at Boulder
Norlin Library
Government Publications
Campus Box 184
Boulder, Colorado 80309

Auraria Library
Government Documents Department
Lawrence at Eleventh Street
Denver, Colorado 80204

Colorado State University Libraries
Document Department
Fort Collins, Colorado 80523

University of Northern Colorado
James A. Michener Library
Government Publications Service
Greeley, Colorado 80639

CONNECTICUT

Bridgeport Public Library
Reference Department
Government Documents
925 Broad Street
Bridgeport, Connecticut 96604

Western Connecticut State University
Ruth A. Haas Library
Government Documents Department
181 White Street
Danbury, Connecticut 06810

Central Connecticut State University
Elihu Burritt Library
1615 Stanley Street
New Britain, Connecticut 06050

University of New Haven
Marvin K. Peterson Library
Documents Department
300 Orange Avenue
West Haven, Connecticut 06516

DELAWARE

Delaware State College
Federal Publications Department
Dover, Delaware 19901

University of Delaware Library
Government Documents and Maps
Reference Department
Newark, Delaware 19717

Widener University School of Law
Library
Post Office Box 7475
4601 Concord Pike
Wilmington, Delaware 19803

WASHINGTON, D.C.

Department of Education
Research Library
555 New Jersey Avenue, N.W.
Room 101
Washington, D.C. 20208

Department of Justice Main Library
Room 5400
10th Street & Pennsylvania Avenue, N.W.
Washington, D.C. 20530

Department of Labor Library
200 Constitution Avenue, N.W.
Room N-2445 FBP
Washington, D.C. 20210

District of Columbia Public Library
Documents Department
901 G Street, N.W.
Washington, D.C. 20001

Georgetown University Library
Government Documents Department
37th and O Street, N.W.
Washington, D.C. 20057

Library of Congress
Serial and Government Publications
Madison Building
1st & Independence Avenue, Southeast
Washington, D.C. 20540

United States Supreme Court Library
1 First Street, Northeast
Washington, D.C. 20543

FLORIDA

Seminole County Public Library
Documents Depository
215 North Oxford Road
Casselberry, Florida 32707

University of Miami
Otto G. Richter Library
Government Publications
Post Office Box 248214
Coral Gables, Florida 33124

Broward County Main Library
Government Documents Department
100 South Andrews Avenue
Fort Lauderdale, Florida 33301

University of Florida Libraries
Documents Department
Library West
Gainesville, Florida 32611

Florida Keys Community College
Key West Campus Library
5901 West Junior College Road
Key West, Florida 33040

Florida International University
North Miami Campus Library
Documents Section
15101 Biscayne Boulevard
North Miami, Florida 33181

Saint Petersburg Public Library
Reference Department
3745 Ninth Avenue North
Saint Petersburg, Florida 33713

Selby Public Library
1001 Boulevard of the Arts
Sarasota, Florida 34236

University of South Florida
Government Documents Department
4202 East Fowler Avenue
Tampa, Florida 33620

GEORGIA

University of Georgia Libraries
Government Documents Department
Jackson Street
Athens, Georgia 30602

Emory University
Law School Library
Documents Office
Gambrell Hall
Atlanta, Georgia 30322

West Georgia College
Irvine Sullivan Ingram Library
Government Documents
Carrollton, Georgia 30118

Chatham-Effingham Library
Regional Library
2002 Bull Street
Savannah, Georgia 31499

Georgia Southern University
Zach S. Henderson Library
Government Documents Department
Statesboro, Georgia 30460

HAWAII

University of Hawaii at Hilo
Edwin H. Mookini Library
Government Documents Department
523 West Lanikaula Street
Hilo, Hawaii 96720

Hawaii State Library
Federal Documents Section
478 South King Street
Honolulu, Hawaii 96813

Maui Public Library
251 High Street
Wailuku, Hawaii 96793

IDAHO

Boise State University Library
Government Documents
1910 University Drive
Boise, Idaho 83725

Idaho State University
Eli Oboler Library
Documents Division
9th & Terry Street
Pocatello, Idaho 83209

College of Southern Idaho
Library
Post Office Box 1238
Twin Falls, Idaho 83303

ILLINOIS

Southern Illinois University at
Carbondale
Morris Library
Documents Center
Carbondale, Illinois 62901

University of Illinois
Law Library
Documents Department
504 East Pennsylvania Avenue
Champaign, Illinois 61820

Chicago Public Library
Government Publications Department
400 North Franklin
Chicago, Illinois 60610

Northwestern University Library
Government Publications Department
and Map Collection
Evanston, Illinois 60208

Western Illinois University
Government Publications & Legal
Reference Library
Macomb, Illinois 61455

Mount Prospect Public Library
Documents Department
10 South Emerson Street
Mount Prospect, Illinois 60056

Illinois Valley Community College
Jacobs Memorial Library
Documents Department
2578 East 350th Road
Oglesby, Illinois 61348

Rockford Public Library
215 North Wyman Street
Rockford, Illinois 61101

Wheaton College
Busweil Memorial Library
Government Documents
Wheaton, Illinois 60187

INDIANA

Anderson University
University Library
Periodicals & Government Documents
Anderson, Indiana 46012

Indiana University Library
Documents Department
10th & Jordan Streets
Bloomington, Indiana 46016

Franklin College Library
Documents Department
Monroe & State Street
Franklin, Indiana 46131

Huntington College
RichLyn Library
Government Documents Service
2303 College Avenue
Huntington, Indiana 46750

Indian State Library
Documents Section
140 North Senate Avenue
Indianapolis, Indiana 46204

Ball State University
Alexander M. Bracken Library
Government Publications Service
2000 University Avenue
Muncie, Indiana 47306

University of Notre Dame
Hesburgh Library
Document Center
Notre Dame, Indiana 46556

IOWA

Iowa State University
Parks Library
Government Publications Section
Ames, Iowa 50011

Iowa Western Community College
Herbert Hoover Library
2700 College Road
Council Bluffs, Iowa 51502

Drake University
Cowles Library
Government Publications Department
2507 University Avenue
Des Moines, Iowa 50311

University of Iowa Libraries
Government Publications Department
Washington & Madison Streets
Iowa City, Iowa 52242

Northwestern College
Ramaker Library
Government Documents Department
Orange City, Iowa 51041

KANSAS

Baker University
Collins Library
Document Department
Baldwin City, Kansas 66006

University of Kansas
Government Documents
6001 Malatt Hall
Lawrence, Kansas 66045

Johnson County Library
Documents Department
8700 West Shawnee Mission Parkway
Box 2901
Shawnee Mission, Kansas 66201

Washburn University of Topeka
Law Library
Government Documents
1700 College Avenue
Topeka, Kansas 66621

Government Documents
Ablah Library
Wichita State University
1845 Fairmount
Wichita, Kansas 67208

KENTUCKY

Western Kentucky University
Helm-Cravens Library
Government Services Unit
Bowling Green, Kentucky 42101

Kentucky Department for Libraries and
Archives
Federal Documents Section
300 Coffee Tree Road
Post Office Box 537
Frankfort, Kentucky 40602

University of Kentucky Libraries
Government Publications
Lexington, Kentucky 40506

University of Louisville
Law Library
Belknap Campus
Louisville, Kentucky 40292

Murray State University
Waterfield Library
Government Documents Department
Fifteenth and Olive Streets
Murray, Kentucky 42071

LOUISIANA

Louisiana State University
Middleton Library
Government Documents Department
Baton Rouge, Louisiana 70803

University of Southwestern Louisiana
Library
Dupre Library
Documents Division
302 East Saint Mary Boulevard
Lafayette, Louisiana 70503

Loyola University
Government Documents Library
6363 Saint Charles Avenue
Box 242
New Orleans, Louisiana 70118

Louisiana College
Richard W. Norton Memorial Library
Government Documents
1140 College Drive
Pineville, Louisiana 71359

Louisiana State University at Shreveport
Library
Documents Department
One University Place
Shreveport, Louisiana 71115

MAINE

Maine State Library
Cultural Building
State House Station
Augusta, Maine 04333

Bowdoin College Library
Documents Department
Brunswick, Maine 04011

Bates College
George and Helen Ladd Library
Documents Department
Lewiston, Maine 04240

University of Maine School of Law
Garbrecht Law Library
246 Deering Avenue
Portland, Maine 04102

MARYLAND

Enoch Pratt Free Library
Documents Division
400 Cathedral Street
Baltimore, Maryland 21201

Frostburg State University Library
Government Documents
Frostburg, Maryland 21532

Western Maryland College
Hoover Library
Westminster, Maryland 21157

MASSACHUSETTS

Amherst College Library
Documents Department
Amherst, Massachusetts 01002

State Library of Massachusetts
Documents Department
442 State House
Boston, Massachusetts 02133

Tufts University
Wessell Library
Government Publications
Medford, Massachusetts 02155

Southeastern Massachusetts University
Library
Documents Section
Old Westport Road
North Dartmouth, Massachusetts 02747

Springfield City Library
Documents Section
220 State Street
Springfield, Massachusetts 01103

MICHIGAN

University of Michigan
Harlan Hatcher Graduate Library
Documents Center
Ann Arbor, Michigan 48109

Cranbrook Institute of Science Library
Documents Department
500 Lone Pine Road
Post Office Box 801
Bloomfield Hills, Michigan 48304

Wayne State University
Arthur Neef Law Library
Documents Department
468 West Ferry Mall
Detroit, Michigan 48202

Michigan State University
Government Documents Library
East Lansing, Michigan 48824

University of Michigan - Flint
Library Documents Unit
Flint, Michigan 48502

Calvin College & Seminary Library
Government Documents Collection
3207 Burton Street, Southeast
Grand Rapids, Michigan 49546

Monroe County Library System
Documents Division
3700 South Custer Road
Monroe, Michigan 48161

MINNESOTA

Southdale-Hennepin Area Library
Government Documents
7001 York Avenue South
Edina, Minnesota 55435

Mankato State University
Memorial Library
Government Publications
MSU Box 19
Mankato, Minnesota 56002

Minneapolis Public Library
Government Documents Department
300 Nicollet Mall
Minneapolis, Minnesota 55401

University of Minnesota, Morris
Rodney A. Briggs Library
Documents Department
Morris, Minnesota 56267

Saint Paul Public Library
Government Publications
90 West 4th Street
Saint Paul, Minnesota 55102

MISSISSIPPI

University of Southern Mississippi
Joseph A. Cook Memorial Library
Southern Station Box 5053
Hattiesburg, Mississippi 39401

Mississippi Library Commission
Documents Section
1221 Ellis Avenue
Jackson, Mississippi 39209

Alcorn State University
J.D. Boyd Library
Post Office Box 539
Lorman, Mississippi 39096

MISSOURI

University of Missouri at Columbia
Ellis Library
Government Documents
Columbia, Missouri 65201

Kansas City Missouri Public Library
Documents Division
311 East Twelfth Street
Kansas City, Missouri 64106

William Jewell College
Charles F. Curry Library
500 College Hill
Liberty, Missouri 64068

Kisker Road Branch Library
Saint Charles City-County Library
District
1000 Kisker Road
Saint Charles, Missouri 63303

Saint Louis Public Library
Documents Department
1301 Olive Street
Saint Louis, Missouri 63103

MONTANA

Eastern Montana College Library
Documents Department
1500 North 30th Street
Billings, Montana 59101

Montana College of Mineral Science and
Technology Library
Documents Division
Park Street
Butte, Montana 59701

State Law Library of Montana
Justice Building
215 North Sanders
Helena, Montana 59620

University of Montana
Maurene & Mike Mansfield Library
Documents Division
Missoula, Montana 59812

NEBRASKA

Midland Lutheran College
Luther Library
Documents Department
900 Clarkson
Fremont, Nebraska 68025

Nebraska Library Commission
Federal Documents Department
1420 P Street
Lincoln, Nebraska 68508

Creighton University School of Law
Library
2500 California Street
Omaha, Nebraska 68178

Scottsbluff Public Library
1809 Third Avenue
Scottsbluff, Nebraska 69361

Wayne State College
United States Conn Library
Documents Division
200 East 10th Street
Wayne, Nebraska 68787

NEVADA

Nevada Supreme Court Library
Supreme Court Building
Capitol Complex
100 North Carson Street
Carson City, Nevada 89710

University of Nevada at Las Vegas
James Dickinson Library
Government Documents
4505 Maryland Parkway
Las Vegas, Nevada 89154

University of Nevada
Reno Library
Government Publications Department
Reno, Nevada 89557

NEW HAMPSHIRE

University of New Hampshire Library
Documents
Durham, New Hampshire 03824

Manchester City Library
Carpenter Memorial Building
405 Pine Street
Manchester, New Hampshire 03104

Nashua Public Library
2 Court Street
Nashua, New Hampshire 03060

NEW JERSEY

Bayonne Free Public Library
Government Documents
697 Avenue C
Bayonne, New Jersey 07002

Rutgers University
Camden Library
300 North Fourth Street
Camden, New Jersey 08102

East Orange Public Library
Government Documents
21 South Arlington Avenue
East Orange, New Jersey 07018

Glassboro State College
Savitz Library
Government Publications
Route 322
Glassboro, New Jersey 08028

Jersey City Public Library
Documents Department
472 Jersey Avenue
Jersey City, New Jersey 07302

Newark Public Library
United States Documents Division
5 Washington Street
Post Office Box 630
Newark, New Jersey 07101

Princeton University
Firestone Library
Documents Division
Princeton, New Jersey 08544

NEW MEXICO

University of New Mexico
General Library
Government Publications Department
Albuquerque, New Mexico 87131

New Mexico State University Library
Government Documents Department
Post Office Box 30006
Department 3475
Las Cruces, New Mexico 88003

Western New Mexico University
Miller Library
Silver City, New Mexico 88062

New Mexico Institute of Mining &
Technology
Martin Speare Memorial Library
Government Documents Department
Campus Station
Socorro, New Mexico 87801

NEW YORK

State University of New York at Albany
University Library
Government Publications Department
1400 Washington Avenue
Albany, New York 12222

State University of New York at
Binghamton
Glenn G. Bartle Library
Government Documents Department
Vestal Parkway East
Binghamton, New York 13902

Fordham University Library
Public Documents Section
Library Annex
Keating Hall
Bronx, New York 10458

Brooklyn College Library
Government Documents Department
Bedford Avenue and Avenue H
Brooklyn, New York 11210

Buffalo and Erie County Public Library
Documents Division
Lafayette Square
Buffalo, New York 14203

State University of New York at Cortland
Memorial Library
Document Section
Post Office Box 2000
Cortland, New York 13045

Elmira College
Gannett Tripp Library Center
Elmira, New York 14901

Queens College
Benjamin S. Rosenthal Library
Documents Department
65-30 Kissena Boulevard
Flushing, New York 11367

Hofstra University
Axinn Library
Documents Department
Hempstead, New York 11550

Cornell Law Library
Myron Taylor Hall
Ithaca, New York 14853

Columbia University Libraries
Documents Service Center
420 West 118th Street
Room 327
New York City, New York 10027

Dowling College Library
Government Documents
Idle Hour Boulevard
Oakdale, New York 11769

State University College at Plattsburgh
Benjamin F. Feinberg Library
Government Documents Collection
Plattsburgh, New York 12901

Skidmore College Library
Documents Department
Saratoga Springs, New York 12866

Union College
Schaffer Library
Schenectady, New York 12308

Syracuse University Library
Documents Division
222 Waverly Avenue
Syracuse, New York 13244

Pace University
Law Library
78 North Broadway
White Plains, New York 10603

NORTH CAROLINA

University of North Carolina at Asheville
D. Hiden Ramsey Library
Government Documents
One University Heights
Asheville, North Carolina 28804

Duke University
School of Law Library
Documents Department
Durham, North Carolina 27706

University of North Carolina at
Greensboro
Walter Clinton Jackson Library
Documents (Microforms Division)
Greensboro, North Carolina 27412

East Carolina University
J. Y. Joyner Library
Documents Department
East 5th Street
Greenville, North Carolina 27858

North Carolina Wesleyan College Library
Government Documents Department
3400 North Wesleyan Boulevard
Rocky Mount, North Carolina 27804

Forsyth County Public Library
Main Government Documents /
Periodical Department
660 West Fifth Street
Winston-Salem, North Carolina 27101

NORTH DAKOTA

Veterans' Memorial Public Library
515 North Fifth Street
Bismarck, North Dakota 58501

North Dakota State University Library
Documents Office
Fargo, North Dakota 58105

University of North Dakota
Chester Fritz Library
Documents Department
University Station
Grand Forks, North Dakota 58202

Valley City State University
Allen Memorial Library
101 College Street, Southwest
Valley City, North Dakota 58072

OHIO

University of Akron
Bierce Library
Government Documents
315 East Buchtel Avenue
Akron, Ohio 44325

Mount Union College Library
Documents Department
1972 Clark Avenue
Alliance, Ohio 44601

Ohio University
Alden Library
Government Documents Department
Athens, Ohio 45701

Cleveland Public Library
Documents Collection
325 Superior Avenue
Cleveland, Ohio 44114

Capital University Library
Documents Department
2199 East Main Street
Columbus, Ohio 43209

Dayton and Montgomery County Public
Library
Documents Department
215 East Third Street
Dayton, Ohio 45402

Marion Public Library
Federal Documents
445 East Church Street
Marion, Ohio 43302

University of Toledo Library
Documents Department
2801 West Bancroft Street
Toledo, Ohio 43606

College of Wooster
Andrews Library
Government Publications Department
Wooster, Ohio 44691

OKLAHOMA

Central State University Library
Documents Department
Edmond, Oklahoma 73034

Metropolitan Library System
Main Library
Documents Department
131 Dean A. McGee Avenue
Oklahoma City, Oklahoma 73109

Oklahoma State University
Edmon Law Library
Documents Department
Stillwater, Oklahoma 74078

University of Tulsa
Government Documents Department
McFarlin Library
600 South College Avenue
Tulsa, Oklahoma 74104

Southwestern Oklahoma State University
Al Harris Library
Documents Department
809 North Custer
Weatherford, Oklahoma 73096

OREGON

Southern Oregon State College Library
Documents
1250 Siskiyou Boulevard
Ashland, Oregon 97520

Oregon State University Library
Documents Division
Corvallis, Oregon 97331

University of Oregon Library
Documents Department
Eugene, Oregon 97403

Blue Mountain Community College
Library
2411 N.W. Carden
Pendleton, Oregon 97801

Oregon Supreme Court Law Library
Supreme Court Building
1163 State Street
Salem, Oregon 97310

PENNSYLVANIA

Dickinson College
Boyd Lee Spahr Library
Government Documents
West High Street
Carlisle, Pennsylvania 17013

East Stroudsburg University
Kemp Library
Government Documents Section
Smith & Normal Streets
East Stroudsburg, Pennsylvania 18301

Thiel College
Langenheim Memorial Library
Documents Department
Greenville, Pennsylvania 16125

Widener University
Harrisburg Campus
School of Law Library
3800 Vartan Way
Harrisburg, Pennsylvania 17110

Mansfield University Library
Government Documents Department
Mansfield, Pennsylvania 16933

Millersville University
Helen A. Ganser Library
Government Documents
Millersville, Pennsylvania 17551

Drexel University
W. W. Hagerty Library
Government Documents Section
32nd and Chestnut Streets
Philadelphia, Pennsylvania 19104

Pottsville Free Public Library
Government Publications Section
16th North Third Street
Pottsville, Pennsylvania 17901

Swarthmore College
McCabe Library
500 College Avenue
Swarthmore, Pennsylvania 19081

West Chester University
Francis Harvey Green Library
Documents Department
High Street & Rosedale Avenue
West Chester, Pennsylvania 19383

PUERTO RICO

University of Puerto Rico
Mayaguez Campus Library
Documents & Maps Collection
College Station
Mayaguez, Puerto Rico 00708

Encarnacion Valdes Library
Catholic University of Puerto Rico
Ponce, Puerto Rico 00732

University of Puerto Rico
J. M. Lázaro Library
Documents/Maps Collection
Box C
U.P.R. Station
Rio Piedras, Puerto Rico 00931

RHODE ISLAND

University of Rhode Island Library
Government Publications Office
Kingston, Rhode Island 02881

Brown University
John D. Rockerfeller Jr. Library
Documents Department
Prospect Street
Providence, Rhode Island 02912

Warwick Public Library
Government Documents
600 Sandy Lane
Warwick, Rhode Island 02886

Woonsocket Harris Public Library
Documents Department
303 Clinton Street
Woonsocket, Rhode Island 02895

SOUTH CAROLINA

University of South Carolina - Aiken
Gregg-Graniteville Library
171 University Parkway
Aiken, South Carolina 29801

College of Charleston
Robert Scott Small Library
Collection Development/Documents
Charleston, South Carolina 29424

South Carolina State Library
Documents Department
1500 Senate Street
Post Office Box 11469
Columbia, South Carolina 29201

Furman University
James B. Duke Library
Government Documents Department
Greenville, South Carolina 29613

Winthrop College
Dacus Library
Documents Department
Oakland Avenue
Rock Hill, South Carolina 29733

SOUTH DAKOTA

Northern State College
Beulah Williams Library
Documents Department
14th & Washington Streets
Aberdeen, South Dakota 57401

South Dakota State Library
Federal Documents Department
South Dakota State Library
800 Governors Drive
Pierre, South Dakota 57501

Augustana College
Mikkelsen Library
29th & Summit
Sioux Falls, South Dakota 57197

University of South Dakota
I.D. Weeks Library
Government Documents
414 East Clark Street
Vermillion, South Dakota 57069

TENNESSEE

E.W. King Library
King College
1350 King College Road
Bristol, Tennessee 37620

Chattanooga-Hamilton County
Bicentennial Library
Government Documents Department
1001 Broad Street
Chattanooga, Tennessee 37402

Stephens-Burnett Library
Carson-Newman College
Documents Department
South Russell Avenue
Jefferson City, Tennessee 37760

Memphis State University Libraries
Government Documents
Memphis, Tennessee 38152

Tennessee State University
Brown-Daniel Library
Government Documents Center
3500 John A. Merritt Boulevard
Nashville, Tennessee 37209

University of the South
Jessie Ball duPont Library
Government Documents
Sewanee, Tennessee 37375

TEXAS

Hardin-Simmons University
Rupert and Pauline Richardson Library
Documents Department
2200 Hickory
Abilene, Texas 79698

University of Texas at Arlington Library
Government Publications
701 South Cooper Street
Arlington, Texas 76019

Texas State Library
United States Documents
Post Office Box 12927
1201 Brazos
Austin, Texas 78711

Lee College Library
Documents Department
511 South Whiting Street
Baytown, Texas 77520

Dallas Public Library
Government Publications Division
1515 Young Street
Dallas, Texas 75201

Houston Public Library
Government Documents Section
500 McKinney Avenue
Houston, Texas 77002

Sam Houston State University
Newton Gresham Library
Government Documents Department
Huntsville, Texas 77341

Texas Art and Industries University
Jernigan Library
Government Documents
Kingsville, Texas 78363

Laredo Junior College
Harold R. Yeary Library
Government Documents
West End Washington Street
Laredo, Texas 78040

Palo Alto College
Government Documents Department
1400 West Villaret
San Antonio, Texas 78224

Baylor University
Moody Memorial Library
Government Documents Department
B.U. Box 7148
Waco, Texas 76798

UTAH

Southern Utah State College Library
Documents Department
150 East College Avenue
Cedar City, Utah 84720

Weber State College
Stewart Library
Documents Department 2901
3750 Harrison Boulevard
Ogden, Utah 84408

Brigham Young University
Law Library
Documents Department
Provo, Utah 84602

University of Utah
Law Library
Government Documents
Salt Lake City, Utah 84112

VERMONT

University of Vermont
Bailey/Howe Library
Documents/Maps Department
Burlington, Vermont 05405

Lyndon State College
Samuel Read Hall Library
Lyndonville, Vermont 05851

Middlebury College
Egbert Starr Library
Middlebury, Vermont 05753

Norwich University
Chaplin Library
Documents Department
South Main Street
Northfield, Vermont 05663

Vermont Law School Library
Chelsea Street
Post Office Box 60
South Royalton, Vermont 05068

VIRGIN ISLANDS

Virgin Islands Division of Libraries
Depository
Florence Williams Public Library
49-50 King Street
Christiansted
Saint Croix, Virgin Islands 00820

University of the Virgin Islands
Ralph M. Paiewonsky Library
Charlotte Amalie
Saint Thomas, Virgin Islands 00802

VIRGINIA

Bridgewater College
Alexander Mack Memorial Library
Documents Department
East College Street
Bridgewater, Virginia 22812

University of Virginia
Alderman Library
Government Documents
Charlottesville, Virginia 22903

George Mason University
Fenwick Library
Government Documents
4400 University Drive
Fairfax, Virginia 22030

Old Dominion University Library
Government Publications Department
Hampton Boulevard
Norfolk, Virginia 23529

University of Richmond
Boatwright Memorial Library
Government Publications
Richmond, Virginia 23173

Clinch Valley College
John Cook Wyllie Library
Documents Division
College Avenue
Wise, Virginia 24293

WASHINGTON

Western Washington University
Mable Zoe Wilson Library
Documents Division
516 High Street
Bellingham, Washington 98225

Eastern Washington University
JFK Library
Documents Department
Mail Stop Number 84
Cheney, Washington 99004

Evergreen State College
Daniel J. Evans Library
Documents Department
Olympia, Washington 98505

University of Washington
Suzzallo Library
Government Publications Division
FM-25
Seattle, Washington 98195

Spokane Public Library
Documents Department
West 906 Main Avenue
Spokane, Washington 99201

University of Puget Sound
Collins Memorial Library
Documents Department
1500 North Warner
Tacoma, Washington 98416

WEST VIRGINIA

Kanawha County Public Library
123 Capitol Street
Charleston, West Virginia 25301

West Virginia University Library
Government Documents Section
Post Office Box 6069
Morgantown, West Virginia 26506

Shepherd College
Scarborough Library
Documents Department
Shepherdstown, West Virginia 25443

WISCONSIN

Lawrence University
Seeley G. Mudd Library
Documents Department
Appleton, Wisconsin 54912

University of Wisconsin - Eau Clair
William D. McIntyre Library
Post Office Box 5010
Eau Claire, Wisconsin 54702

Fond du Lac Public Library
32 Sheboygan Street
Fond du Lac, Wisconsin 54935

University of Wisconsin - Green Bay
Government Publications
Green Bay, Wisconsin 54311

Marquette University Law Library
1103 West Wisconsin Avenue
Milwaukee, Wisconsin 53233

Ripon College Library
Government Documents
Box 248
300 Seward Street
Ripon, Wisconsin 54971

University of Wisconsin - River Falls
Chalmer Davee Library
Government Documents Room
River Falls, Wisconsin 54022

WYOMING

Wyoming State Library
Supreme Court and Library Building
Government Publications
Cheyenne, Wyoming 82002

Campell County Public Library
Documents Division
2101 4-J Road
Gillette, Wyoming 82716

University of Wyoming
Coe Library
Documents Division
Box 3334
University Station
13th & Ivinson
Laramie, Wyoming 82071

Sheridan College
Griffith Memorial Library
Government Publications
3059 Coffeen Avenue
Post Office Box 1500
Sheridan, Wyoming 82801

NOTES

NOTES

7

Workers' Compensation Records

When a search does not reveal a driver's license, vehicle or boat registration, a license for one of the over one hundred professions that require licensing by the state, a military record, evidence that the subject has died or any of the other facets of a normal paper trial, I then turn to the Worker's Compensation Bureau.

Persons who receive benefits from the Workers's Compensation Bureau are those who have suffered injuries during the performance of their jobs. Many cases require that the person not engage in any employment, restrict activity outside the home or not perform routine functions such as driving an automobile. Thus, the reason for a dearth of records.

Many states will provide a complete file which, of course, may yield information including addresses, previous employers, dependents, etc. It is important to remember that states may change their policies on releasing compensation information. Many states, including California, Florida and New Jersey, consider Workers' Compensation files public records, whereas several states will not release information. Write and inquire about the current policy using the following list.

ALABAMA

Workmen's Compensation Division
Industrial Relation Building
Montgomery, Alabama 36130

ALASKA

Workers' Compensation Division
Post Office Box 25512
Juneau, Alaska 99802

ARIZONA

State Compensation Fund
3031 North Second Street
Phoenix, Arizona 85012

ARKANSAS

Workers' Compensation Commission
625 Marshall Street
Little Rock, Arkansas 72201

CALIFORNIA

State Compensation Insurance Fund
1275 Market Street
San Francisco, California 94103

COLORADO

Workers' Compensation Section
1313 Sherman Street, Room 314
Denver, Colorado 80203

CONNECTICUT

Workers' Compensation Commission
1890 Dixwell Avenue
Hamden, Connecticut 06514

DELAWARE

Industrial Accident Board
820 North French Street
Wilmington, Delaware 19801

DISTRICT OF COLUMBIA

Office of Workers' Compensation
Post Office Box 56098
Washington, D.C. 20011

FLORIDA

Division of Workers' Compensation
1321 Executive Center Drive
Tallahassee, Florida 32399

GEORGIA

Board of Workers' Compensation
One CNN Center
Atlanta, Georgia 30303

HAWAII

Disability Compensation Division
830 Punchbowl Street
Honolulu, Hawaii 96813

IDAHO

Idaho Industrial Commission
317 Main Street
Boise, Idaho 83720

ILLINOIS

Illinois Industrial Commission
100 West Randolph
Chicago, Illinois 60611

INDIANA

Industrial Board
100 North Senate Avenue
Indianapolis, Indiana 46204

IOWA

Industrial Commissioner's Office
1000 East Grand Street
Des Moines, Iowa 50319

KANSAS

Division of Workers' Compensation
900 Jackson, Room 651
Topeka, Kansas 66612

KENTUCKY

Department of Workers' Claims
1270 Louisville Road
Frankfort, Kentucky 40601

LOUISIANA

Office of Workers' Compensation
Post Office Box 94040
Baton Rouge, Louisiana 70804

MAINE

Workers' Compensation Commission
State House, Room 27
Augusta, Maine 04333

MARYLAND

Workers' Compensation Commission
6 North Liberty Street
Baltimore, Maryland 21201

MASSACHUSETTS

Industrial Accident Board
600 Washington Street
Boston, Massachusetts 02111

MICHIGAN

Bureau of Workers' Disability
Post Office Box 30016
Lansing, Michigan 48909

MINNESOTA

Workers' Compensation Division
443 Layafette Road
St. Paul, Minnesota 55155

MISSISSIPPI

Workers' Compensation Commission
Post Office Box 5300
Jackson, Mississippi 39216

MISSOURI

Division of Workers' Compensation
Post Office Box 58
Jefferson City, Missouri 65102

MONTANA

Division of Workers' Compensation
5 South Last Chance Gulch
Helena, Montana 59604

NEBRASKA

Workers' Compensation Court
Post Office Box 98908
Lincoln, Nebraska 65809

NEVADA

Department of Industrial Relations
1390 South Curry Street
Carson City, Nevada 98710

NEW HAMPSHIRE

Workers' Compensation Board
19 Pillsbury Street
Concord, New Hampshire 03301

NEW JERSEY

Division of Workers' Compensation
State Office Building, Room 381
Trenton, New Jersey 08625

NEW MEXICO

Workers' Compensation Division
Post Office Box 27198
Albuquerque, New Mexico 87125

NEW YORK

State Insurance Fund
199 Church Street
New York, New York 10007

NORTH CAROLINA

Industrial Commission
430 North Salisbury Street
Raleigh, North Carolina 27611

NORTH DAKOTA

Workers' Compensation Bureau
4007 North State Street
Bismark, North Dakota 58501

OHIO

Bureau of Workers' Compensation
246 North High Street
Columbus, Ohio 43215

OKLAHOMA

Oklahoma Workers' Compensation Court
1915 North Stiles
Oklahoma City, Oklahoma 73105

OREGON

Department of Insurance and Finance
Labor and Industries Building
Salem, Oregon 97310

PENNSYLVANIA

Bureau of Worker's Compensation
1171 South Cameron Street
Harrisburg, Pennsylvania 17104

PUERTO RICO

State Insurance Fund
GPO Box 5038
San Juan, Puerto Rico 00936

RHODE ISLAND

Department of Worker's Compensation
610 Manton Avenue
Providence, Rhode Island 02909

SOUTH CAROLINA

Industrial Commission
1615 Marian Street
Columbia, South Carolina 29202

SOUTH DAKOTA

Department of Labor
700 Governors Drive
Pierre, South Dakota 57501

TENNESSEE

Workers' Compensation Division
501 Union Building
Nashville, Tennessee 37219

TEXAS

Industrial Accident Board
200 East Riverside Drive
Austin, Texas 78704

UTAH

Workers' Compensation Fund
Post Office Box 510250
Salt Lake City, Utah 84151

VERMONT

Department of Labor and Industry
120 State Street
Montpelier, Vermont 05602

VIRGINIA

Industrial Commission
Post Office Box 1794
Richmond, Virginia 23220

WASHINGTON

Department of Labor and Industries
General Administration Building
Olympia, Washington 98504

WEST VIRGINIA

Workers' Compensation Appeal Board
601 Morris Street
Charleston, West Virginia 25301

WISCONSIN

Workers' Compensation Bureau
Post Office Box 7901
Madison, Wisconsin 53707

WYOMING

Workers' Compensation Division
122 West 25th Street
Cheyenne, Wyoming 82002

Workers' Compensation Division
21 Labor & Industries Building, Salem, OR 97310 FAX: (503) 378-6828

February 25, 1993

RE: Claimant: Robert K. Pavella
     SSN: 242/23/8376

     DOB: 6/17/35

This is in response to your letter requesting information on the
above-captioned claimant.

Based on the information provided, the claimant identified in your letter has
not been found in our data system. Claims are submitted to the Department
only when they are disabling or a denial has been issued.

R. Sherwood

Rebecca A. Sherwood
Information Unit
Operations Section

DEPARTMENT OF WORKERS' CLAIMS
Perimeter Park West, Building C
1270 Louisville Road
Frankfort, Kentucky 40601
Telephone (502) 564-5550

Dear Sir or Madam:

The Department of Workers' Claims has received your request for a work history or claim check on the attached individual(s).

Using the information contained within your original letter, such as the employee name and his/her social security number, I checked back to 1978 and have been **unable** to locate any **lost time injuries**, claims or agreements.

If you have any questions concerning this matter, please do not hesitate to contact me.

Sincerely,

Deborah S. Wingate
Open Records Specialist

<u>DATE CHECKED</u>   March 18, 1993

8

Corporations & UCC Filings

Aperson is listed in corporation records because they are an officer, director or registered agent. Since organizations, clubs, teams, churches, associations and clubs require incorporation many times, your subject does not have to be a business person to have an involvement in a corporation.

Write to the corporation division and most states will be able to provide a list of all persons with a particular name, the names of the corporations they are associated with and the addresses of the corporations. Many times the home addresses will be listed for officers and directors in smaller corporations such as the ones noted above.

The corporation division will also conduct a search that will generate a list of all persons with a particular name who have a Uniform Commercial Code transaction. The UCC, in most states, is a transaction that is intended to create a security interest in personal property or fixtures including goods, documents, instruments, general intangibles, chattel paper, and a contract that creates a security interest in a chattel trust, trust deed, equipment trust, conditional sale, trust receipt, and lease or consignment intended as security.

If your subject has, for example, ever lent money or equipment to someone who has opened a business or has borrowed money or equipment, then they would be listed in UCC transactions. When you isolate your subject on the UCC list you will want to order a complete photocopy of the transaction. This will show the business and/or home address of the subject, the names of any witnesses, the name of the business and the name of the other party to the transaction.

ALABAMA

Office of the Secretary of State
Corporations Division
State of Alabama
Post Office Box 5616
Montgomery, Alabama 36103

ALASKA

Division of Corporations
State of Alaska
Post Office Box 110807
Juneau, Alaska 99811

AMERICAN SAMOA

Corporations
Territory of American Samoa
Moata Fona
Pago Pago, American Samoa 96799

ARIZONA

Arizona Corporation Commission
Secretary of State
State of Arizona
1200 West Washington
Phoenix, Arizona 85005

ARKANSAS

Office of the Secretary of State
Corporation Department
State of Arkansas
State Capital
Little Rock, Arkansas 72201

CALIFORNIA

Office of the Secretary of State
Corporate Division
State of California
1230 J Street
Sacramento, California 95814

COLORADO

Department of State
Corporation Section
1560 Broadway, Suite 200
Denver, Colorado 80202

CONNECTICUT

Office of the Secretary of State
Corporations
30 Trinity Street
Hartford, Connecticut 06106

DELAWARE

Secretary of State
Division of Corporations
State of Delaware
Post Office Box 793
Dover, Delaware 19903

DISTRICT OF COLUMBIA

Recorder of Deeds
Recorder of Deeds Building
6th & D Street N.W.
Washington, D.C. 20001

FLORIDA

Office of the Secretary of State
Division of Corporations
State of Florida
Post Office Box 6327
Tallahassee, Florida 32301

GEORGIA

Office of the Secretary of State
Corporations
State of Georgia
#2 Martin Luther King Jr. Drive S.E.
Atlanta, Georgia 30034

GUAM

Corporations
Government of Guam
Post Office Box 2796
Agana, Guam 96910

HAWAII

Department of Regulatory Agencies
Corporations
State of Hawaii
1010 Richards Street
Honolulu, Hawaii 96813

IDAHO

Office of the Secretary of State
Corporations
State of Idaho
Statehouse, Room 203
Boise, Idaho 83720

ILLINOIS

Office of the Secretary
Corporation Department
State of Illinois
Centennial Building, Room 328
Springfield, Illinois 62756

INDIANA

Office of the Secretary of State
Corporation Division
State of Indiana
Statehouse, Room 155
Indianapolis, Indiana 46204

IOWA

Office of the Secretary of State
Corporation Division
East 14th & Walnut Streets
Des Moines, Iowa 50319

KANSAS

Office of the Secretary of State
Corporate Services
Statehouse, Room 200
Topeka, Kansas 66612

KENTUCKY

Office of the Secretary of State
Corporation Department
State of Kentucky
Post Office Box 718
Frankfort, Kentucky 40602

LOUISIANA

Department of State
Corporation Division
State of Louisiana
Post Office Box 94125
Baton Rouge, Louisiana 70804

MAINE

Secretary of State
Bureau of Corporations
State of Maine
Statehouse, Station 101
Augusta, Maine 04333

MARSHALL ISLANDS

Corporations
Post Office Box 100
Republic of the Marshall Islands
Mojuro, M.I. 96960

MARYLAND

Department of Assessments & Taxations
Corporations
State of Maryland
301 West Preston Street
Baltimore, Maryland 21201

MASSACHUSETTS

Secretary of the Commonwealth
Corporations Division
One Ashburton Place, Room 1713
Boston, Massachusetts 02133

MICHIGAN

Department of Commerce
Corporation Division
State of Michigan
6546 Mercantile Drive
Lansing, Michigan 48909

MICRONESIA

Corporations
Department of Resources & Development
FSM National Government
Kolonia, Ponape, E.C.I. 96941

MINNESOTA

Office of the Secretary of State
Corporation Division
State of Minnesota
State Office Building, Room 180
St. Paul, Minnesota 55155

MISSISSIPPI

Office of the Secretary of State
Corporations
State of Mississippi
Post Office Box 136
Jackson, Mississippi 39205

MISSOURI

Office of the Secretary of State
Corporations
State of Missouri
Post Office Box 1159
Jefferson City, Missouri 65101

MONTANA

Office of the Secretary of State
Corporations Bureau
State Capitol, Room 202
Helena, Montana 59620

NEBRASKA

Office of the Secretary of State
Corporation Department
State of Nebraska
301 Centennial Mall South
Lincoln, Nebraska 68509

NEVADA

Office of the Secretary of State
Corporation Department
State of Nevada
Capitol Complex
Carson City, Nevada 89710

NEW HAMPSHIRE

Office of the Secretary of State
Corporate Division
State of New Hampshire
Statehouse Annex, Room 204
Concord, New Hampshire 03301

NEW JERSEY

Office of the Secretary of State
Corporations
State of New Jersey
Statehouse, CN 308
Trenton, New Jersey 08625

NEW MEXICO

Secretary of State
State Corporation Commission
State of New Mexico
State Office Building, Room 420
Santa Fe, New Mexico 87503

NEW YORK

Department of State
Division of Corporations
State of New York
162 Washington Avenue
Albany, New York, 12231

NORTH CAROLINA

Office of the Secretary of State
Corporation Division
300 North Salisbury Street
Raleigh, North Carolina 27611

NORTH DAKOTA

Office of the Secretary of State
Division of Corporations
State of North Dakota
601 East Boulevard Avenue
Bismarck, North Dakota 58501

OHIO

Office of the Secretary of State
Corporations Department
State of Ohio
50 East Broad Street
Columbus, Ohio 43215

OKLAHOMA

Office of the Secretary of State
Corporation Department
State of Oklahoma
State Capitol Building, Room 101
Oklahoma City, Oklahoma 73105

OREGON

Department of Commerce
Corporation Division
State of Oregon
158 12th Street, N.E.
Salem, Oregon 97310

PENNSYLVANIA

Office of the Secretary of State
Corporation Bureau
State of Pennsylvania
North Office Building, Room 308
Harrisburg, Pennsylvania 17120

PUERTO RICO

Corporation Division
Commonwealth of Puerto Rico
Fortaleza Street, #50
San Juan, Puerto Rico 00904

RHODE ISLAND

Secretary of State
Corporation Division
State of Rhode Island
270 Westminster Mall
Providence, Rhode Island 02903

SOUTH CAROLINA

Office of the Secretary of State
Corporation Department
State of South Carolina
Post Office Box 11350
Columbia, South Carolina 29211

SOUTH DAKOTA

Office of the Secretary of State
Corporation Department
State of South Dakota
500 East Capitol
Pierre, South Dakota 57501

TENNESSEE

Office of the Secretary of State
Corporate Section
State of Tennessee
James K. Polk Building, Room 500
Nashville, Tennessee 37219

TEXAS

Office of the Secretary of State
Corporations Section
State of Texas
Post Office Box 13193
Austin, Texas 78711

UTAH

Secretary of State
Corporations
State of Utah
160 East Third Street
Salt Lake City, Utah 84145

VERMONT

Office of the Secretary of State
Corporations
109 State Street, Pavilion Building
Montpelier, Vermont 05602

VIRGIN ISLANDS

Corporations
Territory of Virgin Islands
Charlette Amalie, St. Thomas,
Virgin Islands 00801

VIRGINIA

Secretary of State
State Corporation Commission
Post Office Box 1197
Richmond, Virginia 23209

WASHINGTON

Office of the Secretary of State
Corporations
211 12th Street
Olympia, Washington 98504

WEST VIRGINIA

Office of the Secretary of State
Corporations
State Capitol Building
Charleston, West Virginia 25305

WISCONSIN

Office of the Secretary of State
Division of Corporations
Post Office Box 7648
Madison, Wisconsin 53707

WYOMING

Office of the Secretary of State
Corporation
110 Capitol Building
Cheyenne, Wyoming 82002

ALBERTA

Department of Corporate Affairs
Corporate Registry
10365 97th Street
Edmonton, Alberta T5J 3W7

BRITISH COLUMBIA

Ministry of Corporate Affairs
940 Blanchard Street
Victoria, British Columbia, V8W 3E6

MANITOBA

Department Corporate Affairs
Corporations
10th Floor, Woodsworth Building
405 Broadway Avenue
Winnipeg, Manitoba R3C 3L6

NEW BRUNSWICK

Corporations
348 King Street, Lynch Bldg., 2nd Floor
Post Office Box 6000
Fredericton, New Brunswick E3B 5H1

NEWFOUNDLAND & LABRADOR

Department of Justice
Corporations
Post Office Box 4750
St. John's, Newfoundland A1C 5T7

NORTHWEST TERRITORIES

Department of Justice and Public Services
Corporations
Yellowknife, N.W.T. X1A 2L9

NOVA SCOTIA

Department of the Attorney General
Corporations
1660 Hollis Street
Halifax, Nova Scotia B3J 2Y4

PRINCE EDWARD ISLAND

Department of Justice
Corporations
73 Rochford Street
Charlottetown,
Prince Edward Island C1A 7N8

ONTARIO

Department of Corporate Affairs
Corporations
555 Yonge Street
Toronto, Ontario M7A 2H6

QUEBEC

Bureau de L'Inspecteur General des
Institutions Financieres
800 Place d'Youville
Quebec, P.Q. G1R 4Y5

SASKATCHEWAN

Department Commercial Affairs
Corporations Branch
1871 Smith Street
Regina, Saskatchewan S4P 3V7

YUKON

Department of Corporate Affairs
Corporate Affairs
Post Office Box 2703
Whitehorse, Yukon Y1A 2C6

STATE OF ALABAMA

OFFICE OF THE SECRETARY OF STATE

BUSINESS DIVISION

BILLY JOE CAMP
SECRETARY OF STATE

February 25, 1993

P.O. BOX 5616
MONTGOMERY. AL 36103

Re: Robert K. Pavella

Dear Sir/Madam:

   An examination of the foreign and domestic corporate records
on file in this office discloses no record of a corporation(s) by
the above name.

   With kindest regards, I am

                                  Sincerely,

                                  Billy Joe Camp
                                  Secretary of State

BJC:rj

CORPORATIONS
(205) 242-5324

LANDS & TRADEMARKS
(205) 242-5325

UNIFORM COMMERCIAL CODE
(205) 242-5231

This will be the typical response from most states. You will note that there was no mention of any charge for this search on Robert K. Pavella. When there is information on file about your subject, you will want to order the Articles of Incorporation, which will show the original officers, and the Annual report, which shows current officers. When you receive the paperwork on the corporations of your subject, you will want to look closely for any amendments. Amendments are added after incorporation to change by-laws, but many times amendments will give power of attorney or **full ownership to another person who is not mentioned in any other corporate papers**.

The Abandoned Property Technique

Lf you are searching for a subject that had disappeared abruptly years ago, then the abandoned property files will be a source for you to explore.

The state takes possession of the following if a person has disappeared for, in most states, at least seven years:

> **Bank Accounts**
>
> **State Income Tax Refunds**
>
> **Payroll Checks**
>
> **Overpayment of Insurance Premiums**
>
> **Credit Balance on Credit Cards**
>
> **Utility Refunds**
>
> **Dividend Checks**
>
> **Annuity Checks**
>
> **Telephone Deposit Refunds**
>
> **Safe Deposit Boxes**

Each state maintains an alphabetical listing of all persons that have had property or monies held in escrow by the state. Write to any state where your subject may have lived or had conducted any business in.

If your subject is listed and is due any significant amount of property or monies you can be assured that companies which find persons listed in the abandoned property lists are searching for your subject. These companies assess the person found a percentage, usually 30%, of the money that is held in escrow.

You may check periodically with the state that has your subject listed to see if a research company has located the subject or you can request that the state check the refund file that indicates if a person had been due property or monies and were located. The address that the state sent the refund to is public information.

ALABAMA

Alabama Revenue Department
Unclaimed Property Section
Post Office Box 327350
Montgomery, Alabama 36132

ALASKA

Alaska Department of Revenue
Unclaimed Property Section
Box 8A
Juneau, Alaska 99811

ARIZONA

Arizona Department of Revenue
Unclaimed Property Processing Unit
1600 West Monroe, Sixth Floor
Phoenix, Arizona 85007

ARKANSAS

Auditor of State
Unclaimed Property Department
230 State Capitol
Little Rock, Arkansas 72201

CALIFORNIA

Office of the State Controller
Division of Unclaimed Property
Post Office Box 942850
Sacramento, California 94250

CONNECTICUT

Office of the State Treasurer
Unclaimed Property Division
20 Trinity Street
Hartford, Connecticut 06160

DELAWARE

Delaware State Escheator
Post Office Box 89311
Wilmington, Delaware 19899

DISTRICT OF COLUMBIA

Department of Finance and Revenue
Unclaimed Property Division
300 Indiana Avenue, N.W.
Washington, D.C. 20002

FLORIDA

Office of the Comptroller
Division of Finance
Abandoned Property Section
The Capitol
Tallahassee, Florida 32399

GEORGIA

Georgia Department of Revenue
Property Tax Division
Unclaimed Property Section
405 Trinity—Washington Building
Atlanta, Georgia 30334

HAWAII

Finance Division
Department of Budget and Finance
Post Office Box 150
Honolulu, Hawaii 96810

IDAHO

Unclaimed Property Section
State Tax Commission
Post Office Box 36
Boise, Idaho 83722

ILLINOIS

State of Illinois
Department of Financial Institutions
Unclaimed Property Division
421 East Capitol Avenue
Springfield, Illinois 62706

INDIANA

Unclaimed Property Division
Office of the Attorney General
219 State House
Indianapolis, Indiana 46204

IOWA

Unclaimed Property Division
State Treasurer's Office
Hoover State Office Building
Des Moines, Iowa 50319

KANSAS

Division of Unclaimed Property
Office of State Treasurer
900 Jackson, Suite 201
Topeka, Kansas 66612

KENTUCKY

Miscellaneous Excise Tax Section
Revenue Cabinet
The Capitol
Frankfort, Kentucky 40620

LOUISIANA

Unclaimed Property Division
Post Office Box 91010
Baton Rouge, Louisiana 70821

MAINE

Abandoned Property Division
Treasury Department
Station Number 39
Augusta, Maine 04333

MARYLAND

Comptroller of the Treasurer
Unclaimed Property Division
301 West Preston Street
Baltimore, Maryland 21201

MASSACHUSETTS

Office of the Treasurer
Unclaimed Property Division
50 Franklin Street, Second Floor
Boston, Massachusetts 02110

MICHIGAN

Escheats Division
Michigan Department of the Treasury
Lansing, Michigan 48922

MINNESOTA

Unclaimed Property Office
500 Metro Square Building
Saint Paul, Minnesota 55101

MISSISSIPPI

State Treasury Department
Attention: Unclaimed Property
Post Office Box 138
Jackson, Mississippi 39205

MISSOURI

Unclaimed Property Department
Post Office Box 1272
Jefferson City, Missouri 65102

MONTANA

Department of Revenue
Abandoned Property Section
Mitchell Building
Helena, Montana 59620

NEBRASKA

Office of the State Treasurer
Unclaimed Property Section
Post Office Box 94788
Capitol Building
Lincoln, Nebraska 68509

NEVADA

Department of Commerce
Unclaimed Property Division
State Mail Room
Las Vegas, Nevada 89158

NEW HAMPSHIRE

Abandoned Property Department
State House Annex
Room 121
Concord, New Hampshire 03301

NEW JERSEY

Department of the Treasury
Office of Financial Management
1 West State Street
Trenton, New Jersey 08625

NEW MEXICO

Unclaimed Property Unit
Taxation and Revenue Department
Post Office Box 630
Santa Fe, New Mexico 87509

NEW YORK

New York State Comptroller
Office of Unclaimed Funds
Post Office Box 7003
Albany, New York 12225

NORTH CAROLINA

Treasurer
Escheat and Unclaimed Property
325 North Salisbury Street
Raleigh, North Carolina 27611

NORTH DAKOTA

Unclaimed Property Division
State Land Department
Sixth Floor, State Capitol
Bismarck, North Dakota 58505

OHIO

Ohio Department of Commerce
Division of Unclaimed Funds
77 South High Street
Columbus, Ohio 43266

OKLAHOMA

Oklahoma Tax Commission
Business Tax Division
Unclaimed Property Section
2501 Lincoln Boulevard
Oklahoma City, Oklahoma 73194

OREGON

Division of State Lands
Unclaimed Property Division
1600 State Street
Salem, Oregon 97310

PENNSYLVANIA

Department of Revenue
Abandoned and Unclaimed Property
Bureau of Administrative Services
2850 Turnpike Industrial Park
Middletown, Pennsylvania 17057

PUERTO RICO

Secretary of the Treasury
Unclaimed Property Division
San Juan, Puerto Rico 00940

RHODE ISLAND

Office of General Treasurer
Unclaimed Property Division
Post Office Box 1435
Providence, Rhode Island 02901

SOUTH CAROLINA

South Carolina Tax Division
Post Office Box 125
Columbia, South Carolina 29214

SOUTH DAKOTA

Unclaimed Property Administrator
500 East Capitol
Pierre, South Dakota 57501

TENNESSEE

Unclaimed Property Division
Andrew Jackson Building
11th Floor
Nashville, Tennessee 37219

TEXAS

Office of the State Treasurer
Post Office Box 12608
Capitol Station
Austin, Texas 78711

UTAH

Utah State Treasurer
Unclaimed Property Division
219 State Capitol
Salt Lake City, Utah 84114

VERMONT

Abandoned Property Division
Office of State Treasurer
133 State Street
Montpelier, Vermont 05602

VIRGINIA

Division of Unclaimed Property
Post Office Box 3-R
Richmond, Virginia 23207

WASHINGTON

Unclaimed Property Section
Department of Revenue
Post Office Box 448
Olympia, Washington 98507

WEST VIRGINIA

Office of the Treasurer of State
Division of Unclaimed Property
The State Capitol, Room E-147
Charleston, West Virginia 25305

WISCONSIN

Office of State Treasurer
Unclaimed Property Division
Post Office Box 2114
Madison, Wisconsin 53701

WYOMING

Office of the State Treasurer
Unclaimed Property Division
State Capitol Building
Cheyenne, Wyoming 82002

NOTES

10

Bankruptcy Records

In 1990, 724,867 individuals filed for bankruptcy. If you have reason to believe your subject has ever filed for bankruptcy or will file for bankruptcy then this is an excellent source. Bankruptcy records are public information. The petition file will contain the subject's Social Security Number, date of birth, current and former addresses, bank accounts, stock ownership, employment history including a list of the salaries and fringe benefits earned for the past several years, a list of all property including vehicles and other important financial and personal information.

The Vehicle Identification Number (VIN) of each vehicle listed in the file will be shown. You may access the current address by writing to the appropriate motor vehicle department listed elsewhere in this manual.

Property that the subject will retain because it qualifies as exempt from the bankruptcy will be listed. This property may provide another lead in your search for the subject because the address of property will be listed.

Chapter 7 is commonly known as "liquidation" bankruptcy and any person or business may file. Chapter 11 is a reorganization of debt. Chapter 13 is an adjustment of debts for a wage earner. This option is available to individuals with a regular income and who have fixed unsecured debts less than $100,000 and secured debts of less then $350,000.

Write to the bankruptcy court you feel that your subject may have filed in. If your subject does have a bankruptcy file, then review the file completely and you will be provided with much information that will assist in your search.

ALABAMA

United States Bankruptcy Court
500 South 22nd Street
Birmingham, Alabama 35233

United States Bankruptcy Court
Post Office Box 1248
Montgomery, Alabama 36192

United States Bankruptcy Court
Post Office Box 2865
Mobile, Alabama 36652

ALASKA

United States Bankruptcy Court
222 West 7th Avenue
Anchorage, Alaska 99513

ARIZONA

United States Bankruptcy Court
230 North 1st Avenue
Phoenix, Arizona 85025

United States Bankruptcy Court
110 South Church
Tucson, Arizona 85702

ARKANSAS

United States Bankruptcy Court
Post Office Box 2381
Little Rock, Arkansas 72203

CALIFORNIA

United States Bankruptcy Court
312 North Spring Street
Los Angeles, California 90012

United States Bankruptcy Court
940 Front Street
San Diego, California 92189

United States Bankruptcy Court
1130 O Street
Fresno, California 93721

United States Bankruptcy Court
450 Golden Gate Avenue
San Francisco, California 94102

United States Bankruptcy Court
Post Office Box 5276
Modesto, California 95352

COLORADO

United States Bankruptcy Court
1845 Sherman Street
Denver, Colorado 80203

CONNECTICUT

United States Bankruptcy Court
450 Main Street
Hartford, Connecticut 06103

DELAWARE

United States Bankruptcy Court
844 North King Street
Wilmington, Delaware 19801

DISTRICT OF COLUMBIA

United States Bankruptcy Court
300 Constitution Avenue, Northwest
Washington, D.C. 20001

FLORIDA

United States Bankruptcy Court
51 Southwest 1st Avenue
Miami, Florida 33101

United States Bankruptcy Court
299 East Broward Boulevard
Fort Lauderdale, Florida 33301

United States Bankruptcy Court
227 North Bronough Street
Tallahassee, Florida 32301

United States Bankruptcy Court
4921 Memorial Highway
Tampa, Florida 33634

United States Bankruptcy Court
Post Office Box 559
Jacksonville, Florida 32201

GEORGIA

United States Bankruptcy Court
Post Office Box 1957
Macon, Georgia 31202

United States Bankruptcy Court
75 Spring Street
Atlanta, Georgia 30303

United States Bankruptcy Court
P.O Box 8347
Savannah, Georgia 31412

HAWAII

United States Bankruptcy Court
Post Office Box 50121
Honolulu, Hawaii 96850

IDAHO

United States Bankruptcy Court
Post Office Box 2600
Boise, Idaho 83701

ILLINOIS

United States Bankruptcy Court
219 South Dearborn Street
Chicago, Illinois 60604

United States Bankruptcy Court
Post Office Box 309
East Saint Louis, Illinois 62201

United States Bankruptcy Court
Post Office Box 2438
Springfield, Illinois 62705

INDIANA

United States Bankruptcy Court
46 East Ohio Street
Indianapolis, Indiana 46204

United States Bankruptcy Court
610 Connecticut Street
Gary, Indiana 46402

United States Bankruptcy Court
204 South Main Street
South Bend, Indiana 46601

IOWA

United States Bankruptcy Court
1 Walnut Street
Des Moines, Iowa 50309

KANSAS

United States Bankruptcy Court
401 North Market Street
Wichita, Kansas 67202

KENTUCKY

United States Bankruptcy Court
601 West Broadway
Louisville, Kentucky 40202

United States Bankruptcy Court
Post Office Box 1050
Lexington, Kentucky 40588

LOUISIANA

United States Bankruptcy Court
500 Camp Street
New Orleans, Louisiana 70130

United States Bankruptcy Court
412 North 4th Street
Baton Rouge, Louisiana 70802

United States Bankruptcy Court
500 Fannin Street
Shreveport, Louisiana 71109

MAINE

United States Bankruptcy Court
156 Federal Way
Portland, Maine 04112

MARYLAND

United States Bankruptcy Court
101 West Lombard Street
Baltimore, Maryland 21201

MASSACHUSETTS

United States Bankruptcy Court
10 Causeway
Boston, Massachusetts 02222

MICHIGAN

United States Bankruptcy Court
231 West Lafayette Street
Detroit, Michigan 48226

United States Bankruptcy Court
P.O Box 3310
Grand Rapids, Michigan 49501

MINNESOTA

United States Bankruptcy Court
316 North Robert Street
Saint Paul, Minnesota 55101

United States Bankruptcy Court
330 2nd Avenue
Minneapolis, Minnesota 55401

MISSISSIPPI

United States Bankruptcy Court
245 East Capitol Street
Jackson, Mississippi 39201

United States Bankruptcy Court
Post Office Box 369
Biloxi, Mississippi 39533

United States Bankruptcy Court
Post Office Box 867
Averdeen, Mississippi 39730

MISSOURI

United States Bankruptcy Court
1114 Market Street
Saint Louis, Missouri 63101

United States Bankruptcy Court
811 Grand Avenue
Kansas City, Missouri 64106

MONTANA

United States Bankruptcy Court
273 Federal Building
Butte, Montana 59701

NEBRASKA

United States Bankruptcy Court
Post Office Box 428
Omaha, Nebraska 68101

NEVADA

United States Bankruptcy Court
300 Las Vegas Boulevard
Las Vegas, Nevada 89101

NEW HAMPSHIRE

United States Bankruptcy Court
275 Chestnut Street
Manchester, New Hampshire 03101

NEW JERSEY

United States Bankruptcy Court
15 North 7 Street
Camden, New Jersey 08102

United States Bankruptcy Court
Post Office Box 515
Trenton, New Jersey 08603

NEW MEXICO

United States Bankruptcy Court
Post Office Box 546
Albuquerque, New Mexico 87103

NEW YORK

United States Bankruptcy Court
1 Bowling Green
New York, New York 10004

United States Bankruptcy Court
75 Clinton Street
Brooklyn, New York 11201

United States Bankruptcy Court
Post Office Box 398
Albany, New York 12201

United States Bankruptcy Court
68 Court Street
Buffalo, New York 14202

United States Bankruptcy Court
100 State Street
Rochester, New York 14614

NORTH CAROLINA

United States Bankruptcy Court
Post Office Box 26100
Greensboro, North Carolina 27420

United States Bankruptcy Court
Post Office Box 2807
Wilson, North Carolina 27894

United States Bankruptcy Court
100 Otis Street
Asheville, North Carolina 28801

NORTH DAKOTA

United States Bankruptcy Court
Post Office Box 1110
Fargo, North Dakota 58107

OHIO

United States Bankruptcy Court
1716 Spielbusch Avenue
Toledo, Ohio 43624

United States Bankruptcy Court
201 Superior Avenue
Cleveland, Ohio 44114

United States Bankruptcy Court
2 South Main Street
Akron, Ohio 44308

United States Bankruptcy Court
9 West Front Street
Youngstown, Ohio 44501

United States Bankruptcy Court
201 Cleveland Avenue
Canton, Ohio 44702

United States Bankruptcy Court
85 Marconi Boulevard
Columbus, Ohio 43215

OKLAHOMA

United States Bankruptcy Court
201 Dean McGee Avenue
Oklahoma City, Oklahoma 73102

United States Bankruptcy Court
111 West Fifth Street
Tulsa, Oklahoma 74103

United States Bankruptcy Court
Post Office Box 1347
Okmulgee, Oklahoma 74447

OREGON

United States Bankruptcy Court
Post Office Box 1335
Eugene, Oregon 97440

United States Bankruptcy Court
1001 Southwest Fifth Avenue
Portland, Oregon 97204

PENNSYLVANIA

United States Bankruptcy Court
1602 Liberty Avenue
Pittsburgh, Pennsylvania 15222

United States Bankruptcy Court
197 South Main Street
Wilkes Barre, Pennsylvania 18701

United States Bankruptcy Court
601 Market Street
Philadelphia, Pennsylvania 19106

RHODE ISLAND

United States Bankruptcy Court
380 Westminster Mall
Providence, Rhode Island 02903

SOUTH CAROLINA

United States Bankruptcy Court
Post Office Box 1448
Columbia, South Carolina 29202

SOUTH DAKOTA

United States Bankruptcy Court
Post Office Box 5060
Sioux Falls, South Dakota 57117

TENNESSEE

United States Bankruptcy Court
701 Broadway
Nashville, Tennessee 37203

United States Bankruptcy Court
Post Office Box 2348
Knoxville, Tennessee 37901

United States Bankruptcy Court
969 Madison Avenue
Memphis, Tennessee 38104

TEXAS

United States Bankruptcy Court
1100 Commerce Street
Dallas, Texas 75242

United States Bankruptcy Court
211 West Ferguson Street
Tyler, Texas 75702

United States Bankruptcy Court
501 West 10th Street
Fort Worth, Texas 76102

United States Bankruptcy Court
1205 Texas Avenue
Lubbock, Texas 79401

United States Bankruptcy Court
515 Rusk Avenue
Houston, Texas 77002

United States Bankruptcy Court
Post Office Box 1439
San Antonio, Texas 78295

UTAH

United States Bankruptcy Court
350 South Main Street
Salt Lake City, Utah 84101

VERMONT

United States Bankruptcy Court
Post Office Box 6648
Rutland, Vermont 05702

VIRGINIA

United States Bankruptcy Court
206 North Washington Street
Alexandria, Virginia 22314

United States Bankruptcy Court
Post Office Box 676
Richmond, Virginia 23206

United States Bankruptcy Court
600 Granby Street
Norfolk, Virginia 23510

United States Bankruptcy Court
Post Office Box 497
Newport News, Virginia 23607

United States Bankruptcy Court
Post Office Box 2390
Roanoke, Virginia 24010

WASHINGTON

United States Bankruptcy Court
1200 Sisth Avenue
Seattle, Washington 98101

United States Bankruptcy Court
Post Office Box 2164
Spokane, Washington 99201

WEST VIRGINIA

United States Bankruptcy Court
Post Office Box 3924
Charleston, West Virginia 25301

United States Bankruptcy Court
Post Office Box 70
Wheeling, West Virginia 26003

WISCONSIN

United States Bankruptcy Court
517 West Wisconsin Avenue
Milwaukee, Wisconsin 53202

United States Bankruptcy Court
Post Office Box 548
Madison, Wisconsin 53701

WYOMING

United States Bankruptcy Court
Post Office Box 1107
Cheyenne, Wyoming 82003

John L. Cawler
Name
59 Huser Lane Apt. 23
Street
Nanuet, New York   10954
City, State, Zip
914-675-7723
Telephone

☐ Attorney for Debtor(s)   (If applicable) Attorney's
☒ Debtor In Pro SE   State Bar I.D. No. _____

RECORDED
MAR 2 0 1993
_____ NYC
CLERK OF CIRCUIT

UNITED STATES BANKRUPTCY COURT
Northeast ____ DISTRICT OF __New York____

In re _____ ,

[Set forth here all names including married, maiden, and trade
names used by debtor within last 6 years.]

John L. Cawler   Debtor
Cawler Liquor Store
Cawler Food and Gas Station
Barbara Cawler
Barbara Cawler's Secretarial Service
Social Security No(s). 078-90-0064 _____ and all
Employer's Tax Identification Nos. [If any] _____

Case No. _93-827361-9____

Chapter __Chapter 13____

NOTICE OF AVAILABLE CHAPTERS BY THE CLERK OF THE COURT

1. Section 342(b) of 11 U.S. Code ("The Bankruptcy Code") states:
"Prior to the commencement of a case under this title by an individual whose debts are primarily consumer debts, the clerk shall give written notice to such individual that indicates each chapter of this title under which such individual may proceed."

2. If your debts are primarily consumer ones (as opposed to business debts) and they do not exceed $100,000.00 unsecured or $350,000.00 secured (11 U.S.C. § 109(e)), you are eligible to file under Chapter 13 and to use future income to pay all or a portion of your existing debts.

3. You are also eligible to file under Chapter 11 ($500.00 filing fees) for debt reorganization.

4. You are not eligible to file under Chapter 9.

5. You are eligible to file under Chapter 7 ("straight bankruptcy"), whereby debts are eliminated and your non-exempt assets are liquidated by the trustee for the benefit of your creditors.

6. You may be eligible to file under Chapter 12.

7. All general filing eligibility is subject to 11 U.S.C. §§ 109, 727(a)(8) and (9), and 707(b). Consult your attorney.

_____Robert T. Vernon, Jr._____
Clerk of the Court

I HAVE READ THE ABOVE "NOTICE OF AVAILABLE CHAPTERS".

_____
Signature of Debtor

_____
Signature of Joint Debtor

You will be able to find your subject in the bankruptcy files by name only. When you find the first application to the bankruptcy court, you will note that you now have the case number. Pull the entire file using this number. The subject's Social Security Number is listed along with any other important information, including the address, home telephone number, spouse's name, etc.

11

Child Support Enforcement

Many readers of this book will be able to use the government to conduct a search for them without charge. If an individual has a child support order against a subject, with minimum information (the subject's name and Social Security Number), the Federal Parent Locator Service can search for a current address in the records of the Department of Defense, the National Personnel Records Center, the Social Security Administration and the Veterans Administration.

The Federal Parent Locator Service is a service operated by the Office of Child Support Enforcement within the purview of the United States Department of Health and Human Services to assist the individual states in locating persons for the purpose of obtaining child support payments. This agency is also used in cases of parental kidnapping related to custody and visitation cases.

The first step in seeking the location of a subject that has an obligation to pay child support is to contact your state's Child Support Enforcement office. They will first use the State Parent Locator Service. This service, free of charge, will check the records of other state agencies such as motor vehicle registration, unemployment insurance, state income tax and correctional facilities. If the subject has moved to another state, the above noted Federal Parent Support Service will be contacted.

The Internal Revenue Service, in conjunction with State and Federal Child Enforcement agencies, will disclose information from the tax return of the subject to the child support office which will be of assistance in finding the subject and determining the subject's financial condition.

ALABAMA

Child Support Enforcement Division
Department of Human Resources
64 North Union Street
Montgomery, Alabama 36130
(205) 242-2734

ALASKA

Child Support Enforcement Division
Department of Revenue
550 West 7th Avenue, 4th Floor
Anchorage, Alaska 99501
(907) 276-3441

ARIZONA

Child Support Enforcement
2222 West Encanto
Post Office Box 6123 — Site Code 776A
Phoenix, Arizona 85005
(602) 252-0236

ARKANSAS

Division of Child Support Enforcement
Arkansas Social Services
Post Office Box 3358
Little Rock, Arkansas 72203
(501) 682-8398

CALIFORNIA

Child Support Program Management
Department of Social Service
744 P Street — Mail Stop 9-011
Sacramento, California 95814
(916) 322-8495

COLORADO

Division of Child Support Enforcement
Department of Social Services
1575 Sherman Street
Denver, Colorado 80203
(303) 866-5994

CONNECTICUT

Bureau of Child Support Enforcement
Department of Human Resources
1049 Asylum Avenue
Hartford, Connecticut 06105
(203) 566-3053

DELAWARE

Division of Child Support Enforcement
Department of Health & Social Services
Post Office Box 904
New Castle, Delaware 19720
(302) 421-8300

DISTRICT OF COLUMBIA

Office of Paternity & Child Support
3rd Floor — Suite 3013
425 I Street, NW
Washington, D.C. 20001
(202) 724-5610

FLORIDA

Office of Child Support Enforcement
Health and Rehabilative Services
1317 Winewood Blvd, Building 3
Tallahassee, Florida 32399
(904) 488-9900

GEORGIA

Office of Child Support Recovery
State Department of Human Resources
878 Peachtree Street NE, Room 529
Atlanta, Georgia 30309
(404) 894-4119

GUAM

Office of the Attorney General
Child Support Enforcement Office
194 Hernan Cortez Avenue
Agana, Guam 96910
(671) 477-2036

HAWAII

Child Support Enforcement Agency
Department of the Attorney General
Post Office Box 1860
Honolulu, Hawaii 96805
(808) 548-5779

IDAHO

Bureau of Child Support Enforcement
450 West State Street
Towers Building — 7th Floor
Boise, Idaho 83720
(208) 334-5710

ILLINOIS

Division of Child Support Enforcement
Prescott E. Bloom Building
201 South Grand Avenue East
Springfield, Illinois 62794
(217) 782-1366

INDIANA

Child Support Enforcement Division
Department of Public Welfare
141 South Meridian Street
Indianapolis, Indiana 46225
(317) 232-4885

IOWA

Bureau of Collections
Iowa Department of Human Services
Hoover Building — 5th Floor
Des Moines, Iowa 50319
(515) 281-5580

KANSAS

Child Support Enforcement Program
300 South West Oakley Street
Post Office Box 497
Topeka, Kansas 66603
(913) 296-3237

KENTUCKY

Division of Child Support Enforcement
Department of Social Insurance
275 East Main Street, 6th Floor East
Frankfort, Kentucky 40621
(502) 564-2285

LOUISIANA

Support Enforcement Services
Department of Social Services
Post Office Box 94065
Baton Rouge, Louisiana 70804
(504) 342-4780

MAINE

Support Enforcement and Location Unit
Department of Human Services
State House, Station 11
Augusta, Maine 04333
(207) 289-2886

MARYLAND

Child Support Enforcement
Department of Human Resources
311 West Saratoga Street
Baltimore, Maryland 21201
(301) 333-3979

MASSACHUSETTS

Child Support Enforcement Division
Department of Revenue
215 First Street
Cambridge, Massachusetts 02124
(617) 621-4200

MICHIGAN

Office of Child Support
Department of Social Services
300 South Capitol Avenue, Suite 621
Lansing, Michigan 48909
(517) 373-7570

MINNESOTA

Office of Child Support Enforcement
Department of Human Services
444 Lafayette Road — 4th Floor
St. Paul, Minnesota 55155
(612) 296-2499

MISSISSIPPI

Child Support Division
State Department of Public Welfare
515 East Amite Street
Jackson, Mississippi 39205
(601) 354-0341 EXT. 503

MISSOURI

Division of Child Support Enforcement
Department of Social Services
Post Office Box 1527
Jefferson City, Missouri 65102
(314) 751-4301

MONTANA

Child Support Enforcement Division
Department Rehabilitation Services
Post Office Box 5955
Helena, Montana 59604
(406) 444-4614

NEBRASKA

Child Support Enforcement Office
Department of Social Services
Post Office Box 95026
Lincoln, Nebraska 68509
(402) 471-9125

NEVADA

Child Support Enforcement Program
Department of Human Resources
2527 North Carson Street
Carson City, Nevada 89710
(702) 885-4744

NEW HAMPSHIRE

Office of Child Support Enforcement
Division of Welfare
6 Hazen Road
Concord, New Hampshire 03301
(603) 271-4426

NEW JERSEY

Division of Economic Assistance
Department of Human Services
CN 716
Trenton, New Jersey 08625
(609) 588-2401

NEW MEXICO

Child Support Enforcement Division
Department of Human Services
Post Office Box 25109
Santa Fe, New Mexico 87504
(505) 827-7200

NEW YORK

Office of Child Support Enforcement
Department of Social Services
Post Office Box 14 — 1 Commerce Plaza
Albany, New York 12260
(518) 474-9081

NORTH CAROLINA

Child Support Enforcement Section
Division of Social Services
437 North Harrington Street
Raleigh, North Carolina 27603
(919) 733-4120

NORTH DAKOTA

Child Support Enforcement Agency
Department of Human Services
State Capitol
Bismarck, North Dakota 58505
(701) 224-3582

OHIO

Bureau of Child Support
Department of Human Services
30 East Broad Street
Columbus, Ohio 43266
(614) 466-3233

OKLAHOMA

Child Support Enforcement Division
Department of Human Services
Post Office Box 25352
Oklahoma City, Oklahoma 73125
(405) 424-5871

OREGON

Recovery Services Section
Department of Human Resources
Post Office Box 14506
Salem, Oregon 97309
(503) 378-5439

PENNSYLVANIA

Bureau of Child Support Enforcement
Department of Public Welfare
Post Office Box 8018
Harrisburg, Pennsylvania 17105
(717) 787-3672 or 783-5184

PUERTO RICO

Child Support Enforcement Program
Department of Social Services
CALL Box 3349
San Juan, Puerto Rico 00904
(809) 722-4731

RHODE ISLAND

Bureau of Family Support
Department of Human Services
77 Dorrance Street
Providence, Rhode Island 02903
(401) 277-2409

SOUTH CAROLINA

Child Support Enforcement Division
Department of Social Services
Post Office Box 1520
Columbia, South Carolina 29202
(803) 737-5870

SOUTH DAKOTA

Office of Child Support Enforcement
Department of Social Services
700 Governors Drive
Pierre, South Dakota 57501
(605) 773-3641

TENNESSEE

Child Support Services
Department of Human Services
400 Deadrick Street
Nashville, Tennessee 37219
(615) 741-1820

TEXAS

Child Support Enforcement Division
Office of the Attorney General
Post Office Box 12548
Austin, Texas 78711
(512) 463-2181

UTAH

Office of Recovery Services
Department of Social Services
120 North 200 West
Salt Lake City, Utah 84145
(801) 538-4400

VERMONT

Child Support Division
Department of Social Welfare
103 South Main Street
Waterbury, Vermont 05676
(802) 241-2910

VIRGIN ISLANDS

Support and Paternity Division
Department of Law
46 Norre Gade
St. Thomas, Virgin Islands 00801
(809) 776-0372

VIRGINIA

Division of Support Enforcement Program
Department of Social Services
8007 Discovery Drive
Richmond, Virginia 23288
(804) 662-9297

WASHINGTON

Revenue Division
Department of Social & Health Services
Mail Stop HJ-31
Olympia, Washington 98504
(206) 586-6111

WEST VIRGINIA

Child Advocate Office
Department of Social Services
1900 Washington Street, East
Charleston, West Virginia 25305
(304) 348-3780

WISCONSIN

Division of Economic Support
Bureau of Child Support
1 West Wilson Street — Room 382
Madison, Wisconsin 53707
(608) 266-1175

WYOMING

Child Support Enforcement Section
Division of Public Assistance
Hathaway Building
Cheyenne, Wyoming 82002
(307) 777-7892

REGIONAL OFFICES OF THE
OFFICE OF CHILD SUPPORT ENFORCEMENT

REGION I — CONNECTICUT, MAINE, MASSACHUSETTS, NEW HAMPSHIRE, RHODE ISLAND, VERMONT

OCSE Regional Representative
John F. Kennedy Federal Building
Boston, Massachusetts 02203
(617) 565-2463

REGION II — NEW YORK, NEW JERSEY, PUERTO RICO, VIRGIN ISLANDS

OCSE Regional Representative
Federal Building, Room 4048
26 Federal Plaza
New York, New York 10278
(212) 264-2890

REGION III — DELAWARE, MARYLAND, PENNSYLVANIA, VIRGINIA, WEST VIRGINIA, DISTRICT OF COLUMBIA

OCSE Regional Representative
3535 Market Street, Room 4119 MS/15
Philadelphia, Pennsylvania 19101
(215) 596-1396

REGION IV — ALABAMA, FLORIDA, GEORGIA, KENTUCKY, MISSISSIPPI, NORTH CAROLINA, SOUTH CAROLINA, TENNESSEE

OCSE Regional Representative
101 Marietta Tower, Suite 821
Atlanta, Georgia 30323
(404) 331-5733

REGION V — ILLINOIS, INDIANA, MICHIGAN, MINNESOTA, OHIO, WISCONSIN

OCSE Regional Representative
105 West Adams Street
Chicago, Illinois 60603
(312) 353-4237

REGION VI — ARKANSAS, LOUISIANA, NEW MEXICO, OKLAHOMA, TEXAS

OCSE Regional Representative
1200 Main Tower Building
Suite 1700
Dallas, Texas 75202
(214) 767-9648

REGION VII — IOWA, KANSAS, MISSOURI, NEBRASKA

OCSE Regional Representative
601 East 12th Street
Federal Building, Room 515
Kansas City, Missouri 64106
(816) 426-5159

REGION VIII — COLORADO, MONTANA, NORTH DAKOTA, SOUTH DAKOTA, UTAH, WYOMING

OCSE Regional Representative
Federal Office Building, Room 1185
1961 Stout Street
Denver, Colorado 80294
(303) 844-5646

REGION IX — ARIZONA, CALIFORNIA, HAWAII, NEVADA, GUAM

OCSE Regional Representative
50 United Nations Plaza
Mail Stop 351
San Francisco, California 94102
(415) 556-4415

REGION X — ALASKA, IDAHO, OREGON, WASHINGTON

OCSE Regional Representative
2201 Sixth Avenue
Mail Stop RX-70
Seattle, Washington 98121
(206) 442-2775

NOTES

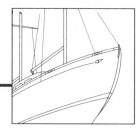

12

Boat & Vessel Registration

The registration of a boat or vessel is a source that is often overlooked but can produce the same desired results as other more commonly used public records. Request an alpha search if you do not have the subject's date of birth. If your subject will be difficult to find and does not have a boat or vessel registration then you may want to order the boat registration of a relative. You will then be able to contact the relative and query them on the location of your subject.

The registration will contain the address, date of birth and the identification number of the boat or vessel. You will be able to order a "Vessel History" and apply the same techniques that are used when accessing vehicle histories.

ALABAMA

Marine Police Division
State of Alabama
State Administrative Building
Montgomery, Alabama 36130

ALASKA

Alaska State Troopers
Department of Public Safety
Post Office Box 6188 Annex
Anchorage, Alaska 99502

ARIZONA

Game and Fish Department
State of Arizona
2222 West Greenway Road
Phoenix, Arizona 85023

ARKANSAS

Boat andVessel Registration
State of Arkansas
Post Office Box 1272
Little Rock, Arkansas 72201

CALIFORNIA

Department of Motor Vehicles
State of California
Vessel Registration Section
Post Office Box 11319
Sacramento, California 95853

CANADA

Ministry of Natural Resources
Whitney Block, Queen's Park
Toronto, Ontario M7A 1W3

COLORADO

Division of Parks and Outdoor Recreation
State of Colorado
Post Office Box 231
Littleton, Colorado 80160

CONNECTICUT

Boat Registration Unit
State of Connecticut
60 State Street
Wethersfield, Connecticut 06109

DELAWARE

Division of Fish and Wildlife
State of Delaware
Post Office Box 1401
Dover, Delaware 19903

DISTRICT OF COLUMBIA

Metropolitan Police Department
Harbor Patrol
550 Water Street, S.W.
Washington, D.C. 20024

FLORIDA

Department of Natural Resources
State of Florida
3900 Commonwealth Boulevard
Tallahassee, Florida 32399

GEORGIA

Department of Natural Resources
State of Georgia
270 Washington Street, S.W.
Atlanta, Georgia 30034

HAWAII

Harbors Division
State of Hawaii
79 S. Nimitz Highway
Honolulu, Hawaii 96813

IDAHO

Department of Parks and Recreation
State of Idaho
2177 Warm Springs Avenue
Boise, Idaho 83720

ILLINOIS

Conservation Department
State of Illinois
524 South Second Street
Springfield, Illinois 62794

INDIANA

Department of Natural Resources
State of Indiana
606 State Office Building
Indianapolis, Indiana 46204

IOWA

Department of Natural Resource
State of Iowa
Wallace Building
Des Moines, Iowa 50319

KANSAS

Kansas, Fish and Game Commission
State of Kansas
R. R. No. 2, Box 54A
Pratt, Kansas 67124

KENTUCKY

Department of Natural Resources
State of Kentucky
107 Mero Street
Frankfort, Kentucky 40601

LOUISIANA

Louisiana Department of Wildlife
State of Louisiana
Post Office Box 14796
Baton Rouge, Louisiana 70898

MAINE

Department of Inland Fisheries
State of Maine
284 State Street
Augusta, Maine 04333

MARYLAND

Department of Natural Resources
State of Maryland
Post Office Box 1869
Annapolis, Maryland 21404

MASSACHUSETTS

Division of Marine Vehicles
Commonwealth of Massachusetts
100 Nashua Street, Room 910
Boston, Massachusetts 02114

MICHIGAN

Boats and Vessel Registration
State of Michigan
7064 Crowner Drive
Lansing, Michigan 48918

MINNESOTA

Department of Natural Resources
State of Minnesota
500 Lafayette Road
Saint Paul, Minnesota 55146

MISSISSIPPI

Mississippi Department of Wildlife
State of Mississippi
Post Office Box 451
Jackson, Mississippi 39205

MISSOURI

Missouri State Water Patrol
State of Missouri
Post Office Box 603
Jefferson City, Missouri 65102

MONTANA

Registrar's Bureau
State of Montana
925 Main Street
Deer Lodge, Montana 59722

NEBRASKA

State Game and Parks Commission
2200 North 33rd Street
Lincoln, Nebraska 68503

NEVADA

Nevada Department of Wildlife
Division of Law Enforcement
Post Office Box 10678
Reno, Nevada 89520

NEW HAMPSHIRE

Division of Safety Services
Department of Safety
6 Hazen Drive
Concord, New Hampshire 03305

NEW JERSEY

New Jersey State Police
Bureau of Marine Law Enforcement
Post Office Box 7068
West Trenton, New Jersey 08625

NEW MEXICO

Natural Resources Department
State Park and Recreation Division
Boating Safety Section
Post Office Box 1147
Santa Fe, New Mexico 87504

NEW YORK

Marine and Recreation Vehicles
Agency Building No. 1
Empire State Plaza
Albany, New York 12238

NORTH CAROLINA

Wildlife Resources Commission
State of North Carolina
512 North Salisbury Street
Raleigh, North Carolina 27604

NORTH DAKOTA

State Game and Fish Department
State of North Dakota
100 North Bismarck Expressway
Bismarck, North Dakota 58501

OHIO

Department of Natural Resources
State of Ohio
Fountain Square
Columbus, Ohio 43224

OKLAHOMA

Boat and Vessel Registration
State of Oklahoma
2501 Lincoln Boulevard
Oklahoma City, Oklahoma 73194

OREGON

State Marine Board
State of Oregon
435 Commercial Street, Northeast
Salem, Oregon 97310

PENNSYLVANIA

Boat and Vessel Registration
Commonwealth of Pennsylvania
Post Office Box 68900
Harrisburg, Pennsylvania 17106

PUERTO RICO

Maritime Department
Ports Authority
GPO Box 2829
San Juan, Puerto Rico 00936

RHODE ISLAND

Department of Environment
Office of Boat Registration
22 Hayes Street
Providence, Rhode Island 02903

SOUTH CAROLINA

Wildlife and Marine Resources
State of South Carolina
Post Office Box 167
Columbia, South Carolina 29202

SOUTH DAKOTA

Wildlife and Marine Resources
Department of Marine Enforcement
State of South Dakota
118 West Capitol Avenue
Pierre, South Dakota 57501

TENNESSEE

Tennessee Wildlife Resources Agency
State of Tennessee
Post Office Box 40747
Nashville, Tennessee 37204

TEXAS

Parks and Wildlife Department
State of Texas
4200 Smith School Road
Austin, Texas 78744

UTAH

Boat and Vessel Registration
Department of Marine Enforcement
State of Utah
1095 Motor Avenue
Salt Lake City, Utah 84116

VERMONT

Marine Division
Department of Public Safety
State of Vermont
103 Main Street
Waterbury, Vermont 05676

VIRGINIA

Commission of Game and Inland
Fisheries
State of Virginia
Post Office Box 11104
Richmond, Virginia 23230

VIRGIN ISLANDS

Department of Planning and Natural
Resources
Nisky Center, Suite 231
St. Thomas, U.S. Virgin Islands 00803

WASHINGTON

Department of Licensing
Division of Title and Registration
State of Washington
Post Office Box 9909
Olympia, Washington 98504

WEST VIRGINIA

Law Enforcement Division
Department of Natural Resources
State of West Virginia
1900 Kanawha Boulevard
Charleston, West Virginia 25305

WISCONSIN

Department of Natural Resources
State of Wisconsin
Post Office Box 7921
Madison, Wisconsin 53707

WYOMING

Game and Fish Department
State of Wyoming
5400 Bishop Boulevard
Cheyenne, Wyoming 82002

Illinois 🚹 **Department of Conservation**
life and land together

Brent Manning
Director

John W. Comerio
Deputy Director

Bruce F. Clay
Assistant Director

LINCOLN TOWER PLAZA • 524 SOUTH SECOND STREET • SPRINGFIELD 62701-1787
CHICAGO OFFICE • ROOM 4-300 • 100 WEST RANDOLPH 60601

Feb. 26, 1993

Mr. Culligan:

This is to certify that we have checked our files and do not find a boat in the State of Illinois registered under the name Robert K. Pavella. We regret we cannot help you further.

If you have any questions, please contact me at 217/782-2138 weekdays from 8:00 A.M. to 4:30 P.M.

Sincerely,

Jim Boyle

Jim Boyle, Supervisor
Regi-Title Section

Signed before me this 26th day of Feb, 1993

Kathryn L. Hill 2/26/93

Kathryn L. Hill   Notary Public

OFFICIAL SEAL
KATHRYN L. HILL
NOTARY PUBLIC, STATE OF ILLINOIS
MY COMMISSION EXPIRES 4-4-93

13

The National Archives

The National Archives preserves and makes available for reference and research the well-known valuable records of the U.S. government. These records include well-known documents, such as the Declaration of Independence and the Constitution, as well as 3 billion textual documents, 2 million cartographic items, 5 million still photographs, 9 million aerial photographs, 91 million feet of motion picture film, and 122,000 video and sound recordings. The National Archives also makes available for research a select number of collections donated to the federal government for that purpose.

Known formally as the National Archives and Records Administration (NARA), the agency operates 14 records centers, 11 field branches and 8 Presidential libraries in 15 states.

GENEALOGICAL RECORDS IN THE NATIONAL ARCHIVES

The National Archives has custody of millions of records relating to persons who have had dealings with the federal government. These records are deposited in the National Archives facilities in the Washington, D.C., area and in the eleven National Archives Regional Archives. These records may contain full information about a person or give little information beyond a name.

The original records may be freely consulted in the National Archives facility that has custody of them. In addition, many of the most heavily used records have been microfilmed, with copies available for research use at more than one facility. Photocopies of most of the records can be supplied for a moderate fee per page. If you are unable to come to the National Archives, you may hire someone to do research for you. Many researchers who work for a fee advertise in genealogical periodicals, which are usually available in public libraries.

RECORDS ABOUT INDIANS

Within the National Archives, there are many records relating to Indians who maintained their tribal affiliation. The original records of the headquarters of the Bureau of Indian Affairs are in the National Archives in Washington, D.C. These records often contain information about specific tribal members. Original records created by the various field offices and Indian schools are among the holdings of the regional archives.

They include the following:

—Lists of Indian tribes include Cherokee, Chickasaw, Choctaw, and Creek. Each entry on these lists usually contains the **name of the head of the family**, the number of persons in the family by **age and sex**, a description of property owned before removal (including the location of real property).

—Annuity Payrolls, showing the **name, age, and sex** of each person who received payment.

—Annual census rolls. These records (available on microfilm) normally show for each person in a family the **Indian or English name** (or both names), **age, sex**, and relationship to the head of the family and sometimes to another enrolled Indian. The records occasionally include supplementary information, such as names of persons who died or were born during the year.

LAND RECORDS

Land records in the National Archives include bounty-land-warrant files, donation land entry files, homestead application files, and private land claim files. The donation land entry files and homestead application files show, in addition to the name of the applicant, the location of the land and the date it was acquired, residence or post office address, **age or date and place of birth, marital status**, and, if applicable, the given **name of spouse** or size of family. If any applicant for homestead land was of foreign birth, the application file contains evidence of naturalization or of intention to become a citizen. Supporting documents show the immigrant's country of birth and sometimes the date and port of arrival. Genealogical information in records relating to private land claims varies from the mention of the claimant's name and location of the land to such additional information as the claimant's place of residence when the claim was made and **the names of relatives**, both living and dead.

NATURALIZATION RECORDS

Naturalization records generally show, for each person who petitioned for naturalization, **name, age, date of birth, nationality**, and whether citizenship was granted. The eleven regional archives hold original records of naturalizations filed in most of the federal courts located in their regions.

The Immigration and Naturalization Service (INS), Washington, D.C., 20536, has duplicate records of all naturalizations that occurred after September 26, 1906. When records relating to citizenship granted after that date are not available in the National Archives, inquiries should be sent to the INS on a form that can be obtained from any of the service's district offices. Local postmasters will give the address of the nearest INS district office.

PASSENGER LISTS

The National Archives series of customs passenger lists and immigration passenger lists of ships arriving from abroad at many Atlantic, Pacific, and gulf coast ports. There are also arrival records for immigration via Canada.

A customs passenger list normally contains the following information for each passenger: **name, age, sex, and occupation**; the country of embarkation; and the country of destination. For one who died in passage, the date and circumstances of death are given. Immigration passenger lists vary in informational content but usually show the place of birth and last place of residence in addition to the information found in the customs passenger lists. Some of the immigration passenger lists include **the name and address of a relative** in the country from which the passenger came.

Microfilm copies of available passenger lists earlier than 1955 can be used in the National Archives in Washington, D.C. Some microfilm copies of lists are also available in the regional archives.

PASSPORT APPLICATIONS

The National Archives in Washington, D.C., has passport applications and related papers. The name of the person who applied for a passport and the place and approximate date of application should be supplied. Requests for information from passport records should be addressed to the Passport Office, Department of State, Washington, D.C. 20520.

PERSONNEL RECORDS

There are records in the National Archives in Washington, D.C., relating to civilian employees of the federal government whose service ended before 1940. These records may contain information about **the date and place of birth of an employee**. The National Archives staff will search for records about employees if given the full name and address of the employing agency and the approximate dates of employment. The personnel records for most civilian employees whose service terminated after 1940 are in Civilian Personnel Records, 111 Winnebago Street, St. Louis, MO 63118.

A veteran's claim will show **his place and date of birth, place of residence after service, and a summary of military service**. A dependent's claim normally includes the **dependent's age and residence**, relationship to the veteran, and information about the veteran's death. A widow's application usually includes her **maiden name, the date of her marriage to the veteran**, and **the names of their children**.

When a claim file is found, documents that normally contain information of a personal nature about the veteran and his family will be selected and photocopied. The inquirer is notified of costs and copies are sent after payment is received. The selected documents furnished generally contain the basic information in the pension file, as the remaining documents rarely contain any additional genealogical data. If an inquirer wishes to have photocopies of all the reproducible papers in the claim file, they can be furnished for a moderate cost per page.

The National Archives has applications or abstracts of applications of seamen on U.S. vessels for "protection certificate," or certificates of U.S. citizenship. Such applications are usually supported by evidence of the **date and place of birth and of the citizenship** of the seaman.

Requests for information about army offices separated after 1916 and army enlisted personnel separated after 1912 should be made on Standard Form 180, Request Pertaining to Military Records, and sent to Military Personnel Records, 9700 Page Boulevard, St. Louis, 63132.

Records of commissioned officers in the U.S. Marine Corps usually show each officer's name and rank and the date of appointment or of acceptance of a commission. They may also give **age** and information about residence. Service records for enlisted marines usually show **name, age**, and **the date, place**, and **term of enlistment**.

The National Archives staff will make a limited search in its naval and marine service records in response to letters of inquiry. If a request concerns a navy or marine officer or enlisted person, his name and the name of the war in which he served or the dates of service should be given.

The U.S. Coast Guard was created on January 28, 1915, which consolidated the former Revenue Cutter and Lifesaving Services of the Department of the Treasury. The Bureau of Lighthouses of the Department of Commerce became a part of the Coast Guard on July 1, 1939. Revenue-Cutter Service vessels were manned by military personnel.

The inspectors of the Lifesaving Service were also military personnel, but the superintendents, keepers, and other employees at the lifesaving stations were civilian employees. The inspectors and engineers of the lighthouse district were officers detailed from the Navy and Army. All other employees of the Lighthouse Service were civilians. Personnel and card records, for civilians formerly employed by the Revenue-Cutter Service, Lifesaving Service and Lighthouse Service are on file at the National Personnel Records Center (Civilian Personnel Records).

Civilian employment records are subject to Office of Personnel Management regulations governing the release of information from federal employees' personnel records under the term of the Freedom of Information Act of 1967 (5 USC 552). Information furnished is limited to **names, position titles, grades, salaries, and duty stations**. Inquiries, with as much identification as possible, should be submitted to Civilian Personnel Records, 111 Winnebago Street, St. Louis, MO 63118.

BIRTHS AND MARRIAGES AT FOREIGN SERVICE POSTS

The National Archives has records of births and marriages of U.S. citizens abroad registered at Foreign Service posts. Birth and marriage records extend through 1941, and reports of deaths extend through 1949. Requests for information should be addressed to the Department of State, Washington, D.C. 20520. Requests for information about earlier registrations should be addressed to the Civil Reference Branch (NNRC), National Archives, Washington, D.C. 20408.

HOW TO SEARCH IN AN ORDERLY FASHION

For records accessioned by the National Archives, the concept of moving from the smallest to the largest citation element (from the record item to the repository) is recommended. Citations may differ because internal record group arrangement is based on the organizational structures of the bureaus, departments, and agencies that created the records; some agencies were organized in more complex structures than others. Citations to records should reflect the hierarchical arrangement of the records as closely as possible.

The citation elements to be used (going from the smallest element to the largest) are:

RECORD: At the National Archives, a record is piece of information or an item in any physical form (e.g. paper, photographic or motion picture film, audio tape, computer tape, etc.) that gives information created or received by a government agency in carrying out its duties and functions. Example: a letter in a pension application file.

FILE UNIT: A file unit holds the records concerning a transaction, person, case, date, or subject. Example: a pension application file based on the military service of one veteran. A pension file often contains record items of various types in addition to the actual application, or claim, such as supporting depositions, affidavits, correspondence, etc.

SERIES: A series consists of file units that deal with a particular subject, function, or activity and that are related by arrangement, source, use, physical form, or action taken. Example: within pension application files for widows and dependents of sailors, pension applications that were not approved constitute one series while pension applications that were approved constitute another series.

SUBGROUP: A subgroup contains two or more series that are related by subject, activity, and source. Example: the two previously mentioned series for approved and unapproved pension applications based on sailors' military service (plus other series of pension applications based on military service in the U.S. Army and the Marine Corps for roughly the same time period) form the subgroup Pension Files.

RECORD GROUP: Subgroups are combined into record groups according to the origin of the subgroup material. Most often, a record group exists for the records of a bureau or other administrative body of an executive department, or for an independent government agency that is equivalent to a bureau in size. Example: the subgroup Pension Files plus other subgroups constitute Records of the Veterans Administration.

REPOSITORY: The repository is the institution in which the cited record is kept. Give the name of the institution and the city in which it is located.

National Archives repositories in Washington, D.C.; Suitland, MD; Alexandria, VA; and other locations in the Washington, D.C., area should be cited as "National Archives, Washington, D.C." A regional archives should be cited as "National Archives — [name of region]."

NATIONAL ARCHIVES REGIONAL
ARCHIVES AND AREAS COVERED

For each of the following, address inquiries to: Director, National Archives — [name of region]

NEW ENGLAND REGION

380 Trapelo Road
Waltham, Massachusetts 02154
Telephone 617-647-8100; Research

Room Hours 8 a.m. to 4:30 p.m., Monday — Friday; 8 a.m. to 4:30 p.m., 1st Saturday of each month. Covers Connecticut, Maine, Massachusetts, New Hampshire, Rhode Island, and Vermont.

NORTHEAST REGION

Building 22 — MOT Bayonne
Bayonne, New Jersey 07002-5388
Telephone 201-823-7252; Research

Room Hours 8 a.m. to 4:30 p.m., Monday — Friday; 8:30 a.m. to 4 p.m., 3rd Saturday of each month. Covers New Jersey, New York, Puerto Rico, and the Virgin Islands.

MID ATLANTIC REGION

9th and Market Streets, Room 1350
Philadelphia, Pennsylvania 19107
Telephone 215-597-3000; Research

Room Hours 8 a.m. to 5 p.m., Monday — Friday; 8 a.m. to noon, 1st and 3rd Saturdays of each month. Covers Delaware, Maryland, Pennsylvania, Virginia, and West Virginia.

SOUTHEAST REGION

1557 St. Joseph Avenue
East Point, Georgia 30344
Telephone 404-763-7477; Research

Room Hours 7:30 a.m. to 4:30 p.m., Monday, Wednesday, Thursday, Friday; 7:30 a.m. to 10 p.m., Tuesday; 9 a.m. to 5 p.m., 2nd Saturday of each month. Covers Alabama, Georgia, Florida, Kentucky, Mississippi, North Carolina, South Carolina, and Tennessee.

GREAT LAKES REGION

7358 South Pulaski Road
Chicago, Illinois 60629
Telephone 312-581-7816; Research

Room Hours 8 a.m. to 4:15 p.m., Monday
— Friday. Covers Illinois, Indiana,
Michigan, Minnesota, Ohio, and
Wisconsin.

CENTRAL PLAINS REGION

2312 East Bannister Road
Kansas City, Missouri 64131
Telephone 816-926-6272; Research

Room Hours 8 a.m. to 4 p.m., Monday —
Friday; 8 a.m. to 8 p.m., 3rd Thursday of
each month; 8 a.m. to 4 p.m., 3rd
Saturday of each month. Covers Iowa,
Kansas, Missouri, and Nebraska.

SOUTHWEST REGION

501 West Felix Street [building address]
Post Office Box 6216 [mailing address]
Fort Worth, Texas 76115
Telephone 817-334-5525; Research

Room Hours 8 a.m. to 4 p.m., Monday —
Friday. Covers Arkansas, Louisiana, New
Mexico, Oklahoma, and Texas.

ROCKY MOUNTAIN REGION

Building 48, Denver Federal Center
Denver, Colorado 80225
Telephone 303-236-0818; Research

Room Hours 7:30 a.m. to 4 p.m., Monday,
Tuesday, Thursday, Friday; 7:30 a.m. to 5
p.m., Wednesday. Covers Colorado,
Montana, North Dakota, South Dakota,
Utah, and Wyoming.

PACIFIC SOUTHWEST REGION

24000 Avila Road [building address]
Post Office Box 6719 [mailing address]
Laguna Niguel, California 92677-6719
Telephone 714-643-4241; Research

Room Hours 8 a.m. to 4:30 p.m., Monday
— Friday; 8 a.m. to 4:30 p.m., 1st
Saturday of each month. Covers Arizona;
the southern California counties of
Imperial, Inyo, Kern, Los Angeles,
Orange, Riverside, San Bernadino, San
Diego, San Louis Obisbo, Santa Barbara,
and Ventura; and Nevada's Clark County.

PACIFIC SIERRA REGION

1000 Commodore Drive
San Brunc, California 94066
Telephone 415-876-9009; Research

Room Hours 7:45 a.m. to 4:15 p.m.,
Monday, Tuesday, Thursday, Friday; 8
a.m. to 8:30 p.m., Wednesday. Covers
Hawaii, Nevada except Clark County,
Northern California, and the Pacific
Ocean area.

PACIFIC NORTHWEST REGION

6125 Sand Point Way N.E.
Seattle, Washington 98115
Telephone 206-526-6507; Research

Room Hours 7:45 a.m. to 4 p.m., Monday
— Friday; 7:45 a.m. to 9 p.m., one
Tuesday each month; noon to 4 p.m., one
Saturday each month. Covers Alaska,
Idaho, Oregon, and Washington.

NOTES

National Cemetery System

The National Cemetery System is a source that is not used to its full potential by finders of missing persons. The National Cemetery System was created by President Lincoln in 1862 and twelve cemeteries were established. In 1933, an Executive Order authorized the transfer of national cemeteries from the War Department (now Department of the Army) to the National Park Service, Department of the Interior. In June 1973, the national cemeteries were transferred from the Department of the Army to the Veterans Administration. Within the Veterans Administration, the National Cemetery System is the responsibility of the Department of Memorial Affairs.

You can request a search to be conducted for your subject but I use the National Cemetery System to find dependents of the subject. If your subject was in the armed forces, the reserves, or a member of the public health service, they may have dependents who are buried in one of the National Cemeteries. Here are the guidelines for the burial of a dependent:

a. The eligible spouse of an active duty member or veteran.

b. The minor children of an eligible active duty member or veteran. For purpose of burial in a national cemetery, a minor child is a person who is unmarried and

(1) Who is under the age of 21 years;

(2) Who, after attaining the age of 21 years and until completion of education or training (but not after attaining the age of 23 years), is pursuing a course of instruction at an educational institution.

c. Unmarried adult children of an eligible active duty member or veteran if they become permanently incapable of self-support because of a physical or mental disability incurred before attaining the age of 21 years.

If your inquiry indicates that your subject, who may be on active status but more likely a veteran for our purposes here, has a family member buried, you want to write and ask for the records of interment. This will yield information about your subject including date of birth, social security number and addresses. A current address is usually available from these records.

The following is a list of all cemeteries in the National Cemetery System:

ALABAMA

Fort Mitchell National Cemetery
Post Office Box 2517
Phoenix City, Alabama 36867

Mobile National Cemetery
1202 Virginia Street
Mobile, Alabama 36604

ALASKA

Fort Richardson National Cemetery
Post Office Box 5-498
Fort Richardson, Alaska 99505

Sitka National Cemetery
Post Office Box 1065
Sitka, Alaska 99835

ARIZONA

Prescott National Cemetery
500 Highway 89N
Prescott, Arizona 86301

National Memorial Cemetery
23029 North Cave Creek Road
Phoenix, Arizona 85024

ARKANSAS

Fayetteville National Cemetery
700 Government Avenue
Fayetteville, Arkansas 72701

Fort Smith National Cemetery
522 Garland Ave. and South 6th Street
Fort Smith, Arkansas 72901

Little Rock National Cemetery
2523 Confederate Boulevard
Little Rock, Arkansas 72206

CALIFORNIA

Fort Rosecrans National Cemetery
Point Loma, Post Office Box 6237
San Diego, California 92106

Golden Gate National Cemetery
1300 Sneath Lane
San Bruno, California 94066

Los Angeles National Cemetery
950 South Sepulveda Boulevard
Los Angeles, California 90049

Riverside National Cemetery
22495 Van Buren Boulevard
Riverside, California 92508

San Francisco National Cemetery
Post Office Box 29012
San Francisco, California 94129

COLORADO

Fort Logan National Cemetery
3698 South Sheridan Boulevard
Denver, Colorado 80235

Fort Lyon National Cemetery
VA Medical Center
Fort Lyon, Colorado 81038

FLORIDA

Barrancas National Cemetery
Naval Air Station
Pensacola, Florida 32508

Bay Pines National Cemetery
Post Office Box 477
Bay Pines, Florida 33504

Florida National Cemetery
Post Office Box 337
Bushnell, Florida 33513

St. Augustine National Cemetery
104 Marine Street
St. Augustine, Florida 32084

GEORGIA

Marietta National Cemetery
500 Washington Avenue
Marietta, Georgia 30060

HAWAII

National Memorial Cemetery of the
    Pacific
2177 Puowaina Drive
Honolulu, Hawaii 96813

ILLINOIS

Alton National Cemetery
600 Pearl Street
Alton, Illinois 62003

Camp Butler National Cemetery
R.R. #1
Springfield, Illinois 62707

Danville National Cemetery
1900 East Main Street
Danville, Illinois 61832

Mound City National Cemetery
Junction — Highway 37 & 51
Mound City, Illinois 62963

Quincy National Cemetery
36th and Maine Street
Quincy, Illinois 62301

Rock Island National Cemetery
Rock Island Arsenal
Rock Island, Illinois 61299

INDIANA

Crown Hill National Cemetery
700 West 38th Street
Indianapolis, Indiana 46208

Marion National Cemetery
VA Medical Center
Marion, Indiana 46952

New Albany National Cemetery
1943 Ekin Avenue
New Albany, Indiana 47150

IOWA

Keokuk National Cemetery
1701 J Street
Keokuk, Iowa 52632

KANSAS

Fort Leavenworth National Cemetery
Fort Leavenworth, Kansas 66027

Fort Scott National Cemetery
Post Office Box 917
Fort Scott, Kansas 66701

Leavenworth National Cemeteries
Post Office Box 1649
Leavenworth, Kansas 66048

KENTUCKY

Camp Nelson National Cemetery
6980 Danville Road
Nicholasville, Kentucky 40356

Cave Hill National Cemetery
701 Baxter Avenue
Louisville, Kentucky 40204

Danville National Cemetery
377 North First Street
Danville, Kentucky 40442

Lebanon National Cemetery
R.R. #1, Box 616
Lebanon, Kentucky 40033

Lexington National Cemetery
833 West Main Street
Lexington, Kentucky 40508

Mill Springs National Cemetery
Rural Route #2, Post Office Box 172
Nancy, Kentucky 42544

Zachary Taylor National Cemetery
4701 Brownsboro Road
Louisville, Kentucky 40207

LOUISIANA

Alexandria National Cemetery
209 Shamrock Avenue
Pineville, Louisiana 71360

Baton Rouge National Cemetery
220 North 19th Street
Baton Rouge, Louisiana 70806

Port Hudson National Cemetery
Route No. 1, Box 185
Zachary, Louisiana 70791

MAINE

Togus National Cemetery
VA Medical and Regional Office Center
Togus, Maine 04330

MARYLAND

Annapolis National Cemetery
800 West Street
Annapolis, Maryland 21401

Baltimore National Cemetery
5501 Frederick Avenue
Baltimore, Maryland 21228

Loudon Park National Cemetery
3445 Frederick Avenue
Baltimore, Maryland 21229

MASSACHUSETTS

Massachusetts National Cemetery
Post Office Box 100
Bourne, Massachusetts 02532

MICHIGAN

Fort Custer National Cemetery
15501 Dickman Road
Augusta, Michigan 49012

MINNESOTA

Fort Snelling National Cemetery
7601 34th Avenue, South
Minneapolis, Minnesota 55450

MISSISSIPPI

Biloxi National Cemetery
Post Office Box 4968
Biloxi, Mississippi 39535

Corinth National Cemetery
1551 Horton Street
Corinth, Mississippi 38834

Natchez National Cemetery
61 Cemetery Road
Natchez, Mississippi 39102

MISSOURI

Jefferson Barracks National Cemetery
101 Memorial Drive
St. Louis, Missouri 63125

Jefferson City National Cemetery
1024 East McCarty Street
Jefferson City, Missouri 65101

Springfield National Cemetery
1702 East Seminole Street
Springfield, Missouri 65804

NEBRASKA

Fort McPherson National Cemetery
HCO 1, Box 67
Maxwell, Nebraska 69151

NEW JERSEY

Beverly National Cemetery
RD #1, Bridge Boro Road
Beverly, New Jersey 08010

Finn's Point National Cemetery
R.F.D No. 3, Fort Mott Road, Box 542
Salem, New Jersey 08079

NEW MEXICO

Fort Bayard National Cemetery
Post Office Box 189
Bayard, New Mexico 88036

Santa Fe National Cemetery
Post Office Box 88
Santa Fe, New Mexico 87501

NEW YORK

Bath National Cemetery
VA Medical Center
Bath, New York 14810

Calverton National Cemetery
210 Princeton Boulevard
Calverton, New York 11933

Cypress Hills National Cemetery
625 Jamaica Avenue
Brooklyn, New York 11208

Long Island National Cemetery
Post Office Box 250
Farmingdale, New York 11735

Woodlawn National Cemetery
1825 Davis Street
Elmira, New York 14901

NORTH CAROLINA

New Bern National Cemetery
1711 National Avenue
New Bern, North Carolina 28560

Raleigh National Cemetery
501 Rock Quarry Road
Raleigh, North Carolina 27610

Salisbury National Cemetery
202 Government Road
Salisbury, North Carolina 28144

Wilmington National Cemetery
2011 Market Street
Wilmington, North Carolina 28403

OHIO

Dayton National Cemetery
VA Medical Center
4100 West Third Street
Dayton, Ohio 45428

OKLAHOMA

Fort Gibson National Cemetery
R.R. #2, Post Office Box 47
Fort Gibson, Oklahoma 74434

OREGON

Eagle Point National Cemetery
2763 Riley Road
Eagle Point, Oregon 97524

Roseburg National Cemetery
VA Medical Center
Roseburg, Oregon 97470

Willamette National Cemetery
11800 S.E. Mt. Scott Boulevard
Portland, Oregon 97266

PENNSYLVANIA

Indiantown Gap National Cemetery
Post Office Box 187
Annville, Pennsylvania 17003

Philadelphia National Cemetery
Haines Street and Limekiln Pike
Philadelphia, Pennsylvania 19138

PUERTO RICO

Puerto Rico National Cemetery
Post Office Box 1298
Bayamon, Puerto Rico 00621

SOUTH CAROLINA

Beaufort National Cemetery
1601 Boundary Street
Beaufort, South Carolina 29902

Florence National Cemetery
803 East National Cemetery Road
Florence, South Carolina 29501

SOUTH DAKOTA

Black Hills National Cemetery
Post Office Box 640
Sturgis, South Dakota 57785

Fort Meade National Cemetery
VA Medical Center
Fort Meade, South Dakota 57785

Hot Springs National Cemetery
VA Medical Center
Hot Springs, South Dakota 57747

TENNESSEE

Chattanooga National Cemetery
1200 Bailey Avenue
Chattanooga, Tennessee 37404

Knoxville National Cemetery
939 Tyson Street, N.W.
Knoxville, Tennessee 37917

Memphis National Cemetery
3568 Townes Avenue
Memphis, Tennessee 38122

Mountain Home National Cemetery
Post Office Box 8
Mountain Home, Tennessee 37684

Nashville National Cemetery
1420 Gallatin Road, South
Madison, Tennessee 37115

TEXAS

Fort Bliss National Cemetery
Post Office Box 6342
Fort Bliss, Texas 79906

Fort Sam Houston National Cemetery
1520 Harry Wurzbach Road
San Antonio, Texas 78209

Houston National Cemetery
10410 Veterans Memorial Drive
Houston, Texas 77038

Kerrville National Cemetery
VA Medical Center
3600 Memorial Blvd.
Kerrville, Texas 78028

San Antonio National Cemetery
517 Paso Hondo Street
San Antonio, Texas 78202

VIRGINIA

Alexandria National Cemetery
1450 Wilkes Street
Alexandria, Virginia 22314

Balls Bluff National Cemetery
Post Office Box 200
Leesburg, Virginia 22075

City Point National Cemetery
10th Avenue and Davis Street
Hopewell, Virginia 23860

Cold Harbor National Cemetery
Route 156 North
Mechanicsville, Virginia 23111

Culpeper National Cemetery
305 U.S. Avenue
Culpeper, Virginia 22701

Danville National Cemetery
721 Lee Street
Danville, Virginia 24541

Fort Harrison National Cemetery
8620 Varina Road
Richmond, Virginia 23231

Glendale National Cemetery
9301 Willis Church Road
Richmond, Virginia 23231

Hampton National Cemetery
Cemetery Road at Marshall Avenue
Hampton, Virginia 23669

Hampton National Cemetery
VA Medical Center
Hampton, Virginia 23669

Quantico National Cemetery
Post Office Box 10
Triangle, Virginia 22172

Richmond National Cemetery
1701 Williamsburg Road
Richmond, Virginia 23231

Seven Pines National Cemetery
400 East Williamsburg Road
Sandson, Virginia 23150

Staunton National Cemetery
901 Richmond Avenue
Staunton, Virginia 24401

Winchester National Cemetery
401 National Avenue
Winchester, Virginia 22601

WEST VIRGINIA

Grafton National Cemetery
431 Walnut Street
Grafton, West Virginia 26354

West Virginia National Cemetery
Route 2, Box 127
Pruntytown, West Virginia 26354

WISCONSIN

Wood National Cemetery
Post Office Box 500
VA Medical Center, Wisconsin

Wood National Cemetery
Post Office Box 150
Milwaukee, Wisconsin 53295

NOTES

15

Medical Boards

The birth certificate of your subject would be one avenue to explore in your search for information but you may want to order the birth records of your subject's children. These particular records will give you the exact date of birth, place of birth and other vital statistics so that you may find the children who may know the whereabouts of the subject. You may also want to contact the physician listed on the birth record for additional information about the location of your subject or the subject's family.

As noted in other chapters, you will be requesting death certificates on persons other than your subject. The reason for this is in order to find a person who has not left much of a paper trail, the best way of finding the subject's current location is to locate the subject's family and make inquiries. Every death record will have a physician's name certifying the cause of death. Many times the family physician will be the official who attests to the cause of death. This physician may be of some assistance in locating your subject.

The following list will assist you in locating the physician because, like many other records you will encounter, years have passed since the date of the issuance of the document. Contact the appropriate medical board and they will give you the current address of the medical practitioner.

ALABAMA

Alabama Medical Board
Post Office Box 36101
Montgomery, Alabama 36101

ALASKA

Alaska Medical Board
Post Office Box D
Juneau, Alaska 99811

ARIZONA

Arizona Medical Board
3601 West Camelback Road
Phoenix, Arizona 85015

ARKANSAS

Arkansas Medical Board
Post Office Box 102
Harrisburg, Arkansas 72432

CALIFORNIA

California Medical Board
1426 Howe Avenue
Sacramento, California 95825

COLORADO

Colorado Medical Board
1560 Broadway
Denver, Colorado 80202

CONNECTICUT

Connecticut Medical Board
150 Washington Street
Hartford, Connecticut 06106

DELAWARE

Delaware Medical Board
Post Office Box 1401
Dover, Delaware 19903

DISTRICT OF COLUMBIA

District of Columbia Medical Board
605 G Street, Northwest
Washington, D.C. 20001

FLORIDA

Florida Medical Board
1940 North Monroe Street
Tallahassee, Florida 32399

GEORGIA

Georgia Medical Board
166 Pryor Street, Southwest
Atlanta, Georgia 30303

HAWAII

Hawaii Medical Board
Post Office Box 3469
Honolulu, Hawaii 96801

IDAHO

Idaho Medical Board
280 North 8th Street
Boise, Idaho 83720

ILLINOIS

Illinois Medical Board
320 West Washington
Springfield, Illinois 62786

INDIANA

Indiana Medical Board
One American Square
Indianapolis, Indiana 46282

IOWA

Iowa Medical Board
1209 West Court Avenue
Des Moines, Iowa 50319

KANSAS

Kansas Medical Board
235 Southwest Topeka Boulevard
Topeka, Kansas 66603

KENTUCKY

Kentucky Medical Board
400 Sherbon Lane
Louisville, Kentucky 40207

LOUISIANA

Louisiana Medical Board
830 Union Street
New Orleans, Louisiana 70112

MAINE

Maine Medical Board
State House, Room 137
Augusta, Maine 04333

MARYLAND

Maryland Medical Board
Post Office Box 2571
Baltimore, Maryland 21215

MASSACHUSETTS

Massachusetts Medical Board
10 West Street
Boston, Massachusetts 02111

MICHIGAN

Michigan Medical Board
Post Office 30018
Lansing, Michigan 48909

MINNESOTA

Minnesota Medical Board
2700 University Avenue, West
Saint Paul, Minnesota 55114

MISSISSIPPI

Mississippi Medical Board
2688 Insurance Center Drive
Jackson, Mississippi 39216

MISSOURI

Missouri Medical Board
Post Office Box 4
Jefferson City, Missouri 65102

MONTANA

Montana Medical Board
1424 9th Avenue
Helena, Montana 59620

NEBRASKA

Nebraska Medical Board
Post Office Box 95007
Lincoln, Nebraska 68509

NEVADA

Nevada Medical Board
Post Office Box 7238
Reno, Nevada 89510

NEW HAMPSHIRE

New Hampshire Medical Board
6 Hazen Drive
Concord, New Hampshire 03301

NEW JERSEY

New Jersey Medical Board
28 West State Street
Trenton, New Jersey 08608

NEW MEXICO

New Mexico Medical Board
Post Office Box 20001
Santa Fe, New Mexico 87504

NEW YORK

New York Medical Board
Empire State Plaza, Room 3023
Albany, New York 12230

NORTH CAROLINA

North Carolina Medical Board
1313 Navaho Drive
Raleigh, North Carolina 27609

NORTH DAKOTA

North Dakota Medical Board
418 East Broadway
Bismarck, North Dakota 58501

OHIO

Ohio Medical Board
77 South High Street
Columbus, Ohio 43266

OKLAHOMA

Oklahoma Medical Board
Post Office Box 18256
Oklahoma City, Oklahoma 73154

OREGON

Oregon Medical Board
620 Crown Avenue
Portland, Oregon 97201

PENNSYLVANIA

Pennsylvania Medical Board
Post Office Box 2649
Harrisburg, Pennsylvania 17105

PUERTO RICO

Puerto Rico Medical Board
Post Office Box 13969
Santurce, Puerto Rico 00908

RHODE ISLAND

Rhode Island Medical Board
3 Capitol Hill Road
Providence, Rhode Island 02908

SOUTH CAROLINA

South Carolina Medical Board
Post Office Box 12245
Columbia, South Carolina 29211

SOUTH DAKOTA

South Dakota Medical Board
1323 South Minnesota Avenue
Sioux Falls, South Dakota 57105

TENNESSEE

Tennessee Medical Board
283 Plus Park Road
Nashville, Tennessee 37247

TEXAS

Texas Medical Board
Post Office Box 13562
Austin, Texas 78711

UTAH

Utah Medical Board
Post Office Box 45802
Salt Lake City, Utah 84145

VERMONT

Vermont Medical Board
Pavillion Building, Room 100
Montpelier, Vermont 05609

VIRGINIA

Virginia Medical Board
1601 Rolling Hills Drive
Richmond, Virginia 23229

WASHINGTON

Washington Medical Board
1300 Quince Street
Olympia, Washington 98504

WEST VIRGINIA

West Virginia Medical Board
101 Dee Drive
Charleston, West Virginia 25311

WISCONSIN

Wisconsin Medical Board
Post Office Box 8935
Madison, Wisconsin 53708

WYOMING

Wyoming Medical Board
2301 Central Avenue
Cheyenne, Wyoming 82002

16

Bar Associations

The following list of Bar Associations will be of assistance because you will retrieve records such as divorce, foreclosures and other legal instruments that have an attorney's name on them. Many of the records will be decades old. You can contact the Bar Association and they will give you the current address and telephone number of the attorney. Explain to the attorney what you are doing and who you are seeking. He or she may be able to provide information heretofore unknown to you.

ALABAMA

Alabama State Bar
Post Office Box 671
Montgomery, AL 36101
Tel: (205) 269-1515

ALASKA

Alaska Bar Association
Post Office Box 279
Anchorage, AK 99510
Tel: (907) 272-7496

ARIZONA

State Bar of Arizona
234 North Central
Phoenix, AZ 85004
Tel: (602) 252-4804

ARKANSAS

Arkansas Bar Association
400 West Markham
Little Rock, AR 72201
Tel: (501) 375-4605

CALIFORNIA

State Bar of California
555 Franklin Street
San Francisco, CA 94102
Tel: (415) 561-8200

COLORADO

Colorado Bar Association
250 West 14th Street
Denver, CO 80204
Tel: (303) 629-6873

CONNECTICUT

Connecticut Bar Association
15 Lewis Street
Hartford, CT 06103
Tel: (203) 249-9141

DELAWARE

Delaware State Bar Association
820 North French Street
Wilmington, DE 19801
Tel: (302) 658-5278

DISTRICT OF COLUMBIA

The District of Columbia Bar
1426 H Street NW
Washington, D.C. 20005
Tel: (202) 638-1500

FLORIDA

The Florida Bar Association
650 Apalachee Parkway
Tallahassee, FL 32301
Tel: (904) 561-5600

GEORGIA

State Bar of Georgia
84 Peachtree Street
Atlanta, GA 30303
Tel: (404) 522-6255

HAWAII

Hawaii State Bar
820 Mililani
Honolulu, HI 96813
Tel: (808) 537-1868

IDAHO

Idaho State Bar
Post Office Box 895
Boise, ID 83701
Tel: (208) 342-8958

ILLINOIS

Illinois Bar Center
424 South 2nd Streeet
Springfield, IL 62701
Tel: (217) 525-1760

INDIANA

Indiana State Bar Association
230 East Ohio Street
Indianapolis, IN 42604
Tel: (317) 639-5465

IOWA

Iowa State Bar Association
1101 Fleming Building
Des Moines, IA 50309
Tel: (515) 243-3179

KANSAS

Kansas Bar Association
Post Office Box 1037
Topeka, KS 66601
Tel: (913) 234-5696

KENTUCKY

Kentucky Bar Association
West Main at Kentucky River
Frankfort, KY 40601
Tel: (502) 564-3795

LOUISIANA

Louisiana State Bar Association
210 O'Keefe Avenue
New Orleans, LA 70112
Tel: (504) 566-1600

MAINE

Maine State Bar Association
Post Office Box 788
August, ME 04330
Tel: (207) 622-7523

MARYLAND

Maryland State Bar Association
207 East Redwood Street
Baltimore, MD 21202
Tel: (301) 685-7878

MASSACHUSETTS

Massachusetts Bar Association
One Center Plaza
Boston, MA 02108
Tel: (617) 523-4529

MICHIGAN

State Bar of Michigan
306 Townsend Street
Lansing, MI 48933
Tel: (517) 372-9030

MINNESOTA

Minnesota State Bar Association
430 Marquette Avenue
Minneapolis, MN 55402
Tel: (612) 335-1183

MISSISSIPPI

Mississippi State Bar
Post Office Box 2168
Jackson, MS 39205
Tel: (601) 948-4471

MISSOURI

The Missouri Bar
Post Office Box 119
Jefferson City, MO 65102
Tel: (314) 635-4128

MONTANA

State Bar of Montana
Post Office Box 4669
Helena, MT 59604
Tel: (406) 442-7660

NEBRASKA

Nebraska State Bar Association
206 South 13th Street
Lincoln, NB 65808
Tel: (402) 475-7091

NEVADA

State Bar of Nevada
834 Willow Street
Reno, NV 89501
Tel: (702) 329-4100

NEW HAMPSHIRE

New Hampshire Bar Association
18 Centre Street
Concord, NH 03301
Tel: (603) 224-6942

NEW JERSEY

New Jersey State Bar Association
172 West State Street
Trenton, NJ 08608
Tel: (609) 394-1101

NEW MEXICO

State Bar of New Mexico
Post Office Box 25883
Albuquerque, NM 87125
Tel: (505) 842-6132

NEW YORK

New York State Bar Association
One Elk Street
Albany, NY 12207
Tel: (518) 463-3200

NORTH CAROLINA

North Carolina State Bar
Post Office Box 25908
Raleigh, NC 27611
Tel: (919) 828-4620

NORTH DAKOTA

State Bar Association of North Dakota
Post Office Box 2136
Bismark, ND 58502
Tel: (701) 255-1404

OHIO

Ohio State Bar Association
33 West 11th Avenue
Columbus, OH 42301
Tel: (614) 421-2121

OKLAHOMA

Oklahoma Bar Association
Post Office Box 53036
Oklahoma City, OK 73152
Tel: (405) 524-2365

OREGON

Oregon State Bar
1776 S.W. Madison
Portland, OR 97205
Tel: (503) 224-4280

PENNSYLVANIA

Pennsylvania Bar Association
Post Office Box 186
Harrisburg, PA 17108
Tel: (717) 238-6715

PUERTO RICO

Bar Association of Puerto Rico
Box 1900
San Juan, PR 00903
Tel: (809) 721-3358

RHODE ISLAND

Rhode Island Bar Association
1804 Industrial Bank Building
Providence, RI 02903
Tel: (401) 421-5740

SOUTH CAROLINA

South Carolina Bar Association
Post Office Box 11039
Columbia, SC 29211
Tel: (803) 799-6653

SOUTH DAKOTA

State Bar of South Dakota
222 East Capitol
Pierre, SD 57501
Tel: (605) 224-7554

TENNESSEE

Tennessee Bar Association
3622 West End Avenue
Nashville, TN 37205
Tel: (615) 383-7421

TEXAS

State Bar of Texas
Post Office Box 12487
Austin, TX 78711
Tel: (512) 475-4200

UTAH

Utah State Bar
425 East First South
Salt Lake City, UT 84111
Tel: (801) 531-9077

VERMONT

Vermont Bar Association
Post Office Box 100
Montpelier, VT 05602
Tel: (802) 223-2020

VIRGINIA

Virginia State Bar
700 East Main Street
Richmond, VA 23219
Tel: (804) 786-2061

WASHINGTON

Washington State Bar Association
505 Madison
Seattle, WA 98104
Tel: (206) 622-6054

WEST VIRGINIA

West Virginia State Bar
2006 Kanawha Boulevard
Charleston, WV 25311
Tel: (304) 346-8414

WISCONSIN

State Bar of Wisconsin
Post Office Box 7158
Madison, WI 53707
Tel: (608) 257-3838

WYOMING

Wyoming State Bar
Post Office Box 109
Cheyenne, WY 82003
Tel: (307) 632-9061

NOTES

17

Foreign Diplomatic Representatives & Foreign Consular Offices In The United States

I use the following list of foreign Diplomatic Representatives and Foreign Consular offices with great success. When I discover that the missing person may be in a particular country I request assistance from the embassy closest to my location. They are ready to assist and can cut through much red tape.

Write and explain in detail what your objective is and give as much information as possible regarding the vital statistics of your subject. Give the reason why you believe your subject may be in a particular country. i.e., employment, extended vacation or simply to hide from others.

AFGHANISTAN

Office of the Embassy, 2341 Wyoming Avenue 20008. Phone, 234–3770

Mr. Miagol, Minister-Counselor (Chargé d'Affaires, a.i.)

ALGERIA

Office of the Embassy, 2118 Kalorama Road 20008. Phone, 328–5300

Mr. Rabah Kerouaz, Counselor (Chargé d'Affaires, a.i.)

ANTIGUA AND BARBUDA

Office of the Embassy, Suite 2H, 3400 International Drive 20008. Phone, 362–5211

H.E. Edmund Hawkins Lake, Ambassador Extraordinary and Plenipotentiary

Consular Office, Florida, Miami

ARGENTINA

Office of the Embassy, 1600 New Hampshire Avenue 20009. Phone, 939–6400

H.E. Enrique J.A. Candioti, Ambassador Extraordinary and Plenipotentiary

Consular Offices:
California:
Los Angeles
San Francisco
Florida, Miami
Illinois, Chicago
Louisiana, New Orleans
Maryland, Baltimore
New York, New York
Puerto Rico, San Juan
Texas, Houston

AUSTRALIA

Office of the Embassy, 1601 Massachusetts Avenue 20036. Phone, 797–3000

H.E. F. Rawdon Dalrymple, Ambassador Extraordinary and Plenipotentiary

Consular Offices:
American Samoa, Pago Pago
California:
Los Angeles
San Francisco
District of Columbia
Hawaii, Honolulu
Illinois, Chicago
New York, New York City
Texas, Houston

AUSTRIA

Office of the Embassy, 2343 Massachusetts Avenue 20008. Phone, 483–4474

H.E. Friedrich Hoess, Ambassador Extraordinary and Plenipotentiary

Consular Offices:
California:

AUSTRIA—Continued

Consular Offices—Continued
Los Angeles
San Francisco
Colorado, Denver
Delaware, Newark
District of Columbia
Florida, Miami
Georgia, Atlanta
Hawaii, Honolulu
Illinois, Chicago
Louisiana, New Orleans
Massachusetts, Boston
Michigan, Detroit
Minnesota, St. Paul
Missouri:
Kansas City
St. Louis
New York:
Buffalo
New York City
Ohio, Cleveland
Pennsylvania, Philadelphia
Texas, Houston
Washington, Seattle

THE COMMONWEALTH OF THE BAHAMAS

Office of the Embassy, Suite 865m, 600 New Hampshire Avenue 20037. Phone, 944–3390

H.E. Margaret E. McDonald, Ambassador Extraordinary and Plenipotentiary

Consular Offices:
District of Columbia
Florida, Miami
New York, New York City

STATE OF BAHRAIN

Office of the Embassy, 3502 International Drive 20008. Phone, 342–0741

H.E. Gahzi Muhammad Al-Gosaibi, Ambassador Extraordinary and Plenipotentiary

Consular Office, New York, New York City

PEOPLE'S REPUBLIC OF BANGLADESH

Office of the Embassy, 2201 Wisconsin Avenue 20007. Phone, 342–8372

H.E. A.H.S. Ataul Karim, Ambassador Extraordinary and Plenipotentiary

Consular Offices:
California, Los Angeles
District of Columbia
Hawaii, Honolulu
Louisiana, New Orleans
New York, New York City

BARBADOS

Office of the Embassy, 2144 Wyoming Avenue 20008. Phone, 939–9200

BARBADOS—Continued

H.E. Sir William Douglas, Ambassador Extraordinary and
Plenipotentiary

Consular Offices:
California:
Los Angeles
San Francisco
District of Columbia
Florida, Miami
Illinois, Chicago
Louisiana, New Orleans
Massachusetts, Boston
Michigan, Detroit
New York, New York City
Ohio, Toledo
Oregon, Portland

BELGIUM

Office of the Embassy, 3330 Garfield Street 20008. Phone,
333–6900

H.E. Herman Dehennin, Ambassador Extraordinary and
Plenipotentiary

Consular Offices:
Alaska, Anchorage
Arizona, Phoenix
California:
Los Angeles
San Diego
San Francisco
Colorado, Denver
District of Columbia
Florida, Miami
Georgia, Atlanta
Hawaii, Honolulu
Illinois:
Chicago
Moline
Indiana, Mishawaka
Kentucky, Louisville
Louisiana, New Orleans
Maryland, Baltimore
Massachusetts, Boston
Michigan, Detroit
Minnesota, Minneapolis
Missouri:
Kansas City
St. Louis
New York, New York City
Ohio, Cleveland
Oregon, Portland
Pennsylvania:
Philadelphia
Pittsburgh
Puerto Rico, San Juan
Texas:
Dallas
Houston
Utah, Salt Lake City
Virgin Islands, Charlotte Amalie
Virginia, Norfolk
Washington, Seattle
Wisconsin, Milwaukee

BELIZE

Office of the Embassy, 3400 International Drive 20008.
Phone, 363–4505

H.E. Edward A. Laing, Ambassador Extraordinary and
Plenipotentiary

Consular Offices:
California, Inglewood
District of Columbia
Florida, Miami
Illinois, Wheaton
Louisiana, New Orleans
Michigan, Southfield

PEOPLE'S REPUBLIC OF BENIN

Office of the Embassy, 2737 Cathedral Avenue 20008.
Phone, 232–6656

H.E. Theophile Nata, Ambassador Extraordinary and
Plenipotentiary

Consular Offices:
California, Los Angeles

PEOPLE'S REPUBLIC OF BENIN—Continued

Consular Offices—Continued
Illinois, Belleville
Missouri, Independence
Texas, Houston

BHUTAN

New York, New York

BOLIVIA

Office of the Embassy, 3014 Massachusetts Avenue 20008.
Phone, 483–4410

H.E. Carlos E. Delius, Ambassador Extraordinary and
Plenipotentiary

Consular Offices:
California
Los Angeles
San Francisco
District of Columbia
Florida, Miami
Georgia, Atlanta
Illinois, Chicago
Louisiana, New Orleans
Missouri, St. Louis
New York, New York City
Ohio, Cincinnati
Puerto Rico, San Juan
Texas, Houston
Washington, Seattle

REPUBLIC OF BOTSWANA

Office of the Embassy, Suite 404, 4301 Connecticut Avenue
20008. Phone, 244–4990

Mr. Cecil I. Manyeula, Counselor (Chargé d'Affaires, a.i.)

Consular Offices:
California:
Los Angeles
San Francisco
Texas, Houston

BRAZIL

Office of the Embassy, 3006 Massachusetts Avenue 20008.
Phone, 745–2700

H.E. Marcilo Macques Moreira, Ambassador
Extraordinary and Plenipotentiary

Consular Offices:
California:
Los Angeles
San Francisco
District of Columbia
Florida, Miami
Georgia:
Atlanta
Savannah
Hawaii, Honolulu
Illinois, Chicago
Indiana, Lafayette
Louisiana, New Orleans
Massachusetts, New Bedford
New York, New York City
Ohio, Cleveland
Pacific Islands, Hong Kong (For the Caroline,
Marshall, and Marianas Islands)
Texas:
Dallas
Houston
Virginia, Norfolk

STATE OF BRUNEI

Office of the Embassy, Watergate, Suite 300, 2600 Virginia
Avenue 20037. Phone, 342–0159

H.E. Dato Paduka Haji *Mohd Suni* bin Haji Idris,
Ambassador Extraordinary and Plenipotentiary

PEOPLE'S REPUBLIC OF BULGARIA

Office of the Embassy, 1621 22d Street 20008. Phone, 387-7969

H.E. Velichko F. Velichkov, Ambassador Extraordinary and Plenipotentiary

Consular Office, Washington, D.C.

BURKINO FASO

Office of the Embassy, 2340 Massachusetts Avenue 20008. Phone, 332-5577

H.E. Paul-Desire Kabore, Ambassador Extraordinay and Planipotentiary

Consular Offices:
California, Los Angeles
Louisiana, New Orleans

BURMA

Office of the Embassy, 2300 S Street 20008. Phone, 332-9044

H.E. U. Myo Aung, Ambassador Extraordinary and Plenipotentiary

Consular Office, New York, New York City

BURUNDI

Office of the Embassy, 2233 Wisconsin Avenue 20007. Phone, 342-2574

H.E. Edouard Kadigiri, Ambassador Extraordinary and Plenipotentiary

Consular Office, Illinois, Chicago

REPUBLIC OF THE CAMEROON

Office of the Embassy, 2349 Massachusetts Avenue 20008. Phone, 265-8790

H.E. Paul Pondi, Ambassador Extraordinary and Plenipotentiary

Consular Offices:
California, San Francisco
Texas, Houston

CANADA

Office of the Embassy, 501 Pennsylvania Avenue 20001. Phone, 682-1740.

H.E. Derek H. Burney, Ambassador Extraordinary and Plenipotentiary

Consular Offices:
California:
    Los Angeles
    San Francisco
District of Columbia
Georgia, Atlanta
Illinois, Chicago
Massachusetts, Boston
Michigan, Detroit
Minnesota, Minneapolis
Missouri, St. Louis
New York:
    Buffalo
    New York City
Ohio:
    Cincinnati
    Cleveland
Pennsylvania:
    Philadelphia
    Pittsburgh
Texas, Dallas
Washington, Seattle

CAPE VERDE

Office of the Embassy, 3415 Massachusetts Avenue 20007. Phone, 965-6820

H.E. Jose Luis Fernandes-Lopes, Ambassador Extraordinary and Plenipotentiary

Consular Office, Massachusetts, Boston

CENTRAL AFRICAN REPUBLIC

Office of the Embassy, 1618 22d Street 20008. Phone, 483-7800

H.E. Christian Lingama-Toleque, Ambassador Extraordinary and Plenipotentiary

Consular Office, Missouri, St. Louis

CEYLON. See Sri Lanka.

CHAD

Office of the Embassy, 2002 R Street 20009. Phone, 462-4009

H.E. Mahamat Ali Adoum, Ambassador Extraordinary and Plenipotentiary

CHILE

Office of the Embassy, 1732 Massachusetts Avenue 20036. Phone, 785-1746

H.E. Octavio Errazuriz, Ambassador Extraordinary and Plenipotentiary

Consular Offices:
Arizona, Tucson
California:
    La Jolla
    Los Angeles
    San Diego
    San Francisco
    Santa Clara
Colorado, Denver
District of Columbia
Florida, Miami
Georgia:
    Atlanta
    Columbus
Hawaii, Honolulu
Illinois, Chicago
Massachusetts, Boston
Michigan, Detroit
New York, New York City
Oregon, Portland
Pennsylvania, Philadelphia
Puerto Rico, San Juan
South Carolina, Charleston
Texas, Houston
Utah, Provo
Washington, Seattle

CHINA

Office of the Embassy of the People's Republic of China, 2300 Connecticut Avenue 20008. Phone, 328-2500

H.E. Han Xu, Ambassador Extraordinary and Plenipotentiary

Consular Offices:
California, Los Angeles
Illinois, Chicago
New York, New York City
Texas, Houston

COLOMBIA

Office of the Embassy, 2118 Leroy Place 20008. Phone, 387-8338

H.E. Victor Mosquera, Ambassador Extraordinary and Plenipotentiary

Consular Offices:
California:
    Los Angeles
    San Diego
    San Francisco
District of Columbia
Florida:
    Ft. Lauderdale
    Miami
    Miami Beach
    Tampa
Georgia, Atlanta

COLOMBIA—Continued

Consular Offices—Continued

 Illinois, Chicago
 Louisiana, New Orleans
 Massachusetts, Boston
 Michigan, Detroit
 Minnesota, Minneapolis
 Missouri, St. Louis
 New York, New York City
 Ohio, Eastlake
 Puerto Rico, San Juan
 Texas, Houston
 West Virginia, Wheeling

COMOROS

Embassy of the Federal and Islamic Republic of the Comoros, 2d Floor, 336 East 45th Street, New York, NY 10017. Phone, 972–8010

H.E. Amini Ali Moumin, Ambassador Extraordinary and
 Plenipotentiary

PEOPLE'S REPUBLIC OF THE CONGO

**Office of the Embassy, 4891 Colorado Avenue 20011.
Phone, 726–5500**

H.E. Benjamin Bounkoulou, Ambassador Extraordinary
 and Plenipotentiary

COOK ISLAND

Honolulu, Hawaii

COSTA RICA

Office of the Embassy, Suite 213, 1825 Connecticut Avenue 20009. Phone, 234–2945

H.E. Danilo Jimenez, Ambassador Extraordinary and
 Plenipotentiary

Consular Offices:
 California:
  Los Angeles
  San Diego
  San Francisco
 Colorado, Denver
 Connecticut, Hartford
 District of Columbia
 Florida:
  Miami
  Tampa
 Georgia, Atlanta
 Hawaii, Honolulu
 Illinois, Chicago
 Louisiana, New Orleans
 Massachusetts, Boston
 Minnesota, Minneapolis
 Missouri:
  Kansas City
  St. Louis
 New Mexico, Albuquerque
 Nevada, Las Vegas
 New York:
  Buffalo
  New York City
 North Carolina, Raleigh
 Ohio, Cincinnati
 Pennsylvania, Philadelphia
 Puerto Rico, San Juan
 Texas:
  Austin
  Houston
  San Antonio
 Washington, Kirkland
 Wisconsin, Milwaukee

CÔTE D'IVOIRE

**Office of the Embassy, 2424 Massachusetts Avenue 20008.
Phone, 483–2400**

H.E. Charles Providence Gomis, Ambassador
 Extraordinary and Plenipotentiary

Consular Offices:
 Arizona, Phoenix
 California:
  Los Angeles
  San Francisco

CÔTE D'IVOIRE—Continued

Consular Offices—Continued

 Missouri, St, Louis
 Oregon, Porland

REPUBLIC OF CYPRUS

Office of the Embassy, 2211 R Street 20008. Phone, 462–5772 and 5773

H.E. Andrew J. Jacovides, Ambassador Extraordinary and
 Plenipotentiary

Consular Offices:
 Arizona, Phoenix
 California:
  Los Angeles
  San Francisco
 District of Columbia
 Georgia, Atlanta
 Indiana, Fort Wayne
 Illinois, Chicago
 Louisiana, Baton Rouge
 Massachusetts, Boston
 Michigan, Detroit
 Minnesota, Rochester
 Missouri, St. Louis
 New York, New York City
 Oregon, Portland
 Pennsylvania, Philadelphia
 Texas, Houston

CZECHOSLOVAKIA SOCIALIST REPUBLIC

Office of the Embassy, 3900 Linnean Avenue 20008. Phone, 363–6315

H.E. Miroslav Houstecky, Ambassador Extraordinary and
 Plenipotentiary

DENMARK

**Office of the Embassy, 3200 Whitehaven Street 20008.
Phone, 234–4300**

H.E. Eigil Jorgensen, Ambassador Extraordinary and
 Plenipotentiary

Consular Offices:
 Alabama, Mobile
 Alaska, Anchorage
 Arizona, Phoenix
 California:
  Los Angeles
  San Diego
  San Francisco
 Colorado, Denver
 District of Columbia
 Florida:
  Jacksonville
  Miami
  Tampa
 Georgia:
  Atlanta
  Savannah
 Hawaii, Honolulu
 Illinois, Chicago
 Iowa, Des Moines
 Maryland, Baltimore
 Massachusetts:
  Boston
  Gloucester
 Michigan, Detroit
 Minnesota, Minneapolis
 Missouri:
  Kansas City
  St. Louis
 Nebraska, Omaha
 New York, New York City
 Ohio, Cleveland
 Oklahoma, Oklahoma City
 Pennsylvania, Philadelphia
 Puerto Rico, San Juan
 Rhode Island, Providence
 South Carolina, Charleston
 Tennessee, Nashville
 Texas:
  Corpus Christi
  Dallas
 Utah, Salt Lake City

DENMARK—Continued

Consular Offices—Continued

Virginia, Norfolk
Virgin Islands:
    Charlotte Amalie
    Christiansted, St. Croix
Washington, Seattle
Wisconsin, Milwaukee

REPUBLIC OF DJIBOUTI

Office of the Embassy, 1430 K Street 20006. Phone, 347-0254

H.E. Roble Olhaye, Ambassador Extraordinary and
    Plenipotentiary

COMMONWEALTH OF DOMINICA

New York, New York

H.E. McDonald P. Benjamin, Ambassador Extraordinary
    and Plenipotentiary

DOMINICAN REPUBLIC

Office of the Embassy, 1715 22d Street 20008. Phone, 332-6280

H.E. Eduardo A. Leon, Ambassador Extraordinary and
    Plenipotentiary

Consular Offices:
    Alabama, Mobile
    California:
        Los Angeles
        Pasadena
        San Francisco
    Colorado, Denver
    District of Columbia
    Florida:
        Coral Gables
        Gainesville
        Jacksonville
        Miami
        Miami Beach
        Panama City
        Sarasota
        Tallahassee
    Georgia, Savannah
    Hawaii, Honolulu
    Illinois:
        Chicago
        Wheaton
    Indiana, Fort Wayne
    Louisiana:
        Baton Rouge
        Lake Charles
        New Orleans
    Maryland:
        Annapolis
        Baltimore
    Massachusetts, Boston
    Michigan, Detroit
    Minnesota:
        Minneapolis
        Rochester
    Missouri, St Louis
    New Mexico, Albuquerque
    New York:
        New Rochelle
        New York City
    Ohio:
        Cleveland
        Columbus
    Oregon, Portland
    Pennsylvania, Philadelphia
    Puerto Rico:
        Arecibo
        Humacao
        Juana Diaz
        Manati
        Marina Station
        Mayaguez
        Ponce
        Ponce de Leon
        San Juan
    Rhode Island, Providence
    Tennessee:
        Memphis
        Nashville

DOMINICAN REPUBLIC—Continued

Consular Offices—Continued

    Texas:
        Corpus Christi
        Dallas
        El Paso
        Houston
    Virginia, Richmond
    Virgin Islands, Charlotte Amalie
    Washington, Seattle

ECUADOR

Office of the Embassy, 2535 15th Street 20009. Phone, 234-7200

H.E. Jaime Moncayo, Ambassador Extraordinary and
    Plenipotentiary

Consular Offices:
    California:
        Los Angeles
        San Diego
        San Francisco
    District of Columbia
    Florida:
        Coral Gables
        Fort Lauderdale
        Miami
        Palm Beach
    Georgia, Atlanta
    Illinois, Chicago
    Louisiana, New Orleans
    Maryland, Baltimore
    Massachusetts, Boston
    Missouri, Kansas City
    Nevada, Las Vegas
    New York, New York City
    Puerto Rico, San Juan
    South Carolina:
        Columbia
        Georgetown
    Tennessee, Nashville
    Texas:
        Dallas
        Houston
    Washington, Seattle

EGYPT, ARAB REPUBLIC OF

Office of the Embassy, 2310 Decatur Place 20008. Phone, 232-5400

H.E. Sayed Abdel Raouf El Reedy, Ambassador
    Extraordinary and Plenipotentiary

Consular Offices:
    California, San Francisco
    District of Columbia
    Illinois, Chicago
    New York, New York City
    Texas, Houston

EL SALVADOR

Office of the Embassy, 2308 California Street 20008. Phone, 265-3480

H.E. Ernesto Rivas-Gallont, Ambassador Extraordinary
    and Plenipotentiary

Consular Offices:
    Alabama, Mobile
    Arizona, Phoenix
    California:
        Los Angeles
        Oakland
        San Diego
        San Francisco
    Colorado, Denver
    District of Columbia
    Florida:
        Coral Gables
        Miami
        Georgia, Atlanta
        Illinois, Chicago
    Louisiana:
        Baton Rouge
        New Orleans

EL SALVADOR—Continued

Consular Offices—Continued

Michigan, Detroit
Missouri, St. Louis
Montana, Billings
New York, New York City
Oregon, Portland
Pennsylvania, Philadelphia
Puerto Rico:
    Bayamon
    San Juan
Texas:
    Houston
    Laredo
    San Antonio

EQUATORIAL GUINEA

Office of the Embassy, Suite 1403, 801 Second Avenue, New York, NY 10017. Phone, (212) 599-1523

H.E. Damaso Obiang Ndong, Ambassador Extraordinary and Plenipotentiary

ESTONIA

Office of the Consulate General, 9 Rockefeller Plaza, New York, NY 10020. Phone, (212) 247-1450

Dr. Ernst Jaakson, Consul General of Estonia at New York City in charge of Legation

Consular Offices:
California, Los Angeles
New York, New York City

ETHIOPIA

Office of the Embassy, 2134 Kalorama Road 20008. Phone, 234-2281

Mr. Girma Amare, Counselor (Chargé d'Affaires, a.i.)

FIJI

Office of the Embassy, 2233 Wisconsin Avenue 20007. Phone, 337-8320

Mr. Abdul H. Yusuf, Counselor (Chargé d'Affaires, a.i.)

Consular Offices:
District of Columbia
New York, New York

FINLAND

Office of the Embassy, 3216 New Mexico Avenue 20016. Phone, 363-2430

H.E. Jukka Valtasaari, Ambassador Extraordinary and Plenipotentiary

Consular Offices:
Alabama, Mobile
Alaska, Anchorage
Arizona, Phoenix
California:
    Los Angeles
    San Diego
    San Francisco
Connecticut, Norwich
District of Columbia
Florida:
    Jacksonville
    Lake Worth
    Miami
    Tampa
Georgia, Atlanta
Hawaii, Honolulu
Illinois, Chicago
Louisiana, New Orleans
Maryland, Baltimore
Massachusetts:
    Boston
    Fitchburg
Michigan:
    Detroit
    Marquette
Minnesota:
    Duluth
    Minneapolis
Missouri, Kansas City
Montana, Butte

FINLAND—Continued

Consular Offices—Continued

New Mexico, Alburquerque
New York, New York City
Ohio, Cleveland
Oregon:
    Astoria
    Portland
Pennsylvania, Philadelphia
Puerto Rico, San Juan
Texas:
    Dallas
    Houston
Utah, Salt Lake City
Virgin Islands, St. Thomas
Virginia, Norfolk
Washington, Bellevue

FRANCE

Office of the Embassy, 4101 Reservoir Road 20007. Phone, 944-6000

H.E. Emmanuel Jacquin de Margerie, Ambassador Extraordinary and Plenipotentiary

Consular Offices:
Alabama, Birmingham
Alaska, Anchorage
American Samoa, Pago Pago
Arkansas, Little Rock
Arizona, Phoenix
California:
    Los Angeles
    Sacramento
    San Diego
    San Jose
    San Francisco
Colorado, Denver
Connecticut, Hartford
Delaware, Wilmington
District of Columbia
Florida:
    Jacksonville
    Miami
    Orlando
Georgia:
    Atlanta
    Savannah
Hawaii, Honolulu
Illinois, Chicago
Indiana, Indianapolis
Iowa, Des Moines
Kansas, Kansas City
Kentucky, Louisville
Louisiana:
    New Orleans
    Shreveport
Maine, Portland
Maryland, Baltimore
Massachusetts:
    Boston
    Fall River
Michigan, Detroit
Minnesota, Minneapolis
Missouri, St. Louis
Montana, Missoula
Nevada, Reno
New Hampshire, Manchester
New Mexico:
    Albuquerque
    Santa Fe
New York, New York City
Ohio:
    Cincinnati
    Cleveland
    Columbus
Oklahoma:
    Oklahoma City
    Tulsa
Oregon, Portland
Pennsylvania:
    Philadelphia
    Pittsburgh
Puerto Rico:
    Mayaguez
    San Juan
South Carolina, Charleston

Consular Offices—Continued

Tennessee, Nashville
Texas:
  Amarillo
  Dallas
  Houston
Virginia, Norfolk
Virgin Islands, St. Thomas
Wisconsin, Milwaukee

GABON

Office of the Embassy, 2034 20th Street 20009. Phone, 797–1000

H.E. Jean Robert Odzaga, Ambassador Extraordinary and Plenipotentiary

THE GAMBIA

Office of the Embassy, Suite 720, 1030 15th Street 20005. Phone, 842–1356

H.E. Oosman A. Sallah, Ambassador Extraordinary and Plenipotentiary

GERMAN DEMOCRATIC REPUBLIC

Office of the Embassy, 1717 Massachusetts Avenue 20036. Phone, 232–3134

H.E. Dr. Gerhard Herder, Ambassador Extraordinary and Plenipotentiary

Consular Office, District of Columbia

GERMANY, FEDERAL REPUBLIC OF

Office of the Embassy, 4645 Reservoir Road 20007. Phone, 298–4000

H.E. Juergen Ruhtus, Ambassador Extraordinary and Plenipotentiary

Consular Offices:
  Alabama, Mobile
  Alaska, Anchorage
  American Samoa, residence at Wellington, New Zealand
  Arizona, Phoenix
  California:
    Los Angeles
    San Diego
    San Francisco
  Colorado, Denver
  District of Columbia
  Florida:
    Jacksonville
    Miami
    St. Petersburg
  Georgia:
    Atlanta
    Savannah
  Hawaii, Honolulu
  Illinois, Chicago
  Indiana, Indianapolis
  Kansas, Kansas City
  Kentucky, Louisville
  Louisiana, New Orleans
  Massachusetts, Boston
  Michigan, Detroit
  Minnesota, Minneapolis
  Missouri, St. Louis
  Nevada, Las Vegas
  New Mexico, Albuquerque
  New York:
    Buffalo
    New York City
  North Carolina, Charlotte
  Ohio:
    Cleveland
    Columbus
  Oklahoma, Oklahoma City
  Oregon, Portland
  Pacific Islands, Manila, Philippines
  Pennsylvania:
    Philadelphia
    Pittsburgh
  Puerto Rico:
    San Juan

Consular Offices—Continued

  South Carolina, Spartanburg
  Tennessee, Memphis
  Texas:
    Corpus Christi
    Dallas
    Houston
  Utah, Salt Lake City
  Virginia, Norfolk
  Washington:
    Seattle
    Spokane

GHANA

Office of the Embassy, 3512 International Drive 20008. Phone, 686–4520

H.E. Eric Kwamina Otoo, Ambassador Extraordinary and Plenipotentiary

Consular Office, New York, New York City

GREAT BRITAIN

Office of the Embassy, 3100 Massachusetts Avenue 20008. Phone, 462–1340

H.E. Sir Antony Acland, Ambassador Extraordinary and Plenipotentiary

Consular Offices:
  Alaska, Anchorage
  California:
    Los Angeles
    San Francisco
  District of Columbia
  Florida, Miami
  Georgia, Atlanta
  Illinois, Chicago
  Louisiana, New Orleans
  Massachusetts, Boston
  Missouri, St. Louis
  New York, New York City
  Ohio, Cleveland
  Oregon, Portland
  Pacific Islands, Tonga
  Pennsylvania, Philadelphia
  Texas:
    Dallas
    Houston
  Virginia, Norfolk
  Washington, Seattle

GREECE

Office of the Embassy, 2221 Massachusetts Avenue 20008. Phone, 667–3168

H.E. George D. Papoulias, Ambassador Extraordinary and Plenipotentiary

Consular Offices:
  California:
    Los Angeles
    San Francisco
  Georgia, Atlanta
  Illinois, Chicago
  Louisiana, New Orleans
  Massachusetts, Boston
  New York, New York City

GRENADA

Office of the Embassy, 1701 New Hampshire Avenue 20009. Phone, 265–2561

H.E. Albert O. Xavier, Ambassador Extraordinary and Plenipotentiary

Consular Offices:
  District of Columbia
  New York, New York City

GUATEMALA

Office of the Embassy, 2220 R Street 20008. Phone, 745–4592

H.E. Rodolfo Rohrmmoser V., Ambassador Extraordinary and Plenipotentiary

GUATEMALA—Continued

Consular Offices:
Alabama, Montgomery
California:
    San Diego
    San Francisco
    San Mateo
Florida, Miami
Georgia, Atlanta
Hawaii, Honolulu
Illinois, Chicago
Kansas, Leavenworth
Louisiana, New Orleans
Maryland, Baltimore
Minnesota, Minneapolis
New York, New York City
Pennsylvania:
    Philadelphia
    Pittsburgh
Puerto Rico, San Juan
Tennessee, Memphis
Texas:
    Brownsville
    Houston

GUINEA

Office of the Embassy, 2112 Leroy Place 20008. Phone, 483-9420

H.E. Dr. Kekoura Camara, Ambassador Extraordinary and Plenipotentiary

GUINEA BISSAU

Office of the Embassy, Care of the Permanent Mission of Guinea Bissau of the UN, 211 East 43d Street, Suite 604, New York, NY 10017. Phone, (212) 661-3977

H.E. Alfredo Lopez Cabral, Appointed Ambassador

GUYANA

Office of the Embassy, 2490 Tracy Place 20008. Phone, 265-6900

H.E. Dr. Cedric Hilburn Grant, Ambassador Extraordinary and Plenipotentiary

Consular Offices:
California, Los Angeles
Florida, Panama City
Indiana, East Chicago
New York, New York City
Texas, Waco

HAITI

Office of the Embassy, 2311 Massachusetts Avenue 20008. Phone, 332-4090

H.E. Pierre Francois Benoit, Ambassador Extraordinary and Plenipotentiary

Consular Offices:
Alabama, Mobile
California:
    Los Angeles
    San Francisco
Colorado, Denver
Florida, Miami
Georgia, Atlanta
Illinois, Chicago
Indiana, Evansville
Louisiana, New Orleans
Massachusetts, Boston
Michigan, Detroit
Missouri, St. Louis
New Jersey, Trenton
New York, New York City
Ohio, Cleveland
Pennsylvania:
    Philadelphia
    Pottsville
Puerto Rico, San Juan

HOLY SEE APOSTOLIC NUNCIATURE

Office of the Embassy, 3339 Massachusetts Avenue 20008. Phone, 333-7121

H.E. The Most Reverend Pio Laghi, Pro-Nuncio

HONDURAS

Office of the Embassy, Suite 100, 4301 Connecticut Avenue 20008. Phone, 966-7700

H.E. Jorge Ramon Hernandez-Alcerro, Ambassador Extraordinary and Plenipotentiary

Consular Offices:
Alabama, Mobile
California:
    Burlingame
    La Habra
    Los Angeles
    San Diego
    San Francisco
Colorado, Denver
District of Columbia
Florida:
    Coral Gables
    Gainesville
    Jacksonville
    Miami
Georgia, Atlanta
Hawaii, Honolulu
Illinois, Chicago
Louisiana:
    Baton Rouge
    New Orleans
Maryland, Baltimore
Massachusetts, Boston
Michigan, Detroit
Minnesota, Minneapolis
Missouri, St. Louis
New York:
    New York City
    Rochester
Ohio, Cleveland
Oregon, Portland
Pennsylvania, Philadelphia
Puerto Rico:
    Cayey
    Ponce
    San Juan
Rhode Island, Providence
Texas:
    Dallas
    Houston
    San Antonio
Washington, Seattle

HUNGARY

Office of the Embassy, 3910 Shoemaker Street 20008. Phone, 362-6730

H.E. Dr. Vencel Hazi, Ambassador Extraordinary and Plenipotentiary

Consular Offices:
District of Columbia
New York, New York City

ICELAND

Office of the Embassy, 2022 Connecticut Avenue 20008. Phone, 265-6653

H.E. Ingvi S. Ingvarsson, Ambassador Extraordinary and Plenipotentiary

Consular Offices:
California, Los Angeles
Florida:
    Hollywood
    Tallahassee
Georgia, Atlanta
Illinois, Chicago
Kentucky, Louisville
Massachusetts, Boston
Michigan, Detroit
Minnesota, Minneapolis
Missouri, Grandview
New York, New York City
Pennsylvania, Harrisburg
Puerto Rico, Guaynabo
Texas:
    Dallas
    Houston
Utah, Salt Lake City
Virginia, Norfolk
Washington, Seattle

INDIA

Office of the Embassy, 2107 Massachusetts Avenue 20008. Phone, 939-7000

H.E. Pratap K. Kaul, Ambassador

Consular Offices:
California, San Francisco
District of Columbia
Hawaii, Honolulu
Illinois, Chicago
Louisiana, New Orleans
New York, New York City
Ohio, Cleveland

INDONESIA

Office of the Embassy, 2020 Massachusetts Avenue 20036. Phone, 293-1745

H.E. Abdul Rachman Ramly, Ambassador Extraordinary and Plenipotentiary

Consular Offices:
California:
Los Angeles
San Francisco
Hawaii, Honolulu
Illinois, Chicago
New York, New York City
Texas, Houston

IRAQ

Office of the Embassy, 1801 P Street 20036. Phone, 483-7500

H.E. Abdul-Amir Ali Al-Anbari, Ambassador Extraordinary and Plenipotentiary

IRELAND

Office of the Embassy, 2334 Massachusetts Avenue 20008. Phone, 462-3939

H.E. Padraic N. MacKernan, Ambassador Extraordinary and Plenipotentiary

Consular Offices:
California, San Francisco
Illinois, Chicago
Massachusetts, Boston
Missouri, St. Louis
New York, New York City

ISRAEL

Office of the Embassy, 3514 International Drive 20008. Phone, 364-5500

H.E. Moshe Arad, Ambassador Extraordinary and Plenipotentiary

Consular Offices:
California:
Los Angeles
San Francisco
District of Columbia
Florida, Miami
Georgia, Atlanta
Illinois, Chicago
Massachusetts, Boston
New York, New York City
Pennsylvania, Philadelphia
Texas, Houston

ITALY

Office of the Embassy, 1601 Fuller Street 20009. Phone, 328-5500

H.E. Rinaldo Petrignani, Ambassador Extraordinary and Plenipotentiary

Consular Offices:
Alaska, Anchorage
California:
Bakersfield
Berkeley
Fresno
Los Angeles
Sacramento
San Diego
San Francisco
San Jose

ITALY—Continued

Consular Offices—Continued
Colorado, Denver
Florida:
Jacksonville
Miami
Tampa
Georgia:
Atlanta
Savannah
Illinois, Chicago
Indiana, Indianapolis
Kansas, Kansas City
Louisiana, New Orleans
Maryland, Baltimore
Masssachusetts:
Boston
Springfield
Worcester
Michigan, Detroit
Missouri, St. Louis
Nevada:
Las Vegas
Reno
New Jersey:
Newark
Trenton
New Mexico, Albuquerque
New York:
Albany
Buffalo
New York City
Rochester
Ohio:
Cincinnati
Cleveland
Pennsylvania:
Philadelphia
Pittsburgh
Puerto Rico, San Juan
Tennessee, Memphis
Texas:
Dallas
Galveston
Houston
Virginia, Norfolk

IVORY COAST. See CÔTE D'IVOIRE.

JAMAICA

Office of the Embassy, Suite 355, 1850 K Street 20006. Phone, 452-0660

H.E. Keith Johnson, Ambassador Extraordinary and Plenipotentiary

Consular Offices:
California:
Haywood
Los Angeles
District of Columbia
Florida, Miami
Illinois, Chicago
New York, New York City

JAPAN

Office of the Embassy, 2520 Massachusetts Avenue 20008. Phone, 234-2266

H.E. Nobuo Matsunaga, Ambassador Extraordinary and Plenipotentiary

Consular Offices:
Alabama, Mobile
Alaska, Anchorage
American Samoa, Pago Pago
Arizona, Phoenix
California:
Los Angeles
San Francisco
Colorado, Denver
District of Columbia
Florida, Miami
Georgia, Atlanta
Guam, Agana
Hawaii, Honolulu
Illinois, Chicago

JAPAN—Continued

Consular Offices—Continued
Louisiana, New Orleans
Massachusetts, Boston
Minnesota, Minneapolis
Missouri:
  Kansas City
  St. Louis
New York:
  Buffalo
  New York City
Ohio, Cleveland
Oregon, Portland
Pacific Islands, Saipan
Pennsylvania, Philadelphia
Puerto Rico, San Juan
Tennessee, Nashville
Texas:
  Dallas
  Houston
Washington, Seattle

JORDAN

Office of the Embassy, 3504 International Drive 20008.
Phone, 966–2664

H.E. Hussein Hammami, Ambassador Extraordinary and
Plenipotentiary

Consular Offices:
  Florida, Palm Beach
  Michigan, Detroit
  Texas, Houston

KENYA

Office of the Embassy, 2249 R Street 20008. Phone, 387–
6101

H.E. Denis D. Afanoe, Ambassador Extraordinary and
Plenipotentiary

Consular Offices:
  California, Los Angeles
  New York, New York City

KIRIBATI
No Ambassador or Chargé d'Affaires

KOREA

Office of the Embassy, 2370 Massachusetts Avenue 20008.
Phone, 939–5600

H.E. Tong-Jin Park, Ambassador Extraordinary and
Plenipotentiary

Consular Offices:
  Alabama, Mobile
  Alaska, Anchorage
  Arizona, Phoenix
  California:
    Los Angeles
    San Francisco
  Colorado, Denver
  District of Columbia
  Florida, Miami
  Georgia, Atlanta
  Guam, Agana
  Hawaii, Honolulu
  Illinois:
    Chicago
    Evanston
  Kansas, Kansas City
  Louisiana, New Orleans
  Massachusetts, Boston
  Michigan, Detroit
  Minnesota, Minneapolis
  Missouri, St. Louis
  New York, New York City
  Ohio, Cleveland
  Oklahoma, Oklahoma City
  Oregon, Portland
  Pennsylvania, Philadelphia
  Puerto Rico, San Juan
  Texas:
    Dallas
    Houston
    San Antonio
  Washington, Seattle

KUWAIT

Office of the Embassy, 2940 Tilden Street 20008. Phone,
966–0702

H.E. Shaikh Saud Nasir Al-Sabah, Ambassador
Extraordinary and Plenipotentiary

LAOS

Office of the Embassy, 2222 S Street 20008. Phone, 332–
6416

H.E. Done Somvorachit, First Secretary (Chargé
d'Affaires, a.i.)

LATVIA

Office of the Embassy, 4325 17th Street 20011. Phone, 726–
8213

Dr. Anatol Dinbergs (Chargé d'Affaires, a.i.)

Consular Offices:
  California, Los Angeles
  District of Columbia

LEBANON

Office of the Embassy, 2560 28th Street 20008. Phone 939–
6300

H.E. Dr. Abdullah Bouhabib, Ambassador Extraordinary
and Plenipotentiary

Consular Offices:
  California, Los Angeles
  Michigan, Detroit
  New York, New York City

LESOTHO

Office of the Embassy, 2511 Massachusetts Avenue 20008.
Phone, 797–5534

H.E. William Thabo Van Tonder, Ambassador
Extraordinary and Plenipotentiary

Consular Offices, Pennsylvania, Philadelphia

LIBERIA

Office of the Embassy, 5201 16th Street 20011. Phone, 723–
0437

H.E. Eugenia A. Wordsworth-Stevenson, Ambassador
Extraordinary and Plenipotentiary

Consular Offices:
  California:
    Los Angeles
    San Francisco
  Colorado, Denver
  District of Columbia
  Georgia, Atlanta
  Illinois, Chicago
  Louisiana, New Orleans
  Michigan, Detroit
  New York, New York City
  Texas, Houston

LITHUANIA

Office of the Legation, 2622 16th Street 20009. Phone, 234–
5860

Mr. Stasys Lozoraitis, Jr. (Chargé d'Affaires, a.i.)

Consular Offices:
  California, Los Angeles
  Illinois, Chicago
  New York, New York City

LUXEMBOURG

Office of the Embassy, 2200 Massachusetts Avenue 20008.
Phone, 265–4171

H.E. Andee Philippe, Ambassador Extraordinary and
Plenipotentiary

Consular Offices:
  California:
    Los Angeles
    San Francisco
  Connecticut, New Haven
  Georgia, Atlanta

LUXEMBOURG—Continued

Consular Offices—Continued

Illinois, Chicago
Louisiana, New Orleans
Michigan, Detroit
Missouri, Kansas City
New York, New York City
Ohio:
  Middletown
  Youngstown
Pennsylvania, Pittsburgh
Washington, Seattle

DEMOCRATIC REPUBLIC OF MADAGASCAR

Office of the Embassy, 2374 Massachusetts Avenue 20008.
Phone, 265-5525

H.E. Leon M. Rajaobelina, Ambassador Extraordinary
and Plenipotentiary

Consular Offices:
California, Palo Alto
Pennsylvania, Philadelphia
New York, New York City

MALAWI

Office of the Embassy, 2408 Massachusetts Avenue NW
20008. Phone, 797-1007

H.E. Robert Mbaya, Ambassador Extraordinary and
Plenipotentiary

Consular Offices:
California, Los Angeles
Texas, Houston

MALAYSIA

Office of the Embassy, 2401 Massachusetts Avenue 20008.
Phone, 328-2700

H.E. Albert S. Talalla, Ambassador Extraordinary and
Plenipotentiary

Consular Offices:
California:
  Los Angeles
  San Francisco
Hawaii, Honolulu
New York, New York City
Oregon, Portland

MALI

Office of the Embassy, 2130 R Street 20008. Phone, 332-
2249

H.E. Nouhoum Samassekou, Ambassador Extraordinary
and Plenipotentiary

Consular Offices:
California, Los Angeles
Massachusetts, Boston
Missouri, St. Louis
New Mexico, Albuquerque

MALTA

Office of the Embassy, 2017 Connecticut Avenue 20008.
Phone, 462-3611

H.E. Salv J. Stellini, Appointed Ambassador

Consular Offices:
California:
  Los Angeles
  San Francisco
District of Columbia
Massachusetts, Boston
Michigan, Detroit
Minnesota, St. Paul
Missouri, St. Louis
New York, New York City
Pennsylvania, Carnegie
Texas, Houston

MAURITANIA

Office of the Embassy, 2129 Leroy Place 20008. Phone,
232-5700

H.E. Abdellah Ould Daddah, Ambassador Extraordinary
and Plenipotentiary

MAURITIUS

Office of the Embassy, 4301 Connecticut Avenue 20008,
Suite 134. Phone, 244-1491

H.E. Chitmansing Jesseramsing, Ambassador
Extraordinary and Plenipotentiary

Consular Office, California, Los Angeles

MEXICO

Office of the Embassy, 2829 16th Street 20009. Phone, 234-
6000

H.E. Gustavo Petricioli, Ambassador Extraordinary and
Plenipotentiary

Consular Offices:
Alabama, Mobile
Arizona
  Nogales
  Phoenix
  Tucson
California:
  Calexico
  Fresno
  Los Angeles
  Oxnard
  Sacramento
  San Bernardino
  San Diego
  San Francisco
  San Jose
  Santa Ana
Colorado, Denver
District of Columbia
Florida:
  Miami
  Tampa
Georgia, Atlanta
Hawaii, Honolulu
Illinois, Chicago
Louisiana, New Orleans
Massachusetts, Boston
Michigan, Detroit
Missouri, St Louis
New Mexico, Albuquerque
New York:
  Buffalo
  New York City
North Carolina, Charlotte
Oregon, Portland,
Pennsylvania, Philadelphia
Puerto Rico, San Juan
Tennessee, Nashville
Texas:
  Austin
  Brownsville
  Corpus Christi
  Dallas
  Del Rio
  Eagle Pass
  El Paso
  Houston
  Laredo
  McAllen
  Presido
  San Antonio
Utah, Salt Lake City
Virginia:
  Norfolk
  Richmond
Washington:
  Seattle
  Spokane
Wisconsin, Madison

MONACO

Consular Offices:
California:
  Los Angeles
  San Francsico
District of Columbia
Florida, Palm Beach
Hawaii, Honolulu
Illinois, Chicago
Louisiana, New Orleans
Massachusetts, Boston
New York, New York City

MONACO—Continued

Consular Offices—Continued

Pennsylvania, Philadelphia
Puerto Rico, San Juan
Texas, Dallas

MOROCCO

Office of the Embassy, 1601 21st Street 20009. Phone, 462-7979

H.E. Ali Bengelloun, Appointed Ambassador

Consular Offices:
California, Los Angeles
Kansas, Kansas City
New York, New York City
Texas:
  Dallas
  Houston

MOZAMBIQUE

Office of the Embassy, Suite 570, 1990 M Street 20009. Phone, 293-7146

H.E. Valeriano Ferrao, Ambassador Extraordinary and Plenipotentiary

NAURU

H.E. T.W. Star, Ambassador Extraordinary and Plenipotentiary (Resident Melbourne, Australia)

Consular Offices:
American Samoa, Pago Pago
Guam, Agana
Hawaii, Honolulu

NEPAL

Office of the Embassay, 2131 Leroy Place 20008. Phone, 667-4550

H.E. Mohan Man Sainju, Ambassador Extraordinary and Plenipotentiary

Consular Offices:
California, San Francisco
Georgia, Atlanta
Illinois, Chicago
Ohio, Cleveland
New York, New York City
Texas, Dallas

NETHERLANDS

Office of the Embassy, 4200 Linnean Avenue 20008. Phone, 244-5300

H.E. Richard H. Fein, Ambassador Extraordinary and Plenipotentiary

Consular Offices:
Alaska, Anchorage
California:
  Los Angeles
  San Diego
  San Francisco
Colorado, Denver
District of Columbia
Florida:
  Jacksonville
  Miami
  Tampa
Georgia, Atlanta
Hawaii, Honolulu
Illinois, Chicago
Louisiana, New Orleans
Maryland, Baltimore
Massachusetts, Boston
Michigan:
  Detroit
  Grand Rapids
Minnesota, St. Paul
Missouri:
  Kansas City
  St. Louis
New York:
  Buffalo
  New York City
Ohio, Cleveland
Oregon, Portland

NETHERLANDS—Continued

Consular Offices—Continued

Pacific Islands, Manila, Philippines
Pennsylvania:
  Philadelphia
  Pittsburgh
Puerto Rico, San Juan
Texas, Houston
Utah, Salt Lake City
Virginia, Norfolk
Virgin Islands, Charlotte Amalie

NEW ZEALAND

Office of the Embassy, 37 Observatory Circle 20008. Phone, 328-4800

H.E. Howard Huyton Francis, Ambassador Extraordinary and Plenipotentiary

Consular Offices:
California, Los Angeles
District of Columbia
New York, New York City

NICARAGUA

Office of the Embassy, 1627 New Hampshire Avenue 20009. Phone, 387-4371

Mrs. Leonor de Huper, Minister-Counselor (Chargé d'Affaires, a.i.)

Consular Office, District of Columbia

NIGER

Office of the Embassy, 2204 R Street 20008. Phone, 483-4224

H.E. Moumouni Adamou Djermakoye, Ambassador Extraordinary and Plenipotentiary

Consular Office, New York, New York City

NIGERIA

Office of the Embassy, 2201 M Street 20037. Phone, 822-1500

H.E. Hamzat Ahmadu, Ambassador Extraordinary and Plenipotentiary

Consular Offices:
California, San Francisco
Georgia, Atlanta
New York, New York City

NORWAY

Office of the Embassy, 2720 34th Street 20008. Phone, 333-6000

H.E. Kjeld Vibe, Ambassador Extraordinary and Plenipotentiary

Consular Offices:
Alabama, Mobile
Alaska, Anchorage
California:
  Los Angeles
  San Diego
  San Francisco
District of Columbia
Florida:
  Jacksonville
  Miami
  Pensacola
  Tampa
Hawaii, Honolulu
Illinois, Chicago
Iowa, Des Moines
Louisiana, New Orleans
Maine, Portland
Maryland, Baltimore
Massachusetts, Boston
Michigan, Detroit
Minnesota, Minneapolis
Missouri, St. Louis
Montana, Billings
Nebraska, Omaha
New York, New York City
North Carolina, Wilmington
North Dakota, Fargo

NORWAY—Continued

Consular Offices—Continued

Ohio, Cleveland
Oklahoma, Tulsa
Oregon, Portland
Pennsylvania, Philadelphia
Puerto Rico:
    Ponce
    San Juan
South Carolina, Charleston
South Dakota, Sioux Falls
Texas:
    Beaumont
    Dallas
    Galveston
    Houston
Utah, Salt Lake City
Virginia, Norfolk
Virgin Islands:
    Charlotte Amalie
    St. Croix
Washington, Seattle
Wisconsin:
    Madison
    Milwaukee

OMAN

Office of the Embassy, 2342 Massachusetts Avenue 20008.
Phone, 939–6200

H.E. Awadh Bader Al-Shanfari, Ambassador
Extraordinary and Plenipotentiary

PAKISTAN

Office of the Embassy, 2315 Massachusetts Avenue 20008.
Phone, 939–6200

H.E. Jamsheed K.A. Marker, Ambassador Extraordinary
and Plenipotentiary

Consular Offices:
California, San Francisco
Illinois, Chicago
Kentucky, Louisville
Massachusetts, Boston
New York, New York City
Texas, Houston

PANAMA

Office of the Embassy, 2862 McGill Terrace 20008. Phone,
483–1407

H.E. Juan B. Sosa, Ambassador Extraordinary and
Plenipotentiary

Consular Offices:
Alabama:
    Mobile
    Montgomery
Arizona, Phoenix
California:
    Beverly Hills
    Burbank
    Long Beach
    Los Angeles
    Sacramento
    San Diego
    San Francisco
Florida:
    Fort Lauderdale
    Miami
    Orlando
    Tampa
Georgia, Atlanta
Hawaii, Honolulu
Illinois, Chicago
Louisiana, New Orleans
Maine, Portland
Maryland, Baltimore
Michigan, Detroit
New York:
    New York City
    Rochester
    Syracuse
Ohio, Cleveland
Oregon, Portland
Pennsylvania:
    Philadelphia
    Pittsburgh

PANAMA—Continued

Consular Offices—Continued

Puerto Rico, San Juan
Texas:
    Corpus Christi
    Dallas
    El Paso
    Houston
Virginia:
    Alexandria
    Norfolk
Washington, Seattle

PAPUA NEW GUINEA

Office of the Embassy, 1330 Connecticut Avenue, Suite 350,
20036. Phone, 659–0856

H.E. Renagi R. Lohia, Ambassador Extraordinary and
Plenipotentiary

PARAGUAY

Office of the Embassy, 2400 Massachusetts Avenue 20008.
Phone, 483–6960

H.E. Marcos Martinez Mendieta, Ambassador
Extraordinary and Plenipotentiary

Consular Offices:
Alaska, Anchorage
California:
    Los Angeles
    San Francisco
Colorado, Denver
Florida, Miami
Illinois, Chicago
Louisiana, New Orleans
Massachusetts, Boston
Michigan, Detroit
New Mexico, Albuquerque
New York, New York City
Puerto Rico, San Juan
Texas:
    Dallas
    Houston
Washington, Seattle

PERU

Office of the Embassy, 1700 Massachusetts Avenue 20036.
Phone, 833–9860 to 9869

H.E. Cesar Guillermo Atala, Ambassador Extraordinary
and Plenipotentiary

Consular Offices:
Arizona, Tucson
California:
    Los Angeles
    San Francisco
District of Columbia
Florida:
    Fort Lauderdale
    Miami
    Orlando
Hawaii, Honolulu
Illinois, Chicago
Louisiana, New Orleans
Maryland, Baltimore
Masschusetts, Boston
Missouri, St. Louis
New Jersey, Paterson
New York, New York City
Oklahoma, Tulsa
Puerto Rico, San Juan
Texas, Houston
Washington, Seattle

PHILIPPINES

Office of the Embassy, 1617 Massachusetts Avenue 20036.
Phone, 483–1414

H.E. Emmanuel Pelaez, Ambassador Extraordinary and
Plenipotentiary

Consular Offices:
California:
    Los Angeles
    San Francisco

PHILIPPINES—Continued

Consular Offices- Continued

    District of Columbia
    Georgia, Atlanta
    Guam, Agana
    Hawaii, Honolulu
    Illinois, Chicago
    Louisiana, New Orleans
    New York, New York City
    Texas, Houston
    Washington, Seattle

POLAND

Office of the Embassy, 2640 16th Street 20009. Phone, 234–3800

H.E. Jan Kinast, Ambassador Extraordinary and Plenipotentiary

Consular Offices:
    District of Columbia
    Illinois, Chicago
    New York, New York City

PORTUGAL

Office of the Embassy, 2125 Kalorama Road 20008. Phone 328–8610

H.E. Joao Eduardo M. Pereira Bastos, Ambassador Extraordinary and Plenipotentiary

Consular Offices:
    California:
        Los Angeles
        San Francisco
    Connecticut, Waterbury
    District of Columbia
    Florida, Miami
    Hawaii, Honolulu
    Illinois, Chicago
    Louisiana, New Orleans
    Massachusetts:
        Boston
        New Bedford
    New Jersey, Newark
    New York, New York City
    Pennsylvania, Philadelphia
    Puerto Rico, San Juan
    Rhode Island, Providence
    Texas, Houston

QATAR

Office of the Embassy, Suite 1180, 600 New Hampshire Avenue 20037. Phone, 338–0111

H.E Ahmed Abdulla Zaid Al-Mahmoud, Ambassador Extraordinary and Plenipotentiary

ROMANIA

Office of the Embassy, 1607 23d Street 20008. Phone, 232–4747

H.E. Ion Stoichici, Ambassador Extraordinary and Plenipotentiary

RWANDA

Office of the Embassy, 1714 New Hampshire Avenue 20009. Phone, 232–2882

H.E. Aloys Vwimana, Ambassador Extraordinary and Plenipotentiary

SAINT CHRISTOPHER AND NEVIS

Office of the Embassy, 2501 M Street, Suite 540, 20037. Phone, 833–3550

Mr. Erstein M. Edwards, Minister (Chargé d'Affaires, a.i.)

Consular Offices:
    District of Columia, Washington
    Georgia, Atlanta
    Texas, Dallas

SAINT LUCIA

Office of the Embassy, 2100 M Street, Suite 309, 20037. Phone, 463–7378

H.E. Dr. Joseph Edsel Edmunds, Ambassador Extraordinary and Plenipotentiary

Consular Offices:
    New York, New York City
    Virgin Islands, St. Croix

SAN MARINO

Consular Offices:
    District of Columbia
    Michigan, Detroit
    New York, New York City

SAO TOME AND PRINCIPE

Office of the Embassy, Suite 1504, 801 Second Avenue, New York, NY 10017. Phone, (212) 697–4211

H.E. Joaquin Rafael Branco, Ambassador Extraordinary and Plenipotentiary

Consular Office, Florida, Miami

SAUDI ARABIA

Office of the Embassy, 601 New Hampshire Avenue 20037. Phone, 342–3800

His Royal Highness Prince Bandar Bin Sultan, Ambassador Extraordinary and Plenipotentiary

Consular Offices:
    California, Los Angeles
    District of Columbia
    New York, New York City
    Texas, Houston

SENEGAL

Office of the Embassy, 2112 Wyoming Avenue 20008. Phone, 234–0540

H.E. Ibra Dequene Ka, Ambassador Extraordinary and Plenipotentiary

Consular Offices:
    Florida, Miami
    Louisiana, New Orleans
    Maryland, Baltimore
    Texas, Houston

SEYCHELLES

Office of the Embassy, Suite 203, 820 Second Avenue, New York, NY 10017. Phone, (212) 687–9766

Mr. Marc R. Marengo, Secong Secretary (Chargé d'Affaires, a.i.)

SIERRA LEONE

Office of the Embassy, 1701 19th Street 20009. Phone, 939–9261

H.E. Dr. George Carew, Ambassador Extraordinary and Plenipotentiary

Consular Offices:
    District of Columbia
    Georgia, Atlanta

SINGAPORE

Office of the Embassy, 1824 R Street 20009. Phone, 667–7555

H.E. Tommy T.B. Koh, Ambassador Extraordinary and Plenipotentiary

SOLOMON ISLANDS

H.E. Francis Saemala, Ambassador Extraordinary and Plenipotentiary (Resident in Honiara, Solomon Islands)

SOMALI DEMOCRATIC REPUBLIC

Office of the Embassy, Suite 710, 600 New Hampshire Avenue 20037. Phone, 342–1575

H.E. Abdullah Ahmed Addou, Ambassador Extraordinary and Plenipotentiary

SOMALI DEMOCRATIC REPUBLIC—Continued

Consular Offices:
District of Columbia
New York, New York City
Texas, Houston

SOUTH AFRICA

Office of the Embassy, 3051 Massachusetts Avenue 20008.
Phone, 232–4400

H.E. Piet G.J. Koornhof, Ambassador Extraordinary and
Plenipotentiary

Consular Offices:
Alabama, Mobile
California, Beverly Hills
Illinois, Chicago
New York, New York City
Texas, Houston
Utah, Salt Lake City

SPAIN

Office of the Embassy, 2700 15th Street 20009. Phone, 265–
0190

H.E. Julian Santamaria, Ambassador Extraordinary and
Plenipotentiary

Consular Offices:
Alabama, Mobile
California:
Los Angeles
San Francisco
Connecticut, Stamford
District of Columbia
Florida:
Jacksonville
Miami
Hawaii, Honolulu
Illinois, Chicago
Louisiana, New Orleans
Maryland, Baltimore
Massachusetts, Boston
Missouri:
Kansas City
St. Louis
New York, New York City
Ohio, Cincinnati
Pennsylvania, Philadelphia
Puerto Rico, San Juan
Texas:
Dallas
El Paso
Houston
Port Arthur

SRI LANKA

Office of the Embassy, 2148 Wyoming Avenue 20008.
Phone, 483–4025

H.E. Susantha de Alwis, Ambassador Extraordinary and
Plenipotentiary

Consular Offices:
Hawaii, Honolulu
Illinois, Chicago
Louisiana, New Orleans
New York, New York City

SUDAN

Office of the Embassy, 2210 Massachusetts Avenue 20008.
Phone, 338–8565

H.E. Hassan Elamin El-Bashir, Ambassador Extraordinary
and Plenipotentiary

Consular Office, New York, New York City

SURINAME

Office of the Embassy, 4301 Connecticut Avenue 20008.
Phone, 244–7488

H.E. Arnold T. Halfhide, Ambassador Extraordinary and
Plenipotentiary

Consular Offices:
Florida, Miami
Georgia, Atlanta

SWAZILAND

Office of the Embassy, Suite 441, 4301 Connecticut Avenue
20008. Phone, 362–6683

H.E. Absalom Vusani Mamba, Ambassador Extraordinary
and Plenipotentiary

SWEDEN

Office of the Embassy, Suite 1200, 600 New Hampshire
Avenue 20037. Phone, 944–5600

H.E. Count Wilhelm Wachtmeister, Ambassador
Extraordinary and Plenipotentiary

Consular Offices:
Alabama, Mobile
Alaska, Anchorage
Arizona, Phoenix
California:
Los Angeles
San Diego
San Francisco
Colorado, Denver
Florida:
Fort Lauderdale
Jacksonville
St. Petersburg
Georgia:
Atlanta
Savannah
Hawaii, Honolulu
Illinois, Chicago
Louisiana, New Orleans
Maine, Portland
Maryland, Baltimore
Massachusetts, Boston
Michigan, Troy
Minnesota, Minneapolis
Missouri:
Kansas City
St. Louis
Nebraska, Omaha
New York:
Buffalo
Jamestown
New York City
Ohio, Cleveland
Oregon, Portland
Pennsylvania, Philadelphia
Puerto Rico, San Juan
Texas:
Dallas
Houston
Virginia, Norfolk
Virgin Islands, Charlotte Amalie
Washington, Seattle
Wisconsin, Milwaukee

SWITZERLAND

Office of the Embassy, 2900 Cathedral Avenue 20008.
Phone, 745–7900

H.E. Klaus Jacobi, Ambassador Extraordinary and
Plenipotentiary

Consular Offices:
Arizona, Phoenix
California:
Los Angeles
San Francisco
Colorado, Denver
District of Columbia
Florida, Miami
Georgia, Atlanta
Hawaii, Honolulu
Illinois, Chicago
Louisiana, New Orleans
Massachusetts, Boston
Minnesota, Minneapolis
Missouri:
Kansas City
St. Louis
New York:
Buffalo
New York City
Ohio:
Cincinnati
Cleveland
Columbus

SWITZERLAND—Continued

Consular Offices--Continued

Pennsylvania:
Philadelphia
Pittsburgh
Puerto Rico, San Juan
South Carolina, Spartanburg
Texas:
Dallas
Houston
Utah, Salt Lake City

SYRIA

Office of the Embassy, 2215 Wyoming Avenue 20008. Phone, 232-6313

Ms. Bushra Kanafani, Counselor (Chargé d'Affaires, a.i.)

Consular Office, Texas, Houston

TANZANIA

Office of the Embassy, 2139 R Street 20008. Phone, 939-6125

H.E. Asterius Hyera, Ambassador Extraordinary and Plenipotentiary

THAILAND

Office of the Embassy, 2300 Kalorama Road 20008. Phone, 483-7200

H.E. Vitthya Vejjajiva, Ambassador Extraordinary and Plenipotentiary

Consular Offices:
Alabama, Montgomery
California, Los Angeles
Colorado, Denver
Florida, Miami
Georgia, Atlanta
Hawaii, Honolulu
Illinois, Chicago
Louisiana, New Orleans
Michigan, Detroit
Missouri, Kansas City
New York, New York City
Oklahoma, Tulsa
Oregon, Portland
Puerto Rico, Hato Rey
Texas, El Paso

TOGO

Office of the Embassy, 2208 Massachusetts Avenue 20008. Phone, 234-4212

H.E. Ellom-Kodjo Schuppius, Ambassador Extraordinary and Plenipotentiary

Consular Offices:
Florida, Miami
Missouri, St. Louis

TRINIDAD AND TOBAGO

Office of the Embassy, 1708 Massachusetts Avenue 20036. Phone, 467-6490

H.E. Angus Albert Khan, Ambassador Extraordinary and Plenipotentiary

Consular Office, New York, New York City

TUNISIA

Office of the Embassy, 1515 Massachusetts Avenue 20005. Phone, 862-1850

H.E. Abdelaziz Ham Zaoui, Ambassador Extraordinary and Plenipotentiary

Consular Offices:
California, San Francisco
Florida, Miami
New York, New York City

TURKEY

Office of the Embassy, 1606 23d Street 20008. Phone, 387-3200

H.E. Dr. Sukru Elekdag, Ambassador Extraordinary and Plenipotentiary

Consular Offices:
California:
Los Angeles
Oakland
District of Columbia
Florida, Miami
Illinois, Chicago
Kansas, Mission Hills
Maryland, Baltimore
New York, New York City
Texas, Houston

UGANDA

Office of the Embassy, 5909 16th Street 20011. Phone, 726-7100

H.E. Stephen Kapimpina Katenta-Apuli, Ambassador Extraordinary and Plenipotentiary

UNION OF SOVIET SOCIALIST REPUBLICS

Office of the Embassy, 1125 16th Street 20036. Phone, 628-7551

H.E. Yuriy Vladimirovich Dubinin, Ambassador Extraordinary and Plenipotentiary

Consular Offices:
California, San Francisco
District of Columbia

UNITED ARAB EMIRATES

Office of the Embassy, 600 New Hampshire Avenue, Suite 740, 20037. Phone, 338-6500

H.E. Ahmed S. Al-Mokarrab, Ambassador Extraordinary and Plenipotentiary

URUGUAY

Office of the Embassy, 1918 F Street 20006. Phone, 331-1313

H.E. Dr. Hector Luisi, Ambassador Extraordinary and Plenipotentiary

Consular Offices:
California:
Los Angeles
San Francisco
District of Columbia
Florida, Miami
Illinois, Chicago
Louisiana, New Orleans
New York, New York City
Puerto Rico, San Juan

VENEZUELA

Office of the Embassy, 2445 Massachusetts Avenue 20008. Phone, 797-3800

H.E. Valentin Hernandez, Ambassador Extraordinary and Plenipotentiary

Consular Offices:
California, San Francisco
Florida, Miami
Illinois, Chicago
Louisiana, New Orleans
Maryland, Baltimore
Massachusetts, Boston
New York, New York City
Pennsylvania, Philadelphia
Puerto Rico, San Juan
Texas, Houston

WESTERN SAMOA

Office of the Embassy, 820 Second Avenue, New York, NY 10017. Phone, (212) 599-6196

H.E. Maiava Iulai Toma, Ambassador Extraordinary and Plenipotentiary

WESTERN SAMOA—Continued

Consular Office, California, Los Angeles

YEMEN

Office of the Embassy, 600 New Hampshire Avenue, Suite 840, 20037. Phone, 965–4760

H.E. Mohsin Ahmed Alaini, Ambassador Extraordinary and Plenipotentiary

Consular Offices:
    California, San Francisco
    District of Columbia
    Michigan, Detroit

YUGOSLAVIA

Office of the Embassy, 2410 California Street 20008. Phone, 462–6566

H.E. Zivorad Kovacevic, Ambassador Extraordinary and Plenipotentiary

Consular Offices:
    California, San Fransisco
    District of Columbia
    Florida, Jacksonville
    Illinois, Chicago
    Kansas, Kansas City
    Louisiana, New Orleans

YUGOSLAVIA—Continued

Consular Offices—Continued
    New York, New York City
    Ohio, Cleveland
    Pennsylvania, Pittsburgh

ZAIRE

Office of the Embassy, 1800 New Hampshire Avenue 20009. Phone, 234–7690

H.E. Mushobekwa Kalimba wa Katana, Ambassador Extraordinary and Plenipotentiary

Consular Office, New York, New York City

ZAMBIA

Office of the Embassy, 2419 Massachusetts Avenue 20008. Phone, 265–9717

Mr. Lazarous Kapambwe, Counselor (Chargé d'Affaires, a.i.)

ZIMBABWE

Office of the Embassy, 2852 McGill Terrace 20008. Phone, 332–7100

Mr. Jonathan Wutawunashe, Counselor (Chargé d'Affaires, a.i.)